CADRES AND CORRUPTION

Studies of the East Asian Institute,
Columbia University

The East Asian Institute is Columbia University's center for
research, education, and publication on modern East Asia.
The Studies of the East Asian Institute were inaugurated in
1961 to bring to a wider public the results of significant new
research on China, Japan, and Korea.

Cadres and Corruption

THE ORGANIZATIONAL INVOLUTION
OF THE CHINESE COMMUNIST PARTY

Xiaobo Lü

STANFORD UNIVERSITY PRESS
STANFORD, CALIFORNIA

Stanford University Press
Stanford, California

© 2000 by the Board of Trustees of the
Leland Stanford Junior University

Printed in the United States of America

Library of Congress Cataloging-in-Publication Data

Lu, Hsiao-po
   Cadres and corruption : the organizational involution of the
Chinese Communist Party / Xiaobo Lu.
      p.   cm. — (Studies of the East Asian Institute, Columbia
University)
   ISBN 0-8047-3958-7 (cloth : alk. paper)
   Includes bibliographical references and index.
   1. Political corruption — China.   2. Chung-kuo kung ch`an tang.
3. China — Politics and government — 1976-.   I. Title.   II. Studies
of the East Asian Institute.
JQ1509.5.C6 L8   2000
324.251'075 — dc21   00-027396

Original printing 2000

Last figure below indicates year of this printing:
09 08 07 06 05 04 03 02 01

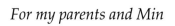

For my parents and Min

ACKNOWLEDGMENTS

I began this book a decade ago, as China was experiencing one of the defining moments in its history. Official corruption had become so endemic that it helped trigger the massive demonstrations that ended in a bloody crackdown. My interest in studying corruption in China, however, goes back further, growing in part out of personal experience. Growing up in a socialist state, I was exposed to various kinds of official misconduct and corruption. I remember vividly how things were routinely accomplished by calling a friend who was in a position to write a *tiaozi* (note) to the right person, and how official privileges were allocated according to one's rank in the political hierarchy. But it was Kenneth Jowitt, from whom I took a graduate seminar at Berkeley some years ago, who inspired my academic interest in corruption. His seminal work on Communist corruption provided a starting point for my research.

I have accumulated many debts to people who have kindly offered advice and assistance over the years. I had the fortune to work with high-caliber political scientists and an established community of China scholars at Berkeley. Robert Scalapino was my first mentor when I came to Berkeley in 1986. He provided my earliest exposure to the systematic study of Chinese politics. Lowell Dittmer gave me much-needed encouragement and guidance throughout the whole process of research and writing. Ken Jowitt, in addition to his usual witty and inspiring words, offered valuable insights that sharpened my analysis. I benefited tremendously not only from Liz Perry's advice but also from her comments on and editing of the early drafts. Tom Gold carefully read every chapter and made copious suggestions. They all deserve my

viii   *Acknowledgments*

sincere gratitude. I wish to thank Lynn White and Jonathan Unger, as well as two anonymous reviewers, who patiently read the whole manuscript and whose comments and suggestions were instrumental in the revision process. I am grateful to many other people, including Kevin O'Brien, Ramon Myers, Thomas Metzger, Mark Selden, Dorothy Solinger, and Christine Wong, who either read parts of the manuscript at different stages or supplied me with references. The Institute of International Studies and the Institute of East Asian Studies at Berkeley, the East Asian Institute at Columbia, and the Hoover Institution at Stanford provided institutional support, which made it possible for me to concentrate on research and writing. The intellectual support of my colleagues at Barnard College and Columbia University nurtured an environment that any junior faculty member would find most desirable. Thomas Bernstein and Andrew Nathan, among others, have given unreserved encouragement since I arrived at Barnard/Columbia. I am especially grateful to them.

Needless to say, for a research project to be successful, firsthand data are crucial, and many people in China kindly helped me during my fieldwork and documentary research. With their assistance, I was able to obtain important information that otherwise would have been unavailable. My thanks also go to those whom I interviewed and who shared candid observations on and personal experiences with a sensitive subject. For many reasons, I cannot list their names here, but they have been an indispensable part of this endeavor.

I am indebted to the staff at the three most comprehensive library collections on contemporary China in the United States—the Center for Chinese Studies Library at Berkeley, the C. V. Starr East Asian Library at Columbia University, and the East Asian Collection at the Hoover Institution of Stanford University. I want to thank especially Annie Chang, C. P. Chen, and Fran Lafleur, who were always resourceful and ready to assist me in my research.

Many friends and colleagues read different parts of the manuscript and offered critical insights that helped me develop my thesis. Others offered editorial assistance. In this regard, I thank Elinor Levine, Tom Bickfield, Patricia Thornton, Pan Wei, Wade Huntly, Martin Rivlin, Kellee Tsai, Cornelia Robart, and Hope Leman. I was fortunate to have

Muriel Bell and Nathan MacBrien at Stanford University Press, who patiently guided me through the various stages of the production process. Sally Serafim provided skillful copyediting with a deft editorial hand and expert care.

My wife, Min, deserves the most credit. There has never been a moment's doubt in my mind that without her understanding and support, this book would never have reached its present shape. Her unsparing, yet apt, comments from a nonspecialist's viewpoint often forced me to rethink my arguments and presentation. She has gone through much during these long, sometimes difficult, times. Her constant encouragement and urging is one source of my drive to accomplish this "core task." I want this book to be a reward for her love and comradeship.

X.L.

CONTENTS

TABLES

The following abbreviations are used throughout the text, Notes, and Bibliography.

BJZ	*Balujun junzheng zazhi* (Journal of military and political affairs of the Eighth Route Army).
BSXZ	*Baishui xianzhi* (Gazetteer of Baishui county). Xi'an: Shaanxi renmin chubanshe, 1989.
BXSDC	*Baixianshi sheqing diaocha* (A survey of socioeconomic conditions in 100 counties and cities). Beijing: Zhongguo dabaike quanshu chubanshe, 1992.
BYT	*Banyuetan* (Bimonthly Forum). Beijing.
CCP	Chinese Communist party.
CCXZ	*Chicheng xianzhi* (Gazetteer of Chicheng county). Beijing: Renmin chubanshe, 1991.
CJRB	*Changjiang ribao* (Yangzi Daily). Wuhan.
CNA	China News Agency wire service. Beijing.
COD	Central Organization Department of CCP.
DBRB	*Dongbei ribao* (Northeast Daily). Shenyang.
DDKH	*Dalu dixia kanwu huibian* (Underground journals in the main land), vols. 1–19. Taipei: Zhonggong yanjiu zazhishe, 1980–84.
FZRB	*Fazhi ribao* (Legal Daily). Beijing.
GJJ	*Guangjiaojing* (Wide-Angle Lenses). Hong Kong.
GMRB	*Guangming ribao* (Guangming Daily). Beijing.
GRRB	*Gongren ribao* (Worker's Daily). Beijing.
HBRB	*Hebei ribao* (Hebei Daily). Shijiazhuang.

HBXZ   *Huaibin xianzhi* (Gazetteer of Huaibin county). Zhengzhou:
          Henan renmin chubanshe, 1987.

HBZTX   *Hebei zugong tongxun* (Bulletin of Hebei province organiza-
          tional work). Hebei shengwei zuzhibu (The CCP organi-
          zation department of Hebei province).

HQ   *Hongqi* (Red Flag). Beijing, official CCP Central Committee
          journal.

HQGZ   *Houqin gongzuo shiliao* (Historical materials of logistical work).
          Beijing Junqu Houqinbu, Beijing: Junshixueyuan chubanshe,
          1985.

JCRB   *Jiancha ribao* (Procurate Daily). Beijing.

JFRB   *Jiefang ribao* (Liberation Daily). Shanghai.

JGFZX   *Jianguo yilai fan tanwu huilu fagui ziliao xuanbian* (Selected anti-
          graft and anti-bribery laws and regulations enacted since
          1949). Beijing: Zhongguo jiancha chubanshe, 1991.

JJCK   *Jingji cankao* (Economic References). Beijing.

JNSH   *Jianguo yilai nongye hezuohua shiliao huibian* (Historical materials
          of the agricultural collectivization since 1949). Beijing: Zhong
          gong danshi chubanshe, 1992.

JYZWX   *Jianguo yilai zhongyao wenxian xuanbian* (A selection of
          important documents since the founding of the nation),
          vols. 1–3. Beijing: Zhongyang wenxian chubanshe, 1992.

KMT   Kuomintang (in pinyin, Guomindang), or Nationalist party.

KSCSX   *Kangri zhanzheng shiqi Jin-Ji-Lu-Yu bianqu caizheng jingji shi
          ziliao xuanbian* (Materials related to the financial and economic
          history of the Shanxi-Hebei-Shandong-Henan border region
          during the anti-Japanese war), vol. 1. Beijing: Zhongguo
          caijing chubanshe, 1992.

KZSGN   *Kangri zhanzheng shiqi Shaan-Gan-Ning bianqu caizheng jingji
          shiliao xuanbian* (Selected historical materials on finance and
          economy during the anti-Japanese war in Shaan-Gan-Ning
          border region). Xi'an: Shaanxi renmin chubanshe, 1981.

LTXZ   *Lintong xianzhi* (Gazetteer of Lintong county). 1990.

NCXB   *Neican xuanbian* (Selected internal materials). Beijing: Xinhua
          News Agency.

NFRB   *Nanfang ribao* (Nanfang Daily). Guangzhou.

NJXZ   *Neijiang xianzhi* (Gazetteer of Neijiang county). Chongqing: Bashu chubanshe, 1987.

NJZWH   *Nongye jitihua zhongyao wenjian huibian 1959–1981* (A collection of important documents of agricultural collectivization, 1959–81). Beijing: Zhongguo nongye chubanshe, 1982.

PDIC   Party Discipline Inspection Commission.

QSND   *Qishi niandai* (The Seventies). Hong Kong.

RMRB   *Renmin ribao* (People's Daily). Beijing.

RMSC   *Renmin shouce* (People's Handbook). Beijing.

RMZG   *Renmin zhongguo* (People's China). Beijing.

SAIC   State Administration of Industry and Commerce.

SFDD   *Sanfan yu feibang de dangnei douzheng* (Three Anti and the inner-party struggle of the Communists). N.p.: Zhongyang Gaizao Weiyuanhui, 1952.

SJRB   *Shijie ribao* (World Journal). New York.

SLXZ   *Shanglin xianzhi* (Gazetteer of Shanglin county). Nanning: Guangxi renmin chubanshe, 1989.

SQGJ   *Siqing gongzuo jianbao* (Bulletin on the Four Cleanup work). N.p.: Office of the Four Cleanup Campaign, CCP Hebei provincial committee.

SXRB   *Shanxi ribao* (Shanxi Daily). Taiyuan.

SYXZ   *Shouyang xianzhi* (Gazetteer of Shouyang county). Taiyuan: Shanxi renmin chubanshe, 1989.

TGGS   *Taihang geming genjudi shigao* (Historical materials of the Taihang revolutionary base). Taiyuan: Shanxi renmin chubanshe, 1987.

TJRB   *Tianjin ribao* (Tianjin Daily). Tianjin.

WAXZ   *Wu'an xianzhi* (Gazetteer of Wu'an county). Shijiazhuang: Hebei renmin chubanshe, 1990.

WCXZ   *Wuchang xianzhi* (Gazetteer of Wuchang county). Harbin: Heilongjiang renmin chubanshe, 1989.

WQXZ   *Wanquan xianzhi* (Gazetteer of Wanquan county). Beijing: Xinhua chubanshe, 1992.

XH   Xinhua News Agency wire service. Beijing.

YYSZ   *Yiyang shizhi* (Gazetteer of Yiyang city). Beijing: Zhongguo wenshi chubanshe, 1990.

ZBSH   *Zhibu shenghuo* (Life in the Party Branches). Beijing.

ZDJCZ   *Zhonggong dangshi jiaoxue cankao ziliao* (Reference materials for
        CCP history teaching), vols. 12–27. Beijing: Guofang daxue
        chubanshe, 1986.

ZGFZB   *Zhongguo fazhi bao* (Chinese Legal Daily). Beijing.

ZGGC   *Zhongguo guoqing congshu* (State of the nation: Socioeconomic
        surveys of 100 counties and cities). Beijing: Zhongguo dabaike
        quanshu chubanshe, 1991.

ZGTX   *Zugong tongxun* (Bulletin of organizational work). Beijing: CCP
        Central Organization Department (COD).

ZJDZ   *Zhonghua renmin gongheguo jingji dang'an ziliao xuanbian*
        (Selected archives of economy of the PRC, 1949–52), vol. 1.
        Beijing: Zhongguo chengshi jingji shehui chubanshe, 1990.

ZJQG   *Zhongguo renmin jiefangjun qunzhong gongzuoshi* (The history of
        mass work in the People's Liberation Army). Zongzhengzhibu,
        Beijing: Jiefangjun chubanshe, 1989.

ZLRN   *Zhongguo laodong renshi nianjian 1949–1987* (Almanac of
        Chinese labor and personnel affairs, 1949–87). Beijing:
        Laodong renshi chubanshe, 1989.

ZYSXB   *Zhongyang geming genjudi shiliao xuanbian* (A collection of
        historical materials on the central revolutionary base).
        Nanchang: Jiangxi renmin chubanshe, 1982.

CADRES AND CORRUPTION

CHAPTER ONE

Introduction: Organization, Cadres, and Corruption

Why Study Corruption?

Some half a century ago, Mao Zedong addressed the question of how the Communists could avoid falling into the "clean-legitimate-corrupt-demise" cycle, a fate to which other regimes in Chinese history have fallen prey. He declared that "we have found a new path that enables us to break this historical cycle. This is the path of democracy. Only when people participate in monitoring the government does the government become hardworking and non-corrupt. Only when everyone participates will the regime be preserved."[1]

Today, many sectors of Chinese society echo similar concerns. Many question whether the cycle of decline brought about by corruption has been broken and, indeed, whether the People's Republic has progressed very far at all along the new path of democracy envisioned by Mao. Despite the economic achievements of the last two decades, in 1997 China was rated as one of the world's most corrupt countries.[2]

In the 1970s, corruption among officials had become endemic in Communist regimes worldwide. The anti-corruption *cri de coeur* that sounded from Beijing to Bucharest to Budapest in the late 1980s caught the attention of both the leaders of these Communist regimes and of outsiders. It may even be reasonably claimed that corruption played a crucial role in triggering the social and political upheavals in China and the European Communist countries in the late 1980s.[3] Today, both China and Russia, countries under drastic transitions from state socialism, are still experiencing a high degree of corruption in their societies.

Leaders in these countries are, to be sure, well aware of the magnitude of the problem and its potential danger. The Chinese Communist party (CCP) published an open directive on the problem of the deterioration of the relationship between the party and the masses soon after the 1989 Tiananmen protests.[4] It admitted the seriousness of the corruption among party cadres and called for more anti-corruption measures and for the restoration of the old "mass line." Underneath the rhetoric, there was a desperate need for the CCP to refine, and eventually to redefine, the relationship between state and society. Despite the economic successes China has achieved since 1989, its Communist leaders never stopped trying to fight off any potential dangers brought about by rampant corruption among public officials. In the first half of 1999, a new round of "three emphases"—on political commitment, righteousness, and study—was launched among the party and government officials. In effect, it is a campaign to reduce corruption in the public administration and party organization.

Can the CCP succeed in its efforts to control corruption? How do vanguards, who are supposed to be well-disciplined and deployable, become corrupt? What is to blame for the growing tension between the state and society? How well do we really understand the nature, patterns, and extent of official corruption in Communist countries including China? There is much yet to be learned and communicated about official corruption as well as about the nature and fate of Communist regimes, including those that are in transition.

Asking these questions of an ordinary person on the street in China today will get vastly different responses. A peasant interviewee once remarked to a Western scholar, "Chairman Mao said that the scriptures were good, except that from time to time they had been recited by monks with crooked mouths. I wonder about these scriptures; it seems that they have distorted the mouths instead."[5] However, when I asked a retired urban worker what was to blame for the rampant corruption of late, he made a somewhat different point. "The Communist party is a good party," he replied, "but this bunch of monks has distorted the scriptures when reciting them." The differences of opinion reflected by the metaphor are evident: while some still have faith in the party leadership and its policies and place blame for the problem of corruption on the rank and file, others have doubts about the infallibility of the party.

Similarly, within the scholarly community such questions remain a source of contention. Despite growing interest among scholars, however, so far only a few studies have been done on the subject of corruption in China.

Corruption, of course, is nothing new to human society. For a long time people have realized that anyone in a position to exercise public power may be tempted to use such power for purposes other than those allowed by prescribed norms. Corruption has received a considerable amount of attention from the ancient philosophers down to contemporary social scientists. Confucius contended that "only when those who govern remain clean, upright, and unseduced by greed can common people refrain from stealing."[6] Aristotle wrote: "There are three kinds of constitutions, or an equal number of deviations, or as it were, corruption of these three kinds. . . . The deviation or corruption of kingship is tyranny."[7] Corruption has been on the social science research agenda for well over a century, and the intellectual discourse on corruption has become a highly developed, if not yet fully refined, component of social science. Yet despite such efforts, many questions about corruption remain unanswered, making this field an attractive target for scholars. As society develops, old paradigms often fail to supply adequate explanatory and predictive contemporary models. Political corruption remains, therefore, one of the most intriguing and challenging issues in social science research and public policy, perhaps because although it occurs in virtually all polities, its causes, patterns, and consequences often seem unique to each circumstance.

OBJECTIVES OF THIS STUDY

This book has a twofold purpose: it examines official corruption in China, and it also studies the organizational development of the Chinese Communist party in the last five decades since coming to power in 1949. As in other social science inquiries, studies of corruption often attempt to answer all the questions that pertain to the phenomenon: Why does it happen (causes); How does it happen (patterns, forms); What effects does it have (consequences, impacts); and How to control it (solutions, remedies). While it is important to address all of these questions, the complexity of the problem and the difficulties involved in overambitious research projects have often resulted in unconvincing analyses. First, let me make it clear that in this book I intend to focus only on the questions of *why* and *how* — that is, the nature, dynamics, and changing pattern of official corruption in China. The ultimate objective is to offer an explanation of why corruption has become one of the most pervasive problems in Chinese society today.

Second, my underlining assumption, unlike that of many other studies, is that we cannot understand corruption as an isolated phenomenon, but should place it within a broader political and social context. Corruption is not just a problem of administrative or political ethics but also a reflection of political development and changes in regime; for this reason we should study it in the widest possible context. To the extent that this study examines changes in the behavior of China's ruling elite (broadly defined as the officialdom of the ruling Communist party/state), it also seeks to address another issue of even broader significance: the nature of the Chinese Communist regime and its evolution. A central question is what kinds of changes are associated with a revolutionary organization in post-revolutionary times, and how such changes have affected the behavior of its cadres. The principal line of investigation that I will pursue involves the nature of the CCP and the changes in its integration, maintenance, and evolution as a ruling party. These, I suggest, are the underpinnings of elite behavior, normal or deviant, in a Communist context. In other words, I will attempt to analyze the cause of official corruption in China by tracing the organizational development of China's officialdom from the beginning of the Communist regime in 1949 to the present.

Third, on the theoretical level, I hope through this case study to arrive at viable conclusions with implications for comparative as well as Chinese studies. Like many other important aspects of post-1949 China, the issue of elite corruption rekindles an old debate: how much of the problem is uniquely Chinese, and how much is common to all developing regimes, Communist or otherwise? Does corruption in a Communist setting differ from that found in other political systems? The problem of official corruption offers us an opportunity to revisit the question of whether the Communist revolution did after all transform Chinese society. Using a historical approach, this study will make inquiries about not only corruption in contemporary China under market reforms—a popular subject—but also official deviance in PRC history since 1949 under both radical and developmental Maoism.[8]

THE SCOPE AND METHODS OF RESEARCH

Let me emphasize that my focus in this study is *official* or *cadre* corruption, that is, corrupt acts committed by public officials. Corruption by non-officials bears a relation to official corruption but should be treated differently. Students of corruption have noted an important factor: the independent power of the bureaucratic elite, as distinguished from that of the political elite. They have argued that corruption is likely to occur when a bureaucratic elite is intermeshed with the political elite or is dominated by it to such an extent that the interests of top politicians dictate the activities of top bureaucrats in the performance of their duties.[9] But this argument has limited analytical power in the case of a political system ruled by a cadre party, where the distinction between "political" and "bureaucratic" elite bears little conceptual meaning because of "the collapsing of the official and political realms."[10] In this sense, the concepts of "electoral corruption," "administrative corruption," "bureaucratic corruption," or even "political corruption" (in its narrow sense) that are common in the Western literature on elite corruption lack relevance to Communist politics.

In studies of corruption in China, ample attention is often given to reported cases involving high-ranking officials such as the automobile smuggling case of a deputy governor of Hainan province in 1987 and the corruption case of a former mayor of Beijing in 1996. Through pursuing these well-publicized cases, the government intends to show its resolve to curb official corruption and to ease tensions between the state and society. However, I believe that these high-profile cases do not excite the discontent and alienation of the people nearly as much as does the deviant behavior of lower-level officials who have daily interaction with and direct supervisory power over ordinary citizens. In this study, therefore, I give attention to lower-level cadres, including officials in positions below the county level in rural areas and the *ju* (bureau) level in urban areas.

Corruption is a politically sensitive subject in all societies, for obvi-

ous reasons. Studying it in an authoritarian country is even more difficult. Serious methodological challenges are thus posed to those who
take on such studies. As a scholar studying bribery once noted, there is
always the temptation to quantify, yet quantification in corruption studies has never been systematically attempted.[11] There are no existing sets
of figures by which one could conclude that the Qing dynasty was more
or less corrupt than the People's Republic of China or the Roman
empire. Corruption studies need not rest on a statistical basis, however.
Researchers have adopted various approaches to address the issue,
such as relying on legal case studies of economic crimes, news media
reports, émigré interviews, participant observation, and so on. My own
experience with investigating and collecting information on corruption
cases shows that much depends upon how one defines corrupt behavior and whom one investigates. In this study, I use both textual and
interview sources of information. I have interviewed many people during several field trips to China between 1991 and 1996, including both
party cadres and non-party members. Given the sensitivity of the subject, I have omitted names of informants.

When corruption in the PRC is under study, textual work can com-
pensate for inaccuracies and sometimes for the reluctance of interview-
ees to speak about cases in which they are directly involved. In the
study of the post-1949 period, the conventional reliance on news reports
and other official publications of the time is problematic due to the
dearth of reports critical of the party/state. One source I have utilized is
local gazetteers (*difangzhi*) that were updated in the last decade. Local
gazetteers are official or unofficial records of social, economic, communal, cultural, and political history. Traditionally, they were updated reg-
ularly by the local literati. After the Communist revolution, most local
gazetteers ceased to be updated until the early 1980s. The last decade
has seen scores of counties publish their updated version of county
gazetteers, based on classified local official archives and given official
blessing. While some of them omit discussion of sensitive political
issues, they provide an invaluable source of information on local history during political campaigns such as the Great Leap Forward, the
Four Cleanup Campaign, and the Cultural Revolution.

One of the obstacles that often confront students of Chinese politics is
the unavailability of *neibu* (internal) publications, which are meant

either for specified ranks of officials or for circulation inside China only. Cadres' deviant behavior often was, and to some extent still is, a sensitive subject that the party would prefer to keep to itself. Many materials which contain such cases are classified for internal use only. Although in recent years a number of historical documents containing information about several major post-1949 periods have been published, they are usually strictly for internal use and circulation. Few, if any, scholarly works in the West have used these sources. Even many of the official archives and records of the Great Leap Forward and the Four Cleanup Campaign periods are still classified and access to them is very difficult, if not impossible. Nevertheless, I was able to consult some case materials and data from internal documents and reports, which I cite in this study.

Another often-neglected primary source of information, *baogao wenxue* (reportage)—along with *jishi wenxue* (literature that records facts) and *zhuanji wenxue* (biographical literature)—has provided a valuable source for my study. I have gone over hundreds of articles of reportage published since 1979, when reportage became a medium through which investigative reporters and writers could publish while avoiding political censorship and repercussions, claiming that the article was only a literary work or a report based on investigation.[12] Reportage was, understandably, often used to expose the dark side of the system and society. It is no coincidence that such exposés have sometimes caused political backlash against those who wrote or published them. To search for useful empirical evidence in *baogao wenxue* can be a time-consuming job, for aside from a half dozen or so journals that carry mostly this type of work, exposés are scattered in hundreds of literary journals. To be sure, one has to be very cautious when using materials from *baogao wenxue,* because there is some literary coloring of the facts; I have thus tried not to use any suspiciously detailed descriptions of cases that took place long ago.

What Is Corruption? The Issue of Definition

As many students of corruption have noted, the generic concept of corruption has been one of the most complex, problematic, and changeable in the literature of the political and social sciences. The term has been used to cover everything from the commonsense idea of the "putrid rot of body politic" to the very abstract technical-legal definition of official malfeasance.

There are two main schools of thought on corruption. The first can be called "universalist" and seeks to define corruption using certain common properties; the premise is that such properties make certain behavior "corruption" in all societies. The second is "relativist," and contends that what is corrupt in one society may not be in another. Most contemporary scholars on corruption agree, though, that a working definition of corruption that can be applied across country boundaries should be, and indeed is, possible.

One type of definition is centered on the *public interest*. Scholars who apply this kind of definition maintain that the concept of the public interest is useful, even necessary, to demonstrate the essence of concepts such as corruption. Carl Friedrich contends that the pattern of corruption can be said to exist "whenever a power holder who is charged with doing certain things . . . is, by monetary or other rewards not legally provided for, induced to take actions which favor whoever provides the rewards and thereby does damage to the public and its interests."[13]

Corruption involves a deviation from certain standards of behavior. The question is, what criteria shall we use to establish these standards? Here the relativists point out quite rightly that a practice—nepotism, for example—may be regarded in some societies as corrupt and forbidden but may be acceptable and expected in others. Certain practices may be "corrupt" at one time but not at another. For this reason, a concept based on public interest tends to be subjective. Indeed, in terms of workability alone, the public interest criterion poses great difficulties. As James Scott has commented, a standard of public interest would require an unambiguous definition of the public interest in order "to classify acts according to whether or not they serve that interest."[14] In countries such as China and the former Soviet Union, where the Communist polity blurred the demarcation of the public and private spheres, the viability of such a definition is weak and only tenuously relevant to our study.

Even within a single society, particularly one that lacks a general consensus on the definition of "public" and "private," what the society perceives as normal and permissible behavior may not be so regarded by its government. Again, this definition can merit little acceptance because it would represent an attempt to resolve an essentially normative or ideological question.

Another type of definition—*market-centered*—is more popular among economists. Definitions of corruption that focus on the market have been developed on two grounds. One is the axiom of self-interest maximization of *homo oeconomicus*, which denies normative constraints; the other is the belief held by those dealing with premodern Western and contemporary non-Western societies that norms governing public officeholders are not clearly articulated or are nonexistent. For example, the German historian Jacob Van Klaveren claims that "a corrupt civil servant regards his public office as a business, the income of which he will . . . seek to maximize. . . . The size of his income depends upon the market situation and his talent for finding the point of maximal gain on the public's demand curve."[15]

Ironically, those who apply market-centered definitions and the rationalist/political economics approach join those who take the social-cultural approach in criticizing public-interest-centered definitions as being subjective and ethnocentric. On the other hand, market-centered definitions and the rationalist approach are also criticized as "unacceptable because by definition they preclude the existence of a distinct political realm with distinct norms and so on."[16] The most commonly adopted definition is *public-office-centered*. It views corruption in political-institutional terms. To Joseph Nye, corruption refers to "behavior which deviates from the normal duties of a public role because of private-regarding (personal, close family, private clique) pecuniary or status gains; or violates rules against the exercise of certain types of private-regarding influence."[17]

Public-office definitions are often associated with explanations that trace the cause of corruption to structural and institutional causes. Nye's definition identifies the basic components of official corruption at the individual level. It stresses the behavioral element of intentional deviation for personal gain. This definition will constitute the starting point of this study, although I will need to make some revisions to render it more relevant to the contemporary Chinese situation.

TOWARD A RECONCEPTUALIZATION OF CORRUPTION

In addition to the theoretical contentions regarding a definition of corruption the issue of how to make the concept operational, that is, what to include and what not to in a study of corruption, also arises. In today's social science vocabulary, as we can see from the variety of definitions discussed above, the word "corruption" has been used either too broadly—including everything from malfeasance, scandals, and the usurpation of power to bribery, embezzlement, and extortion—or too narrowly, referring primarily to *material* corruption, that is, deviant practices in return for receiving some kind of material benefits. The issue of definition remains highly confusing and hampers the efforts to study the problem.

The broad usage of the term "corruption" has existed for many years. Robert Brooks, in an essay published early in the twentieth century on corruption in America, defined corruption as "the intentional misperformance or neglect of a recognized duty, or the unwarranted exercise of power, with the motive of gaining advantage more or less personal."[18] Such a broad application raises the question of whether to consider as corrupt all forms of particularistic behavior in public organizations, or only those forms that involve pecuniary gain for public servants. Some scholars have recommended that all forms of bureaucratic behavior in which personal roles take precedence over organizational roles be deemed a problem of organizational control, and that corruption be viewed as a subtype of this more general organizational problem.[19]

In China, the concept of corruption also poses difficulties in practical usage. Narrowly defined, it refers only to actions that violate the penal code and other statutes generally falling under the rubric of graft—including both taking (*shouhui*) and giving (*huilu*) bribes—the peculation of public funds (*nuoyong gongkuan*), embezzlement (*tanwu*), and, until the early 1990s, speculation and profiteering (*touji daoba*).[20]

In studies of corruption in China, often a narrowly defined, economic-oriented definition of corruption is applied.[21] These studies tend to trace the first appearance of corruption in the Communist party/state to the end of the Maoist era, or roughly around the late 1970s when the economic reforms began, and treat corruption as if it were a problem unrelated to the broader political and social context. The patterns of corruption, we are told, are mainly related to official abuses of power for tangible interests, and such abuses really only became possible on a large scale after the market began to emerge. Early studies were greatly influenced by the study of corruption of the Soviet apparatchik modeled after the "second economy" theory of Grossman.[22] This approach has led researchers to bury themselves in a seemingly endless maze of economic crimes, including embezzlement, bribery, profiteering, extortion, and the like, and to lose sight of the equally, if not more, important issue of official deviance that is *political* in nature. Naturally, researchers' attention was drawn to areas like Guangdong, Fujian, and other "open" regions of China, where tremendous wheeling and dealing goes on, as well as to cases of officials in positions where they are likely to be involved in power-for-money games, such as foreign trade, officials-turned-businessmen, and official firms.

From another standpoint, people also tend to perceive a whole spectrum of other behavior by officials as "corrupt" (*fubai*) in China. This broad definition of corruption can also be found in the official literature. Numerous terms more often metaphoric than explicit have been used to describe corrupt behavior, including *fubai* (decay, corruption), *fuhua* (immoral or scandalous activities), *buzheng zhifeng* (unhealthy tendencies), and *dangfeng wenti* (problems in party work style).[23] Any disciplinary problem in the party organization could be regarded as a corruption problem.

In the Chinese context, then, an operational concept of corruption should facilitate the following considerations. First, it should be broad enough to include not only narrowly defined corrupt acts such as bribery, embezzlement, and backdoor deals (*zouhoumen*, literally "going through the backdoor") but also such practices as nepotism, patronage, and statistical falsification, which do not necessarily involve monetary exchange or material gains. Second, it should emphasize the deviation of a public servant's action from prescribed norms, legal or organizational. Thus, both "economic crimes" and *buzheng zhifeng* ("unhealthy tendencies") would be treated as forms of corruption. Third, it should concern behavior deviant from prescribed norms that is also aimed at private gain. For this reason, concepts such as *guanliao zhuyi* (bureau-cratism), *tuoli qunzhong* (detachment from the masses), and *wenshan huihai* (excessive directives and meetings), which are usually regarded by the regime as problems of wrongful work-style, would not be included.

Instead of applying an ambiguously defined concept of corruption, I propose a broad conceptualization of *official deviance*, which refers to all forms of behavior that deviate from the prescribed norms of a regime, in which individuals or groups exploit the formal organization instead of working for it, and in which personal roles take precedence over organizational roles. The behavior itself, as conducted by public agents, may not be for private purposes. Official deviance so defined includes both corrupt conduct and non-corrupt misconduct. Deviant modes of operation such as statistical falsification and forming and using personal connections (*la guanxi*) are examples of official deviance that are not necessarily corruption per se.[24] Corruption, then, can be conceived as a type of official deviance: all corruption by public officials is official deviance, but not all forms of official deviance are corruption.

Corruption by public officials renders itself mainly in two forms, economic and non-economic corruption. They in turn consist of three subtypes: *graft*, *rent-seeking*, and *prebendalism*.

Graft. Graft, the most common form of corruption, can be found in almost all countries. In its narrowest sense, corruption is often defined as graft. Conduct such as bribery, illicit kickbacks, embezzlement, and peculation of public funds belongs to this type of deviant behavior. What characterizes this type of deviance is that it often involves something of value given to, and accepted by, public officials for dishonest or illegal purposes. It may also involve officials engaging in fraudulent expenditures or diversion of public funds for private benefit.

Rent-seeking. Since the concept of "rent-seeking" first appeared in analyses of corruption by economists, it has been used to refer to all forms of corrupt behavior by people with monopolistic power.[25] In conventional rent-seeking literature, however, the rent-seekers are private citizens with privileged access to a monopoly. Public officials, through granting a license or monopoly to their clients, create "rents"—extra earnings obtained by virtue of a restricted market. They are regarded as rent-generators and are involved in corruption to the extent that rents are granted discriminatorily to people they favor. It is akin to what some scholars call "cronyism" in Old Regime France, namely, the phenomenon in which officeholders and their cronies enjoyed monopoly rents not available to other social classes.[26] In the Chinese case, however, public officials are both rent-generators and rent-seekers in that they both generate rent opportunities for others and seek such opportunities to benefit themselves by virtue of a monopoly. When officials become rent-seekers they are in effect putting non-official rent-seekers in a disadvantageous position. The concept is employed to refer to the behavior by public officials or agencies of seeking illicit profits through a monopoly over critical resources or regulatory power. It includes profiteering by officials or official firms, and extortion in the forms of illicit impositions, apportionments, fees, and other kinds of charges. The rent-seeking type of corruption is marked by its usurpation of a monopoly over critical resources. Although in the economic literature the term was originally used to depict the activities by private citizens who had obtained certain monopolies from the state, in this study it mainly refers to the conduct exhibited by public officials who have direct control over, and wield, government authority in the economy.

Prebendalism. Prebendalism refers to the practice where incumbents of public office receive privileges and perquisites tied to that office.[27] Incumbency or control of an office entitles the holder to rents or payments for undertaking real or fictitious duties.[28] It occurs when "organizations are transformed from places of work to resource banks whereby individuals and informal groups pursue their own goals."[29] In its extreme form, such as is found in some contemporary African countries, prebendalism provides a context in which the state is perceived as congeries of office susceptible to individual *cum* communal appropriation.[30] If the other two subtypes of corruption are pecuniary and tangible, prebendal corruption is not necessarily about monetary gains. That is, it may not involve economic corruption. It manifests itself in such forms as usurpation of official privilege, backdoor deals, clientelism, cronyism, and nepotism.[31] Prebendalistic behavior deviates from the norms of public office—in this case the party/state—with a goal of private gain that is primarily non-economic and political in nature.

Not all corruption is transactional in nature, that is, involving two parties, as in its most common manifestation, bribery. Whereas in briberies two parties exchange favors, other non-transactional forms may involve only one party, the incumbents of public office themselves.[32] It is the latter who should arouse our attention, for under a regime in which political power is not only very much concentrated but even omnipotent, the usurpation of power by public officials for private purposes does not always involve give-and-take dyadic relations, and it may be more prevalent than bribery.

This broad re-conceptualization not only includes more forms of deviant behavior by public officials but sharpens the distinctions among various kinds of corruption. It enables us to investigate and analyze cadre corruption and organizational change in a country where the boundaries between public and private have shifted at different times and the official definition of corruption has remained vague.

Explaining Corruption

A survey of the social science literature in the field produces a long list, which, nonetheless, can be categorized into three major approaches to explaining corruption: institutional, actor-centered rationalist, and sociocultural.

INSTITUTIONS AND CORRUPTION

The main assumption of the *institutional approach* is that the cause of corruption is to be found in the political system and its processes. There are two main lines of argument. One views corruption as induced by bureaucratization, by permanent bureaucratic inertia; the other takes an opposite position, that corruption is a consequence of "maladministration," of the lack of an impersonal and universalistic bureaucratic system. The former is most often found in case studies of Britain, the United States, and other capitalist industrialized countries. In these societies, corruption is viewed as a consequence of the shift from the impersonal logic of the market to bureaucratic impersonalism. A typical argument in this vein can be found in the treatment of "machine" politics in early twentieth-century urban America. Corruption is seen here as a functional equalizer providing access to resources for various disadvantaged groups in the face of a blindly impersonal and inefficient bureaucracy.

The bureaucratization thesis of corruption corresponds to one important strand of thought in comparative Communism that contains both Marxist and non-Marxist components. Central to the Marxist component is Marx's somewhat ambivalent view of the state. On the one hand, the state is not an independent and autonomous force in history, but rather an instrument of the ruling classes. However, Marx implied at the same time that certain socio-historical situations are conducive to the autonomy of the state. The classic stand of Marx on the capitalist state bureaucracy, that it is *not* a separate class in and of itself but rather a reflection of the class relationships within society, finds a variant in Marx's own analysis of a Bonapartist bureaucracy that had the freedom to manipulate societal interests politically. This latter line of argument was first applied to the socialist state by Trotsky.[33] Other Marxist theorists, however, were more sanguine than Marx in positing the socialist state as an autonomous entity and bureaucracy, a class not only in but for itself. Well-known to Western students of Communist politics is the thesis of the "new class" expounded by Milovan Djilas. The theory that not only echoed Djilas's view, however, but also put it into practice to forestall the forming of a socialist bureaucratic class was the Maoist version of "continuing revolution under the dictatorship of the proletariat." According to the Maoist notion, which was shared by some Chinese social democrats in the short-lived democratic movement of the late 1970s, the bureaucratic class inside the party was "worse than the capitalists in sucking the blood of the workers."[34] It was no coincidence that the Cultural Revolution was described by those same people as "a major struggle waged between the proletariat and the bureaucratic class," and a necessary revolution to eliminate the new privileged and corrupt class."[35] In addition, there was the non-Marxist criticism of "a highly bureaucratized" regime and society that was regarded as the source of corruption in Communist countries.[36] The "maladministration" argument is commonly found in the literature on corruption in developing nations. According to this concept, the roots of corrupt behavior lie in the politicization of bureaucracy. As Kempe Hope explains, "the saliency of political dominance over bureaucratic values created a style of administrative behavior that is highly politicized despite the formal acceptance of a career system of administration based on a high degree of professionalism."[37]

If the "bureaucratization" and "maladministration" theories of corruption in Communist countries focus on the nature of bureaucracy, another line of argument pays attention, instead, to institutions other than the bureaucracy itself. Its adherents suggest that the causes of corruption can be found, for example, in the lack of any market and in the prevalent scarcity that led to a "second economy";[38] or in the weak, imperfect legal systems and lack of rule by law that often fails to sanction and prevent corruption;[39] or in the socialist state structure and power relations that make the socialist regimes "more prone to graft";[40] or, finally, in the reform policies that "easily triggered" corruption.[41]

THE MARKET AND CORRUPTION

While some scholars try to explain corruption by establishing links between institutions and bureaucratic behavior, others search for economic reasons accentuated by the rational calculation of people involved in corrupt transactions. Studies of competition for a public contract by Rose-Ackerman and MacRae's game theoretical model on "transaction costs" represent examples of the microeconomics approach. Attempts were also made to employ a principal-agent model in a study of corruption by Chinese fiscal bureaucrats in the late imperial period.[42] This kind of reasoning tends to be formal and methodologically rigorous and capable of analyzing the costs and benefits of corrupt actions. It helps us to understand the process of a given *bribery* action from initiation to the bargaining stage for establishing a transaction, also. However, the approach is limited in its scope of application to more subtle forms of corruption that involve not two actors or two actors in power relationships, but equal bargainers. As indicated below, corruption in pre-reform China, and for that matter, in other Communist societies, usually is rendered in the form of "auto-corruption," that is, the non-transaction type. The main weakness of the microeconomic approach, though, is that by focusing mainly on why and when corruption is profitable, "the answers often have to be trivial,"[43] ignoring the larger and more significant socio-political environment in which corruption occurs.

Another rationalist variant operates on the macro-structural level, represented by studies that apply the theory of rent-seeking.[44] The basic argument is that when circumstances allow (usually when the market is not well nurtured and is mediated by strong administrative manipulation), people attempt to use legal or illegal means to gain, extend, and protect monopoly positions, special treatment, and privilege. Doing so inevitably leads to corruption. Government restriction is seen as the source of the problem. The more extensive the government's control and intervention, the more rents it creates and the more rent-seeking will follow. The consequence of rent-seeking is the waste of social resources consumed by competition for rent.

This mode of reasoning claims essentially that the lack of economic development and the presence of restrictive government intervention are the main structural factors leading to corruption. Corruption is seen primarily as a consequence of scarcity, artificially created by government desires to promote economic growth. Proponents of this theory assert that corruption takes place when there is a shortage of supply under government dispensation facing a growing demand. This gap between supply and demand creates a situation in which the market price for these goods is above their official price. Individuals who desire the scarce values will be willing to buy at a higher market price. Robert Tilman puts it this way: "Corruption involves a shift from a mandatory pricing model to a free-market model. The centralized allocative mechanism, which is the ideal of modern bureaucracy, may break down in the face of serious disequilibrium between supply and demand."[45]

A somewhat similar argument is advanced by some economists who study Communist economy and corruption. They see dysfunctionality in corrupt activities, as with the "second economy" theory mentioned earlier.[46] In recent years, some Chinese authors have taken a similar approach but added a sophisticated theoretical dimension when, in the

late 1980s, rent-seeking theory was introduced to Chinese reform economists. They blame the dual-track pricing system—the legitimate coexistence of state-controlled and market prices—in the reform economy
as the source of pervasive *"guandao,"* a phenomenon of speculation by
public officials or state agencies buying goods at fixed state prices and
selling at higher market prices.[47]

Models along the same lines as the macroeconomic rent-seeking theory provide a convincing explanation for the establishment of certain
links between scarcity, monopoly, government control, and corruption.
Particularly illuminating is their sobering analysis of the waste of social
resources that corruption causes, in direct contrast to those "revision-
ists" who regard corruption as driven by a market that equalizes the
chances of participation in bureaucratic decision-making. The problem,
as Margaret Levi points out, is that the focus of these neoclassic political
economists is too narrow.[48] In her view, those who see the "negative
impact of government on the economy normatively advocate a competitive market as the most socially effective means of producing goods
and services, turning a blind eye to the fact that inefficiencies are often
caused by the market itself."[49] That is, those who ardently present themselves as value-free in studying corruption by criticizing the cultural
approach cannot escape the very pitfall they are trying to avoid—the
market is not neutral after all. More serious flaws, however, lie in the
reductionist tendency of the "market" approach, in that it overlooks the
political realm and corruption in non-economic activities not entirely
driven by pure economic considerations. Paradoxically, that is the very
reason why this approach is so fruitful: it latches precisely onto cases in
which incentives override public norms.[50]

CULTURE AND CORRUPTION

The sociocultural approach can be found most often in the literature on
corruption in developing countries,[51] and sometimes in the treatment of
Communist[52] and early capitalist countries.[53] Although somewhat different in their analytical units, some studies being more psychological
and attitudinal at the individual level while others are more macro-
structural at the societal level, the analytical focus of this approach,
influenced by Fred Riggs's ecological treatment of public administra-

tion, is generally the sociocultural milieu of corruption.[54] They pay great attention to values, ethos, and "cultures of corruption." This strand of scholarship is labeled "populist theories" because it explains corrupt practices on the basis of certain traits of the public, such as, according to James Scott, a large immigrant population not steeped in the political culture of democracy, widespread poverty, or low levels of education.[55] Studies of this kind argue that these countries lack a well-developed market or institutionalized bureaucracy with strong pressures coming from society; they generally depict a weak state permeated by strong, often traditional, societal values and norms.[56] This approach is closely related to modernization theories, and some authors view corruption as in some ways functional. They stress the need for rapid development of the economy in developing countries, in a context that still lacks comparable and compatible political and administrative institutions to facilitate and sustain the resulting economic growth. This disparity creates pressure for finding solutions that are short of reform and forestall violence.

Some Western scholars of Chinese corruption follow this line of reasoning. They emphasize that the "genesis of corruption" is the mixture and incompatibility of Marxist virtues imported from the West and a traditional Confucian ethos still residing in the deep structure of society.[57] They consider that Chinese culture has a tendency to engage in corrupt practices because individuals do not internalize norms, and thus outside judgments circumscribe their behavior, creating a "culture of shame" as opposed to a "culture of guilt." In the PRC, the Communist party has in fact failed to transform such a culture.[58] Thus, they argue, corruption cannot be stopped until the party successfully replaces the current value system with a stable and *new* "articulated moral element."

Cultural theories of corruption have found their counterparts in China, especially in the 1980s. A typical article on corruption by Chinese scholars would usually blame "feudal influence" as the source of unhealthy tendencies in the party and society.[59] While some Chinese scholars have been concerned with the existence of a "culture of corruption" that persisted for generations even after the Communists took over, others soberly pursue the question of why "feudal"[60] values have not only survived but thrived. They generally point to the fact that in the Maoist era the main objective of many political campaigns was always "anti-capitalism" rather than "anti-feudalism." This thrust, they argue, has permitted the residual cultural elements of the small-production-oriented peasantry to survive.[61]

A simple and unbalanced cultural explanation of corruption contains pitfalls such as are often found among cultural theories, that is, assigning too much unwarranted explanatory power to the value system as an independent variable. Cultural theories identify significant factors but fall short of asking the more fundamental questions of *how* and *what* values have survived changes in society. In general, such theories provide a powerful answer to the question of why people do what they do, but they are often criticized as static and unable to encompass change. Questions of why and in what way the corruption-prone values and ethos survived the revolutionary changes remain unanswered.

ORGANIZATION AND CORRUPTION

In addition to these three schools of mainstream scholarship, there is an often-overlooked *organizational approach* to corruption. This viewpoint regards corruption as a problem innate to all formal bureaucratic organizations, where the "irrationality, uncontrolled behavior, and unanticipated consequences that constantly exist" are derived from the "bureaucratic vicious cycle."[62] Rooted in post-Weberian organizational theories, it considers corruption as a consequence of over-rationalization and over-institutionalization. Insightful as this approach is in calling for a closer look at organizational structures and operational modes, however, herein also lies its weakness. Criticizing the Weberian thesis of rational technical organization, proponents of this viewpoint suggest that informal human relations exist within a formal organization and require the attention of the organizational leaders. These relations need not be dysfunctional, and indeed may be beneficial to the achievement of organizational goals. While these post-Weberian organization theorists made contributions in highlighting the importance of human factors and informal organization, they fall short in accounting for the detrimental effects of informal modes of organizational development.

Kenneth Jowitt offers another organizational approach to analyzing corruption inherent in a particular type of organizational change, that of

Communist regimes. His approach explores the nature of corruption at the organizational level, which typifies corruption peculiar to Communist regimes. According to Jowitt, "*Corruption* refers to an organization's loss of its specific competence through failure to identify a task and strategy that practically distinguish between rather than equate or confuse, (particular) members with (general) organizational interests."[63] To Jowitt, corruption in Communist societies is not so much a problem of improper behavior of individuals as a problem of what he calls "regime corruption." Corruption becomes widespread and systemic when an evolving Communist regime reaches a historical developmental stage of "neotraditionalism."[64]

This approach not only captures the very nature of corruption in post-revolutionary movements but also is useful in interpreting the changes of a Communist polity. It points to one of the generic features of Communist systems, that is, the importance of an organization that has the capability to define and manipulate the interests of members. The focus on a ruling party organization (the Communist party/state) that Jowitt advocates for studying corruption in Communist states promises potent analytical power in understanding this phenomenon, and I have adopted it in this study. However, two aspects of the thesis require some reformulation. The first concerns his conceptualization of corruption. By defining it in organizational terms, Jowitt's arguments tend to confuse two kinds of corruption—corruption *of* organization and corruption *in* organization—while at the same time trying to address both issues. This confusion makes it unclear how one may distinguish the weakening capacity of the organization, Communist or other, to set norms for its members (corruption *of* the organization) and the increasing deviance by members of the organization (corruption *in* the organization). The main problem, then, is operational rather than theoretical. Questions remain as to how to find the connections between the two situations, for, after all, corruption at the individual level or the sub-organizational level is what most studies of corruption are concerned with. I suggest that an individual-oriented definition of corruption can be associated with an organizational approach, and that the two processes, corruption of the organization and corruption in the organization, are linked. Indeed, it is on this ground that I raise the basic question of this study: how would corruption *of* an organization affect corruption *in* an organization, and vice versa?

The second aspect needing reformulation goes to the strength of Jowitt's theory, which lies in his historical view of the Communist regimes. It points to both the nature and change of these regimes over time.[65] Jowitt correctly places great significance on informal structures such as political culture and organizational ethos. However, the predestined developmental profile that he construed about Communist regimes, with neotraditionalism being one of the stages, is overemphasized, whereas the *unintended* consequences of short-term policy and institutional changes are overlooked. In this regard, the question that needs to be examined is this: how did certain rules, codes of conduct, and policies of the party result in unintended consequences in cadre behavior?

Organizational Involution

To address these questions and to understand the relationship between the organizational development of a ruling Communist party and the corruption of its elite, I propose a thesis of "organizational involution" based on the theory of Communist neotraditionalism and conceptually informed by the anthropological theory of agricultural involution.[66] Organizational involution refers to a process whereby a revolutionary party, while adopting and expanding many "modern" (i.e., rational, empirical, impersonal) structures, refuses and fails to adapt itself to, and be transformed by, the routinization and bureaucratization that characterize modern bureaucracy; at the same time, it is unable to maintain its original distinctive competence and identity. Its members make adjustments and adaptations neither through revolutionary ideologies nor modern institutions and practices, but through reinforced and elaborated traditional modes of operation. Rather than evolving toward regularization and rationalization, the regime becomes indefinitely patrimonial.

Drawing on Jowitt's theory, the organizational involution thesis is based on the premise that the nature of Communist organizations can inform us about inherent contradictions with an impact on political and social development after their coming into power, and that the results of such development are far from what totalitarian theories originally predicted.

The involutionary change of a post-revolutionary regime results in a neotraditionalism characterized by informal modes of operation, cellular institutions, personalistic networks, a ritualistic ethos, and corruption of non-economic forms. Organizational involution is unique in that it differs from other possible directions of change—*evolutionary* development, which maintains revolutionary integrity, and *devolutionary* development, which results in bureaucratization and abandonment of the revolutionary ideology and its goals.[67] It produces neither modern bureaucrats who are rational, role-conscious, and rule-oriented, as a *devolutionary* development of revolutionary organization would,[68] nor well-maintained, disciplined, and committed revolutionary cadres, as an *evolutionary* process of continuous revolution ideally should; instead, it produces disillusioned, status-conscious, and undisciplined cadres,[69] who, in the manner of pre-revolutionary (i.e., traditional) local officials, put the interests of more intimate secondary and primary groups above those of the regime.

As a result of the process of organizational involution, the movement grows into an organization that upholds its formal revolutionary goals, operating under a set of formal, impersonal, and routine procedures; in fact, however, many of its own patterns of behavior and relationship mirror traditional, informal modes. The discrepancies between the prescribed organizational ideology and norms, the formal structures and rules, and the value system of its members become increasingly salient. A unique revolutionary movement that was once perceived by Lenin and some Western scholars as an "organizational weapon" and, in the terms of the human relations school of organization theory, prized as an "institution" rather than an "organization," gradually becomes *de*institutionalized.[70] It is precisely the conscious choice of anti-routinization, anti-bureaucratization measures, which were to fulfill the goal of "continuous revolution" under socialism, that is responsible for the occurrence of the involution. Under just such circumstances, the corrupt behavior of those Helen Siu calls "socialist peddlers and princes" becomes prevalent, and "state involution" becomes possible.[71]

During the developmental period of a regime, as long as the need for routinization and functionalization grew and rationalization in the sense of effective social engineering was desired, regimes that took this involutionary path did not simply replicate traditional or pre-existing norms, as depicted by Clifford Geertz's involution model. Organizational involution results in *reinforcement*, not simple replication or expansion, of some traditional modes. Indeed, all modern organizations reflect a complex pattern of continuity and change with regard to their traditional social structures and the consequences of modernization, however limited.[72] In one sense, *all* organizations bear certain traditional and modern patterns. The question, rather, is why institutional and cultural patterns common to premodern settings are more apparent and prevalent in some organizations than in others. The resistance to the revolutionary integrative force by cadres and the rejection of bureaucratic routinization by the leadership did not merely stem from the extra-organizational cultural patterns of society. It arose mainly from the paradox that the regime created for itself, namely, a structure that reinforces traditional ways rather than sustaining new norms, and from the precariousness of revolutionary values that can not successfully transcend, transform, and, more important, maintain even the regime's own rank and file as loyal and deployable agents.

FOCUS ON ORGANIZATION

The organizational involution thesis focuses on the ruling (regime) organization and officialdom rather than the residual elements of societal values that supposedly survived the revolution. It is thus predicated on the means and contents of organizational integration and on the logic of actual operation of the organization. The dynamics of maintenance of organizational integrity is seen as a source of change. The questions we ask are: What policies, institutions, or code of conduct have affected the behavior of rank and file cadres? In what way did cadres follow or deviate from these rules and policies?

This thesis examines how the Communist regime operates not only as an autonomous power vis-à-vis society. But also, and more important, it looks at the inner dynamics of the organization itself: how it has created, maintained, and regenerated organizational integrity and the legitimization of authority and how such integration has affected the behavior of its members, namely, the cadres. Our attention now shifts back to the regime and its staff.

Rather than merely concerning itself with structural causes of organizational change and cadre behavior, this framework takes into account both formal and informal, procedural and substantive aspects that define patterns of belief and behavior of the organization and the elite members belonging to it.[73] Questions to be asked are: What are the contents, not merely the forms, of the organizational ethos, such as modes of operation, by the organization and by the cadres? To be more specific, we ask whether the cadres, the elite members of Communist organizations, individually and as a whole have been maintained as committed, disciplined, uncorrupted, and deployable agents.

Organizational involution is a framework intended not merely to capture the nature of a regime by analyzing a novel conceptual type (as Andrew Walder's earlier work tried to accomplish) but also to capture better the *change* in Communist regimes after revolutionary movements seize power. Thus, this framework provides a remedy for the lack of a dynamic analysis of changing institutions, policies, and norms, which affected in their own ways the behavior of elite and masses alike. It also posits the predicaments and dilemmas that many Communist organizations have faced. On the one hand, these were movements with revolutionary goals and ideologies, and some of them had already formed distinctive competencies and identities during civil wars. Early on, when the movements first seized power, these revolutionary features provided the raison d'être for the organization and helped forge organizational coherence. The ultimate tools for organizational integration—"pure" and "practical" revolutionary ideologies[74]—continued to be upheld even during the post-revolutionary stage. On the other hand, faced with nation-building and developmental tasks, the Communist organizations as ruling parties encountered problems such as the changing social composition of members, increasing needs for new kinds of competencies of its cadres, and a functional inclination to routinization that posed a challenge to revolutionary values. The various Communist regimes responded to these challenges and handled difficulties differently. Some were more adaptive than others. To some, particularly the Chinese leaders, and notably Mao among them, the path of routinization did not appear attractive. Instead of adapting to the needs of modernization or simply retreating to residual patterns of traditional relations, they attempted to create new revolutionary situations, combat tasks, and ideological discourses, striving to maintain the revolutionary nature of the organization despite changing conditions.

IMPETUS FOR ORGANIZATIONAL CHANGE

As a revolutionary movement becomes a ruling party, it faces an impetus for organizational change arising from two directions. Both routinization/bureaucratization and continuous revolution have affected the developmental course of Communist organizations. In China during the Maoist era, organizational change was driven primarily by the thrusts intended to maintain the radical charismatic mission, the "uninterrupted revolution." An involution emerged with conscious revolutionary goals, goals that, ironically, were intended precisely to prevent situations such as routinization or involution from taking place. In fact, involution of the Chinese regime began first as a consequence of revolutionary mobilization and the "combat task"[75] of anti-bureaucratization. It was only later that the involutionary process received another impingement, that of modernization of the economic and managerial systems. Viewed as such, the process is not a simple cyclical replication of a historical event in a given society. Rather, it affects the stability and development of a regime that does not repeat history. To the extent that all Communist regimes have faced at one time or another the problem of routinization and have often opted to prevent it, organizational involution may well be a generic Communist phenomenon.[76] However, because of the dominant concern of the CCP leadership to carry out continuous revolution, the Maoist emphasis on the compatibility of a cultural "superstructure" with a new political regime, and the conviction of the power of moral discourse over institutional elements (itself rooted in the traditional Chinese belief in moral indoctrination and cultivation), the propensity toward routinization that charismatic movements may often face[77] was much more consciously and constantly disrupted, suppressed, and even reversed in China than in any other Communist regimes.

THE FORMAL AND THE INFORMAL

The main contribution of the involution theory to anthropology has been to reveal the discrepancy between the façade of modern forms as a result of revolution (in the sense of drastic departures from traditional forms) and the informal, traditional patterns that actually dominate courses of action. But in our current framework the divergence is not seen as one between "the attitudes, aims, and methods of the government . . . and those of the society in which they operate,"[78] but between the prescribed formal norms and the informal modes of operation of the elite. When such a disparity exists we may speak of the existence of an *elite culture*[79] that deviates from organizational values and norms. In organizational terms, when a deviation happens, organizational integrity—an *ésprit de corps* into which the regime and elite cultures are supposed to merge—fails to be established or sustained. The proliferation of informal relations and modes of operation is an important component of organizational change in Communist regimes. Formal institutional arrangements confine the behavior of institutions and the individuals within them; thus, informal rules and relations become established as a response to formal structural changes.

On the one hand, organizational involution depicts a "dysrhythmic course of change."[80] Even though it results in reinforcing traditional or preexisting norms, there is no lack of rational institutions. Organizational involution reveals an irony: Communist regimes assign paramount importance to the substantive over the procedural component of rationalization and minimize informal group ties; consequently, not only are formal procedures not fully operational and dominant, they are at the same time *ritualized* with no comparable and complementary substance, casting the familiar profile of a bureaucratic organization with predominant emphases on procedural rather than substantive rationality. What makes the development of Communist organizations unique is that ritualization occurs not only in the realm of formal procedures but also in that of substantive revolutionary ideology and values. The latter process is sometimes called "ritualization of charisma."[81] The one seemingly unsolvable problem of official deviance that has often confronted the Chinese regime, *xingshizhuyi* (formalism, ritualism), can and should be analyzed in this light. An organization may not only experience a "displacement of goals" in which "an instrumental value becomes a terminal value," as Robert Merton and others have noted,[82] but also a "displacement of rules," where ends become means. The former, manifested in the ritualization of the charismatic mission, is prone to what is called in the Communist context "bureaucratism"—that is, red tape, losing touch with the public, and the like, thus decreasing the efficacy of members. The latter, epitomized by ritualization of routine regulations, is prone to non-compliance and particularistic behavior such as nepotism, patronage, and corruption.

On the other hand, formal rules and policies are also *informalized*, or simply replaced by rules and policies that have been routinely practiced but never formally approved. The informalization of formal institutions is another trait of organizational involution. Like ritualization, it is a response of members to an organization's ineffective and confusing attempts to reconcile the goals of revolution and modernization. But unlike ritualization, which depletes the substance of formal institutions, informalization changes, and substitutes new modes of behavior for, formal institutions. An organization may involute to the extent that the old modes subvert and substitute for new ones (such as the creation of combat tasks, ideological symbols, and heroic role models) that the organization seeks. Official deviance, including corruption, can be regarded as resulting from such informalization.

ORGANIZATIONAL INVOLUTION AND CORRUPTION

The existence and evolution of cadre corruption in Communist organizations testify to the lack of institutionalized procedures and regulations sustained by an internalized organizational ethos. Official deviance in a Communist political system is intimately related to the involutionary development of the organization of the regime. Organizational involution is causally related to cadre corruption, with the organization losing its ability to maintain committed and disciplined cadres and a widening gap between the intended formal organizational objectives and the unintended informal response of members of the organization. This widening gap is the key to understanding official deviance, including corruption in various forms, in Communist regimes. Cadre corruption, like other forms of official deviance, is an informal response to formal institutions and norms. The regime itself "transposes the expected purposes of the organization, forced to follow what otherwise would be termed unacceptable ways, and actually punishes those who resist."[83] When this happens, we may indeed begin to speak of "systemic corruption" or "regime corruption," as Jowitt put it.

None of the arguments involving the disappearance or the reappearance of the market, or those based on bureaucratization or feudal tradition, can sufficiently explain the cause of official corruption in contemporary China. In this study, official deviance is treated as a problem that has been present ever since the Communists came to power. My main assumption is that, while the Communist party has been encountering official deviance all along, it has created for itself, first, in the absence of a market, corruption of cadres, mainly, but not exclusively, in forms of prebendalism. Later, with the weakening of the planned economy and advent of the market, cadre corruption mainly, but not exclusively, is manifested in forms of rent-seeking. Political corruption, although often overlapping with economic corruption, always preceded it, and it may well be a part of the reason for the very appearance of economic corruption at all. Thus we can claim that corruption in the PRC did not begin with the advent of the economic reforms, nor did it perish when the reforms brought institutional and cultural changes.

Organization of Chapters

I have organized the chapters of this study both chronologically and analytically. Chapters 2, 3, and 4 explore official corruption in three major periods in PRC history: the socialist transformation of the early 1950s, the radical Maoist developmental drive of the late 1950s, and the chaotic anti-revisionist mid-1960s. Four major events that have affected the organizational integrity of the CCP and cadre behavior are given detailed discussion: the Three Anti Campaign, the Anti-Rightist Campaign, the Four Cleanup Campaign, and the Cultural Revolution. I argue that the organizational involution of the Chinese ruling party, the CCP, began in the late 1950s when the party refused to subject the regime to the propensities of routinization and bureaucratization.

Informal practices including official deviance began to appear on a large scale during and after these combat-like campaigns, unfolding around non-routine "core tasks" and "storming approaches" to socialist reconstruction.

Chapters 5 and 6 examine organizational development and cadre behavior in the post-Mao reform era. Rather than treating corruption as a novel phenomenon particular to the marketization resulting from the economic reforms, I show that corruption has been a continuing problem, occasionally offering some new twists and incentives. To be sure, official corruption in contemporary China is both qualitatively and quantitatively different from earlier patterns, yet the fundamental causes remain constant. It appears that the reforms have not until recently fundamentally changed the neotraditionalism resulting from organizational involution.

In the concluding chapter, I summarize my basic findings and the arguments of previous chapters regarding organizational development and official corruption under the Communist regime. To further drive home my points about organizational involution and official deviance, I make some comparisons between patterns of corruption in China and those found in former Communist regimes, third world states, and China's own pre-revolutionary past. In addition, I discuss a few themes from my empirical analysis, including the importance of refocusing our attention on the agents of the state, the changing role of the state and state agents in the transition to a market economy, and the characterization of Chinese officialdom under reform.

CHAPTER TWO

Sugar-Coated Bullets from Enemies: Corruption in the Early Years

The Chinese Communist party came to power in 1949 as a rural-based, war-worn revolutionary movement. As its corps of cadres entered the cities victoriously, their role took a dramatic turn—saboteurs became rulers and guerrilla fighters became state functionaries. The party organization as a whole faced the similar challenge of redefining its nature from revolutionary movement to ruling institution. From the very beginning, the maintenance or transformation of its organizational integrity became predominant for the party. The new regime faced many formidable undertakings including overcoming economic crisis, building a new administration, quelling residual opposition from the *ancien régime*, and stabilizing a society still recovering from years of civil wars. All required an effective and loyal official corps to carry them out. The Leninist tenet "cadres determine all" appeared increasingly relevant to this reality. The first major problem concerned the existing group of revolutionary cadres. These men and women were mainly from rural backgrounds and poorly educated, and they were seriously inadequate both in numbers and by training to handle the complexity of administering the new urban settings.[1] A rapid expansion of the administrative staff was inevitable. To overcome the shortage of personnel and expertise, new recruits had to be found and former bureaucrats and technical personnel retained.[2] In many urban areas, in fact, the majority of the staff in government organs consisted of retained personnel.[3] In 1948, there were some 600,000 Communist cadres with district (*qu*) or higher rank. By 1952, the number had increased to 3.9 million— more than quadrupling in less than five years.[4]

The problems of administrative reconstruction soon shifted to other areas. With the injection of new recruits, mostly middle or high school graduates, and personnel retained from the old regime, organizational boundaries were open and susceptible to societal influence and conflicting personal motives. An official survey was conducted of trainees in the North China Revolutionary University near Beijing, a school especially designed to train the retained personnel in the new ideology. It showed that only 15.5 percent of trainees had been inspired by a desire to re-educate themselves and break with the past; in contrast, 32.2 percent were opportunists seeking jobs, 18.9 percent had enrolled for the education, 10.4 percent wanted to protect themselves from persecution by the new regime, and 9.8 percent were simply looking for free board and lodging.[5] A party rectification campaign was set in motion soon after the Communists came to power in 1949. It especially targeted so-called "opportunist elements," who were believed to have joined the revolutionary ranks primarily out of career or other economic motives without tests of hardship and risk. Transforming and remolding these "flawed elements" entailed intensive training in ideology and political commitment, but training alone would not guarantee successful transformation.

The new recruits and retained personnel were only part of the problem. Veteran cadres (*lao ganbu*)—seasoned revolutionaries from the guerrilla period—now had to face a fundamental change of role. Before coming to power they had endured hardship and survived dangerous battles or risked their lives in covert struggles in cities under enemy control, but now as victors they had to leave the field for offices in the cities, where the new urban setting demanded more educated and skilled public officials.

Spoils of Victory: Veterans and Decadent Lifestyles

Mao, wary of potential problems of waning commitment and corruption among the cadres, warned before the Communist victory that "because of the victory, meritorious and arrogant attitudes as well as longings for comfortable lives may grow in the party. . . . Some Communists were never defeated by enemies armed with weapons and were real heroes in front of these enemies. But once hit by the bullets coated with sugar, they will be defeated. We must prevent this situation from taking place."[6]

Mao's worry was not unfounded. As with all Communist revolutionary parties, the organizational capability to integrate members and turn them into able and loyal agents was pivotal to the success of the CCP. However, the party was never to be free from members' deviance, even during the civil war, when it fought for its very survival. The selfsame party that claimed to be fighting against a corrupt regime was itself infected by corruption.

In a 1939 article, a senior CCP leader wrote about corruption among the cadres who were working in the base-area government in Yan'an: "The administrative staff of the [Shaanxi, Gansu, and Ningxia] border region, from the Chairman on down, all receive the lowest allowance. Yet, we, like all other human beings, have the tendency to enjoy ourselves. Now that we have had three years of peace, some comrades have immersed themselves in personal life, which requires more than the little allowance they receive. Thus 'skimming', misappropriation, graft, etc. occurs."[7]

Another CCP official noted similar problems in the Red Army in the same period:

> A capitalist mentality is looming in the army, which can be detected from the following facts: due to individualistic and private-ownership thinking, some party members place personal life above everything else. They demand a new suit today and will want a blanket issued to them tomorrow. If their superiors refuse to meet their demands, they will slow down their work or stay in bed for many days. If they feel a bit sick, they ask for fish oil (vitamin E) and health enhancement items or force the doctor to issue a sick-leave request. Individualism is also manifested in personal indulgence and a decadent lifestyle. Naturally, when economic difficulties preclude the fulfillment of their insatiable appetites, they would resort to embezzlement and graft.[8]

Corruption was not associated only with cadres working in the government and army units of the major base areas. Cadres who worked more independently in smaller base areas were even more prone to deviant behavior due to their lack of systematic training and proper monitoring. A study of the township level cadres in the Huaibei base area found that in some townships over half the cadres were corrupt and decadent (*tanwu fuhua*); in one place corruption among cadres was as high as 98 percent.[9]

Even as the Communists saw their hard-fought struggle nearing its final stage, deviant acts such as desertion and corruption took place in the ranks of the People's Liberation Army (PLA). The most serious problems were desertion and refusal of new assignments. In a telegram to the central command during the Northeast Campaign in 1945, General Huang Kecheng reported that one division left Jiangsu province with a force of 32,500. Along the way to Northeast China, some 3,000 men deserted. In the same campaign, by the time it arrived in the Northeast, a regiment from central Hebei province had lost half of its 4,000 soldiers to desertion. When some officers were asked to set up patrols to prevent escapes, they themselves deserted.[10] In the three years (1945–48) of the Northeast Campaign, desertion was the main reason for the depletion of personnel in the PLA, and the tendency continued to be of concern. In a telegram to the Central Military Commission and Chairman Mao, General Lin Biao reported:

> After the liberation of the Northeast, there were a lot of discussions in the ranks. Many soldiers, even officers, from the Northeast were afraid of going to battle in other regions, and feared leaving their hometowns. They felt that after land reform, they have not yet enjoyed peaceful lives. Therefore, desertion has increased recently. The 5th Army lost some 300 men during its move to Yi county; the 11th Army lost 600 in six days while moving to East Hebei, and the 11th Division of the 4th Army lost 200 in five days.[11]

As in many of the Chinese millenarian movements in history, peasant followers of the revolution did not know how to deal with a successful outcome in the fighting, and would typically desert on the eve of victory. This phenomenon illustrates to some extent how precarious the values and goals of the Communist revolution were among peasants-turned-soldiers. The peasants' motivation for joining the revolution was often simply to escape poverty and the harsh living conditions of China's rural areas.[12] In 1943, a party leader in a Huaibei base area wrote about the discrepancy between party and peasant interests in an internal party journal:

Cadres recruited from the villages, peasants and hired hands, after the outburst of the resistance war still have a low cultural level. They joined the revolution mostly because of concrete benefits of rent and interest reduction. For this reason, it is easy to connect class struggle with national struggle in daily life. They tend to give undue emphasis to the smallest economic benefits. They are also very susceptible to the influence of bad habits brought from the city by urban cadres.[13]

According to a 1946 document from the department of political affairs of the PLA Northeast Command, over half of the soldiers in one company who had previously worked for the puppet Manchukuo regime joined the PLA because of economic reasons, to escape hunger, to avoid farm labor, or to find work after the defeat of the Japanese.[14] Soldiers and officers with such motives were not the tested revolutionaries that the party hoped to mold. As combat tasks decreased, the party was confronted with the challenge of how to recast these soldiers, who were not necessarily revolutionaries, into committed, self-conscious agents of the party and state. On May 24, 1946, shortly before the PLA took over the entire Northeast, General Huang Kecheng wrote to the Central Committee about problems in the victory-bound army:

All except a small number of advanced army and civilian cadres are generally weary of war and aspire to peace. They want to sink into urban decadence and lavish lifestyles. None of the cadres from Chengde [of Hebei province] are willing to accept jobs in rural areas. Everyone wants to go to big cities like Changchun and Harbin. Many army officers want to retire to work in civilian positions in non-combat areas.[15]

Once in the cities, some veteran cadres immediately strived to enjoy the booty and spoils. They demanded higher positions and more perquisites.[16] The party criticized veterans for their desire to enjoy at last a better material life after many years of sweat and blood, which the party assailed as "unhealthy thinking." Even before the victory was achieved, many cadres of the newly liberated areas engaged in activities such as lavish banquets, searching for good housing and furniture, and hiring chauffeurs, all at official expense. As early as 1950, the CCP leadership expressed alarm about the growing corruption among veteran cadres and the bureaucratic squandering in state agencies. In many of the cases, the officials reprimanded were linked to lavish lifestyles or indecent behavior such as extramarital affairs, divorcing wives of peasant backgrounds to marry young, educated urban girls, and sexual harassment.[17] Profiteering of military goods and materials was common in the ranks of the Northeast PLA units, according to a military history of the three-year civil war.[18] In Beijing, of the 650 people involved in "corrupt and decadent conduct" (*fuhua duoluo*) in the period 1949–51, 79 were veteran cadres, according to a report to the Central Committee from the party's Beijing Municipal Committee.[19] In Shanghai in 1950, the first year after the city was taken over by the Communists, 319 party members were found to have committed graft or other misconduct; a massive anti-corruption campaign was later inaugurated.[20]

The Chinese Communist experience of governing guerrilla base areas contrasted with that of most other Communist organizations in that it had a direct impact on its post-revolutionary organization building. The coexistence of a system of free supplies for veteran cadres and a more advantageous salary system for new personnel, including both retained and newly recruited officials, created discrepancies in income and standard of living among lower-ranking officials and state administrative staff. These discrepancies caused a considerable amount of discontent among veteran cadres, although many felt it politically "glorious" to be on the supply list. A veteran cadre who came from a poor peasant family background admitted after being disciplined for corruption:

> After coming to Shanghai, what I saw were high-rises, electric lights, telephones, automobiles . . . , everything. But gradually I became dissatisfied with living conditions. I noticed some comrades and new cadres were on salary, which made their life better than mine. They have fountain pens and wristwatches. I have nothing besides an old pen. I brought my bed cover from the countryside and am still using it. I felt that taking part in revolutionary work "has cost me a lot."[21]

Many revolutionary veterans shared these feelings. When the new government was established in 1949, a large number of cadres who had been in the revolutionary ranks at the time of the founding of the PRC continued to remain on the supply list. Not only were their basic daily needs provided for by the state, members of their families also enjoyed free supplies and education. The veterans on the free-supply list accounted for 83 percent of the total cadre corps in 1950, and was gradually reduced to 37 percent by 1955, when all personnel on the state payroll were converted to the salary system.[22] Still, in what remained largely a market economy, many veterans were envious of the "retained personnel"—former public servants from the Kuomintang regime—who continued to receive salaries.[23] The veterans, who remembered the hardship they had endured during the civil war, felt they were now regarded as "country bumpkins" with little money to spend and were being treated unfairly. Years before, when the free supply system was implemented, its intention was to enhance egalitarian treatment in the revolutionary ranks and to better allocate limited resources. However, treatment was not absolutely equal even during wartime.[24] Such unfairness had the unexpected consequence of propelling cadres to vie for higher positions, and thus get better treatment and more privileges. The free supply system lasted into the early years of the "New China," and thus the problem of cadres seeking higher positions and better treatment persisted, fueled by the contrast with personnel on the state payroll, who had more cash at their disposal than did those on the supply list.[25]

To further understand why this dual-track payment system became a source of cadre misconduct and corruption, we have to look into the origins of the free supply system and other institutions established during wartime that the Communist party led people to believe contributed to curbing corruption in the Communist ranks.

Revolutionary Legacy and Corruption

A notion often propagandized by the party is that in the early years of the new government, corruption by officials was caused mainly by the untransformed society and residual elements of hostile forces. The party/state has said little about how its own institutions and legacies may have accounted for violations of party discipline and administrative malfeasance, and neither have scholars. One element previously ignored by scholars was the encouragement of economic production by party and government units, a supposedly revolutionary tradition that had been instrumental in the survival and expansion of Communist forces. Positive economic and political contributions notwithstanding, many irregularities and deviant practices of individual cadres in the

Communist base regions were rooted in such practices as the "small institutional economy" (*xiaogong jiawu*), which was essentially sustained by the economic activities of government and army units.

Agency production (*jiguan shengchan*) was a product of the economic shortfalls due to the Japanese blockade of the Communist base regions and the lack of material supplies from the Nationalist government in the late 1930s. In 1938, some army units began experimenting with production activities such as planting vegetables, raising pigs, and making shoes, mainly for the purpose of improving the soldiers' livelihood.[26] By 1939, the financial situation of the Communists had worsened, due both to a decrease in supplies from the Nationalists and to an increase in the number of government agencies and other public units and their staffs. In January 1939, Mao Zedong formally advocated the idea of "letting the army produce for itself."[27] In early 1940, a large-scale production movement (*dashengchan yundong*) was launched in a directive by the Central Military Commission; it called on every military unit to participate in production of all kinds, including commercial businesses. The slogans at that time were to "feed and dress ourselves by self-reliance," and to "develop the economy in order to guarantee supplies."[28] At first, only army units were mobilized to engage in self-sufficiency production activities. Soon other non-military units such as government units, public schools, and hospitals in Yan'an and the surrounding Shaan-Gan-Ning border region were all participating. These activities were given the name "agency production" (*jiguan shengchan*). Similar production movements were also launched in other Communist-controlled base areas in 1942 and 1943. Although set in motion in mass campaign style, the movement took on a permanent character. Encouraged by the CCP leadership, economic activities of military and administrative units lasted not only throughout the anti-Japanese resistance and civil war periods but also after 1949. In fact, it can be argued that the contemporary commercial frenzy of "taking a plunge into the ocean" of business[29] by government agencies finds its origins in this revolutionary tradition.

THE FREE SUPPLY SYSTEM

In order to comprehend the imperatives of production activities in the guerrilla bases, one has to understand the free supply system (*gongjizhi*), the institution that sustained the Communist guerrillas throughout the civil wars. Under this system, essential supplies were provided at almost no cost to members of the revolutionary rank and file, including non-combat personnel and administrative staff. To a large degree, it was as much a product of economic necessity as a reflection of Communist egalitarian principles, for a salary system would have required a much stronger revenue base than the Communists had. When it was first inaugurated in the Red Army bases in 1927, the system basically covered meals, with no difference in standards for officers and soldiers. From army commanders on down to cooks, everyone was on a five-cent daily meal plan.[30] In the early years, the sources of revenue and food supply of the Communists came largely from confiscation of the possessions of rich landlords, apportioned levies, and donations. Later, when some base areas had been established, Communist authorities also relied upon taxation and revenues from a limited number of small-scale industries run by the base-area authorities. When the Communists formed a united front with the Nationalists, they also received funding and some regular supplies from the Nationalist government.[31]

Although the items on the supply list varied from time to time and place to place, some key items remained throughout the whole period. Living allowances usually covered everything from food and miscellaneous daily allowances to a health allowance for women and subsidies for childcare and children's clothing. All servicemen and non-military personnel also received uniforms or other clothing and a number of other daily necessities in kind. One basic tenet of the free supply system was relatively equal treatment of officers, soldiers, officials, and staff in the Communist army and government.

The anti-Japanese war (1937–45) saw the development of the free supply system in a number of Communist base regions. The system evolved from a non-differentiated system to one that had several scales according to one's position. Besides free meals, a four- or five-tiered meal allowance was provided to members of the army and administrative staff. There appeared two (and later, three) different eating locations—and levels of dining standards: the Big Kitchen (*dazao*) for commanders and higher-ranking officials and the Small Kitchen (*xiaozao*) for solders and general staff. Later, the Medium Kitchen (*zhongzao*) was added to further differentiate treatment. Sometimes, different treatment was in kind rather than in quantity or convenience. In a Communist-controlled Northeast area before the war ended, for instance, the local PLA garrison issued an instruction suggesting that officers above regimental rank drink cow's milk and officers of battalion and company rank drink soybean milk. Soldiers did not have such privileges.[32] In a few base areas, Communist government officials also received living allowances. For instance, the chairman of the Jin-Cha-Ji Regional Government received a monthly allowance of 18 *yuan* and the administrative staff earned 10 *yuan*.[33] This system was to continue after 1949. A large number of cadres who had been in the revolutionary ranks at the time of the founding of the PRC continued to remain on the supply list until 1955.

SELF-RELIANCE AND ECONOMIC ACTIVITIES OF UNITS

In times of economic difficulty, the free supply system entailed "self-reliance production" by Communist base area government agencies, army units, and other non-production units. Although called "production," the economic activities were not confined to farming and manufacturing. Commercial retailing activities were also common.[34] The achievements of the production movement were impressive. It greatly helped to solve the economic difficulties caused by the Japanese blockade. By 1942, about half of the major subsistence necessities in the Shaan-Gan-Ning border region could be produced locally.[35] The Communist forces survived in part due to the economic activities of the units. In many instances, such activities provided supplements and funds to units insufficiently supplied by the central authorities. In other cases, they even generated a surplus. In 1941, the worst year the Communist forces experienced in terms of outside aid and supplies, 70 percent of all supplies came from the individual units themselves.[36] The revenues from production by the 21 units directly under the auspices of the CCP Central Committee could meet 48 percent of these units' total expenditures in 1942. The proportion of revenues from self-sufficient production in the Shaan-Gan-Ning region increased to 64 percent in 1943, 63 percent in 1944, and 61 percent in 1945. If the accumulated collective assets (funds and materials) of these units were included, their financial needs would be fully met by agency production.[37]

Collective assets or "minor public family holdings" (*xiaogong jiawu*) varied in amounts and kinds. Some Red Army units had in their possession several dozen taels of gold. A government agency might operate several shops and small businesses.[38] Such activities were dubbed "building up institutional households" (*gao jiawu*), an expression that reflected the needs and nature of guerrilla warfare. In Yan'an, each army company (as a combat unit) had a production manager, who was often an experienced farm hand. In addition to farm production there were small factories and other lines of business.[39] In one instance, an army regiment in the Jin-Cha-Ji border region operated its "production" mainly in the form of a convenience store, a restaurant, a small food-processing factory, and transportation.[40] The production campaign helped to improve the quality of life in the base region and to reduce the financial burden on local peasants. The campaign played an indispensable part in the survival and expansion of the Communist troops and the base area government.[41]

In order to stimulate more active involvement of servicemen and administrative staff in production, incentives were also provided to individuals in the units. Contrary to the assumption that Communist ideology and guidelines forbade the existence of private interests in the revolutionary ranks, the experience of the guerrilla period indicates that during the production campaign private interests were not only condoned but encouraged, as manifested in the policies of "attending to private interests while taking care of public interests" (*gongsi jiangu*) and "public interests first, private interests second" (*xiangong housi*).[42] The introduction of these two principles was even billed as "a revolution" in changing the attitude of cadres toward private interests.[43] In what was later known as the "Teng-Yang Plan,"[44] the leadership of the Taihang base area actually criticized those who "take the future perspectives of communism as reality, regarding accumulation through labor as economism (*jingji zhuyi*) and a rich-peasant mentality."[45] The plan, issued in April 1943, provided that products from spare-time production by individual staff members should be purchased by the mess unit they belonged to, and that 70 percent of the income from this source was to be retained by the producers, with 30 percent going to the unit.[46]

Encouraged by this plan, the livelihood of the army and agencies of the Taihang region greatly improved. In the Red Army, 9,411 people had personal savings totaling 1.67 million *yuan*.[47] The famous 359th Brigade, which to this day symbolizes the spirit of the Great Production Movement, actually encouraged soldiers to participate in production by allowing them to retain one-fifth of the income if they borrowed public tools, or one-third if they did not.[48] During the production campaign, one of the "model production heroes" was Guo Jin, who used to be chief of the administrative affairs section of the CCP's Northern Bureau's Party School. In 1942, Guo began farming land near his unit. By 1944, he used his fifty thousand *yuan* savings as an investment to open a small restaurant, several shops with 30 employees, and a hat factory that hired twelve people. Eventually, he made over a million *yuan*, half of which he gave to the unit. Guo, who was perhaps the first millionaire among Communist ranks in history, was named a first-class labor hero for his accomplishment.[49]

PRIVATE, UNIT, AND PUBLIC INTERESTS

Recognition of private interests and material incentives had other consequences. Production activities were linked in an interesting way to anti-corruption and austerity drives by the authorities in the base areas. A directive issued by the Communist administration and army command of the Hebei-Shandong-Henan border region in 1944 alleged that there were two types of misconduct in the production movement. One was the failure to encourage people to engage in production; the other was an overemphasis on public interest and neglect of private interests. The previous anti-corruption and austerity drives, carried out simultaneously, this directive instructed, had been unsuccessful because they failed to consider the private interests in the army and government units.[50] In order to successfully combat corruption, it went on, material incentives had to be provided for those who reported any wrongdoing.

Such documents indicate a strong inclination to attend to private interests on the part of the CCP authorities. The same directive stipulated that after part of the output of the production quota had been saved for reinvestment in the unit's production, 80 percent of the profits should be retained by the unit to be used as funds for collective livelihood, and 20 percent was to be distributed among the individual producers. The surplus beyond the output quota could be evenly divided between the individual and the unit.[51] The irony is that the production campaign, which was launched to sustain and improve the egalitarian free supply system, produced something else: scaled salaries and other incentives more like those found in modern factories than in an egalitarian guerrilla base.[52]

By recognizing the economic interests of individual units, the Communists in effect created a realm of interests distinguished from both the public and private realms. This was the realm of the *danwei* (unit) or *xiaogong* ("minor public," as it was called in the Yan'an era) interests.[53] In that period, the demarcation between the "greater public" and the "minor public" was very clear. For example, by allowing units to have their own legitimate "institutional household," the distinction between what belonged to the public (*gongjia*) and to the unit was prescribed. There were "graft of public property" and "graft of unit property," both of which belonged to the category of corruption, yet any funds and materials recovered would be returned to different locations, according to an official directive.[54] Regarded as deviant behavior, though not categorized as "graft" per se, concealment by units of what should be reported and turned over to the authorities, such as grain seized from the enemy and fines, was a main target of the anti-corruption campaign carried out in conjunction with the production campaign.[55]

As indicated in several official documents, corruption seems to have been a problem particularly associated with the production drive as economic stakes for units and individuals became increasingly important. In the Hebei-Shandong-Henan border region, an anti-corruption campaign was launched in 1944 in which all army, administrative, and educational units were ordered to have a three-to-four-month-long "confession campaign" for personnel to confess any corrupt behavior. Those who failed to confess would be subjected to denunciation at a later stage of the campaign.[56] What made it more than an ordinary political mobilization was the fact that in this campaign not only were individuals required to confess, or be exposed of their wrongdoing, but units were also required to do so. In order to encourage people to expose corruption, an incentive was created: 20 percent of the amount recovered would be rewarded to informants.[57]

Ye Jizhuang, who was in charge of logistics of the Eighth Route Army, wrote about irregularities by army units that were pertinent to the supply system and production:

> Due to residual departmentalism, the phenomenon of under-reporting income and over-reporting expenditure and other kinds of concealment (*da mai fu*)[58] could not be eliminated. Although these are not corrupt acts by individuals, there exists an erroneous belief that the illegal acts of under- or over-reporting can be legal if the income is retained by *the public of a small unit,* not by individuals *privately.* This is the main source of concealment.[59]

The following passage from Mao Zedong's "On Economic and Financial Problems" indicates how he viewed the seriousness of the problem:

> Units of lower levels run their own show separately. There is little or no unified leadership, or coordinated plans and orchestrated inspections from above on policy guidelines and work content. Thus individual units do not know what is allowed or pretend they do not. . . . Economic units not only refuse to assist each other, they fight and obstruct each other. They cheat both superiors and subordinates. Concealment and forged reports occur. . . . What is especially serious is the graft and gambling among some cadres. Some of the cadres have become totally corrupted by material things. All these evil phenomena can be found among the cadres in some army units, agencies and schools to various degrees. From now on, the superiors of all army units, administrative agencies, and schools must take measures to make sure that general interests are attended to and policies well grasped. They must enforce integrated plans and inspections for the production activities of work units. Practices such as autonomy-seeking, each unit pursuing its own path, breaching laws and policies, in-fighting among units, graft and gambling among cadres are absolutely prohibited. . . . This is what rectification in economic work is all about.[60]

This speech, delivered in 1942, indicates the extent to which irregularities and cadre corruption had to do with agency production activities. It also indicates that the official attitude toward the so-called "minor public" interests was often ambiguous, particularly when irregularities and misconduct associated with them were common. Clearly, the policy of self-reliance and production during this period laid an institutional foundation for units to pursue their own tangible interests, legitimately or illicitly.

Agency Production and the Corruption of Victors

In the first few years after achieving nationwide victory, the new regime used production activities by army and administrative units to respond to the pressing tasks of social and economic recovery, as we have seen above, and at the same time to bolster the morale and commitment of the cadres in the rapidly expanding administration. Businesses ranged from legal (construction, small-scale milling, and farming) to illegal (retailing,[61] money-lending, and speculation). At the time, there was a distinction between two kinds of public industrial enterprises: state-owned enterprises (*guoying gongye*) and public–unit owned enterprises (*gongying gongye*). Both were promoted by the new government.[62] In the Northeastern region, for example, the *gongying gongye*, which included 792 economic entities run by administrative agencies involving 28,096 people, contributed 10 percent of the total industrial output by the public sector in 1949.[63]

Legitimate business activities by public units were in fact promoted by Mao himself. In December 1949, soon after the establishment of the People's Republic, Mao personally drafted a party directive instructing PLA units to launch a new production campaign in order to reduce state expenditure, and to improve living standards in the military.[64] Declaring the rule, Mao wrote, "Production should be operated according to the principle of benefiting both public and private interests. Forty percent of the profits should go to individuals and the rest to the unit and the state *in order to build up both the revolutionary public family economy and the revolutionary private family economy*. This way, not only the army can be self-sufficient, but individuals can also enjoy profits."[65]

Even after the Communists had won the war, Mao seemed to regard the economy as still under the "special conditions" he had spoken of some years earlier. Unit economic activity, therefore, was still necessary. Mao did, however, caution against unwarranted kinds of business activities. It appears that in the beginning, due to "commercial and business activities including illegal speculation by government agencies, army units and public schools in the name of production," and in a time of high inflation and severe shortages, the government found it difficult to regulate the market in general and prices in particular.[66] Besides posing a challenge to the state's control of the economy, the new government perceived that the main problem associated with such commercial activities was corruption by individuals or units. According to a circular of the CCP West Manchuria Bureau issued on May 18, 1946, many agencies and army units in the base areas under its jurisdiction were involved in smuggling, tax evasion, and illicit commercial businesses.[67] In September of the same year, another directive from the CCP Northeast Bureau ordered a prohibition of commercial activities by administrative agencies and army units.[68] In April 1950, the new national government similarly issued a directive to prohibit government agencies and army units from engaging in commercial business (*shangye jingying*).[69]

Bo Yibo, the chief overseer of the Three Anti Campaign, spoke about the problem of agency production: "There are many cases where public units deliberately forge their books to advance their departmental interests. Agency production has had its positive role in the past. Now it has become an important source of subverting the fiscal system and corrupting cadres."[70] An editorial in the *People's Daily* further drove home the point: "The sources of many agencies' production were not clean. They either transfigure the 'greater public' into a 'minor public,' or impound the budget surplus, or exaggerate the need for funds and divert them for agency production use. These are all in violation of the party's policy."[71] Eventually the government decided to take over all the businesses run by state agencies. It also confiscated all cash and material assets that had "accumulated over the years as a part of the 'small public household' belonging to various units."[72] From then on, until the reappearance of a market after the reforms began in the late 1970s, businesses operated by state agencies and other non-production organizations were banned.[73] But even after production activities by state agencies were banned during the Three Anti Campaign, the military continued to operate some production and businesses such as farming and mining, which were not part of regular military logistics.[74]

The new government recognized the irregularities that agency production had caused in this regard. Embezzlement of funds that belonged to units for personal use was not uncommon. In one instance, six commanding officers of the Tianjin army garrison spent about 40 percent of the garrison's production funds for personal purposes.[75] A resolution issued by the Council of Administrative Affairs (*zhengwu yuan*) ordering government agencies and administrative units to close down all their businesses, pointed out that

> operated in the dispersed rural environment of the revolutionary war, agency production once had a positive impact on supporting our struggle and overcoming the difficulties in staff's daily lives. However, after the nationwide victory, such needs have been gradually reduced. The fragmentation and lack of planning in agency production has put it in conflict with the centralization and planning of the national economy. The degenerating effects of the bourgeois mentality have led state agents to immerse themselves in profit seeking and pleasure seeking. It has caused serious corruption and waste. It is the *most pervasive problem* in the current Three Anti Campaign that must be resolutely dealt with.[76]

A decision of March 12, 1952, ordered that all the agricultural, commercial, manufacturing, transportation, and construction businesses (including all real estate, investment, and cash assets) run by state agencies, military units, public schools, and other not-for-profit organizations be immediately turned over to the Special Commission on the Dissolution of Agency Production, which had been set up by the government at various levels.[77] Although no national statistics are available, it is reasonable to assume that the assets of individual units were very large. In one province, Heilongjiang, assets of "institutional households" from 36 county-level units and 26 provincial units turned over to the state treasury were worth, in total, 500,000 *yuan*.[78] Similar decisions were issued by some local authorities. For example, the municipal party committee of Harbin issued a directive requiring that "all except financial, trade and business sectors be prohibited from running commercial or business activities; all the personnel in state agencies and army units who participate in industrial or small businesses dress in civilian clothes and the expenses of the production units [affiliated with these agencies and army units] be paid from the profits of production, not from public funds (*gongkuan*) or be reimbursed by the state."[79]

"Minor Public" Versus "Greater Public"

After years of sporadic operation in fragmented base areas facing fiscal and economic difficulties with a rapidly expanding administrative corps, the Communists found that local economic interests were increasingly at odds with the need to unify national economic and fiscal operations and to establish a viable central treasury.[80] Contradictions between "general interests" (represented by the central government) and "partial interests" (of localities and individual units) became salient, especially when the government tried to stabilize the market and gain full control of the economy. Opposition from local leadership was also present. A case of concealment of grain output by local officials in Jiangxi province offers a telling example. In this case, three of the top leaders of Jiangxi province were criticized for permitting and even encouraging concealment of resources because they feared budget cuts by the central government. Their self-criticism of "departmentalism" stated that they were still influenced by "vestiges of the old outlook of scattered management . . . which single-sidedly stressed local difficulties and failed to realize the circumstances of a unified national political system."[81]

Establishing a demarcation between the "greater public" and the "minor public," as well as their relationship with private interests, continued to pose a vexing question for the new regime. It was not a novel problem, to be sure. Even during the production campaign of the Yan'an period, agency production already had created a realm that held vested interests and had a life of its own. The discrepancy between greater public and minor public had become significant. Economic survival in scattered, blockaded base areas, however, entailed tolerance and even promotion of "economic departmentalism," which, in practical terms, might have benefited the whole army in one way or another. Once it took over the official realm, the party found itself in need of redefining the boundaries that effectively separated official (the greater public), collective (the minor public), and private interests. The CCP, like other Communist parties operating in the setting of a socialist state, never succeeded in making a clear distinction either in ideological terms, or, even more significantly, in practice. While a practical distinction between state, collective, and private realms continued to be recognized, ideological studies were also meant to lead people to believe that minor publics were *part* of the (greater) public, not *independent* of it. Practically, though, things were not this simple. The bona fide collective sector (e.g., cooperatives, Russian *kolkohz*, Chinese *jitiqiye*) notwithstanding, it is the minor publics in the state sector, particularly state agencies, that invoke deviance. When these agencies are supported by public budgets, and are at the same time allowed to raise revenues of their own, conflicts of interest between greater public and minor public inevitably occur. The damaging effects of these minor publics lie in their encroaching upon the "greater public" and preying upon private interests at the same time, even though not all actions of the minor publics are predatory or corrupt in nature.[82]

Ideological and practical contradictions and confusion arising from this task of defining (or redefining) affected how people regarded graft and the "theft of public property." On the one hand, in some cases corruption was defined in a broad manner: many of the denounced and prosecuted cases involved actions stemming from a conflation of public and private interests (*gongsi bufen*). A large number of officials were disciplined for misappropriation of public funds and *jiagong jisi* (benefiting the private by pretending to benefit the public). For example, a senior official in Guangzhou was disciplined for using public funds to buy a car and motorcycle for personal use, even though the car belonged to the agency, and for hiring two housekeepers at public expense.[83] Although there had been calls for curbing *benwei zhuyi* or "departmentalism" during the Yan'an era, the anti-corruption campaign in the early 1950s made it a serious transgression to attend to the interests of small units.[84] On the other hand, many cadres who had used illicit methods such as fraudulent reporting, padding of the books, and collusion with private businessmen to promote the interests of the "minor public" were regarded not as violators of the rules but rather as "competent" and "good at managing business."[85]

Murky, sometimes self-contradictory, definitions of corruption affected the results of the anti-corruption drive in 1951, when pressures to meet higher quotas and revolutionary élan were at their peak. Fifteen percent of the cases initially treated as serious graft but later acquitted by the end of this campaign (which I will discuss in detail later) were "due to unclear definitions of graft, convolution of public and private properties and interests (*gongsi bufen*), malfeasance, waste or political problems."[86] Some local leaders pointed out that one of the most serious transgressions at the time was collusion, through such means as bribery and kickbacks, involving officials who represented "minor publics" and private businesses in order to prey on state assets.[87]

Usually, those who benefited the most from government agencies' involvement in economic activities and accumulated assets were veteran cadres on the supply list. One official implicated in a corruption case confessed that he thought the money he used "was money made from agency production, *not part of state property*, so it was all right to spend some."[88] To those revolutionary veterans who were used to living in a totally deprived environment, where nothing belonged to them yet every necessity was provided for, the demarcation between public, collective, and private was not readily clear. As another senior cadre put it, "I am a part of the supply system. Even I as a person belong to the 'public family' (*gong jia*). It does not really matter if I use some of the stuff belonging to the public family."[89] Thus, the key was to have a clear delimitation of what belonged to the public (greater or minor) and private. Yet it was not easy. At the beginning of the campaign, standards were set high: anything a public official or staff used or took from the "public family" (i.e., the state) without approval was an action of graft. But later, such restrictive criteria were relaxed. In the early reports about the results of the campaign, the total number of grafters (*tanwu fenzi*) nationwide who took more than 1,000 *yuan* was 292,000. Later it was reduced to 105,000. Fifteen percent of these "embezzlement" or "graft" cases belonged to either "*gongsi bufen*" or malfeasance.[90]

The situation was best summarized by the governor of Hebei province, where the most serious corruption case in the early years of the new regime allegedly took place:

> For us, it was a profound change from war to peace and from the countryside to cities. Along with this change, there were changes in the minds of some cadres. For instance, they [now] compete for better housing, to be "generous" and "elegant" in spending public money. They always feel

not quite as elegant as others. Other problems [have arisen] such as over-reporting budget needs, impounding extra funds, promoting interests of the minor public at the cost of the greater public. . . . [A] serious phenomenon of graft was growing to the point where people committed graft collectively. . . . Evidence shows that government staff were affected by a combination of the *supply system mentality* and decadent thinking, and they developed the abominable behavior of "grabbing": grab personnel, grab money, grab materials.[91]

The First Anti-Corruption Campaign

To address the growing problems among the growing government staff and reduce administrative costs, the CCP decided to expand a party rectification campaign started in 1950 and launch a mass campaign against corruption, squandering, and bureaucratism. The campaign, known as the *sanfan* or the Three Antis, was first carried out in urban government agencies in the fall of 1951 and lasted until May 1952.[92] Although combating administrative waste and bureaucratism was a part of the campaign, the main target was graft, which, according to Teng Daiyuan, then minister of railways, included "all actions in which public funds, property or materials are retained by individuals for private reasons, as well as the usurpation of power to steal, extort, and take bribes."[93]

THE CAMPAIGN METHOD

The most significant feature of this anti-corruption drive was the all-out mobilization of both party cadres and the general public.[94] As with previous political campaigns, this mobilization became a "core task"; thus, all routine work must give way to the anti-corruption drive. Like all mobilizations, the campaign defied regular procedures and routines. Streamlining and promoting production, eliminating corruption, and implementing economic austerity were declared as the main objectives of the campaign in a December 1, 1951, resolution by the CCP central committee.[95] To lead the anti-corruption work, a special commission, the Austerity Inspection Commission, was formed at each level. All of the regular institutions, such as the party disciplinary inspection commissions, the administrative supervision commissions, the procurate, and the courts, were to follow the directions of this ad hoc body. Special courts were set up *within* each government agency or other public units above the district level (*qu*) or the military equivalent, the regimental level. These irregular courts had the power to subpoena, detain, arrest, impose fines, and sentence corruption suspects found in their own units. According to a resolution passed by the State Council on March 28, 1952, the heads of the agencies that set up these courts should serve as the chief judges and the other judges were to be selected from among non-party activists.[96]

The hallmarks of this revolutionary mobilization approach to corruption were manifested in other facets of the campaign as well. From the outset, Mao's personal involvement reinforced the campaign process. All major reports and telegrams from various provinces and ministries on anti-corruption efforts were read and commented on by Mao personally. It was Mao who sent several telegrams to provincial leaders, insisting that "in every agency that disposes of large amounts of money and materials, there must be a large number of grafters who embezzled a large amount of money or materials." Mao urged provinces to search for these "big tigers." It was also Mao who gave final approval to the execution of two senior officials found guilty of graft and embezzlement.[97]

Well-planned and carefully coordinated campaign tactics were employed in the Three Anti Campaign. Peng Zhen, then mayor of Beijing, spelled out these step-by-step tactics:

> Methods are to mobilize all the forces to vehemently attack corruption. Initially, mutual inspections between superiors and subordinates as well as between units of the same level should be organized by the austerity inspection commissions. Next, we should call on people, from leading cadres on down, both party members and non-members, who have committed corrupt or wasteful actions, to make confessions and self-criticism. Then, we must mobilize everyone, especially the state administrative staff, to report and denounce any corrupt and wasteful behavior to the authorities.[98]

In the confession phase, pressure was put on those cadres alleged to have committed misconduct, including embezzlement and graft, to confess rather than to conceal their actions. In Shanghai, the campaign was set in motion with self-criticisms by the chairman and deputy chairman of the city's austerity commission, followed by self-criticism by department heads. The climax was reached when the municipal government convened a confession meeting attended by over 10,000 officials. By then, 3,147 people had already "confessed" their corrupt acts.[99]

The denunciation phase mobilized the otherwise passive masses, including lower-ranking officials and staff, to confront their corrupt superiors and expose wrongdoing, which they would otherwise not have dared to do. Mass meetings provided a chance for people to speak out without fear of repercussions. As a retired official recalled, "many cadres, particularly young, new cadres, felt that no other political parties would have let lower-rank staff openly chastise (*douzheng*) their superiors."[100] People were encouraged to write letters exposing or denouncing any wrongdoing committed by anyone they knew. Special post boxes were set up for this purpose. In many instances, face-to-face denunciation of allegedly corrupt or squandering officials at mass meetings was also common. Mass mobilization exerted tremendous pressure on people who were suspects in cases of corruption and squandering. Suspects were given an opportunity to confess their wrongdoing in the initial stage. Otherwise, they would be denounced by others and suffer more severe penalties. This technique of "confession leads to lighter penalties, while resistance leads to heavier penalties" has been repeatedly used in political campaigns throughout the history of the PRC up through recent anti-corruption drives.

After the confession and denunciation phase, the campaign entered the critical phase of going after suspected major grafters who had not confessed, the "tiger hunting" or investigation phase. Like other Communist mobilizations on economic and social fronts, this campaign had pre-set targeted numbers to fulfill. In two telegrams (January 23 and February 4, 1952), Mao repeatedly instructed party committees of provinces, army garrisons, and central ministries that an estimated "budget" [*sic*] of exposed "grafters" should be made by each unit within three days of receiving the February fourth telegram.[101] "Tiger hunting teams" were sent with quotas of "tigers" that each unit was to hunt.

The effectiveness of the mass mobilization against corruption, as in the case of the Three Anti Campaign, could be realized in the short term, but in the long run it was limited. Mass mobilizations such as those used in anti-corruption efforts often had unintended consequences, including backlash and personal vengeance. The director of the CCP's central organization department (COD) made the point when he summarized the situation soon after the Three Anti Campaign:

> After a mass campaign is over, many flaws and errors assailed during the campaign may re-emerge. They may even re-emerge to a greater degree. Some people self-congratulate themselves for having discovered some patterns from repeated campaigns. They would get prepared before a new campaign began and pretend to be active and honest. Sometimes they could even shed a few drops of tears while making self-criticisms or confessions. Yet no sooner is the campaign over than they would return to their old selves.[102]

He particularly pinpointed the problem of post-campaign vengeance by officials who had received criticism or denunciation from subordinates, an action known as *"zheng ren"* (to fix someone) or *"chuan xiaoxie"* (literally, "to give someone tight shoes to wear," i.e., make things hard for someone). This practice became familiar to many Chinese in the many political campaigns that were to follow.[103]

Opposition to corruption in the ranks was nothing new when the CCP launched its first campaign after taking power in 1949. Already by the early 1930s, during the Chinese Soviet Republic period (1927–35), the Communists had designed mechanisms to combat corruption in the government of the Jiangxi base area. Although the actions in these two periods differed in many ways, this early experience did have some impact on later methods. One difference from later campaigns was that, during the early period, the anti-corruption mechanisms followed the more institutionalized Bolshevik model. For instance, two types of organized teams participated in by the masses—Shock Teams and Light Cavalry—were set up as regular monitoring devices. Under the leadership of the procurate, the Shock Teams were initiated in August 1932 to fulfill the mission of supervising the Communist government and monitoring citizens. Members of the team, usually three, used their spare time to conduct this work. They might pay a surprise visit to an agency or a public enterprise, or pretend to be in need of help from a government agency.[104] The Light Cavalry was organized and primarily manned by the Communist youth organization to monitor corruption, waste, and work slowdowns in revolutionary organizations. They were affiliated with various organizations and operated under the leadership of the youth organization branch.[105]

Another device that was implemented at the time was the system of "worker and peasant reporters," who acted in effect as monitors (*jianchayuan*) and informers in lower-level units, reporting corruption cases to procurators at various levels.[106] Irregular and mass-oriented as they seemed, they were nonetheless an effective deterrent against potential violators in government agencies. These methods were later replaced with more ad hoc measures, such as inner-party rectification and mass campaigns in the Yan'an period. The anti-corruption campaign of the early 1950s bore imprints of the organization building of the CCP in the 1940s rather than that of the Jiangxi soviet in the early 1930s.

THE TIGERS

Though the severity of the problem varied, as reflected in figures now available, petty graft was common among officials at all levels. In some places, as many as 43 percent of all cadres in county-level government agencies were involved in graft.[107] In Shanghai, China's largest city, 38 percent of cadres in government agencies and state enterprises at the time were found in the Three Anti Campaign to have committed graft/embezzlement to various degrees, of which 3 percent were cases that involved more than 1,000 *yuan*.[108] Nationwide, among 3.85 million cadres in government agencies above the county level who took part in the campaign, 1.23 million were found to have committed graft, or 31.4 percent of the total number of cadres. Among the "grafters" were offenders who committed serious graft (*tanwu fenzi*) and "those who committed lapses of graft" (*fan tanwu cuowu*); 196,000 were CCP members (16 percent). Of the total of 1.23 million people, 8.8 percent were "tigers" who embezzled more than 1,000 *yuan* (see Table 2.1).[109]

Given the pressure from above and the revolutionary enthusiasm, lower-level officials were reluctant to reduce budgeted quotas, even when it was apparent that in fact there were few "tigers."[110] As a result,

TABLE·2.1

Statistics of the Three Anti Campaign, by Region

Region	Total participants	Persons embezzling > 1,000 yuan	
		Number	*% of participants*
Central agencies	88,427	822	0.9%
North China	890,231	16,107	1.8
Northeast	755,271	18,569	2.5
Northwest	289,647	2,478	4.3
Eastern China	797,272	15,411	1.9
South Central	496,716	13,843	2.8
Southwest	492,419	28,810	5.9
Inner Mongolia	40,530	1,790	4.4
TOTAL	3,850,513	107,830	2.8%

SOURCE: *ZJDZ*, vol. 1.

many minor misconduct cases were treated as corruption, and initial numbers of reported corruption cases from each province and major city had to be drastically adjusted. For instance, in Hebei, one of the most active (i.e., radical) provinces in the campaign, 10.5 percent of the initially designated corruption cases were later dropped for lack of evidence. In other provinces, final numbers were revised at the later stages of the campaign due either to miscalculations of the amount of money involved (33 percent), overly severe punishment of minor cases (47 percent), lack of a clearly defined demarcation between graft and malfeasance or other misconduct (15 percent), or simply wrong judgments (5 percent). Eventually, by the end of the campaign the nationwide number of corruption cases by party/state officials involving 1,000 *yuan* or more was reduced 65 percent, from 292,000 to 107,830, of whom 10,009 were sentenced to prison terms and 42 executed—fewer than Mao had anticipated.[111] Many who were initially accused of graft were spared of any disciplinary action (see Table 2.2).

The Three Anti Campaign was mainly confined to urban areas and to government administrative personnel. While a relatively successful campaign was concluded in the cities, the party could not neglect

TABLE 2.2

Disciplinary Actions Against Graft, by Region

Region	% of total cases	Criminal charges	Administrative charges	Exempted	Death penalty cases
Central	1.3%	3.4%	26.9%	69.8%	4
North China	15.6	4.2	24.0	71.8	10
Northeast China	14.9	3.7	22.9	73.4	3
Northwest	9.1	4.1	22.7	73.2	2
Eastern China	26.5	2.0	18.9	79.1	5
South Central	12.8	4.9	20.7	74.4	13[a]
Southwest	18.9	4.6	17.6	77.8	14
Inner Mongolia	0.9	3.1	24.8	72.7	0
TOTAL	100.0%	3.6%	20.8%	75.6%	51[b]

SOURCE: *ZJDZ*, vol. 1.

[a] Figure does not include Guangdong province.

[b] Forty-two people were executed.

another even larger group of cadres: low-level officials in the country-side, where the anti-corruption campaign was preceded and over-lapped by a party rectification. Rural cadres, particularly grassroots cadres (*jizeng ganbu*), were not mobilized to take part in the Three Anti Campaign, on the premise that corruption was less of a problem in the countryside.[112] However, the party leadership was aware that, despite the success of the Three Anti Campaign in the cities, among the rural cadres from the county level on down there still existed serious prob-lems of bureaucratic misconduct in the form of "bureaucratism, com-mandism, and violations of law and discipline." The "New Three Anti" Campaign was thus commenced in the rural areas in 1953.

Violations of law and discipline (*weifa luanji*) and abuses of leader-ship authority were at the center of this campaign. These were attrib-uted to the conceit and arrogance of old party cadres and to the remain-ing influence of the KMT style of governance on newly recruited cadres and retained personnel. Abuses included cursing, beating, illegal arrests, torture and other physical abuse, interference in the freedom of marriage, and persecution of those making criticisms. In Lintong county, Shanxi province, 51 officials were disciplined for disobeying party policies (*weifan zhengce*) during the anti-corruption and rectification campaign, while 730 cadres were sanctioned for graft or decadent lifestyles.[113] The anti-corruption campaign targeted mainly cadres in the cities, even though more than 100,000 specially trained cadres were dispatched to the countryside to lead the rectification of the problems in grassroots party organizations.[114] On the whole, the rural campaign was much less intense and was not given high priority.

THE LIU-ZHANG CASE

The corruption case of Liu Qingshan and Zhang Zishan in 1950–52 during the Three Anti Campaign was billed as "the first serious criminal case of New China"[115] and offers a compelling example of how the practice of agency production precipitated official corruption. Liu, the party secretary of a northern prefecture, and Zhang, the administrative chief of the prefecture, both veterans of the anti-Japanese war, were found guilty and executed for, among other things, embezzling state funds, leading decadent lifestyles, and sabotaging defense construction projects. This case has been used by the party/state time and again as an instance where the party was determined to punish anyone, including senior officials who were veteran revolutionaries with meritorious records, who was found guilty of corruption. But a closer look at this case reveals that most of the alleged embezzlement and diversion of state funds was in fact for the purpose of developing agency production, rather than for strictly personal use. According to the indictment, of the 171 million *yuan* in state and other funds Liu and Zhang embezzled, only about 30,000 *yuan* was for "personal purposes." This amount included 4,500 *yuan* spent on "extravagance and waste in the agency" and 16,360 *yuan* on "bribes and gifts." The rest was used in "agency production."[116] Liu often boasted of his experience in managing agency production and preached to his subordinates: "All county party secretaries should promote agency production. Only when agency production is doing well, can the general work be carried out well. This is based on my years of experience."[117] Under Liu and Zhang, the prefecture government had its own "agency production management office," which legitimately ran ten commercial or manufacturing businesses.[118]

According to one account, "the main graft and theft Liu and Zhang committed on water projects was the diversion of the workers' living allowance fund to invest in agency production."[119] Some of the money was later paid back. Bo Yibo also pointed out that Liu and Zhang could so fearlessly embezzle funds because they had agency production as a cover. Bo wrote, "Liu and Zhang often diverted funds specified for particular uses, concealed the books and failed to separate what was private and what was public in daily life."[120] When state policy decreed that agency production was not only allowed but actually advocated, a question arose: should officials who were engaged in such activities be held accountable for promoting production when their methods violated laws and regulations (*feifa shouduan*)?[121] In fact, until the end of the anti-corruption campaign, no clearly defined legal statutes or regulations existed that banned activities such as diverting funds from their designated use (e.g., public works) to another use (e.g., agency production).[122]

The prosecution of major cases involving high-ranking officials like Liu and Zhang, and the Three Anti Campaign in general, helped to boost the legitimacy of the new regime among urbanites. To many people, the campaign showed the resolve of the Communist party to stamp out corruption in its ranks—in impressive contrast to the rampant corruption of the incompetent Nationalist government in its waning days on the mainland. The party's concern with its image as clean and selfless underlined the early struggle against corruption. In many highly publicized cases, high-ranking officials who were involved in corruption received heavy penalties. In interviews with the author, a number of people who had experienced the anti-corruption campaign of the early 1950s spoke about the appeal the party had among people familiar with the corrupt bureaucracy of the *ancien régime*.

"CONTAMINATION" FROM SOCIETY AND THE FIVE ANTI CAMPAIGN

In the socioeconomic environment of this period, the private sector still dominated and central planning was not yet the main regulating mechanism. For the party/state, whose veteran cadres were mostly from peasant backgrounds and whose functionaries were mostly retained personnel from the old regime, the unreformed private sector obviously represented a dangerous "environmental contamination." From the regime's perspective, if cadres were not totally committed and able to resist the temptation to live a better life, they were likely to be "pulled into the water" (*la xia shui*) by unlawful capitalists. Not only did the society remain essentially "bourgeois," but the remaining influence of the old regime was also at work within the officialdom. In the Three Anti Campaign, the primary targets were of auto-corruption—i.e., corrupt acts involving public officials only, such as graft, diversion of public funds for private purposes, and embezzlement. Later, the focus was switched to transactional forms of corruption involving not only public officials but also private businessmen, such as kickbacks, commissions, honoraria, outright bribery, sinecure salary, and gift shares to a company. In large measure, the old, often illicit, ways of doing business from the pre-Communist period remained the order of the day. It turned out later that many cases of graft, bribery, and tax evasion exposed during the anti-corruption campaign involved state tax agents, who, like traditional Chinese local tax collectors, accepted bribes and helped private businesses evade taxes.[123] The private sector soon became the main target of the anti-corruption campaign.

In a November 1951 report on the anti-corruption, anti-waste, and anti-bureaucratism campaigns to the Central Committee, the CCP Northeast Bureau reported that "from the corruption cases exposed in the last two months we can detect a common feature: all the serious graft cases involve the collusion of private businessmen and corrupt elements in the government who collaborated to steal state property."[124] In the urban areas and some county seats, the Three Anti Campaign was expanded in January 1952 to the Five Anti Campaign: opposing bribery, tax evasion, the theft of state property, cheating on government contracts, and stealing state economic secrets for private speculation.[125] The Central Committee, with Mao directly involved, decided to "launch a counterattack against the capitalists who in the last three years have vehemently attacked this party," especially in major metropolitan areas.[126]

The Five Anti, or *wufan*, Campaign was conducted almost concomitantly with the Three Anti Campaign and party rectification. In Shanghai, a 1951 audit by the city tax bureau found that out of the 9,100 businesses investigated, 81 percent had committed tax evasion.[127] The

Five Anti Campaign started in late March of 1952 in Shanghai, and the methods were similar to those used in the Three Anti Campaign. First, the masses were mobilized to report unlawful businessmen; then the authorities organized business owners to "assess and help each other" to "actively confess wrongdoing"; and finally some 1,000 inspection teams led by cadres with crash training pressured businessmen who refused to confess.[128] In Shanghai alone, the authorities received over 240,000 accusations of unlawful acts by businessmen.[129]

The results of the *Wufan* were mixed. On the one hand, the campaign did accomplish the objectives of inhibiting illicit practices such as bribery and tax evasion. Thus, the external sources of economic corruption by Communist cadres were seriously neutralized, if not totally eradicated. More important, many old "normal," that is, informal and often illicit, business practices of the private sector were now deemed irregular and deviant. As Kenneth Lieberthal has pointed out, this was the first time the new government successfully penetrated private firms, and it paved the way for later socialist transformation of the industrial and commercial sectors.[130] On the other hand, the ambiguous long-term strategy of the CCP leadership and Mao in particular resulted in sweeping attacks on the capitalist class by local authorities and mobilized masses, who often bore grudges against business owners and managers. The campaign in Shanghai even lodged allegations about the luxurious lifestyles of the capitalists, and some became so desperate that they committed suicide.[131]

The economy, which still depended a great deal on the private sector, took a hard hit. Even state-owned businesses were affected. Much of the urban private sector was either shut down or saw its operations sharply cut back. The economy became sluggish. In the spring of 1952, the monetary flow fell by 13 percent compared to the same quarter in 1951. In the North China region, tax revenues for February 1952 decreased by 50 percent from the month before. In Tianjin, a major industrial and commercial center, 4,000 private businesses closed their doors, thus affecting some 400,000 people.[132] Deng Xiaoping, then military governor of the Southwest China region, reported to Beijing the near-crisis situation in the Southwest provinces on February 22, 1952: the first quarter tax revenues would decrease 50 percent, and many tax agencies were already out of work. Due to the recession caused by political pressure on the private sector, a large number of people became unemployed and the livelihood of already impoverished city dwellers further deteriorated. In one district alone of Chongqing, in Sichuan province, some 20,000 residents (one-third of the district's population) were on the verge of starvation and became resistant to the *Sanfan* and *Wufan* campaigns.[133]

The problems caused by the Five Anti Campaign actually manifested a deep contradiction. On the one hand, the party/state organization needed to thwart attempts to influence and infiltrate it by the capitalist class, and, on the other, it aimed to maintain a tolerant and cooperative posture toward the private economy during the period of economic recovery. According to the "New Democracy," the general policy adopted by the CCP on the eve of the national victory, the private economy was to be protected and not to be replaced by socialism for some time to come. The Five Anti Campaign, however, brought about such changes to these plans that it expedited the socialist transformation of commerce and industries, a goal that had not been planned to be undertaken for some time.[134] The radical anti-capitalist stance toward private business owners received a measure of support from urban workers and veteran cadres, who wanted to eliminate the private economy once and for all.

Building a Post-Revolutionary Ruling Party

The deviance and corruption among the officialdom that appeared in the early 1950s led the CCP to seriously reconsider the overall strategy of building an effective and disciplined elite corps able to lead the national socioeconomic transformation. The CCP had two choices available to it: it could transform the officialdom from a closed group of revolutionary cadres operating in accord with the tenets of wartime military communism to a Soviet-type bureaucracy through routinization and rationalization. The other choice was to maintain the elite as a non-routine, combat-dependent, and politically mobilizable group. Although the CCP remained determined to continue to maintain the party organization as a non-routine cadre corps, as epitomized by the mobilization methods employed in the anti-corruption campaigns, the main thrust in the early years of the new regime was to embark on the Stalinist path.

TOWARD ROUTINIZATION

It was generally recognized, during the first few years of the new regime, that it lacked both institutionalization and enforcement of regulations. The disregard for and lack of compliance with rules and regulations on the part of public officials made existing regulations even less effective. The official press drew an image of such a government official: "He abides by the regulations of the state only in principle. He rejects mechanical compliance—when the rules benefit him he will obey them, otherwise he will not. He calls this flexibility."[135] Indeed, in the action code book of Communist cadres, flexibility in carrying out policies handed down from above is allowed and encouraged under certain circumstances. As a cadre, one was expected to act obediently yet not dogmatically, as Franz Schurmann noted.[136] Thus a Leninist cadre has a certain inherent quandary: how flexible should he or she be without infringing upon the essence of the policy? Herein lies the ultimate difference between a Leninist *cadre* mode of action, which is predicated on what Chalmers Johnson called a "goal culture," which defies rigid procedures, and a Weberian *bureaucratic* mode, which places paramount importance on procedural adherence.

There is ample evidence that the Chinese regime was moving toward routinization in the first half of the 1950s. Between 1950 and 1956, some four thousand legal statutes, ordinances, and regulations, new financial and accounting rules, and a personnel management system were drafted, passed, or implemented.[137] In the first few years of the regime, the judiciary and prosecutory institutions were directly under the leadership of the party and administration. The first National People's Congress in 1954, which produced the PRC's first constitution, marked the formal beginning of attempted institutionalization. The power and limited autonomy of the court and procurate systems were recognized by the new constitution.[138] With the establishment of a regular court system, the special courts composed of officials and citizen representatives that had been set up during the anti-corruption campaign were abolished. Initial drafting of criminal and civil codes was also commenced in 1957.[139] State and party supervisory systems, which are crucial to the maintenance of administrative and party discipline, were instituted following the Soviet model as well.

THE SUPERVISORY INSTITUTIONS

The origins of supervisory agencies in the PRC can be traced to the Communist government in the soviet regions during the civil war in the 1930s. These agencies were modeled after the Soviet system. One of the main functions of the Worker-Peasant Supervisory Commission was to prevent corruption and bureaucratism. After the Communists came to power, a state supervisory apparatus was first established in November 1949 under the name of Central Supervision Commission; it was one of the four major commissions of the State Council, enjoying a higher status than ministries. It had the power to supervise and review the actions of state agencies and agents and to investigate accusations from the public against state agencies and agents for malfeasance and other unlawful actions. Local commissions were also set up from the administrative region (i.e., composed of several provinces) level down to the county level. During the PRC's first three years, the commission's functions were limited. Although it was involved in some regular inspections and investigations in 1950 and 1951, the massive mobilization of the Three Anti Campaign overshadowed the commission's routine functions. Ad hoc organizations were set up to lead campaigns such as the Austerity Inspection Commission. Among the 100,000 or so cases of graft/embezzlement that were handled during the Three Anti Campaign, only about 9,000 were discovered by supervisory agencies.[140]

One problem facing the new system was the lack of regular procedures for administrative sanctions. Different localities had different practices. For example, when reporting cases of administrative misconduct, some local supervision commissions sent them to the Central Commission, others to the administration of the same level, or to the personnel offices of local government, or directly to the State Council.[141] These practices were changed in 1953, as the First Five-Year Plan began to be implemented and the Communist party/state moved toward further routinization and institutionalization. The supervision apparatus underwent a major expansion: not only was each county required to set up a supervisory agency but government financial agencies of provinces and large state enterprises were also required to establish internal supervision offices. By the end of 1953, there were 3,586 supervisory agencies nationwide and a 18,000-strong force of full-time and part-time supervisory officials, plus 78,000 more "people's supervision correspondents."[142] The 1954 constitution, which established the Ministry of Supervision, mandated the supervisory agencies with routine supervision, investigation, and recommendation for further disciplinary measures against administrative wrongdoing by public officials.

PERSONNEL MANAGEMENT

Another major organizational development directly influenced by the Soviet system was a change in personnel management. As the CCP became a ruling organization, routine management of administrative personnel became a pressing task. Before 1949, the CCP had operated under the principle of undivided (*yilanzi*) control of all cadres by the party Central Committee and the party organizational affairs departments at various levels. In the wake of the first post-Liberation rectification (1949–53) and the Three Anti Campaign, a second national conference on CCP organizational work was held in September 1953. The meeting focused on how to effectively manage the rapidly growing cadre corps.[143] A resolution was proposed to the Central Committee to implement a "cadre position list" (*bianzhi*) system, a copy of the Soviet *nomenklatura* system. Under this system, implemented soon afterward, all party/state cadres were classified into nine categories and put under the supervision of party committees of various sectors (*fen bumen*) and levels (*fen ji*) and their management was rationalized and institutionalized.[144] Other complementary systems, such as the personal dossier system and the cadre statistics report system, were also put into place after this meeting.[145]

To be sure, routinization did not replace all the non-routine methods that the Communists had adopted to maintain a strong organization during the armed struggle to topple the old regime. One such method was the continuing application of *tiba*, or promotion without going through regular procedures. The term originated in the imperial bureaucracy, where, following the recommendations of high-ranking officials, the emperor at times would promote bureaucrats outside of regular bureaucratic ranks. (*Jinsheng,* the more usual word for promotion, reflects a routine, regularized promotion according to merit and rules.) In the Chinese Communist system, to *tiba* a cadre means to find someone among a pool of cadres or activists and to promote the person to a higher position. This irregular method of promoting officials, controlled largely by upper-echelon supervisors and ignoring normal procedures, fitted well with a revolutionary organization that had a cadre corps based on loyalty, commitment, and *biaoxian* (performance or manifestation of loyalty and commitment).[146]

The nature of the *tiba* method had much do with the revolutionary cadre system. One of the drastic changes that the Communists brought with them when they took over in 1949 was in the way of recruiting personnel for managing the state. The traditional merit system of examination and promotion gave way to a new set of methods and criteria. Speaking of how to find, train, and promote officials in 1951, the director of the central organizational affairs department of the CCP, An Ziwen, who was also minister of personnel, said that "now everybody claims there is a serious shortage of cadres, but nobody knows where to find them, only with their eyes on the people working in the bureaus. The main source of cadres is the society where there is a large pool of activists. We should find and train them into cadres, and *tiba* those who are qualified through work and study."[147]

During the first few years of the PRC, the CCP promoted 160,000 cadres to *ke* (section) and higher ranks through *tiba*. In 1951, there were 123,000 cadres who held positions above the *ke* and its county-level equivalent. By 1954, they increased to 280,000.[148]

Tiba as an organizational technique remained one of the enduring aspects of the personnel system in China during the Maoist period. After the reforms began in the late 1970s, there was an absence of large-scale drives to promote lower-level officials by way of *tiba*. Still, in the first decade of the reforms, retired veteran cadres were often called upon to act like "Bo Le," a legendary figure who was said to have sharp eyes for good horses, by recommending reliable and able young people for promotion to leadership positions. Sensing the possibility of cronyism and irregularity, some changes were made. Instead of calling on retired cadres, the organizational affairs departments of the party and the personnel departments of administrative agencies were later expected to serve in the "Bo Le" tradition. As reforms deepened in the 1990s, the gradual implementation of the new civil service system has now begun to diminish the significance of *tiba*.

By 1956, the regime had succeeded in establishing the basic institutions of government. Many routine regulations were put into place. As part of the integration effort, the cadre system was to change direction, for, as Liu Shaoqi pointed out,

> The time for large-scale promotion (*tiba*) of officials is over. The institutions of the state have been established and the normal operation of the state is on track now. The positions and officials of every sector and department are now all in place. For most cadres, now is the time to settle in to their positions and be determined to work there for ten, twenty years and maybe a whole life time.[149]

THE SALARY SYSTEM

The problem of corruption in the new administration and among party cadres pointed to the incompatibility of the inherited free supply system with new, post-Liberation conditions. One major step taken by the government after the Three Anti Campaign was to begin drafting and implementing a replacement for the supply system, a scaled salary system. In late 1951, the supply system was first converted into a "wage point system" with 46 grades by which basic daily necessities were distributed. In 1954, with the help of Soviet advisers, the government drafted a wage reform plan that was later put into effect. A major target of this reform was the supply system of administrative personnel. Starting in July 1955, all supplies were converted to salaries. Along with announcing its decision to eliminate free material supplies (including grain, fabric, cooking oil, salt, and coal), the state stopped supplying officials with free non-material perks such as domestic help and in-house child-care services.[150]

With these efforts to regularize administrative routines, the Chinese regime in the mid-1950s appeared to be on a track of qualified bureaucratization very similar to that of the Soviet Union. Yet, as Harry Harding pointed out, within the CCP leadership the Soviet model was not enthusiastically received and was short of adequate commitment.[151] A deeply rooted distrust of and animosity toward bureaucracy (which was linked to bureaucratism) was ever-present among CCP leaders, who perceived a danger of breeding a privileged bureaucratic stratum out of touch with the masses. By late 1956, events in Eastern Europe had alerted the CCP to the serious consequences of a growing privileged cadre corps disengaged from ordinary citizens. Liu Shaoqi spoke of the possibility of nurturing an "aristocratic stratum" in the party at a CCP meeting that year.[152]

Not long after this brief flirtation with routinization, the party and administrative organizations were thrown into another revolutionary situation, which was followed by political and economic chaos that was to last for over two decades. Underlined by a common theme of organization vs. officialdom, these stormy political campaigns all centered around party/state cadres.

Cadres and Corruption in the Early Years

The CCP underwent a transition from a revolutionary, rural-based organization emerging from years of guerrilla war to a ruling party managing a vast country and a large population. Although the Chinese Communists had a relatively larger cadre corps at the time of taking over power than the Bolsheviks had had, they, too, needed a large number of experienced bureaucrats from the old regime to staff the administrative apparatus. In a sense, the early years of the regime were marked by an intense campaign by the state to put the officialdom under total control, creating a cohesive party/state able to perform the task of social transformation. The persistent influences of pre-revolutionary (non-Communist) institutions, Soviet methods of reconstruction and governing, and the CCP's own past were all at work during this period, each contributing to the occurrence of official deviance and corruption. These three factors sometimes clashed, but they also reinforced each other.

The influence of pre-revolution institutions mainly came from outside the party. Many personnel from the Nationalist government had to be retained due to the shortage of Communist cadres, and carried with

them some of the old habits of pre-revolutionary bureaucrats. More significantly, the private sector was still a strong pillar of the economy.
Using personal ties was a common mode of private business. A large
number of corruption cases took place in institutions where corruption
rates had run high in the pre-revolutionary era. In Beijing, for example,
among 650 people who committed graft between 1949 and 1951 (before
the Three Anti Campaign), 514 were new recruits, including a large
number of retained personnel. Besides those who worked in financial or
business departments, the largest group of offenders came from the
police department (112 cases). A common feature of police corruption
was *shezhang buhuan* (i.e., not paying back debts they owed to the
department's accounts); this vice, according to an internal report by
Beijing city authorities, dated from the pre-Communist period.[153] Similar
patterns were found in Shanghai.[154] Other types of misconduct—seeking and accepting kickbacks from private contractors, accepting bribes,
forging books and receipts, and profiteering off state-controlled materials and goods—also bore salient imprints from the past and the untransformed socioeconomic order. The new regime was well aware of the
danger posed by a "contaminating" society. Many old institutions were
still in force and many old relational modes still prevalent. The attack on
the capitalist class in the Five Anti Campaign was grounded in the belief
that urban capitalists were partly responsible for corrupting the revolutionary ranks and disrupting the economic order.

The influence of some institutions and operational modes that the
new regime inherited from the Communist base area administration
was also at work. Facing the new challenge of national unification and
consolidation of power, these institutions and practices required review,
revision, or repeal. However, the question of how much of the "revolutionary tradition" to maintain and how much to eliminate was initially
not well addressed. Much of the cadre corruption had its roots in the
murky and sometimes self-contradictory boundaries between the
greater public, the minor public, and the private interests, which
reached back to the Yan'an period.

There was Soviet influence in centralizing administrative authority,
formalizing chains of command, and creating a division of labor among
specialized agencies in this period, particularly after the Three Anti

Campaign.[155] Direct Soviet impact on deviant and corrupt behavior was less consequential than the pre-revolution and guerrilla institutions. The tendency to continuously push the boundaries of the public realm and to expand the administrative corps led to administrative waste and usurpation. But even though the Chinese Communists had always been vigilant against "bureaucratism," they did not fear bureaucratization as they did later in the late 1950s and afterward. One lesson the party drew from the Three Anti and Five Anti campaigns was that much of the existing party/state structure needed to be standardized, with core tasks and organizational strategies redefined. It was in the institutionalization of the new administrative structure that the CCP looked to the Soviet model. Among many institutions that were set up with direct assistance from the Soviets, the most significant were the administrative personnel management (i.e., the nomenclatura), supervisory, control, and administrative salary systems.

As the Communists tried to consolidate power, the new environment rendered the task of maintaining a loyal, effective, and disciplined cadre corps a formidable one. As Ezra Vogel put it, revolutionaries who had provoked disorder became functionaries preserving order; publicists who had been criticizing authorities took on the responsibility of defending authority.[156] The cadre was becoming a bureaucrat. Such drastic reversals of roles and transitions of status undoubtedly contributed to disciplinary problems.[157]

The anti-corruption efforts of the CCP in the early period of the PRC have been interpreted as attempts not only to fence off "contamination" from the bourgeois class and a hostile social environment, but also to transform society as part of a broader program.[158] Such an interpretation certainly sheds light on the intentions of the leadership and nature of the early anti-corruption campaigns. What this chapter presents, however, is that although politically motivated to strengthen party organization and the new administrative corps, the anti-corruption, waste, and bureaucratism campaign was initially regarded as part of the overall economic recovery program, driven both by political and economic necessities.

In the beginning, economic considerations were, in fact, more salient than political ones. The initial CCP Central Committee resolution on launching the Three Anti Campaign and other official documents regarded the Three Anti Campaign as part of an austerity and production-promotion campaign. The resolution to provincial and military regional garrison CCP committees, issued on December 1, 1951, stated that "to carry out the core task of administrative streamlining, austerity and production promotion, a struggle against corruption, waste and bureaucratism must be conducted."[159] Economic considerations were also evident in the leading office, the Austerity Inspection Commission, which was formed to supervise the Three Anti Campaign. This campaign, however, soon turned into a political mobilization centered on organizational rectification of the party and the new administration. The campaign took yet another turn to focus on the capitalist class, which the party held responsible, at least partially, for the erosion of revolutionary élan among the cadres. The new regime invoked a typical mobilization-style mass campaign to address the problem of corruption, one that set a precedent for anti-corruption drives to follow. In this campaign, cadre corruption, which mainly manifested itself in cases of petty graft, embezzlement, and taking bribes from private businessmen, was treated as a critical component of organizational development. That is, the issue was dealt with not simply in economic terms but also in political and organizational terms.

How bad was the problem of cadre corruption in the early days of the Communist regime? In any country, 1.23 million people found guilty of graft in a short period of time would be a tremendous figure. However, one factor to take into consideration is that many of these cases were so minor that in a different time and place they would not have been so designated. The term "graft lapses," denoting relatively minor faults of this kind, was used by the CCP leadership to categorize one large group of cadres who were alleged to have committed wrongdoing. Two major considerations may have affected the seemingly huge number: first, with a majority of cadres on the free supply list living quite literally "in a big revolutionary family," the practical distinction between public and private was indeed minimal. Second were the legitimized "institutional households" or "small public families," which further blurred the criteria of what could be legitimately possessed by "members of the family," be they individuals or institutions. Another qualification lies in the unique features of mass mobilization. One feature was the pressure generated by genuine or pretended enthusiasm of leaders in an agency to designate a sufficient numbers of "tigers." Another was the pressure for their peers to denounce those whom they suspected; yet a third was for cadres who feared for their careers to confess to even minor economic transgressions. It is one of the reasons why political campaigns in China have always been followed by waves of large numbers of petitioners clamoring for re-evaluation of the allegations against them or, better yet, complete rehabilitation. The Three Anti Campaign was no exception.[160]

As a result of the efforts to build a post-revolutionary ruling party and to strengthen discipline among cadres, some of the immediate structural causes of economic corruption were eliminated. With the private sector weakened after the socialist transformation of commerce and industry up through the mid-1950s, corrupt practices involving the private sector such as bribery and profiteering were contained, if not eliminated. More significantly, the institutionalization efforts by the party/state put into place many formal monitoring and supervisory mechanisms to control official deviance. As the ruling party, the CCP organization appeared to be evolving in the direction of transforming from a revolutionary, combat-dependent, cadre organization to a routinized, post-revolutionary bureaucracy oriented toward running a centralized command economy. This trend did not last long, however.

CHAPTER THREE

The Great Leap Forward:
The Beginning of Involution

Organizational involution takes place when a ruling party, in dealing with change of environment, opts to retain preexisting modes and ethos rather than to adopt new ones. The CCP's rejection of the bureaucratic mode of organizational integration embedded in the Stalinist model of state socialism and its adoption of the radical Maoist model of continuous revolution were crucial to its organizational development and cadre behavior. The involutionary development began in the wake of the Anti-Rightist Campaign. It was an unintended consequence of the reconfirmation of revolutionary goals and methods, after the party found itself facing increasing domestic dissent and international pressure due to the instability of the European Communist regimes.

The Anti-Rightist Campaign in 1957 marked the end of the party's brief flirtation with organizational rationalization, bringing with it the first breaches in the newly established rules and in the accompanying legality in order to pursue radical policies.[1] Among the chief targets were intellectuals as well as cadres who were recruited shortly before or after the 1949 victory. Even though this campaign lessened their immediate concerns for the moment, the CCP leadership continued to be preoccupied by its organization and cadres. The prevailing belief among the CCP leadership was that the popular displeasure over mid- and lower-level officials revealed during the Hundred Flowers Campaign could not be solved by further bureaucratization and regularization. They believed instead that the problems had to be solved, first, by a return to the old ways of organizational integration that had been effective during wartime and, second, by devising new techniques to remedy bureaucratic problems. In the "Directive on the Rectification

Campaign" (April 27, 1957), the CCP Central Committee claimed that the growing problems of bureaucratism, factionalism, and voluntarism were alienating the masses.[2] The same directive stipulated that, as a permanent rule, leading officials at all levels of the party and state apparatus should spend some time in activities involving manual labor. For the first time since the founding of the PRC, the CCP raised the possibility of administrative officials participating in manual labor.[3] Its concerns over an increasingly bureaucratic cadre corps seemed genuine. Mao spoke on several occasions about the "fading revolutionary enthusiasm" among cadres and the increasing problems of "rank-seeking (*nao diwei*), reputation-seeking (*nao mingyu*), and competing for higher salaries."[4] In early 1958, Mao for the first time proposed the idea of "uninterrupted revolution," at whose core he saw technological revolution.[5] To accomplish such a task, he concluded, concomitant progress must be also made in "production relations," of which the organizational integration of the party/state was a significant part. With the arrival of a socialist high tide, the CCP embarked upon a road of organizational integration aimed at maintaining the old revolutionary ideological commitment. This shift from the Soviet-type centralized planning system was marked by a re-injection of revolutionary methods used during the guerrilla war. Mao confidently believed the CCP could do better than the Soviet Union with its own tradition of "mass work" and "mass campaigns."[6] The party's revolutionary tradition, along with revolutionary inventions by the masses, it was believed, were the ways to fulfill the requirements of rapid industrialization and "uninterrupted revolution."

This crucial period in the history of the Chinese Communist regime, particularly of its party organization, left a major imprint on organizational development over the next two decades. Some significant institutional features of the Chinese regime and cadre behavioral traits since the 1970s can be traced back to the Great Leap Forward period (1958–60). In many ways, the Great Leap Forward marked a beginning of Maoist attempts to avert what were perceived as the bureaucratic tendencies of post-revolutionary societies. The results, however, were far from what the party leadership had intended. Today, the devastating impact of the Great Leap Forward on economic and social development is well known. Yet more aspects of the radical mobilizations in this period were assumed than documented in existing studies, including the behavior of cadres during and after the Great Leap Forward.[7]

Deregulation and De-regularization

Intensifying the frustration of the CCP leadership and especially Mao over an increasingly "bureaucratic" officialdom influenced by the Soviet model was rapid industrialization. When the goals of "catching up with the UK in 15 years and the US in 20 years" (which later were adjusted to seven and fifteen years respectively) were set,[8] they had decided that such goals could be accomplished only by the unrestrained efforts of millions of daring cadres and the people at large. Conventional wisdom, such as technical expertise, routine, and bureaucratic methods of modernization, was discarded as too conservative and too organizationally ineffective to achieve such radical objectives. New methods and institutions had to be used, among which the most far-reaching was the drastic elevation and expansion of the power of the party in administrative affairs. (Some of the same practices and the cadre behavior induced by them still exist today.) In order to strengthen its "unified" leading role in the Great Leap Forward, the Central Committee decided to establish several small groups in the Central Committee to take charge of finance and economics, legal affairs, foreign affairs, science, and culture and education. Lower levels of the party apparatus were soon to follow suit. A September 1958 announcement from the Shanghai Municipal Party Committee noted:

> In order to strengthen the unified leadership of the party and to enforce
> the principle of non-separation of the party and administration (*dang zheng
> bu fen*). . . . From now on, all government bureaus should report directly to
> the respective departments and offices of the Municipal Party Committee,
> and all the district and county administrations should directly report to the
> Municipal Party Committee. They should no longer report to the Municipal
> Administration. . . . No administrative meetings, regular mayoral meetings
> or meetings of district and county administrative chiefs are to be convened
> by the Municipal Administration. Meetings of the Municipal
> Administration itself will be only for the purpose of discussing the
> decisions already made by the Party Committee.[9]

This formal replacement of the authority of administrative agencies by the power of the party apparatus lasted for at least four years, until the economic and political retrenchment of 1962. However, even after the formal announcement to discontinue the 1958 arrangement, the extension of party authority into administrative affairs was not forestalled or reversed. Some functional departments and offices in the party apparatus established during the Great Leap Forward remained intact. Strictly speaking, the Great Leap Forward period witnessed the substitution of active administration by the party (*yi dang dai zheng*), whereas thereafter the practice was routine intervention by the party in administrative affairs or *dangzheng bufen*.

'XIAFANG' AND MANUAL LABOR

After 1957, Mao expressed on several occasions his disdain of public officials and his high expectations of the ordinary citizens. He criticized Stalin for promoting the practices of "cadres decide all" and "technology decides all."[10] As a part of the concern over the "bureaucratism" of the various levels of cadres, regarded in the post-revolutionary times as an unsolved problem of organizational maintenance, in early 1957 during the rectification and anti-rightist campaigns the CCP first raised the issue of high-ranking officials taking part in manual labor. To Mao, the best practical means for cadres to be both "red" and "expert"—an idea Mao raised at the third plenary meeting of the eighth Central Committee in 1957—was to take part in farm work or manufacturing, because not only could they acquire technological know-how, but they could temper their revolutionary commitment and remain in touch with ordinary people. When the Great Leap Forward began to unfold, many places had already instituted a routine manual labor program for all party/state cadres working in urban public agencies. In Shanghai, municipal agencies canceled their regular meetings on Thursdays so that cadres could go to industrial or service units to take part in manual labor.[11] In February 1958, the Central Committee issued another directive calling for a large-scale cadre "downward transfer" (*xiafang*) to the countryside. All cadres in government, administrative, and enterprise units were required to spend at least one month a year participating in manual labor.[12] By 1962, two million cadres had been transferred to rural areas to work in local governments and participate in manual labor. Eventually, among the ten million or so cadres, about one-third either had been transferred or were signed up to do so.[13]

The origin of *xiafang* can be traced back to the 1940s during the Yan'an era, but only in 1957 did it become a widely used, regular practice in Communist cadre policy.[14] A unique method of combating what Leninist regimes call "bureaucratism," *xiafang* became an important mechanism serving several consequential purposes. First, it was used for selecting cadres for promotion: those who participated actively could expect to return to the cities and receive promotion, and those who lacked manual labor experience or took part grudgingly had less of a chance.[15] Another of its purposes was to try out cadres who were already designated to be promoted but had little experience working in local governments. While manual labor is no longer regarded as a necessary part of cadre character building, to this day the use of *xiafang* for future promotion is still frequent. At times, *xiafang* served other purposes: to streamline party/state institutions and downsize excessive government staff (as in the 1956–57 *xiafang* drive), to punish those with problems in personal background or in political commitment (as in the Cultural Revolution), and to strengthen grassroots leadership by organizing mass campaigns and monitoring and disciplining those sent down.

Despite the streamlining and downsizing of redundant state agencies it brought about, *xiafang* had a negative impact on effective administration. Instead of providing well-trained and capable bureaucrats, it acted against the need for rapid development in urban areas. During the retrenchment after the Great Leap Forward (1961–63), the more urgent needs of government work kept back most of the two million cadres originally slated to be transferred to the countryside. Only some 100,000 actually went.[16]

DEREGULATION

Another target of the Great Leap Forward was the existing regulations and rules. The Central Committee proposed to reform those that were, according to the leadership, obsolete, conservative, and inefficient, hindered socialist development, and inhibited the revolutionary initiatives of the masses. The committee's concerns were with "relations of pro-duction which are lagging behind the development of the productive forces and therefore are interfering with the development of the pro-ductive forces."[17] Mass mobilization was deemed the most effective method to achieve rapid development.

The Central Committee launched a thorough review and overhaul of existing rules and regulations. In his speech at a Central Committee meeting in May 1958, Mao asserted that "the vulgar are the most intel-ligent and the noble the most stupid." He argued that non-experts such as petty intellectuals, workers, peasants, and old cadres could and should supervise experts. He called on non-experts not to be afraid to challenge any authorities in certain fields, and to dare to think, speak, and act.[18] Two major decisions were made about government structure, on the grounds that some existing institutions (e.g., the state supervi-sory apparatus and the People's Procurate) had become overly inde-pendent of the party's unified leadership and that many of the func-tions of these institutions could be fulfilled by the general public through mobilization: to decentralize and to deregulate. As a conse-quence, a trend toward *de-regularization* (in the sense of breaking away from existing modes of conduct) and *deregulation* (in the sense of aban-doning some existing rules and institutions) emerged.

Soon after the May 1958 meeting, the deregulation of "old" systems began in earnest. In August, the Central Committee, convening in Beidaihe (later known as the Beidaihe Meeting), decided to abolish some existing government institutions, including some legal ones; the assumption was that, because of the heightened Communist conscious-ness among the general public, the policies and resolutions of the party could maintain social order in place of laws and administrative rules. According to a directive drafted by Mao personally and first circulated within the party, the initiatives from the ordinary citizens should not be constrained by existing rules and institutions. On the contrary, they should be encouraged. Rules and institutions were to be broken.[19]

In April 1959, the Ministry of Justice, the Ministry of Supervision, and the Bureau of Legal Affairs of the State Council were eliminated by the National People's Congress (NPC) upon the recommendation of the CCP. In his proposal to the NPC, Premier Zhou Enlai reasoned thus:

In the past few years, the Ministry of Supervision has done a great deal in maintaining discipline and checking state agents in administrative organs. Our experience shows, however, that this work must be done under the leadership of party committees, with state agencies in charge, and relying on the masses. . . . From now on, all the work of supervision of the state administrative staff should be done by the concerned state agencies themselves.[20]

The most telling example of the trend was the leadership's serious criticism of the People's Procurate, an agency that survived the mass mobilizations that were to come, but with its power reduced. After the 1949 victory, the Chinese Communists, following the Soviet Union, established a legal system that included three major branches: public security, the public procurate, and the court. Besides prosecuting criminal cases, the public procurate had another important role—to monitor (*jiandu*) law enforcement by the public security agency and prosecute administrative wrongdoing by public officials. Like the state supervision apparatus, it was one of the early targets of political radicalism because of its ambiguous role as a "state legal control agency" in line with Lenin's idea of the authority of the socialist state to supervise the legal system. The procurate, Lenin pointed out, was not merely a public prosecuting agency; it should also inspect, review, and supervise all adjudicative decision-making and execution by state agencies.[21] In writing, at least, in their 1954 Constitution the Chinese had established this broad authority of the procurate to be similar to the Soviet 1936 Constitution. In reality, the Chinese procurate never really got into the business of broad legal (i.e., constitutional) supervision, mainly because it was suspected of being independent of party leadership.[22]

During the fourth national conference of chief public procurators, held from June through August of 1958, the Central Committee instructed the participants to *wuxu* ("engage in discussing ideological issues") so as to encourage them to identify weaknesses of the institution.[23] In concluding, the meeting criticized the procurate system as seriously flawed for its undue emphasis on controlling state agencies and agents, and for the overly complicated regulations and procedures that tied its own hands.[24] Based on this assessment of the public procuracy, a major reorientation and reorganization was undertaken and its functions were greatly reduced. According to one account, in 1957 eight provincial procurates prosecuted 21,304 criminal cases such as embezzlement and administrative malfeasance, an average of 2,663 per province. In 1959, a similar group of nine provinces prosecuted only 6,010 cases, an average of 668. This reduction did not reflect a more lawful society and less crime; the same report pointed out that as soon as the Great Leap Forward began to emerge as a great disaster, many people became disgruntled and crimes increased.[25]

At the county level, the authority of police chiefs, the public procurate, and the courts was integrated into an "area responsibility" in which the head of one agency dealt with all the work that used to be in the others' jurisdiction. This meant a police chief could act as the chief public procurator and judge at the same time.[26] In 1959, the three agencies in many prefectures and counties actually began to merge into the "department of political, legal, and public security affairs" (*zhengfa gong'an bu*). By 1961, nothing but a name was left of the procurate system.

Mao's attempt to dismantle existing institutions did not stop there. He tampered with an even more basic bureaucratic institution that was established after the Communists came to power—the salary system. At the Beidaihe meeting of 1958, Mao spoke highly of the *gongjizhi* (system of free supplies) that the Communist guerrillas had instituted during wartime. In Mao's words, the Long March and the civil wars were won not by salary but by political guidance and the *gongjizhi*. He explicitly indicated that it was because of the influence of the bourgeois class that the *gongjizhi* was replaced by a salary system after the Liberation in 1953.[27] Mao blamed the salary system, which he viewed as a part of "bourgeois rights," for the problem of selfish pursuit of higher rank among cadres.[28] He wanted to reinstate the *gongjizhi* and abolish the salary system over the next few years. Mao's distaste and hostility toward routinization and bureaucratization could not be better exemplified.

The reinstitution of the free supply system was not only discussed; it was later put into practice, albeit only briefly. After the communization in rural areas, the portion of the government personnel who were on the supply list swelled to almost 50 percent of those who had been previously on the state payroll.[29] In urban areas, many industrial enterprises followed suit and installed a "half-salary, half-supply" system among industrial workers. In some instances, supplied items included groceries, meals, clothing, and other daily necessities.[30] But unlike the rural communes, where the supply system lasted over a year and even longer, in urban factories it generally lasted only several months.

A related development was the decentralization of fiscal and other economic power from the center to localities and individual units. The discretionary power of officials in grassroots units was greatly enhanced by this tendency. An urban residency registration system (*hukou*) was implemented, and a widespread drive was inaugurated to construct new walls around urban factories and other institutions, resulting in the conversion of these urban units into enclosed *danwei*, which would function as all-encompassing physical and administrative entities. This development marked a distinctive turn toward involution in the existing system, which for a while seemed to be becoming a modern organization.[31]

DE-REGULARIZATION

In the view of the Maoist leadership, not only did some institutions and rules nourish an increasingly bureaucratic officialdom and become a hindrance to rapid development, but also the established modes of routine operations fed the bureaucratic tendency. Thus, in addition to reducing or dismantling existing institutions the party also took aim at regular procedures. Evidence of such de-regularization included both an increase in the number of non-legal, informal yet binding and effective forms of conveying official policy decisions and the substitution of formal legislation and regulations with more ad hoc "policies" (*zhengce*). Reliance on various types of "documents" (*wenjian*) from the CCP Central Committee or government agencies mushroomed after 1957. Sometimes written in ambiguous terms, they were often issued after an official meeting and were often replaced by other, sometimes contradictory, documents. Many major policy decisions were announced in such forms as "drafts" (*cao'an*, e.g., "Sixty Work Methods [Draft]," issued by the Central Committee), "preliminary opinions" (*chubu yijian*, e.g., "Preliminary Opinion [Draft] on Implementing Part-Supply, Part-Salary

System in Some Enterprises," issued by the Ministry of Labor), "discussion minutes" (*huiyi jiyao*, e.g., "Discussion Minutes on the Issue of Rural Rectification Policies," from the Central Committee), and "instructions" (*pishi*, e.g., "Instruction on the Issue of Sending Down Cadres," also from the Central Committee). The most intriguing example is "An Intra-Party Open Letter" (*dangnei gongkaixin*) that Mao wrote to officials at all levels in April 1959. On a number of occasions the Central Committee handed down an "approved report with instructions" (*pizhuan baogao*) as a form of directive. In it, the leadership, usually Mao himself, would make comments and/or give instructions about the report, which was often used as model case for others to emulate. For example, Mao commented in 1959 on a report from a provincial party school about how the "anti-rightist-orientation campaign" should unfold through heated debates: "Comrades, please learn from this and organize debates at provincial, prefecture and county levels . . . combine reading with debate and engage in a new round of rectification."[32] This short instruction along with a model case would provide the goal and methods as well as the timetable for the new campaign, during which the Central Committee issued more than a dozen such "reports with instructions or comments."

As tentative and provisional as they may sound, the authority and normative power of these documents should not be dismissed. How clearly they were interpreted and implemented by cadres is another matter. It was very difficult for officials at lower levels to understand fully what the policies of the center really meant or how soon they would be replaced. Soon after the CCP Central Committee ordered a halt in the radical leveling and equalization drive (*yi ping er diao*) in 1959, it launched the Anti-Rightist-Orientation Campaign (*fanyouqing*) and a new round of party rectification to further attack those who had doubts about or had spoken against the previous radicalism. Local officials had begun to have "false illusions" and misjudgments, so they continued to enforce the leveling policy.[33] Lower-level officials, however, saw in the *wenjian* a certain "spirit" (*jingshen*) of leadership intention that they knew they were expected to execute. Such informality and short-lived effects, however, made it difficult and risky to do so. A commune party secretary of that period recalled his experience in an interview with the author:

> There were so many *wenjian* during that period that we had to attend meetings or organize meetings all the time. We had to take all *wenjian* from above seriously as if they were laws. Sometimes they were very vague, so we had to figure out what was the hidden message behind them (*linghui jingshen*). The thing is, if you executed a policy that turned out to be successful, then it was because the policy was good. If you "foolishly" executed a policy that was later repealed or replaced, the error most likely was yours.[34]

This characteristically non-bureaucratic reliance on informal policy decisions and opinions rather than formal laws and procedures contributed to the timidity and arbitrariness of the officials, causing conservatism and opportunism of a different kind, distinctive from the usual inundation in the oceans of paperwork and vast sloughs of minutely detailed rules and regulations found in Western bureaucracies.

Pingbi: *Politicizing the Officials*

During the Great Leap Forward, organizational work was propelled by a radical utopian thrust. The guiding principles of organizational work were contained in a Central Committee directive issued in January 1958, "Sixty Work Methods (Draft)." Ironically, these methods, meant to improve the discipline and effectiveness of the party/state organizations, actually became the fertile ground from which grew later cadre misconduct and corruption. Among these "work methods," one of the most significant was "competition and assessment," or *pingbi*.

Pingbi as a mode of operation was not a Chinese Communist invention.[35] It was, however, refined and extensively developed by the Chinese leadership. It was used to boost the competitive spirit and diligence of individuals and work units by applying non-pecuniary incentives. During the Great Leap Forward, it was widely adopted by party/state organizations at all levels and had a significant impact on cadres' attitudes and behavior. *Pingbi* was first endorsed in "Sixty Work Methods," which explained that the correct way to apply it was to encourage competition between provinces, cities, counties, communes, and factories, "with or without a written agreement," and with regular reviews.[36] Following this instruction from the CCP leadership, the whole nation was soon engaged in *pingbi* activities. Three categories of designations based on achievements individuals and work units made would be bestowed: advanced, mediocre, and backward—or "red flag," "gray flag," and "white flag."[37] Officials at various levels scrambled hard to avoid being labeled as a "white flag." A county official of the time recalls his experience of being caught up in the *pingbi* frenzy:

> That year, we pooled all our able hands together to work on water well drilling, leaving spring farming unattended. The prefecture party committee held a *pingbi* meeting at which we received a "red flag" for well drilling and a "white flag" for spring farming. I went back to the county party committee to report this result and got blasted by the party secretary: "how could you have left with a red flag but come back with a white flag!" I realized then that the problem was very serious. I myself could be picked as a "white flag." Thus I had to leave my sobbing wife who was due to give birth soon and my dying sister who was infected with tetanus to go back to the work site in the mountains.[38]

Pingbi was intended as a method to enhance the work ethic and efficiency in economic development. However, one unintended consequence of it was to create a frantic pursuit of planned objectives, even if one had to cheat to claim certain results. What made this method so uniquely important in the development of Chinese politics is that it was applied not only to fulfill economic plans but also to build organizations. To "compete for leadership art" was another objective of *pingbi* first put forth during the Great Leap Forward. Beijing was, in February 1958, the first city to apply it to the competition among and assessment of party branches and party members. In March, the CCP Central Committee issued a directive calling for general adoption of the Beijing experience.[39] As the competition progressed, it became clear that *pingbi* had led to a formalistic emphasis on arbitrary, unrealistic demands, such as so-called "ten-*izations*" and "three standards (*sanding*) and five goods (*wuhao*)"; they included regularization of political work, routinization of the mass line, regularization of organizational life, self-cultivation of the Communist spirit, regularization of political studies, routinization of manual labor for cadres, combatization of work style, popularization of the party school, courageous innovation, and vanguardization of party members.[40] Although after the Great Leap Forward the prerequisites of competition were dropped for their negative effects, the method remained a regular feature of party organization building. In the post-Mao reform era, *pingbi* took on a somewhat different form—*dabiao* (attaining certain goals or standards), which will be discussed later in this book.

Pingbi was only a part of a response by the regime to the demands of the Great Leap Forward on a larger, more radical scale. The organization department of the CCP Central Committee (COD), which was in charge of recruiting, training, and deploying party and state cadres, played an active role. An Ziwen, its director at the time, spoke about how to "prepare our party organization for the upcoming transition to communism" at several meetings of local party organization department chiefs in 1958. At these meetings, the issues of changing the cadre salary system to a free supply system and of minimizing the discrepancies between each salary scale of cadres were discussed.[41]

Cadres were called upon to eliminate selfishness and to acquire the Communist spirit of "working without consideration of compensation." A major decision that emerged from these meetings and went out through a COD directive to all party/state organizations concerned the rapid expansion of party membership. Based on the assumption that the progressive activists among the non-party members were about one-third of the total work force, the COD instructed grassroots party branches to recruit new members; party members should be 10 percent of the total population.[42] Each branch was asked to set a high target of recruitment and to compete for a "red flag." As indicated in Table 3.1, in the Great Leap Forward period party membership surged by nearly five million, even though it was still far from the goal of 10 percent of the population.[43]

Other popular methods included "joining the party in combat," "launching satellites," "working hard a few days and nights," and "doubling the number of party members." Because of the paramount importance of demonstrating political activism (*zhengzhi biaoxian*), the

TABLE 3.1
CCP Membership, 1937–1998

Year	Number	Year	Number
1937	40,000	1958	12,450,000
1940	800,000	1959	13,960,000
1942	730,000	1961	17,380,000
1944	90,000	1964	18,011,000
1945	1,210,000	1965	18,954,000
1946	1,350,000	1966	22,144,000
1947	2,700,000	1969	22,000,000
1948	3,000,000	1973	28,000,000
1949	4,500,000	1977	35,070,000
1951	5,800,000	1979	37,000,000
1952	5,980,000	1981	38,900,000
1953	6,389,000	1982	39,650,000
1954	6,500,000	1987	46,000,000
1955	9,000,000	1997	58,000,000
1956	10,730,000	1998	61,000,000
1957	12,720,000		

SOURCES: *RMRB*, July 1, 1951, September 14, 1956, July 1, 1953, February 18, 1954, February 17, 1956, October 19, 1957, September 28, 1959, July 8, 1997, June 28, 1999; Ma and Huang, *Zhongguo de zuotian yu jintian*; Zhao Shenghui, *Zhongguo gongchandang zuzhi shigang*.

real commitment of this cohort of new recruits was questionable. In late 1962, the COD reported to the Central Committee that some 15 to 20 percent of the seventeen million party members were not qualified as Communists, and that after an ideological indoctrination, members should be re-evaluated and re-registered. This report was later distributed as an internal directive in the party.[44]

'BIAOXIAN' AND 'PAIDUI'

Closely related to the *pingbi* method were two other concepts that were key to this period of highly politicized organizational life. The first was *biaoxian* (demonstration of performance) and the second *paidui* (classification). *Biaoxian* was an important criterion for *pingbi*. It had both performance and manifestation aspects: to perform one's duty well or do work not necessarily required, and to display one's political commitment and activism to a certain audience. Andrew Walder has aptly analyzed the significance of these aspects: "*Biaoxian* is an ambiguous concept. . . . Its official, 'public' definition [concerns] employee conduct during campaigns and political meetings, their 'work attitude' and political loyalty toward the leadership and the party line. . . . There is an irreducible personal, 'private' aspect to the act of assessing *biaoxian* as well. One has to make a personal impression on the people who do the evaluating."[45]

As Walder noted, *biaoxian* became an important criterion for evaluating individuals with the advent of the Anti-Rightist Campaign and the Great Leap Forward in the late 1950s.[46] In addition to serving as a criterion for evaluating individuals, *biaoxian* also had a collective dimension. Evaluation of work units for their *biaoxian* was closely tied to the *biaoxian* of the units' leaders. A unit could show good *biaoxian* and receive high marks in *pingbi* by fulfilling the tasks assigned to it by superiors or by reaching certain political or economic objectives.

Competition and assessment (*pingbi*) also led to a resulting classification (*paidui*, to put a person or a work unit into its proper category or order). Classification as practiced by the Communists was not solely related to *pingbi*, however. Open competition and assessment gave the authorities a legitimate reason to categorize people or units. Leninist parties share the practice of classifying people into social classes and groups by economic status, which determines the kind of treatment each person received. What was novel about the classification system originated in the Great Leap Forward was its use to gauge not only class (*jieji*) status but also performance (*biaoxian*).[47] Thereafter, the classification system used by the Chinese Communists had both dimensions to it. For instance, the well-known "five black categories" (landlords, rich peasants, counter-revolutionaries, bad elements, and rightist cadres) used both kinds of classification (the first two categories being based on social class and the other three on political *biaoxian*); people in these categories became constant targets of political campaigns after 1957. As in the *pingbi* of economic activities, grassroots organizations were also evaluated for their performance and classified into groups. In the 1959 rural rectification campaign, communes were classified into "three categories"—the good, the not-so-good, and the bad—according to their performance and the organizational loyalty of cadres in power. Later, in the Socialist Education Campaign, party branches, brigades, and production teams were also classified, but into three similar categories based on yet another set of criteria. Even among the supposed vanguard of the progressive class, party members and branches were divided into different classifications. There were "Excellent Party Members" and "Advanced Party Branches" as well as "Third Category (i.e., backward) Branches" and "Third Category Members."[48] This practice, particularly the tripartition, still goes on today.

Pingbi and classification were often manipulated through the use of very concrete and vivid symbols. The encounters such as the following were not rare in the years of the Great Leap Forward. According to Yang Zhigong,

> a village party secretary went to attend a commune cadre meeting about production output. Upon entering the gate of the commune headquarters, he noticed a gigantic board on the front wall. It had a huge diagram on it, marked with rockets, airplanes, automobiles, wagons pulled by cattle, and turtles, which symbolized the speed of progress. It was entitled "the *Pingbi* Diagram of the Autumn Output of the Shilipu Commune." He concluded that soaring rockets might cause dizziness and riding a turtle would look stupid. So he decided to follow the upper-middle range reports others had made and received an airplane.[49]

Using this classification system significantly affected the behavior of cadres as well as ordinary people. People or units in different categories received different political and economic treatment. To be an "advanced worker" (*xianjin gongzuozhe*) or to "compete for the best" (*zheng shangyou*) were used as effective tools in mass mobilization. There was great pressure on "third-category cadres" or "third-category party branches" that had not fared so well. At the Beidaihe Meeting in August 1958, the Central Committee made some tough disciplinary rules regarding cadres who could not meet the lofty goals of expanding steel and iron production. There were six degrees of sanctions: warning, issuing demerits, deprivation of position with probation, probation within the party, deprivation of position, and expulsion from the party.[50] Many grassroots-level officials received punishment of various degrees for their "conservative," "cowardly" behavior. To cadres, performing well, or at least appearing to do so, was more important than adhering to rules and procedures. The practice of classification thus contributed to strengthening the goal orientation, and weakening the rule orientation, of the party.

Pingbi and related methods also reinforced status-consciousness among officials and the general public. Prestige, a heroic aura, and special political treatment—which were all the more significant in a society where material incentives were not tied to the marketplace but to political status—were used to induce loyalty and conformity. Consequently, status-consciousness became more dominant than the role-consciousness that is characteristic of a legal-rational bureaucracy.

Cadre Misconduct: The Five Tendencies

The revolutionary utopianism and anti-routinization attitudes of the leadership during the Great Leap Forward altered the beliefs and behavior of the rank and file, but not completely to Beijing's liking. Cadres at various levels received vague general guidelines from the center that were very politicized. As one former official put it sarcastically years later, "everyone said 'revolution means to leap forward,' but nobody, common folk and leaders alike, knew exactly how to leap."[51] For officials at various levels, the dominant concern became to fulfill the planned targets and avoid being singled out as conservative "rightists" protecting their political careers. The term *feng* (tendency) appeared in the Chinese political vocabulary for the first time since 1949.[52] It referred to a widespread, usually negative, behavioral pattern by a large number of people. The most prevalent and perhaps most detrimental to the party/state organization was the *fukua feng* (tendency toward exaggeration and cheating). *Fukua feng* suggests a pattern of dissimulation, intentional cheating, and Janus-faced behavior, which according to Jowitt is highly typical of Communist mobilization regimes.[53]

STATISTICAL FABRICATION

To answer the call for the courage to think, speak, and act and to fulfill the goals of rapid development, cadres competed for better records. One popular phrase at the time was "high production satellite." Some of these "satellites" were launched to absurd heights. Beginning with a yield of 3,530 *jin* (1 *jin* = 0.5 kilogram) wheat per *mu* (1 *mu* = 1/15 of a hectare) announced in the *People's Daily* on June 12, 1958, reported wheat production output reached as high as 8,585 *jin* per *mu*.[54] The highest rice output per *mu* was reported at 130,434 *jin* by the Red Flag Commune in Huanjiang county, Guangxi province.[55] In a report on how the CCP leadership communicated and interacted with local cadres, a *People's Daily* reporter wrote:

> Zhang Guozhong, the county party secretary [of Xushui], told Chairman Mao that the county planned to produce 1.2 billion *jin* of grains, an average 2,000 *jin* per *mu*. Chairman Mao opened his eyes wide [in surprise] and smiled at the people around him:
>
> "You are going to produce so much grain! But you just got 90 million *jin* for the summer harvest, you have to have another 110 million. You have 310,000 people in your county, how can you consume so much grain! What are you going to do with it?"
>
> No one in the room was prepared for such a question. After some hesitation, Zhang replied, "We can use it in exchange for machines."
>
> "It's not only you who have more grain, every county has surplus grain," Chairman Mao said. "It's good to have more grain. The state may not want it. Peasants themselves can eat more. Well, they can eat five times a day."[56]

Five times a day they did eat. But the problem was that there was not enough grain, let alone a surplus. The result, as we all know today, was devastating. According to one account, the national population, including the newly born, was reduced from 672.07 million in 1959 to 662.07 million in 1960 and 658.95 million in 1961.[57] Thus, during that time at least ten million people died due to unnatural causes. In one county alone, the population decreased from 378,144 in 1959 to 266,166 in 1960,[58] with one-third of the population having either perished or migrated (which was unlikely due to restrictive regulations on migration). The very county under Mao's personal inspection, Xushui, where he had conversations with local officials reported as above by the *People's Daily*, suffered heavy human loss as a result of the 1959 famine—329 died of starvation and 2,447 had severe edema due to malnutrition.[59] Arbitrary conduct by officials, with orders and directives ignoring empirical conditions, was largely responsible for this devastation, as the passages that follow will show.

The *fukua feng* encouraged local cadres in rural areas to behave in an irrational manner so as to keep up with the speed of socialist development and not to be left behind. Did they know they were cheating when reporting production outputs and other required tasks? One interviewee, once a party committee member of a rural commune, offers a good answer to that:

> All those so-called "steel satellites" and "steel aces" were fabricated. They had to be forged because of the pressure from above. Reports on progress [of steel] production had to be made twice daily. Of course the officials knew what they were doing. But if they could not report higher results in the evening, they would be subject to criticism and not be allowed to go to bed. So in the end, each level cheated the level above it, just like the saying goes today—"*Sheng, di, xian, qu, xiang; hezhe hunong dangzhongyang*" (province, prefecture, county, district and administrative village; they all try to cheat the center). The only difference is that today the lower level officials consciously choose to cheat; then they were forced to do so.[60]

Indeed, statistical fabrication, both exaggeration and under-reporting, has been a long-standing problem associated with command economies. The Great Leap Forward may not have originated this practice, but it certainly marked the beginning of its becoming widespread and entrenched. Today, some twenty years after the reforms began, statistical fabrication still exists, albeit for different reasons. Officials in 1958 may well have believed what they were doing was at least partly justified by revolutionary enthusiasm and the party's call, but they also knew they had to do it. It is not that these party cadres were unaware of the actual situation, but two major factors influenced them. One was the pressure to avoid being labeled as a "white flag"—a symbol of a conservative, slow-paced and sometimes reactionary unit or person. The other was the pressure to be a "red flag" in the competition for more glory and commendations.

In the fall of 1959, the party committee of Shanglin county, Guangxi province, held a production assessment meeting at which most of the commune and brigade leaders initially provided the real outputs of their own units. However, the party committee decided that the figures were not high enough. So it ordered a re-assessment with a double-edged sword: those who reported high production figures would get awards, whereas those who still reported the real figures would wear the hats of "rightists" or "anti-Three Red Flags"[61] and be subject to severe criticism. The meetings did not adjourn until the Party Committee was satisfied with higher figures. In the end, the total production output of the county was reported at 257 million *jin,* instead of the actual 144 million *jin.*[62] The pressures to satisfy higher demands from above were felt everywhere and by almost all rural cadres. A well-known maverick journalist made a colorful description of such pressures:

> Nothing was dealt with routinely anymore. For instance, meetings—the professional activity with which rural cadres were most familiar in the years after the Liberation—were also conducted in an unusual manner. A meeting itself had become a process of "great production." After one meeting was over, production output could go up several times. Such production did need hard work. Superiors pressed hard, grassroots level cadres tried hard to come up with the "correct output" . . . until an unprecedented output was reached, a satellite was launched. Then meetings could adjourn and cadres could go home.[63]

The source of such pressures probably should be traced all the way to Beijing. Even among provincial officials, instances of false statistical reporting were not isolated. In a little-known incident, a provincial party secretary, who was a Central Committee member present at the Lushan Meeting, half-jokingly pointed out that there were only three kinds of provincial officials in 1958: those who were bureaucratic, those who cheated, and those who trimmed sails from time to time.[64] As local officials became accustomed to making exaggerated reports as a way of keeping in line with the party's general policies, the problem became more than a concealed one. In Henan province, one of the places where the most exaggerated outputs were reported and (not totally by coincidence) the worst famine-ridden areas were located, a county party secretary openly noted in a speech at a provincial party conference that "without exaggerated reports, the motivation and productive forces of the masses can not be fully activated; without exaggerated reports, the momentum of the Great Leap Forward cannot be furthered; without exaggerated reports, the masses will feel humiliated." Naturally, his conclusion was that for the leap forward to occur, exaggerated reports were indispensable.[65] There were so many cadres telling lies and so few speaking honestly that Mao later made a plea in an inner-party letter to officials from the provincial level on down to the production team to speak truthfully.[66]

THE USE OF COERCION

Under strong pressure from above to achieve higher goals and fulfill production plans that had been set absurdly high, local officials had to resort to coercive, sometimes even forceful, methods—the so-called *qiangpo mingling feng* (tendency to use coercive means). According to a report from the public procurate of Guangdong province, among the 665 cases prosecuted involving local officials in 22 counties in the period of 1959–60, 150 involved death by beating or other forceful methods by officials; there were 96 cases of serious wounds inflicted by heavy beating, 156 rape cases, 34 illegal house searches, 21 embezzlement cases, 11 cases of illegal detention and forced labor, and 17 personal assault cases.[67] Years later, Wang Guangmei, the widow of Liu Shaoqi, recalled the widespread physical assaults by local officials that she and her husband witnessed in 1961 when they visited Hunan: "every agency and cadre could detain or beat up someone at will, not bound by any rules."[68] The cases of violation of law and discipline by officials, particularly in the rural areas, were so widespread that the Supreme People's Procurate issued an internal directive in December 1960 to all local agencies calling for relentless prosecution of such cases.[69]

In Anguo county, Hebei province, a district party secretary and a village party secretary convened a meeting of villagers to force them to join the public canteen with their private grain inventories. Before the meeting, it was ordered that two horses be prepared ready to drag those who failed to hand over their grain. At this meeting alone, 5 peasants were dragged by horse, 18 were beaten, and 20 more were physically abused (e.g., tied to trees and exposed to chilly winter winds). In the same county, among 609 officials at the commune level, 181 were involved in beatings and physical abuse of peasants. In one village, 70 percent of the peasants received some kind of physical abuse.[70] In the model county Xushui that Mao personally helped promote to national prominence, "the words of county party secretary Zhang Guozhong (who presented his county to Mao) became laws." One of his lesser known "achievements," as it came to light years later, was to have arrested 4,643 people in 1958 alone. All this was done during the time his county was praised by the party and official media as one of the first to leap a step closer to communism. Zhang, speaking to another county party official, could not conceal his bewilderment at what he had been able to achieve: "Detention is so effective! It can stimulate activism in production."[71]

One of the worst incidents took place in Shouyang county, Shanxi province, where under orders from the county party secretary a target of collecting 98 million *jin* of grain and one million *yuan* of cash was set, despite the fact that falsified reports and exaggerated plans had already caused a shortage of food in the fall of 1959. Commune and brigade officials went out to search for grain and money using forceful methods such as illegal detention, beating, and torture. In the end, 167 people lost their lives to "unnatural causes," 48 were disabled, and 842 people suffered from hunger-induced edema.[72]

CADRE PRIVILEGE

With all the revolutionary zeal and appeals for inculcation of the Communist spirit, one would suspect there would have been less privilege-seeking by grassroots-level officials. Evidence shows this was apparently not the case. Collectivization, particularly communization, elevated these cadres, as agents of the state, to powerful positions and made them highly susceptible both to political pressure and abuse of power. Another deviant official tendency, *ganbu teshuhua feng* (widespread privilege among cadres) was a direct result.

Examples of this hellish combination of deviant zeal and indifference to the people it was meant to serve abound. Anguo county, for example, was one of the many locales that suffered a serious famine in the winter of 1959. While the disaster was taking its toll, the families of the county party secretary and administrative chief passed the time in a resort, with chefs, doctors, and servants at their disposal. In a village where 80 people died of famine and some 300 left home to try to survive elsewhere, the home of the party secretary retained its own kitchen and never stopped cooking, although no one else in the village was allowed to maintain such private facilities.[73]

In Xushui County, the first county in China that claimed to have entered the communist stage, communization brought the free supply system into the life of the peasants. It turned out later that not only did the new lifestyle not last long, there were many cases where local officials abused power for private purposes. The following conversation between an official investigating cadre wrongdoing and a peasant who experienced the "communist heaven" shows how powerful officials at the grassroots level exploited communization for their own personal interests:

"Did the officials also eat in the public canteen?"

"Yes. They ate inside the canteen and ate good stuff. We common folks ate outside and ate thin soup."

"Have you heard sayings like 'those who work get meals, those who do not also get them'?"

"We had many sayings like that. Here is one: *gongjizhi, hunjizhi, ganbuzhi, bujizhi.*"

"What do *ganbuzhi* and *bujizhi* mean?"

"*Ganbuzhi* means cadres had the power of distributing supplies. They held in their possession the things belonging to all of us. *Bujizhi* means they supplied nothing to us."[74]

BLIND COMMANDISM

Previously I mentioned another serious misdeed of grassroots-level officials during the Great Leap Forward: *xiazhihui feng* or blind, sometimes absurd, commandism in agricultural activities by local officials.

A 1962 report by a county government made this assessment of its own errors:

> The errors we made in blind commandism of production during 1959 and
> 1960 were very serious with detrimental consequences. . . . For the planting
> plan, high-yield crops and conformity were emphasized without enough
> consideration given to local conditions. This has led to a lack of food for
> animal stocks and hence starvation. . . . The leadership style of the county
> government was bureaucratic. Orders and directives were not based
> on careful investigation of empirical conditions. When new work was
> assigned (*buzhi gongzuo*), it was always directed that a few days of hard
> fighting (*dazhan*) was required to realize this and that dissemination, this
> and that clean, or this and that -ization (*hua*). Lower levels were ordered
> to report their good news and battle victories. What would follow were
> a series of inspection teams and on-the-spot meetings (*xianchanghui*). We
> made both improper commendations and criticisms which led to cheating
> by lower level officials. Some of them only planted the fields by the road
> sides for inspection teams to see while leaving large squares of farm fields
> unattended. . . . Commandism not only existed in agriculture but also in
> other areas of work as well.[75]

The problem of commandism was rooted in the conviction among
the CCP top leadership, notably Mao, that daring and innovative thinking could boost agricultural and industrial production. When Mao discovered that in some areas high planting densities and deep plowing
could help raise grain production, he personally advocated these techniques for the whole country as an efficacious way of farming. However, what this candid self-criticism really shows is that in a system that
was highly politicized, officials only looked upward. Rather than being
regarded as a "bureaucratic" loss of touch with reality, it should be seen
as an innate behavior of cadres who were responsible only to their superiors to keep in step with the general political line.

LEVELING

Feverish collectivization also caused what Mao himself called *gongchan
feng*, which literally means "a tendency to communize properties."
Local officials, out of revolutionary enthusiasm or not, confiscated the

private property of peasants, including land, houses, cash, grain, cattle, and even furniture, so that everyone could live as equals. Such leveling swept the whole countryside at the peak of the Great Leap Forward, as we now know. According to a 1961 report by the Department of Agricultural Work of the CCP Central Committee, the estimated value of properties and materials taken away by communes was 2.5 billion *yuan*, an average of 48.89 *yuan* per peasant in a nation where the annual average consumption by peasants was 68 *yuan*.[76]

What previous studies of the leveling during this period have overlooked is that public institutions in the state sector also took part in this frenzy of leveling and property taking. Both state agencies above the county level and local communes extracted property from peasants. Due to the shortage of consumer goods caused by economic mismanagement, state units, including governmental agencies, army units, and schools, began in 1959 to operate their own "grocery production bases" (*shipin shengchan jidi*). As a matter of fact, in the beginning they were encouraged by the central government to do so.[77] They acquired land and other production materials free of charge from the communes.[78] It was revealed that during this period 312 military and central government agencies requested from Hebei province a total of 1.2 million *mu* of farm land for their own production purposes. Some units even demanded seeds, fertilizer, and labor, all for free. Another investigation found that in four counties in Gansu province, 90 percent of county governmental agencies and schools acquired land from local villages to run their own production; similar requisitioning occurred in many other provinces.[79] Although the practice of obtaining land and other materials from villages by public units was later banned, evidence indicates that as late as 1962 many units still possessed what they had taken by eminent domain.[80]

These practices were very detrimental to the party organization, which, to be sure, never called for cheating and false reporting or physical abuse. Yet its own policies and endorsed practices resulted in misconduct. When it did not and could not admit it had erred in its policies, the party looked away from its unrealistic agenda of rapid industrialization and social change. It chose to ignore or tolerate outdated modes of operation such as the "Three Great Weapons" (*sanda fabao*, the mass line, the united front, and putting theories into practice). It cast a blind eye on the reactionary esprit de corps of the wartime guerrillas, the peasants' desperate survivor mentality, and the cadres' irregular work styles.[81] Instead, it viewed the problems as stemming from a lack of revolutionary commitment and a failure to follow the party line on the part of individual cadres. Blame was eventually to fall on officials at lower levels rather than the party's radical policies. Even after all the failures, the party's refusal to reevaluate and discard these revolutionary means of organizational maintenance in post-revolutionary times could not be more salient.

Caught in Between: Cadres Take the Blame

The CCP leadership blamed the cadres at various levels, particularly those at the grassroots, for the "five tendencies" and the other deviations of this period. In an instruction on a six-level[82] cadre meeting in Shandong province on March 23, 1960, the CCP Central Committee severely criticized officials at the commune level:

> Some of the commune cadres are very arrogant. They defy discipline and dare to implement equalization (*pingdiao*) policies without the approval of their superiors. Some engaged in embezzlement, squandering, and bureaucratism which jeopardize the interests of the people. They could care less about equal exchange. All of these are committed by cadres at the commune level. The problem may be not very prevalent but it is not an isolated incident. It must be investigated to see whether one-third of the communes are involved in such irresponsible actions.[83]

Mao, in a remark written on a central committee report, explicitly blamed grassroots-level officials in the countryside for the difficulties during the Great Leap Forward. The problem appeared, he wrote, because "bad elements are in power": "they beat people to death and reduced grain production; they hated socialism, obstructing socialist production relations and productive forces."[84]

A common theme of interviews and documents about the period is how demoralized cadres became as the debacle of the Great Leap Forward unfolded. Despite widespread official deviance such as fraudulent reporting and coercion of the masses, the cadres were committed and deployable to the course of a rapid transition to communism, if not totally controllable. As agents of the state, they did what they thought the party wanted them to do, with great enthusiasm—rapid industrialization through mass mobilization. Many of them acted, voluntarily or not, in line with the interests of the state even when they were at odds with local interests. However, in the end, their fate was no better than those who tried openly to protect local interests. Both got the blame. In this period, local officials were under dual pressures from both society and the state.

"Those who got the axe were usually outspoken and dared to stand up for truth," commented one official who had worked during that time in the party committee of a small county in Hebei province; "they were responsible people who were devoted to the party." The case of Zhang Xidong from this same county is typical. Zhang was an "old revolutionary," who joined the movement in 1938 and the party in 1955. He was the head of the county coking factory. Very outspoken, Zhang often uttered incautious words that might sound unpleasant to his superiors. During the Anti-Rightist-Orientation Campaign in the late 1950s, he was expelled from the party and stripped of all his positions for his "rightist stands," on the evidence of two dozen sentences spoken on various occasions. Statements such as "meetings can not feed people, production does" and "workers have a better living than peasants, so it's natural for peasants to go to the cities while the urban people are coerced to come down to the countryside" cost him his political career. In the same county, in a period of three years, 138 people were purged as "rightists," 76 as "anti-socialists," and 45 as "possible rightists" in 1957. Sixty-eight officials were labeled as "rightist opportunists" in 1959, most of them cadres in various positions.[85]

However, the party did not acknowledge that the commune structure and the restriction on peasant mobility provided tremendous power to local officials in the countryside. Almost all aspects of peasant life were under their control. As one high-ranking party official put it, they "hold other people's rice-bowls (i.e., daily meals of peasants) in their hands."[86]

Ironically, one of the major targets of the Anti-Rightist-Orientation

Campaign of 1959 was cheating and fraudulent reports by local officials. Yet after the campaign, wary of political persecution of this sort,
cadres, including high-ranking officials, became more afraid of speaking the truth or what they really had on their minds. It was revealed
later, at a national conference of party/state officials in 1962, that a
prevalent mode of operation among cadres was the "three looks and
three don't-speaks": look for the direction of the wind (*kan fengxiang*),
when it is not clear where the wind is blowing from, don't speak; look at
the color of the eyes of supervisors (*kan lingdao yanse*), when the color is
not right (that is, not in the right mood), don't speak; look into the intentions (*kan yitu*), when the intentions of superiors are not clear, don't
speak.[87] A report circulated inside the CCP revealed that whenever local
officials spoke publicly, they did so "without failing to mention three,
six, and nine": namely, "long live the *Three* Red Flags," "based on the
needs of *six* hundred million people," and "*nine* fingers vs. one finger"
(a metaphor for sacrificing local interests for those of the nation).[88] A
pattern of behavior among cadres had already become pervasive: out
of fear of political persecution, officials tended to do whatever was necessary, including dissimulation, to protect and promote themselves.

Mao was as concerned with mid-level party/state officials as he was
with grassroots-level officials. He wrote in an internally circulated letter
to party secretaries of ministries, provinces, and major municipalities:

> In making and executing major policy decisions, the grassroots-level
> officials (party branch secretaries, workshop chiefs, and floor leaders)
> and activists must be consulted. Party committee secretaries, factory
> party leaders, district party secretaries in cities, leaders of city party
> committees and the government, as well as the bureau chiefs of the
> central government cannot always be trusted. Many of them have
> almost totally separated themselves from the masses, becoming arbitrary
> and dictatorial. When instructions coming down from above are not to
> their taste, they would act with double-dealing or simply ignore them. . . .
> Only when they are attacked from both their superiors and subordinates
> can their wrongful views be corrected. After listening to them long enough,
> we may even be assimilated and make mistakes.[89]

Mao's distrust of mid-level officials is apparent in this letter, originally written in March 1959. But he was only partially right in his

assessment of the cadres in a time of revolutionary change. Mid-level officials were indeed failing to feed policy makers in Beijing with accurate information, a practice that broke down the critical information flow between the party leadership and the grassroots. Mao warned, "it is so dangerous if information from above can't reach down and information from below can't go up" (shangqing buneng xiada, xiaqing buneng shangda). However, these officials acted in this way not because they were hopelessly out of touch with reality but because their vision and information were limited by the political demands from Beijing. Some of them were clearly aware of the real situation and the needs of the masses. But most of these mid-level party/state officials had few choices in making decisions about such issues as future plans for their own units. A case in point is the dilemma that officials of Shahe county in Hebei province had to face.

In August 1958, the CCP central leadership made an appeal to the whole nation to engage in a mass campaign of producing iron and steel. Shahe, like many other counties then, organized an army-like command headquarters for the campaign with the county party secretary as political commissar and the county head as commander-in-chief. All went well, with over a hundred cadres from all levels working with forty thousand strong laborers day and night. Officials of the county party committee worked their hearts out to execute the decision of the leadership. In the beginning they received some commendations from provincial and prefecture leaders. However, trouble came when Shahe reported their already exaggerated daily production output of 50 tons of iron in a local newspaper while other counties reported over 1,000 tons per day. The prefecture party secretary personally called the county party secretary and asked bluntly if he felt shamed by the reports. At the county party committee meeting that followed, the county party secretary conveyed the phone message from above. For ten minutes, there was dead silence. Nobody wanted to speak out. Their dilemma was captured by one of the participants who recalled the event:

> Nobody wanted or dared to tell lies because the Communists were supposed to be truthful; yet without telling lies, the pressure was on and everyone could feel it. At that time, everyone was scared of being

a "rightist," for the Anti-Rightist Campaign was just over with several hundred people in governmental agencies and schools in that county having lost their jobs and/or having been sent to labor camps after being labeled as "rightists."[90]

Sure enough, the next day a report of daily production output of over one thousand tons was made to the provincial party committee, and the county leaders called a meeting of communes, brigades, and production team leaders to make detailed plans for their part in enforcing the new production target.[91]

Mid-level officials were later hit hard by a major political assault during the new round of the Anti-Rightist-Orientation Campaign after the Lushan Meeting in the summer of 1959. In Henan province, where the most radical leap to communization took place, among the 150,000 officials at prefecture, city, and county levels, 8.6 percent were averred to be "rightist opportunists." Among officials holding positions of county chiefs or party secretaries or higher, 22.4 percent were accused of being "rightist oriented" (*youqing*). In Hunan province, one-fourth of the 10,000 county officials who attended the campaign meetings were criticized as having the problem of "losing sight of the correct line."[92] A similar fate befell many cadres who worked in central government ministries. According to a report by the Second Machinery Ministry, a few months after the Anti-Rightist-Orientation Campaign began in August 1959, 472 division chiefs (*chuzhang*), section chiefs (*kezhang*), and other rank-and-file cadres—7.6 percent of the total number of administrative staff—were accused and criticized. The disciplinary actions these cadres received included expulsion from the party, dismissal from their posts, and expulsion with probation.[93]

Thus the overly politicized cadre corps took blows primarily from the CCP leadership and the party organization rather than from the society, as had been the case in 1957. Even though many of the officials who suffered in the Anti-Rightist-Orientation Campaign were later rehabilitated, the campaign and accusations nonetheless had some lasting effects on their attitudes and morale. A major turnover of grassroots-level cadres followed in the 1960–61 period. Many who lost their posts were cadres since the civil war and had been actively involved in the post-revolutionary campaigns. The turnover was largely a result of the campaign launched in the winter of 1960 to rectify rural party organizations. According to a provincial party directive, the campaign was to "take back power" from class enemies such as former landlords, rich peasants, counterrevolutionaries, bad elements, and rightist officials—the so-called "five bad elements"—in the so-called "third category" (i.e., politically unreliable) communes and brigades. In other places, reorganization was ordered to replace "deadwood bureaucrats and cadres who are muddleheaded and incompetent."[94] In one typical case, a work team was sent down to a commune to solve problems of organization and leadership. The local officials were brushed aside and political activists were mobilized to carry out the work of "remaking the class order." All the cadres in that commune had to be examined on their class background, personal history, *biaoxian*, and social relations to determine their niche in the classification of the "five elements." Harsh treatment of officials was not isolated. A party secretary was forced to stand on the legs of an upside-down table and then spat on by passers-by. In this commune alone, half the twelve members of the commune party committee were accused of being a "bad class element." Among the brigade and village officials, 34 percent received severe public criticism (*pidou*) and disciplinary action.[95]

Years later, An Ziwen, the director of the COD during the Great Leap Forward, spoke about the detrimental effect on cadre ranks of the Great Leap Forward, pointing to the heart of the problem:

> The worst mistake [in the post-1949 history] was the Anti-Rightist-Orientation Campaign after the Lushan Meeting in 1959. It made people so scared that they no longer dared to speak the truth. The damage done by this campaign to the mode of operation of the party was worse, in some respects, than the harm the Great Leap Forward had done to the economy. It took a long time and a lot of effort to heal the trauma it caused in the party ranks.[96]

As the revolutionary radicalization of officialdom reaching an unprecedented height in the late 1950s, a startling number of officials underwent either severe criticism or disciplinary action between 1958 and 1961: according to the statistics of 23 provinces, 4.34 million cadres received some sort of disciplinary action (not including those who were treated as "class enemies" through legal actions).[97] The political performance of party members in administrative or leadership positions was closely scrutinized. Many were criticized and punished by the party for a lack of "revolutionary enthusiasm" and for being insufficiently active in carrying out the party's policy of rapid socioeconomic transformation. In 1958 alone, half a million party members (both cadres and non-cadres) received disciplinary action; the number of people expelled from the party at that time equaled 80 percent of the total number of expulsions from 1951 to 1957.[98]

The party organization felt the impact of the Great Leap Forward immediately after the economic catastrophe. During this period some pre-revolutionary forms of official deviance, which differed from the irregularities induced more directly by the revolutionary fever during the Great Leap Forward, began to occur on a large scale at the grassroots. A case in Shulu County shows how the Great Leap Forward affected rural officials. An internal investigation report by a prefecture "Four Cleanup Workteam" in 1965 reported widespread gambling among county and commune officials, a social problem that had been contained, if not wiped out, after 1949. It noted that such activities first reappeared in 1960 and then gradually got out of hand. In fact, 167 work units, or 23 percent of the units of that county, were involved in *providing* gambling venues. A commune party secretary always brought along a set of playing cards whenever he went to villages to inspect work. Another official lost all his money in gambling and had to offer to stand guard outside the gambling house in exchange. All told, 139 county or commune officials took part in gambling activities—almost a quarter of the cadres in the county. It was not hard to understand why such illicit activities could last several years when, in 29 of the 31 communes, either the party secretary or commune director or both were involved.

As one indication, cadre corruption and misconduct cases prosecuted in the wake of the Great Leap Forward increased, particularly in the early 1960s. Table 3.2 is an example of the kind of cases that were prosecuted.[99]

Official corruption and misconduct were perceived by the leadership not simply as transgressions by individual cadres, but rather as serious *political* threats to the existing socialist order. After the mid-1950s de-Stalinization in the Soviet Union, the Chinese party began to be more

TABLE 3.2

Cases Prosecuted by the People's Procurate
of Heilongjiang Province, 1963

Embezzlement	Abuse of power[a]	Graft	Other
Law enforcement officials[b]	2	5	4
Economic and financial officials	151	39	5
Other state agents	74	65	16
Grassroots-level officials	156	90	51
Other	21	27	1
TOTAL	404	226	77

SOURCE: *Dangdai Zhongguo de jiancha zhidu.*
[a]Includes illegal searches, illegal interrogations, and torture of detainees.
[b]Includes staff in public security, the court, and the procurate.

alert to a possible "revisionist" threat in China. In the wake of the failure of the Great Leap Forward and the open Sino-Soviet split, the CCP took new cognizance of the sources of Soviet "revisionism": stratification in the socialist countryside had enabled cadres to become the rich and privileged.[100] Containing disciplinary problems among cadres was regarded as crucial to preventing similar revisionism from gaining ground in China. Deng Zihui, a major figure in agricultural affairs in the 1950s and 1960s, expressed a concern that represented the stand of the CCP leadership:

> Privilege seeking by cadres most seriously alienates the masses. Common folks are discontented with them. . . . This is very dangerous. If these cadres do not change, they will become the fertile grounds for future revisionism. Twenty years from now, China may see revisionism. Don't think it is impossible. After the old generation passes away, these guys are likely to become Khrushchevs. The chairmen of Soviet collective farms, belonging to the privileged strata, earn a high salary. They are scared of war and combat. We have to solve the problem, otherwise it can become very dangerous.[101]

The leadership was correct to place the focus of attention on cadres; after all, the party's ability to control its agents was weakened after the damage to the organization inflicted by the Great Leap Forward, and the cadres were demoralized and devastated. The leaders' solution to the problems, however, was to further revolutionize the "superstructural domain" of the system. For the first time in post-liberation history, cadres who carried out policies that turned out to be disastrous were later blamed for many of the consequences. Many learned a lesson not taught in party schools or training classes: to survive in a politically sensitive and dangerous game, it was not enough to follow orders and meet goals. They had to find protection by utilizing particularistic and informal relations or strategies that the revolution had intended to destroy. Ironic as it may sound, the "revolutionary" character of the party and the conscious choice of the leadership to counter the erosion of revolutionary ethos among its ranks, however ineffectively, were what compelled cadres to seek shelter under the guise of politically correct formalities.

The Great Leap Forward and the Party Organization

One often-noted development of the Great Leap Forward period is the decentralization of economic authority initiated by Mao and his associates.[102] Less noted were trends toward the deregulation and deregularization of established institutions and the impact of these trends on the party organization and its cadres. Organization building, perceived as an important part of the superstructure of relations of production, was a high priority of the CCP leadership. Prior to the Great Leap Forward, there were serious concerns about the direction in which the party organization was heading. A *People's Daily* editorial went so far as to point out that the most dangerous enemy was not the KMT, the U.S., or the bourgeoisie, but bureaucratism.[103] The party believed that a change in the institutions and ethos of the administrative apparatus must be made, together with a socioeconomic transformation. Some of the existing administrative structures, it was believed, were overly independent of the party's leadership. They had become increasingly "bureaucratic" and inefficient in the sense that they had lost touch with the masses and reality.[104] Revolutionary institutions and methods such as mass mobilization, the leadership believed, could replace many existing bureaucratic institutions—notably institutions of supervision, control, and inspection.

The leadership's determination led to measures that would affect the party organization as a whole: elimination or reform of some established structures and regulations, as well as installation of "revolutionary," non-conventional mechanisms specifically designed to remedy bureaucratic problems (e.g., *xiafang*, *pingbi*, and new rounds of rectification campaigns). The CCP leadership chose these methods to overcome the problems of growing routinization, alienation from the people, and autonomy of cadres working in functionary roles. They chose revolutionary means rather than a further bureaucratization of the cadre corps. However, although the intention of the party was to reduce and remedy bureaucratic problems as well as to accommodate economic development, in the end it found itself not only falling far short of these two goals but faced with even more serious problems concerning cadres and organization.[105] Ten years into the complex task of socialist reconstruction, the party experienced its first major economic and organizational setbacks.

The methods employed to reduce what the leadership perceived as the problem of "bureaucratism" were effective only in certain ways. They may have helped to keep the post-revolutionary party/state agents closely in touch with the masses. But in the long run, they induced non-professionalism and produced highly politicized administrative staffs who were not only timid politically but also inefficient and incapable professionally. At the individual level, these methods served to nurture deviant behavior by officials represented in the prevalent "five tendencies." Consequently, when it appeared that the Great Leap Forward was a failure, individual cadres were blamed. They were caught between revolutionary idealism and cruel reality, and were demoralized. This was the beginning of the organizational involution of the party.

In times of rapid change, the role of the organizational leaders, as Selznick has noted, is to steer a middle course between opportunism—"the pursuit of immediate, short advantages in a way inadequately controlled by considerations of principle and ultimate consequence"—and utopianism.[106] Opportunistic behavior leads to aimless drifting and, worse, to attenuation of organizational character. Utopian leadership often arises in an attempt "to avoid hard choices by a flight to abstraction." Paradoxical though it may sound, utopianism may join hands with opportunism:

> Utopian wishful thinking enters when men who purport to be institutional leaders attempt to rely on overgeneralized purposes to guide their decisions. But when guides are unrealistic, yet decisions must be made, more realistic but uncontrolled criteria will somehow fill the gap. Immediate exigencies will dominate the actual choices that are made. In this way, the polarities of utopianism and opportunism involve each other.[107]

In the case of the CCP organization, opportunism was reflected in the deviant behavior of officials who, to the leadership, either were too slow to take the lead or even to follow others in the Great Leap Forward—doubting the "Three Red Flags," hesitating in collectivization, being unwilling to set higher production targets, and the like, or fraudulently reported and ignored difficult realities to suit the taste of their supervisors. Utopianism, on the other hand, existed in almost everyone's mind; the Chinese had for a very long time sought the attractive and at that time seemingly reachable goals of national development.

In the Great Leap Forward, opportunism involved utopianism in that cadres took an opportunistic approach in order to meet the utopian needs of their superiors all the way up to the Central Committee. They joined hands to reinforce each other. Under a utopian banner, opportunism became the predominant mode of operation. This situation was not what organizational leaders intended. Furthermore, when it eventually led to devastating consequences, the people who took the blame were those rank-and-file officials who acted opportunistically but were not the real sources of such opportunism. Thus, the Great Leap Forward was followed by political campaigns almost all of which were aimed at investigating and disciplining party cadres. The distrust Mao and other CCP leaders felt toward grassroots-level cadres mainly originated in this period and found its ultimate expression in the launching of the Cultural Revolution in 1966.

The debacle of the Great Leap Forward clearly reflects the failure of organization leaders to balance revolutionary idealism with a realistic assessment of the situation. Despite its lofty intentions, the party as a whole could not move forward without being compromised by the uncontrolled reactions of the rank and file, which were due, precisely, to its refusal to give up revolutionary utopianism while rapidly modernizing the economy. The party leadership applied a radical "storming" approach to economic development, but it refused to let the routinization of a charismatic revolutionary organization occur or continue. Mass mobilization, as Mao put it at the time, was "still a premium method to be relied upon in doing everything, including the production of steel."[108] Cadres who were incapable, not innovative enough in following policy lines, and unfaithful or unreliable in communicating information up to the central leadership were seen in political terms and led to what Harry Harding calls an "internal remedial approach."[109] This Maoist approach to the "bureaucratic problem" was based on one of the most important philosophical tenets of Chinese revolutionaries— the significance assigned to subjective human agency in determining an objective outcome. It was believed that only by changing the internal human condition could an effective and committed organization be maintained and the socialist revolution be accomplished. External constraints on human behavior were secondary. Methods such as making officials take part in manual labor, *xiafang*, and dismantling existing rules and regulations, Mao noted, were all intended to change people's worldview.[110] He criticized Stalin's overemphasis on economic development and neglect of the superstructure. Yet the outcome of this "institutional" (in the Selznickian sense) approach to organizational integration was far from what Mao and the CCP leadership desired. Although they reduced the problem of "bureaucratism," other problems related to the cadre corps appeared as a result.

Studies of the Great Leap Forward period have often neglected the impact of radicalization on organization building. I document here evidence that at the beginning with the rectification campaign of 1957, the Chinese regime entered a period of fluctuation and uncertainty in terms of its organization and cadres that was to last for at least another two decades. One line of argument about the Great Leap Forward claims that behind the radical push for rapid economic development was the politics played out among different bureaucratic agencies and between the party and bureaucratic sectors. According to this view, the functional bureaucracy at the top was as much responsible for the catastrophe of the Great Leap Forward as were Mao and the party leaders who were constrained, and later frustrated, by it. Thus, David Bachman concludes, "this may be nothing more than that bureaucracy in China differs little from bureaucracy in other countries."[111] Bachman's argument criticizes the existing literature on the Great Leap Forward for its general neglect of the organizational sources of political behavior, andpresents a strong case for going beyond common assumptions of pure leadership miscalculation and judgment or factional infighting. It pits a "fluctuating political coalition" against a "stable" bureaucratic coalition. While I agree with him that the organizational origins and effects of the Great Leap Forward should not be neglected, I suggest that it is not *factional, judgmental,* or *coalitional* politics that limited the choice of the CCP leadership, but rather its own *organizational* politics. By "organizational politics" I do not mean the contradictions and bargaining between political and administrative leaderships, but those between leadership and rank and file, and between organizational goals and the mode of elite behavior. After all, "organization" is not only about central leadership; it also includes the whole echelon of members. Although there is evidence that Mao was disgruntled over the increasingly uncontrollable ministries in Beijing,[112] the launching of the Great Leap Forward and its attendant mass mobilization were not simply a result of bureaucratic bargaining. Findings in this chapter support the notion that the CCP leadership, particularly Mao, sincerely believed that the "engineering approach" (i.e., routinized, rationalized institutions) adopted since early 1950 "had matured *a new type of cadre,* whose narrow professional/bureaucratic interests caused one to lose sight of the revolutionary mission."[113] Many of the measures implemented in this period, both economic and political, were based on this belief rather than on the outcomes of bureaucratic politics played out in Beijing.

Studies of the Great Leap Forward have shown that this failed attempt seriously undermined the legitimacy of the regime, particularly in the countryside.[114] However, it is worth pointing out that the discontent and estrangement were directed more toward local officials and activists than toward Mao and the party itself. Peasants still believed that Mao did not know "their plight and he was their last hope and ultimate savior."[115]

It is often argued that bureaucracies everywhere tend to have stable preferences and to be conservative. In the case of the party/state during the Great Leap Forward, heavy pressures came from the leadership for *de*-bureaucratization with a goal of radical change.[116] Mao "seemed to believe that rationalization had gone too far, not that it remained incomplete, and that bureaucratization was producing conservatism."[117] But there is little evidence that the bureaucracy had any head-on conflict with the party, at least concerning policy execution by agents of the party/state. On the contrary, the officialdom itself was very politicized and enthusiastic, whether out of real personal conviction or not, at the height of this "revolutionary storming" on both economic and political fronts. Cadres, political and functional alike, felt the heat of revolutionary enthusiasm and became active participants. The problems of official deviance that occurred during and after the Great Leap Forward were more related to the politicization of officialdom than to the loss of revolutionary goals by cadres, which is how the leadership perceived it. In a revisionist argument about the Maoist discourse and practice on bureaucratization, Martin King Whyte contends that "a major push toward further structural bureaucratization of Chinese society was launched during the period of Mao's ascendancy during the Great Leap Forward . . . and seemed most infected by Soviet 'gigantism.'"[118] No evidence that I have found substantiates such an argument. On the contrary, the Maoist leadership, despite the gigantic size of "bureaucratic" organizations—rural communes—experimented with a novel form of organization sustained by revolutionary norms, and bearing little resemblance to the "structural bureaucratization" Whyte attributed to the Soviet patterns.[119]

Unlike the typical bureaucratic problem of conservative "rigidity and an inability to adjust readily" that is usually caused by what Robert Merton has called "the displacement of goals," officialdom during the Great Leap Forward was plagued by a lack of clearly defined rules and regulations to which it could render conformity. Conformance in this case was judged not by adherence to rules but by adherence to revolutionary goals. This development led to "formalism" of a different kind—the *displacement of rules* fostered by the tremendous symbolic significance of ends, an antithesis of Merton's theory.[120] Hence the serious organizational problem that bothered the leadership was not rigidity or inefficiency but deviant behavior characterized by disinformation and unpredictability.

Even if we assume that cadres *do* pursue stability and security, the history of the Great Leap Forward demonstrates that the Chinese bureaucracy under Maoism was more vulnerable to political pressure. Before the Great Leap Forward there indeed had been a tendency in routinization of the party/state, but it was not yet "mature," as Mao incorrectly perceived. Early on, this tendency was resisted and fought with great effort by the CCP. The common image of bureaucracies as "conservative structures, oriented toward maintaining the external as well as the internal status quo"[121] does not fare well in this case, not because the generalization is wrong, but because China's was not a modern bureaucracy in the Weberian sense.[122] Franz Schurmann's distinction among four types of administrative leadership, of which cadre leadership is a unique type, is illuminating here:

> The manager and the cadre agree in defining their environment as one of constant change and challenge. . . . They must act innovatively and creatively in order to survive personally and keep the organization moving ahead. Both types of bureaucrats, on the other hand, are primarily oriented to routine, maintenance, and stability. . . . Modern bureaucrat and manager agree that techniques and expertise are the basic means for organizational integration. In contrast, the traditional bureaucrat and the cadre regard human organization as most significant for achieving this goal.[123]

It was the intention of the CCP leadership to sustain a *cadre*, not *bureaucratic*, mode in its post-revolutionary administrative staff, in spite of changing tasks and environment. To that end, new objectives and a new environment were manipulated through revolutionary symbols into combat situations. Cadres were expected to be daring and capable agents in this new round of struggles. Seen in this light, change and radicalism, rather than the status quo and conservatism, were the main dynamics behind the actions of party/state agents. These agents acted in the way they did not because they resisted the change and radicalism that originated in the organization's leadership, but because they tried to be in line with the leadership and did what they thought they were supposed to do. In the end, when the objectives could not be reached, the leadership did not question its own organizational principles imposed upon changing reality but blamed the rank and file. The two intertwined factors—politicization and insecurity of the officialdom—induced certain behavioral patterns. Ironically, although the goal of the organizational leaders was to eliminate what Mao saw as bureaucratic conservatism, a different kind of conservatism was actually fostered by such purposeful anti-bureaucratization. This new form of conservatism compelled officials to take a sluggish course of action, guess the intentions of superiors from ambiguous policy pronouncements, and avoid taking responsibility—all exactly the opposite of what the party had intended to do by politicizing the cadre ranks. The organizational problems of the late 1950s and onward lay not in intra-bureaucratic conflict and bargaining between the political leadership and functionaries, but in the sharp contradiction between the goals of rapid industrialization, on the one hand, and systematic deregularization on the other. What underlined the tension was a growing gap between the interests of the organization and those of the rank-and-file cadre members, rather than a divergence of the interests of the bureaucracy (and different interests among various agencies within it) and the interests of the party. All these factors point to a commencement of the involutionary development of the ruling party, which was to intensify as Mao began to resort to an even more drastic method of solving organization problems—an out-and-out attack on the party/state organizations brought about by mobilizing society against them. This revolutionary impingement on the organization would reach its peak during the Cultural Revolution.

CHAPTER FOUR

Political Mobilization and the Cadres

In Mao's overall discourse concerning "continuous revolution," the cadre question occupied a prominent place.[1] The integrity, discipline, and capability of the party organization and its cadres became a top priority after the failure of the Great Leap Forward. Throughout the 1960s, major political and economic events were highlighted by attempts to adopt a Maoist radical remedy to bureaucratic problems, including cadre indiscipline and corruption. These attempts were part of the Maoist response to the question of how to maintain organizational integrity and competence in post-revolutionary times. The failure of the Great Leap Forward did not lessen the leadership's belief that the evolution of the party/state to a bureaucratic organization was most dangerous, or the leadership's determination to avert it. Political mobilizations were still regarded as the most effective means to answer all challenges, including rectifying cadre misconduct. The belief was that only by infusing more revolutionary doctrines and carrying out continuous revolution could the party succeed in rooting out deviant behavior among its cadres. A series of major political mobilizations was launched: a new Anti-Rightist-Orientation Campaign, the Socialist Education Campaign (also known as "the Four Cleanups," or *siqing*), and the Cultural Revolution, as well as a number of smaller, lesser-known anti-corruption campaigns.[2] All these campaigns shared one difference from earlier campaigns: the party leadership went outside the party to mobilize the masses to attack party/state officials who, it believed, after many years of governing, "had become bureaucratic and corrupt" and "a part of the new bourgeois class elements or their allies."[3] Yet, despite the intensified mobilization to instill the revolutionary ethos and reverse the tendency toward routinization, the results of the Maoist efforts were far from sufficient; however, it did not go back to the pre-Leap bureaucratization mode. Instead, the prevailing organizational ethos and relational modes turned into more informal and formalistic ones. Organizational involution continued as the leadership insisted on halting and reversing the propensity toward bureaucratization in the party/state with high-pressure tactics and the cadres reacted to such pressure by resorting to informal strategies both political and economic. Official deviance including corruption—as much as it was the target of these intense political mobilizations—became even more pronounced.

Continuous Revolution and Officialdom

The Maoist discourse on "continuous revolution" and "class struggle" derived initially from concerns about post-Stalin reforms in Eastern Europe. The Great Leap Forward, as part of an ambitious economic development program, failed to produce the results Mao had envisioned. A brief period followed, during which the blind fever for rapid industrialization at all costs somewhat cooled and the subsequent economic readjustments were somewhat assimilated. But the CCP leadership became increasingly uneasy about sagging morale, lingering doubts about Beijing's policies, and discipline problems among lower-level officials, particularly those in the countryside. Zhou Enlai assailed the cadre disciplinary problem in a speech about twenty "evil phenomena occurring in the party." He mentioned, among others, "disregarding organizational discipline, willfully promoting one's favorite staff, forming cliques to pursue selfish interests and shield each other, maintaining feudal relationships and sharing factional interests, and maximizing private interests and letting the interests of a 'minor public' encroach upon the interests of the greater public."[4]

One of the leadership's gravest concerns was the pervasive practice of dissimulation by individual cadres and public units, a byproduct of the highly charged mobilizations of the Great Leap Forward. As Deng Xiaoping, then a member of the CCP Politburo, put it at the well-known "Conference of Seven Thousand Officials" in 1962, "intra-party struggle had made some errors during several campaigns, harming a number of cadres. In some regions, a large number of cadres were unnecessarily harmed. Due to a lack of implementation of the rule of democratic centralism, and the over-hostile attitude toward officials, there developed in the Party a vicious tendency not to speak or report the truth out of fear."[5] Chen Yun, who declined Mao's invitation to speak at the plenary meeting of the same conference, warned at a smaller session later of the danger of officials' concealing the truth: "Intra-party life has not been normal in the past few years. The phenomenon of 'speaking out only one-third of what one wants to say and reserving the rest' is very dangerous. For the party, it ought to be fine for people to say something wrong, but it is dangerous when people do not speak out. The revolutionary course is doomed to fail if this continues."[6]

Reporting only what higher-level officials wanted to hear and omitting the negative became extremely prevalent in the bureaucratic hierarchy, so much so that when CCP leaders were preparing the 1962 budget, they discovered that in the previous period (1958–61), all of the annual fiscal revenues reported had been exaggerated and deficits had been concealed by the State Council's financial officials.[7] Such cheating at the very top showed that it was indeed pervasive and that the worry of CCP leaders was justified.

The leadership was divided on what were the root causes of the problem, however. Some, such as Deng Xiaoping and Chen Yun, believed that the source of such dissimulation was the intensified political mobilizations themselves, and they called for relaxed treatment of cadres. Others voiced their concerns regarding the advent of an increasingly bureaucratic administrative corps similar to that of the Soviet Union, where the Communist Party under Khrushchev had become an organization of "the high-salary and rural rich strata."[8] Liu Shaoqi offered a more direct criticism of the cadre ranks: "We have all kinds of official status. Not only is resident housing allocation done according to ranks, but so are the number of desks, sofas, and chairs one can get [at no charge from the state]. Such a system of status fosters the tendency among officials to seek special treatment."[9]

Mao was even more blunt: officials were becoming increasingly "lazy," which might lead to "greediness" (*chan*), "grabbiness" (*zhan*), "graft" (*tan*), and eventually "decay" (*bian*).[10] He saw the sources of the problem as lying in the officialdom's "mentality of seeking a comfortable life," and in the cadres' lack of ideological commitment. Whether or not the cadre problems were regarded as grounded in the politicization of officialdom (as Deng and Chen seemed to think), or the lack of it (as Mao, Zhou, and Liu believed), the predominant theme in Chinese politics of the 1960s was to maintain political vigilance against Soviet-type revisionism among the cadres by carrying out "continuous revolution."[11]

The Maoist leadership attempted two solutions to prevent cadre degeneration: to invoke the revolutionary wartime experience, or to use ideological indoctrination and political mobilization. Mao had already tried the first method once during the Great Leap Forward, when he took issue with the salary system that had completely replaced the free supply system. He championed the idea of a self-sufficient, egalitarian community in his famous "May Seventh Instruction" of 1966, in which he recalled the army during wartime, and called on all sectors, including industry, agriculture, education, commerce, and government, to turn themselves into a "grand school," where "people can learn politics, military skills, and science as well as engaging in agricultural productions." In this place, "small factories can also be run, which can produce certain items to meet their own needs and items exchangeable with the state at a comparable price."[12] In separate speeches in late 1966, Zhou Enlai and Jiang Qing hinted that Mao had again raised the issue of reinstalling the free supply system. On May 14, 1967, during a meeting of the Leading Group of the Cultural Revolution—an ad hoc organization set up beside the regular Politburo—Mao expressed his desire to "discuss at some point the issue of eliminating the ranking system."[13] Evidently, Mao still savored the image of wartime military communism and desired a more egalitarian, self-sufficient economy and organization. To him, these revolutionary institutions were the ultimate way to prevent the emergence of a bureaucratic class. He contended that cadres in party and government organizations had become so bureaucratic that they had lost touch with reality and with the masses. One way to resist bureaucratization, Mao believed, as he did during the Great Leap Forward, was to engage cadres in manual labor. In his words, "most of the staff in the administrative apparatus should work part-time in the office, and part-time in manual labor. Laziness is one of the sources of revisionism."[14]

More significantly, the leadership's other solution—political mobilization based on the Maoist emphasis on class struggle and continuous revolution, which was purported to become "in command" (*zhengzhi guashuai*)—was seen as more effective in rooting out bureaucratization. The economic crisis caused by the Great Leap Forward did little to motivate the CCP to reassess its "storming" approach to industrialization. Instead, the party continued to search for an answer in the "superstructure of the relations of production," key among which was the commitment of cadres to revolutionary goals and ideology.

Based on the assumption that an independent bureaucratic class was forming and becoming the most dangerous force of the post-revolutionary socialist order, the priority of the CCP switched from economic development to political struggle against the "degenerating elements" in officialdom. If in the 1950s class enemies were perceived as outside of the party, in the 1960s they were viewed as being within the party, and even more dangerous to the regime than those outside. Mao, commenting on an internal report from one province, explicitly pointed to the existence of a new class:

> The bureaucratic class is the class whose interests are in absolute conflict with the working class and poor peasants. . . . Those leaders who take a capitalist road have become or are becoming bourgeois elements sucking blood from the workers. They are the targets of struggle and revolution. The socialist education campaign most definitely cannot rely on them. We can only rely on those cadres who maintain revolutionary spirit and whom workers do not hate.[15]

This stance represented a reversal of Marx's classic argument that the ruling class is but a reflection of production relationships in society, and that the bureaucracy is not a class for and of itself, although the state may in certain situations be autonomous. The CCP leadership's view of Chinese officialdom was derived from its broader perspective on "revisionism" in the post-revolutionary Soviet Union and Yugoslavia.[16] Clearly, the driving force of the Socialist Education Campaign, and later the Cultural Revolution, involved the concern that Chinese cadres might evolve in similar directions.

"Catching Fleas": Cleaning Up the Cadre Ranks

The Maoist "continuous revolution" thesis did not remain just an ideological discourse. It was put to use as a guide to address the problems of the beleaguered cadre ranks, in order to, as Mao put it, "pull up the roots of revisionism."[17] The initial efforts were made by the provincial officials in Hunan and Hebei, where a "rectification of communes and cadre work styles" was implemented in 1963. The Hunan provincial party committee reported to the Central Committee that 7 percent of county officials, 10 percent of commune officials, and an even larger proportion of grassroots cadres "had serious problems."[18] Hebei province went further and invented the Four Cleanups: cleaning up public accounts, storage and inventory, funds and materials, and work points.[19] The CCP central leadership later in effect endorsed the Hebei model for the entire nation, setting in motion a new anti-corruption campaign.

If the metaphor for the corrupt elements in the Three Anti and Five Anti campaigns was "tigers"—referring to corrupt high officials and businessmen—the new metaphor in the 1963–66 anti-corruption campaign was "fleas"—petty corruption by lower-rank officials—reflecting the change of targets. Both metaphors appear to have been invented by Mao, who had a tendency to use unsophisticated metaphors, for instance, such terms as "taking a bath" and "washing hands" in the Four Cleanup Campaign. On several occasions, Mao used "fleas" to refer to those who committed graft or other violations.[20] Such a choice of words, casual as it may seem, reflected Mao's assessment of the situation in the cadre ranks: "tigers" were limited in number but big and powerful, whereas "fleas" were small yet great in number and hard to catch. As he put it at a high-level meeting on the anti-corruption drive, "the more graft cases that are exposed, the happier I am. Have you ever caught fleas on your body? The more you catch, the more pleased you are."[21] The Socialist Education Campaign, which had two components—the New Five Anti Campaign in urban areas and the Four Cleanup Campaign in the countryside—was intended to avert "revisionist tendencies within the party" as reflected in the discipline problems among lower-level officials.[22]

In the cities, a new Five Anti Campaign—opposing graft and pilferage, speculation and profiteering, extravagance and waste, departmentalism (*fensan zhuyi*), and bureaucratism—commenced in March 1963 to rectify problems of official deviance.[23] The campaign was mainly carried out in government agencies, the commercial sector, and consumer industries, where, in the period of post-Leap consumer-product shortages, misconduct and irregularities such as graft and backdoor deals were most prominent.[24] During this campaign, special efforts were made—with instructions from Beijing—against graft/pilferage and speculation/profiteering. According to an internal report from the central supervisory commission, in the 1,800 units where the anti-graft and anti-speculation drive was under way, 15,100 people (3 percent) out of a total of 410,000 people who took part in the campaign were found to have committed graft or speculation.[25] In some places, as many as 7.6 percent of those who took part in the campaign were found to have been involved in graft or "stealing state assets."[26]

Some aspects of official deviance of this period resembled those of the previous anti-corruption drive, the Three Anti Campaign. One example was the seemingly perpetual problem of extravagance and banqueting with public funds by and in government agencies. In Heilongjiang province, for example, a survey of 23 public units found that between January 1962 and August 1963, there had been 224 such dinner parties or banquets.[27]

Another target, "departmentalism"—a synonym for deviant behavior and irregularities committed by public units—was a persistent problem with roots in the guerrilla period. The internal instructions from the Central Committee to launch the campaign pointed to practices of concealment, "enriching the minor public by encroaching on the greater public," and the involvement of government agencies in commercial activities.[28] In Heilongjiang province, for example, an investigation found that the provincial post and telecommunication administration fraudulently reported the number of telephone operators in order to receive more fabric to make uniforms. A reported 1,000 additional operators in whose names additional fabric was received by the agency in fact did not exist. Cases such as this, where government agencies tried through various means to build up "small coffers" by cheating on the higher authorities, were common in other provinces as well.[29]

As in earlier periods, there were fuzzy boundaries between the greater public, the minor public, and the private. This situation intensified after additional "socialist elements"—such as communal dining halls in both rural and urban areas—were introduced during the Great Leap Forward. Another such change was the rural commune structure, in which officials enjoyed both political and economic power and, which, by virtue of size, were beyond the reach of popular supervision and monitoring. This concentration of power in the hands of commune officials played a significant role in inducing illicit behavior. According to a Four Cleanups investigation of misappropriations averaging 300,000 *yuan* in Shanghai's suburban counties in 1963, each of the 21 communes "had no clear explanation as to what the money had been spent on."[30]

A familiar type of misconduct by officials in the anti-corruption campaigns throughout the Maoist period was *duochi duozhan* (eat more than one's share and take more than one is entitled to). In the urban Five Anti and the rural Four Cleanup campaigns, *duochi duozhan* was often cited in the official press and internal reports. It was treated as a serious transgression because the violator took advantage of either the public or collective interests at a time of economic difficulties. But it was never clear how much was too much. Many of the transgressions were marginal cases of "conflation of public and private interests" (*gongsi bufen*), "gaining petty advantages" (*zhan xiaopianyi*), or "taking more than one is entitled to" (*duochi duozhan*). Even Mao, speaking about how to make officials pay back what they had taken, admitted at a high-level party leadership meeting that "*duochi duozhan* is a very complicated matter. It's mainly because people like us have cars and houses with heating. I cannot afford a chauffeur plus a secretary with my own salary."[31] The broad targets set at the onset of the campaign notwithstanding, confusion prevailed as to what constituted "graft and theft of public property" and "speculation and profiteering." Ultimately, this confusion adversely affected anti-corruption efforts.

Two factors may account for the differences between this Five Anti

Campaign and that of 1951–52. First, the material shortages during the post-Leap period appear to have been much greater than during the early post-1949 period, due partly to the Great Leap Forward's attempt to industrialize, which had created demand for production inputs. This was evidenced by the fact that during the first Five Anti Campaign, the sectors in which the most grafters were caught were the tax bureau and the police department, whereas in the later campaign the most misconduct-plagued sector was commerce.[32] Second, whereas in the early years of the PRC, the private sector was still a viable part of the economy, the vitality of private business in the national economy had been drastically reduced by the end of PRC's first decade, after the socialist transformation had been accomplished. The state had monopolized the power of allocation and redistribution of resources as well as products. The legitimate sphere of non-controlled purchases and sales was kept at a minimum, much smaller than in 1952. Whereas in the early years the most common forms of illicit business practice were those inherited from pre-revolutionary times, such as tax evasion and using low-quality production materials, which are also illegal in a capitalist market economy, the targets of the 1960s campaign were defined by the then-current system of state socialism. More significantly, the new Five Anti Campaign was intended to tighten up organizational control over public units and individual cadres emboldened by the decentralization and weakened institutions of the Great Leap Forward.

THE "SECOND ECONOMY"

After the failure of the Great Leap Forward, the CCP was forced to retrench from its unrealistic industrialization policies in early 1961. The economy was plagued by severe shortages of production materials and consumer goods despite a good agricultural harvest in 1962. This period of retrenchment saw the emergence of free markets and other activities of the "second economy." In Wuhan, for example, nearly 100 farmers' markets had sprouted by February 1961. Additionally, by the end of 1961 as many as 140 large production material trading warehouses, which had disappeared after the state monopolized the allocation of all production materials, reappeared in thirteen major cities.[33]

At the same time, the number of "underground" or unlicensed private businesses (*dixia heigongchang*) increased rapidly. Black markets in the selling and buying of ration coupons for grain, fabric, and other rationed goods were booming. At the end of 1962, it was estimated that three million people were active in this "underground" sector, and, according to official criteria, 10 percent of them were involved in illegal profiteering.[34]

Unlike the previous Five Anti Campaign in the early 1950s, the 1960s campaign was aimed heavily at profiteering practices, which by official definition included illicitly obtaining or purchasing state- or collective-controlled materials that were then sold at higher prices (*daomǎi daomài*); long-distance transporting and marketing of goods in other places (*changtu fanyun*); organizing "underground production" (for example, unlicensed factories, shops, and construction teams); and other "illegal commercial activities." Mao estimated, during a meeting with North Korean leader Kim Il Song in February 1964, that some ten million people were engaged in such "underground work."[35] In addition to the targets in the state sector, campaign activities were also directed toward the growing private sector, including black marketeers and private businessmen who profited from state-controlled commodities obtained illegally (*taogou*, i.e., purchases outside the state plan). During the 1951–52 campaign, the private sector was still strong enough to resist the government's attacks, which, though heavy-handed, were sometimes limited. By the early 1960s, the economic structure had drastically changed. The private sector represented a small, if not totally insignificant, share of the national economy and, resilient and persistent as it might be, was too fragile to clash with the state head-on. In the short term, it had to fold its banners.

Another form of "second economy" to emerge during this period were "extra-plan" (*jihuawai*) and "extra-budgetary" (*yusuanwai*) economic activities engaged in by both individuals and (mostly industrial and commercial) organizations. Many studies of the "second economy" under the state socialist systems have pointed out that activities of this type represented a rational response by public units, productive or nonproductive, to survive and to fulfill production plans when the state was not able to meet all their needs for raw materials and capital goods supplies. A phenomenon shared by other state socialist countries—enterprises' use of powerful purchasing expediters (known as *caigouyuan* in China and *tolkachi* in the Soviet Union)—also emerged in the Great Leap Forward period, when rapid industrialization inflicted production material shortages and economic planning was left with numerous loopholes. Supplies often could not meet the needs of production as laid out in government plans. Thus a policy known as "searching for rice to cook" (*zhaomi xiaguo*) was advocated by the authorities. As a result, extra-plan purchasing and selling activities became widespread. Price gouging and profiteering naturally occurred. Armed with funds or materials, hundreds of thousands of expedited purchasing and sales agents were floating around in major cities, in effect creating a "gray market" of their own. Soon such practices were out of state control. Despite the government's attempt in 1959 to rectify what it called "the chaotic situation in purchasing work," extra-plan purchases and sales continued to increase. According to a survey in Shanghai, there were more than 50,000 *caigouyuan* temporarily stationed in the city, and they brought in some 100 million *yuan* for procurement in the city in 1960.[36] The practice continued well into the 1970s.[37]

During the same period, representative offices (*banshichu*) of provincial governments in Beijing also proliferated, with similar offices of government agencies and large enterprises in major cities. These offices functioned to develop useful connections in the central ministries and lobby for more in-plan and extra-plan material and fund allocations. Some provincial offices in Beijing also ran their own guest rooms, serving the needs of visiting officials from their own local government.[38]

The "second economy" is a complex historical phenomenon associated with state socialism.[39] It is difficult to categorize it as either legitimate (in that it was functional for the units) or illegitimate (in that it was harmful to central planning and general interests). In some parts of the country and in some periods, governments acquiesced. Except for a brief period in 1961–62, throughout the 1960s the government perceived the second economy as an "illegal undertaking that hampers the economic order, further galvanizing shortages, and undermining people's interests."[40] It reflected the Chinese government's ambiguous stand toward extra-plan activities: at times restrictive and hostile, at others tolerant and acquiescent.

TROUBLED RURAL CADRES

In rural areas, the anti-corruption campaign was even more pronounced. The economic crisis caused by the Great Leap Forward had left scars on the Chinese rural landscape, where millions of peasants had died or suffered from hunger and malnutrition. The party's brief embrace of private farm plots and a relaxed policy on the rural free market in the first two years of the 1960s made local officials and peasants who had maximized the opportunity better off than others. More significant factors that affected the behavior of rural officials included rapid changes in policy and the lack of institutional stability—such as the lack of a well-established accounting system and frequent turnovers of rural officials as a result of political purges. The anti-corruption drive that began as a new Three Anti (anti-graft, squandering, and bureaucratism) Campaign was launched in rural areas in 1960.[41] Unhappy with the results of this campaign and facing continuing problems among rural cadres, the CCP leadership decided to expand it to a broader "socialist education campaign" in November 1961, which eventually evolved into the now well-known Four Cleanup Campaign in 1963.[42] The primary targets of the Four Cleanup Campaign were local officials who took advantage of their official positions and control of collective funds. In Shanghai's suburbs, for example, the initial stage (i.e., self-confession) of the campaign exposed that local officials had embezzled or peculated large sums of money. In the 175 communes that were involved, embezzled or peculated funds amounted to 3.1 million *yuan*, an average of 18,000 *yuan* per commune.[43]

The central leadership was concerned with growing social inequality resulting from the abuse of office by officials for personal gain. Investigations found that officials were the ones most likely to be prosperous, despite the economic plight suffered by the rural population after the Great Leap Forward. In Hebei province, a survey of 71 families of "poor and lower-middle peasant background" showed that 28 families in which someone who worked as a village official lived a better life; the 43 families in which no one held an official post suffered from "exploitation" by the "four-unclean officials" (*sibuqing ganbu*) and their lives were "increasingly impoverished."[44] The same investigation detected the presence of abuse of power by officials from patterns of redistribution of housing, food, clothing, income from family sideline farming and education of children. It found that in another village in Baxian county, 571 poor and lower-middle peasant families on average lived in one-room housing, mostly built with clay blocks, while 233 officials' families lived in 1.9 rooms, mostly built of more expensive bricks. Eighty-nine of 167 newly built houses since 1961 belonged to officials' families. Some of these houses were built using disaster or poverty relief funds impounded by village officials.[45] In Longhua county, the officials of a village sold over one thousand *jin* of surplus grain at (higher) market prices in 1963; meanwhile, some poor peasants from the same village had to *buy* grain in order to feed their families. In Zhaoxian county, a medium-income county in Hebei, in one village seven peasant families made do with four winter jackets and one pair of trousers for every three persons; the four cadre families had seven winter jackets per individual. In Baxian County, there was one child in school for every 18 cadre families; for every 71 poor peasant families, one child was in school.[46] These numbers, which were provided in internal reports circulated in the party organizations, revealed the significant gap between the living standards of officials and peasants.[47]

Lower-level officials again bore the brunt of the new campaign, which applied similar but more radical techniques than the previous anti-corruption drives. A number of new features distinguished this campaign from previous anti-misconduct campaigns. First, it viewed corruption and other forms of official deviance as a reflection of the growth of "new exploitative elements" or a "new bourgeois class" within the party. The leadership perceived that the party had lost one-third of its grassroots party organizations to class enemies or enemy sympathizers.[48] Those who committed graft or profiteering were defined as being part of this new class.[49] The campaign was therefore regarded as a class struggle, bearing serious political connotations. A second feature of this campaign was the recruitment and training of non-party-member activists to join the work teams (*gongzuodui*) sent down from provincial or county governments. Non-party-member peasants in rural areas were also mobilized to form Poor Peasants Associations, which, for a short period, were empowered with personnel and allocative discretion to be reckoned with.[50] Rural cadres were put under strong pressure. Many of them resisted either actively, by threatening or buying off villagers, or passively, by quitting their positions. In one county, 63 of the 177 cadres in a brigade quit before the campaign even reached their unit.[51] The words of a production team head indicate the mental state of rural cadres during the Four Cleanup Campaign: "To be a cadre costs too much. Family plots are not well taken care of, and my wife complained a lot. Every year, I would get fixed (*zheng*, i.e., criticized and/or reprimanded). I may as well quit once and for all."[52]

Consequently, a large number of cadres were reprimanded with various disciplinary measures. In many places nationwide during the Four Cleanup Campaign of 1963–66, the statistics indicate that the annual average number of cadres to receive disciplinary actions was higher than in any other political campaign to date. No national figures are available, but the cases in Tables 4.1 and 4.2 offer evidence that the numbers of cadres reprimanded were matched only by those reproved in the earlier Anti-Rightist-Orientation Campaign of 1959–62.

Many cadres were relieved of their positions and replaced by newly recruited activists. This campaign resulted in a major surge of newly admitted CCP members and newly promoted grassroots officials. The use of the *tiba* method lived up to its full expectations.[53] In the later stages of the Four Cleanups, the CCP admitted 940,000 new members (in 1965) and 3.23 million (in 1966), most of whom had been activists in the campaign.[54]

ANTI-CORRUPTION AS CLASS STRUGGLE

As efforts to strengthen grassroots organization, the Four Cleanup and Five Anti campaigns went far beyond the limits of a narrowly defined anti-corruption drive. Their function as part of class struggle and continuous revolution was underscored by more comprehensive purges. It is for this reason that the results of the anti-corruption aspects of the campaign are difficult to assess. Among the cadres subject to disciplinary action or stripped of their positions, many were purged simply because of "impure" family or personal backgrounds (*chushen buhao*). In an internal report, the "Office of Four Cleanups" of the Hebei provin-

TABLE 4.1

Cases of Disciplinary Violations and Misconduct
in Xiaogan County, Hubei Province

Year	CASES		CASES INVOLVING CCP MEMBERS	
	Total	Per year	Total	Per year
1951–56	363	73	169	34
1957–62	1,212	202	1,063	177
1963–66	1,136	284	1,136	284
1967–79	363	30	363	30

SOURCE: Based on data from *BXSDC* (*Xiaogan*).

TABLE 4.2

Cases of Disciplinary Violations and Misconduct
in Wuchang County, Heilongjiang Province

Year	CASES		CASES INVOLVING CCP MEMBERS	
	Total	Per year	Total	Per year
1951–56	353	59	353	59
1957–62	837	140	837	140
1963–66	354	89	354	89
1967–79	335	28	335	28

SOURCE: Based on data from *WCXZ*.

cial government lists the elements of "a completely rotten (*landiao le*)
commune," in which not only was the commune leadership "totally
degenerated" but most of the top officials of brigades and local enterprises were corrupt:

> (1) In this commune the [party] organizations were impure and were con-
> trolled by bad elements. Among the ten party secretaries and commune
> heads over the years, six have problems in their class background or past
> [i.e., pre-liberation] experience; (2) profiteering by commune leadership
> through a farming machine factory run by the commune; (3) graft, theft,
> and extortion; (4) gifts and banquets at public expense; (5) moral degenera-
> tion and sexual promiscuity.[55]

These venal actions were not without connection to each other. The belief was that if someone engaged in corrupt acts, he must be from an impure class background, and vice versa. This belief was especially strong in rural areas, where class categorization was much more comprehensive.

As chaotic and destructive as it was, the Cultural Revolution kept up the constant theme of anti-corruption, anti-waste, and austerity, part of almost every political mobilization in PRC history. No sooner was the initial stage of the Cultural Revolution over in late 1969 than a series of articles appeared in the official press, such as *Red Flag* and *People's Daily*, on "class struggle in the economic realm," assailing existing waste, graft, and speculation in "every sector of our society."[56] This series marked the inauguration of a new "One Attack, Three Anti" campaign (*yi da san fan*)—attacking counter-revolutionaries, anti-graft and theft, anti-profiteering and speculation, and anti-waste and lavishness—in many localities in early 1970. However, because constant political mobilization and reconstruction of the badly damaged institutions remained the core task of the day, problems related to economic misconduct were not given priority. During this new anti-corruption campaign, which was based on the assumption that waste and graft were "intentionally caused by a small clique of class enemies,"[57] the importance of containing graft, speculation, and waste was again overshadowed by the political "core task" of purging political dissidents. Many who were found guilty of corruption were also accused of being "counterrevolutionary." In Baishui county, Shaanxi province, for example, the campaign lasted more than twenty months. By the end of 1971, about one-third of 3,003 "corruption" cases were deemed to be "politically oriented," including "vicious verbal assaults on the leadership," and 2,057 had to do with economic crimes.[58] In many places, the campaign was completely intertwined with factional in-fighting among officials and activists. Once a faction was ousted from power, the one that took over would accuse the people of the other faction of having been "corrupt." As with campaign-style anti-corruption efforts, numbers were often exaggerated and cases mishandled. In Chicheng county, Henan province, an initial 6,656 people were implicated for having "economic problems," but after further assessment the number was later reduced to 766. This process of re-examination and consequent reduction happened frequently during anti-corruption campaigns in the PRC.[59] Officials were frequently later found to have been unfairly wronged. Thus, at the height of political radicalism, every wrongdoing became politically motivated and the goals of prosecuting economic crimes were often lost in the political power struggle waged at all levels of the system in the wake of the Cultural Revolution.

Zouhoumen: *Opening the Back Door*

In the state socialist economic order, characterized by a lack of markets and the existence of perennial shortages, the practice of making deals or obtaining things (usually consumer products) through personal connections was common; it was known in China as *zouhoumen* (going through the back door) or *kaihoumen* (opening the back door). Many thought that this practice first appeared in the wake of the Cultural Revolution in the early or mid-1970s. However, its origins can actually be traced back to the early 1960s, when the debacle of the Great Leap Forward left its imprint on the daily life of urban residents. Unbalanced industrial development and agricultural failure resulted in a scarcity of basic daily necessities and consumer products in retail stores. Many consumer and food items were either rationed or put on controlled access.

The shortages were particularly acute in large cities such as Shanghai and Tianjin, where residents sought other means to obtain hard-to-buy goods. Their strategies included purchasing from acquaintances or relatives working in the commercial sector. Since retail shops had only empty shelves, and coming out the front door with goods would elicit suspicion, people with connections bought merchandise literally through the back door. Hence the beginning of *zouhoumen*. The earliest evidence of *zouhoumen* appears in an internal directive from the Department of Commercial and Financial Work of the CCP Central Committee in June 1959.[60]

Zouhoumen thus began as an informal response, by both individuals and institutions, to economic problems caused by the failure of the command economic system. To the party organization, *zouhoumen* added to an array of informal modes of operation that were detrimental to orga-

nizational integrity and discipline. It was an important element of organizational involution. For the most part, the people able to buy rationed
or scarce items through the back door were cadres. Even more alarm-
ingly, *zouhoumen* was also used by the privileged group of high-ranking officials who enjoyed "special supplies" (*tegong*) during the most
difficult economic times.

Despite early warnings from the government, *zouhoumen* continued
to spread in the commercial sector. In 1959, the city of Anshan in
Liaoning province launched a local campaign against backdoor dealing
in the commercial sector. The CCP Central Committee transmitted to
the whole country a report from the Anshan municipal party committee
on how the campaign had proceeded.[61] Ironically, the appearance of
zouhoumen also had a lot to do with official privilege. High-ranking officials and senior scholars had been provided with special supplies of
goods that were generally in short supply. In order to obtain these
goods, some local governments tried to include more officials on the
special supply lists. Lower-ranking officials, on the other hand, tried to
get the goods through the back door. In October 1960, the Central
Committee issued a directive titled "Reforming the System of Special
Supplies for High-Ranking Officials and Prohibiting Backdoor
Dealing,"[62] attempting to halt the practice. Nevertheless, the situation
did not improve. Liu Shaoqi wrote after reading a report on the
zouhoumen phenomenon in August 1961: "If not rectified immediately, it
will damage all of our programs. How to put an end to *zouhoumen* in
the commercial and grain sectors and let the masses monitor the distribution of grains and consumer products is one of the most pressing
tasks for us."[63] The practice became so widespread that the central government convened a special meeting to counter back door dealings, corruption, and speculation in October 1961.[64] Li Xian-nian, the vice-pre-
mier in charge of finance and commerce in the State Council, spoke
about the problem of *zouhoumen* at this high-level meeting: "*Zouhoumen*
is caused by the shortage of commercial items. There are different man-
ifestations of *zouhoumen*: some are for personal need, some for eating
and taking more than one's own share. The most serious ones are speculation, profiteering, and corruption."[65]

Li revealed that the phenomenon was not confined to the commercial sector. "It exists in every sector," he warned. "There are so many case materials submitted by local governments that one can hardly read them all."[66] Despite this meeting and an anti-*zouhoumen* campaign in the commercial sector, the practice did not disappear, but actually spread beyond the commercial sector. In 1962, Premier Zhou Enlai spoke about it in his speech at the National People's Congress meeting.[67] On May 9, 1962, the CCP Central Committee, in a report on the anti-*zouhoumen* campaign conducted in the commercial sector of 21 provinces, instructed that "the campaign has far-reaching impact and must be carried out to the end." The report criticized some local governments for failing to curb the practice: "People at the higher level continue to have access through [the back door], while people at the lower level are hard pressed not to use it" (*xiafan shangzou, bianfan bianzou*).[68] In 1963, after issuing a directive that regarded *zouhoumen* as one of the problems existing in the commercial sector,[69] the CCP Central Committee issued another directive[70] to curb illicit practices, including the *zouhoumen*, in all walks of life. Zhou Enlai, in a 1963 speech depicting twenty "bureaucratic traits," again underlined the problem of "seeking enjoyment and avoiding difficulty, stretching out a long hand and *zouhoumen*; one person being an official, the whole family benefits; giving gifts and throwing banquets."[71] As a typical informal and deviant practice, *zouhoumen* existed through the early 1980s, when reforms opened many other doors. Even during the Cultural Revolution the practice did not cease. In 1968, for example, the CCP Central Committee warned against *zouhoumen*, mainly in consumer items, in an urgent announcement on fiscal austerity.[72]

Why did *zouhoumen* occur? *Zouhoumen* in its original form entailed a transaction through informal channels, in the absence of the market, between the staff of a state-run store who had discretion over certain goods, and a buyer who might have something to offer in return or simply had a close relationship with store clerks. The official view at the time on the cause of such a practice was both political and practical. Liu Shaoqi voiced a typical Maoist opinion on a problem related to the party organization, that it was "a struggle between two lines. We should bring this practice which may corrupt our ranks and damage our course up to such a high level of ideological consideration."[73] Li Xian-nian, in his speech on *zouhoumen*, echoed this view and added:

Indeed there are objective conditions where there is a material shortage due to the two-year famine. But all the people have suffered from shortages. When the nation is facing difficulties, state agents are being tested.

There are many reasons why *zouhoumen* occurred. First, in the last few years political indoctrination work was superseded by busy professional work. Second, both the quality and quantity of the staff in the financial and commercial sectors declined because they were sent to assist industry and agriculture. Third, we *revoked some rules and regulations*, an action which may not have been rational. Some of those revoked regulations have not been replaced by new ones. In order for the "back door" to be shut closed, the "front door" must be kept open. Yet we do not have well-established institutions in place.[74]

Evidently, the shortage of consumer products could not by itself explain the appearance of the practice. Before the Great Leap Forward, there were also times when consumer goods were scarce, yet *zouhoumen* did not become a common method of acquiring things. The cause may also lie in the rapid nationalization in the 1950s of the commercial sector, which peaked during the Leap when all urban industrial and retail businesses were forced to merge with, or switch to, state-owned businesses.[75] State-run retail shops and department stores were the only places where people could buy daily necessities.

The rise of informal strategies and the "second economy" could not all be attributed to the economic impulse and rational calculation. Informal modes occur (and at times prevail) when formal mechanisms fail to instruct and constrain the behavior of organizational members. The deregulation and deregularization during the Great Leap Forward led to a significant degree of confusion of norms in the wake of a major economic and political crisis. What the Great Leap Forward did was as detrimental to the organization as to the economy. It is arguably the beginning of a trend toward increasing separation between the organization's goal of keeping the revolutionary combat spirit alive and its members' own search for certainty and routine. Cadres, in the political crossfire and with minimal certainty about formal institutions, would find new possibilities in such informal or deviant practices as *zouhoumen*, *guanxi*, or graft. Similar patterns could be found in the ensuing years following the Cultural Revolution, when instances of *zouhoumen* again rose to a new level of intensity.

The Cultural Revolution and Its Impact on Cadre Behavior

The Cultural Revolution began, according to the Maoist interpretations, as a continuation of the efforts to rectify the party organization weakened by the post-revolutionary propensity to routinization. Though the causes and original objectives of the Cultural Revolution are disputed,[76] it is beyond question that Mao's discontent with the growing bureaucratization of the party and its officialdom was a major reason for him to launch such a political campaign. More significant are the results of the campaign and its impact on officialdom during its course and immediately afterward. If Mao's goal was to provide a fundamental solution to the problem of bureaucracy by such radical measures as dismantling the old establishment, the outcome of the Cultural Revolution failed him.

The breakdown of formal institutions and existing norms during the early phase of the Cultural Revolution gave rise to new configurations of organizational and social relations. Among them, political struggle participated in by cadres at various levels created a deeply divisive factionalism that was to last for many years. It provided the basis for one of the most notable informal ties of the early post–Cultural Revolution period. Ironically, political campaigns were intended to foster impersonal, ideologically correct, and universal relationships. In reality, they facilitated a kind of comradeship among activists and cadres who shared similar political views and interests, and, to a certain degree, close ties among both the accused and the prosecuted. As a result of political mobilization, inter-personal relationships became such that comradeship was actually infused with friendship. Yet such friendship was not the revolutionary new type the party had hoped for through a transformation of cultural values, but a kind of relationship that sprang from revolutionary bonding and was embedded in more personal attachments that often were invoked instrumentally.[77] This consequence of the Cultural Revolution was easily detectable in its late stage and in the period that immediately followed. A retired official who used to work in a provincial public security bureau said in an interview, "after several decades of working in this place and constantly going down to 'squat' in grassroots units (*xiaqu dundian*), who would not have some people with whom you share some special relations? You must have a few people, in or outside of your own *danwei*, whom you can trust and count on for help in case troubles occur."[78] Similar experiences in rural China were also recorded in ad hoc organizations (e.g., work teams) or informal groups (e.g., factions) where a close personal bond was forged during political campaigns.[79] Although the Cultural Revolution was intended to be a sweeping experience that would establish a new type of human relations, in effect it created a foundation for some long-lasting informal relations, thanks partly to the blurred boundaries of formal organizations. The cellular nature of Chinese social control through the *danwei* system, which generated cellular social and political dynamics, precluded collective action organized across organizational boundaries. When during the Maoist period actions such as labor protests occurred, they were organized and participated in only by employees from the same enterprise.[80] Rarely were these employees organized by unions or joined by workers from other enterprises. During political mobilizations such as the Cultural Revolution and the Socialist Education Campaign, the routine confines of the work unit were broken for the sake of an overriding "core task." People from different institutions were able to have non-routine interactions, participating in ad hoc groups across formal unit boundaries.

Another important objective of the Cultural Revolution was to eradicate people's selfishness and the private realm in the economic and social arenas. A repeated theme during the most radical years was *dagong wusi* (augmenting the public, nullifying the private). An editorial reflecting the views of the radical faction in Shanghai, the testing ground for urban socialist transformation, struck the chord of anti-private interest, anti-selfishness rhetoric:[81]

> Shanghai in the old days before 1949 was a heaven for the capitalist class. The idea of private property rights had a strong hold among people. In the eighteen years since 1949, "*si*" (the private) was constantly under severe attack every year. Yet it still had a lot of influence. The Cultural Revolution is a great revolution of thoughts which emphasizes "breaking the private

[realm], establishing the public [realm]" (*posi ligong*). It is a proletarian revolution intended to weed out the values of exploitative classes, replacing
them with communist values or what may be called "*public*-ism."[82]

It has become a widely accepted assertion that the Cultural Revolution did more to impair than reintegrate the purportedly bureaucratic
and ineffective party/state. However, its perverse effects on the normative behavior of millions of cadres are still not fully appreciated. Some
aspects of the aftermath of the Cultural Revolution, such as the resurgence of informal relations in the Chinese politics and society in general, and the illicit transactions based on those relations, have been more
assumed than carefully documented and analyzed. Some have suggested that the resurgence of informal, instrumental relationships
rooted in traditional Chinese values was a direct result of people's
needs in an environment where the marketplace was under state control.[83] Such an assessment points out one important structural cause of
deviant behavior in Chinese society, that of satisfying material needs in
a non-market economy. But there were also more complex institutional
causes, such as weakening organizational control, confusion of norms,
volatile political mobilizations, and, most significant, the inherent contradictions between the routinization propensity of a post-revolutionary organization and the conscious attempts to resist such tendencies.

Guanxi: *The Utility of Personal Connection*

Not only did the Cultural Revolution fail to eradicate the private realm,
it further nourished more informal, personal relations and modes of
operation, among which were the pervasive exercise of *guanxi* and
zouhoumen by cadres and ordinary citizens alike. *Zouhoumen* as a widely
invoked strategy and a "subculture" grew to new proportions during
the period after 1969, when the Cultural Revolution entered its recon-
structive phase. *Zouhoumen* entailed personal connections that facilitated access to the right person who could have things done. It was
closely related to *guanxi*, which became an informal behavioral mode
commonly adopted among both the elite and members of the society
only after the Cultural Revolution. The prevalent use of *guanxi* during
this period helped to weaken further many of China's already frail insti-

tutions and organizational norms.[84] The term *guanxihu* (or "units that one has informal ties with") was practically unheard of before the Cultural Revolution. The novel facet of the practice of *zouhoumen*, a practice that had existed before, was the extensive use of *guanxi*. When *zouhoumen* first appeared in the early 1960s, state agents were involved in exploiting their control over scarce resources by going through the back door within the confines of their own sector. In these instances, the practice was more approximate to profiteering involving transactional exchanges than had been the case in the post–Cultural Revolution period, when it involved *guanxi* to obtain items and favors from agencies or agents.

Guanxi, an informal and often instrumental dyadic relationship, is not always corrupt. It can be non-corrupt when the purpose of engaging in such a relationship does not involve public office and the power derived from it. But in the Chinese social context, the two are often intimately related. *Guanxi* as an informal institution is a deviation from formal institutions that the regime sanctions. In the political realm, *guanxi* as a mode of social exchange provides a mechanism for people who collude to abuse the power entrusted to state agents.

The notion and practice of *guanxi* did, in fact, exist before the Cultural Revolution, but only when formal institutions and rules had proven ineffective did it become so widely exploited as to attain both tangible and intangible personal goals. At the onset, the practice of "going through the back door" was driven by consumer product shortages following the debacle of the Great Leap Forward. The pursuit of material goods was the main impulse behind such an action undertaken by officials and staff in the economic and commercial sectors. By the time the Cultural Revolution was running out of steam, however, the function of using personal connections and going through the back door also shifted, though not exclusively, to non-material purposes, despite the existence of similar consumer product shortages. *Zouhoumen* was employed to serve other purposes, in addition to obtaining material goods, such as to advance a career or to rehabilitate purged officials—and, in the case of urban youths, to avoid being sent to the countryside, to obtain urban residency or college admission, to return to cities, and to join the military. Many of these were personal efforts related to redressing the wrongs and destruction of the Cultural Revolution.

Influence peddling was another important objective for people weaving a network of connections. As one media report put it, "If you strain the relations [with a senior official] to the extreme breaking point, he can turn off the engine of your car and stall your movement. . . . But he can also lubricate the engine well and make it go fast."[85] A popular saying at the time captured the essence of *guanxi* as an effective tool: "An official seal does not count as much as a few good words put in by someone whom you know."[86]

Guanxi was not only cultivated and utilized to optimize personal gain; it was also increasingly used by organizations (i.e., work units) to achieve goals, economic and otherwise.[87] One purchase and sales agent of a textile machinery factory averred that to cultivate *guanxi* "is vital and legitimate because others do it for private purposes, I do it for public (*gong*) purposes, for my work unit. Leaders in my unit fully support me."[88] He also made a cogent observation about the thin line between the corrupt facet of *guanxi* and the non-corrupt (but nonetheless deviant) one:

> I had spent two years in prison for embezzlement. Still, the leaders of my unit wanted me because I have an uncle who is an official in a state timber mill and they need lumber. Now I have realized that only fools embezzle. They have to do it illicitly at the risk of breaching the law. Smart ones do it openly. Now I am living a luxurious life but do not have to pay for it. It is all covered by the entertainment expenses. It is not embezzlement.[89]

The official view regarding the utility of *guanxi*, particularly when used in place of formal relationships, has always been negative. A 1980 newspaper commentary applied strong words in analyzing *guanxi*: "What is the nature of the relationship of so-called '*guanxihu*'? It is a relationship of giving and taking bribes in disguised form. In the old society, 'buying your way through' was everywhere in the bureaucracy. Today, to rely on *guanxihu* to have things done is in essence a kind of 'buying your way through.' "[90]

The same commentator also admitted that to inhibit the *guanxihu* problem is no easy job, acknowledging that such bribery relationships not only show themselves "horizontally" (i.e., between sector and sector, unit and unit) but also "vertically" (i.e., between superiors and their subordinates, leaders and the led). The majority of the people who operate through *guanxihu* would probably only be subject to criticism and education, not disciplinary or legal actions.[91] An official decree of the CCP Central Party Discipline Inspection Commission (PDIC), issued in July 1981 and specifically on *guanxihu*, acknowledged that there was a prevalent "tolerant, and sometimes, supportive attitude of some party organizations and leading officials toward the *guanxihu* practice," and called for strong disciplinary actions against it.[92]

The pervasiveness of *guanxi* indicated a loss of the party's ability to integrate its members using formal relational modes. "The connections are established to mutual advantage," a newspaper editorialized; "people trying to establish such connections must possess something— power, money, or material objects—to offer, or they are not qualified to join the club."[93] Practice of this sort should be indeed regarded as official deviance when a state agent, or cadre, is involved, particularly because it harmed the efforts to re-institutionalize the bureaucracy.

What makes the use of *guanxi* an action that often eludes punishment by law or discipline is that it does not directly violate either of them. Also, although the action itself can be a process of delayed and potential bribery, the potentially venal elements can be easily disguised. *Guanxi* further blurs the line between gift-giving and bribery. Instrumental as it often is, *guanxi* can be an innocent, non-power relationship between people without any intention to exploit official power. The delay in seeking reciprocation can be long or short. Sometimes, it is important to cultivate *guanxi* for a long time before one claims its fruits. The experience of a mid-level official at a provincial bureau of cultural relics, who expressed his frustration as a newly appointed deputy section chief, offers an example of a short-term *guanxi* deal:

> As soon as I was appointed to the position, I found myself besieged by
> all kinds of gifts and well-wishers. People came to me with booze and
> cigarettes. But they would always want something in return even if they
> did not say it. Once a guy from a county cultural affairs bureau came
> with a big fish, a two-footer. It turned out that the next day, my agency
> was going to decide on the 4 million *yuan* budget. He came for the purpose
> of getting more funds from the province. . . . It is sometimes hard to refuse
> the gifts because of face.[94]

Rediscovering the Value of Power

The party/state organization came out of the Cultural Revolution with great damage to its organizational integrity and discipline. Purged officials gradually reemerged during the later, post–Red Guard period.[95] Many returned to their old positions as the result of post-mobilization "rehabilitation" and "liberation," an idiosyncratic aspect of the Maoist regime. One thing they had learned from the Cultural Revolution was the insecurity of their positions and the precariousness of their power. Among those who had endured the constant pressure of continuous political campaigns and party rectification drives, especially those who suffered to various degrees, the power of office had never been so valuable. For new cadres, who had been activists from humble backgrounds incorporated into the leadership ranks, the power that attached to their new positions appeared especially tempting.[96] Power (*quanli*), they discovered, could be used in dictating to the formal chain of command in the organizational hierarchy for official purposes or in disposal of resources. It could also be used informally to attain personal objectives. A popular dictum in the late Maoist period was *"youquan buyong guoqi zuofei"*—"power has to be used, otherwise it will expire."[97] The correlation between the post–Cultural Revolution reconstruction of the party organization and the apparent increase of official deviance was aptly noted by Liu Binyan. In his well-known investigation and exposé of the Wang Shouxin corruption case, he found that 1972 "was an historic year in modern Chinese history, [because in Bin county] banqueting and drinking as well as pilfering, seizures of property, embezzlement, and misappropriation by officials all reached a new height that year."[98] It is not pure coincidence that in the 1990s the age group of officials who are most likely to commit corruption is close to sixty—a practice sarcastically dubbed the "fifty-nine phenomenon." According to a 1994 survey of the corruption cases involving bureau-rank officials in Shanghai, two-thirds of the officials were almost sixty years of age. Another survey in Zhejiang province showed a similar pattern: 29 of the 58 officials indicted in corruption cases in 1996 involving county-rank officials were older than fifty.[99] The reason is not difficult to discern—the regulations stipulate that once a county-rank (or the urban equivalent, bureau-rank) official reaches sixty years of age, he or she must retire unless promoted. Power will expire when one retires. As a deputy chairman of the People's Congress of Guangdong province confessed to the Central PDIC investigators, "To retire from leadership position means giving up power. By 'grabbing' more, one can keep a psychological balance. I felt that after I step down from the mayor position in Dongguan [and move to the provincial congress], no one will watch me. I didn't have to care."[100]

OFFICIAL PRIVILEGE

An increasingly pervasive pattern of official deviance in this period is elite *teshuhua* (special treatment) or *tequan* (official privileges). A high-school teacher used a popular saying of the mid-1970s to summarize the situation of the time: "*gaogan song shangmen, zhonggan zouhoumen, laobaixing zong qiuren*" (high-ranking officials have goods delivered at their front door, and mid-level officials go through the back door to get things, while common folks always beg for help).[101] The prevalent pattern of cadre corruption in the 1970s was a "socialist mode of corruption," or prebendalism, which encompassed more subtle usurpation of power for private purposes—such as official privileges and *zouhoumen*—as opposed to a "capitalist mode of corruption"—things like bribery and embezzlement, for example, which were the primary patterns of corruption in the early 1950s. Official perquisites had long existed among the Communist ranks before but they were granted to officials according to positions or rank. What was different now was that officials actively sought privileges and other preferential treatment. Ironically, official privilege in China became prevalent after the leadership's intense criticism during the Cultural Revolution of Soviet apparatchiks for indulging in official privilege. Official privilege was so common among high- and middle-ranking officials that by the end of the 1970s, it had become a key reason for popular discontent and the declining legitimacy of the regime. As a matter of fact, the Democracy Wall Movement of 1978–80 was partly a reaction to this type of corruption. The government realized the gravity of the problem but was unable to curb it. An official newspaper commentary admitted: "due to the profound negative impact of the Cultural Revolution and the long-existing flaws in our system, unhealthy tendencies of seeking various kinds of privileges have become a chronic disease hard to cure and a serious social problem potentially threatening."[102] An urban youth who spent several years in the countryside wrote about the officials: "Their children happily flew out of the countryside. *It was then* [1971] *that the legitimacy and appeal of the party among the masses and youths began to deteriorate rapidly.* The phenomenon of official corruption that caused a lot of discontent also originated in this period."[103]

Official privileges included watching foreign movies, reading restricted documents, and access to restricted books, enjoyed by officials of certain ranks and denied to ordinary citizens. These materials were officially claimed to contain "unhealthy or improper content," were regarded as "reference materials" for study purposes among officials, and thus were not available to the general public. This period saw a boom in privileges of party/state officials who, depending on their rank and position, had access to items designated as *neibu* (internal). *Neibu* movies were mostly foreign-made (often Hollywood) features such as *Gone with the Wind*, *Star Wars*, and *White Nights*, screened only in "internal" theaters inside the compounds of government or military units; public movie theaters outside only had a few reruns of propaganda films. The term *neibu* in Chinese public life first appeared in the early 1960s. Although the CCP had used various designations for classified materials (such as "top secret," "secret," and "classified") as did any other political party or government, it devised the unique category of "internal" for a restricted audience. The term first appeared in official documents designated to be read only by CCP members or certain levels of officials. It may well indicate that after the late 1950s, the CCP consciously upheld a demarcation between the internal (i.e., the party/state) and the external (i.e., the general public). The delineation was perhaps seen as necessary out of distrust in the civil society, where class enemies were perceived to still exist. Political intentions aside, the term became widely used in other than official documents in the mid-1960s. It also began to appear stamped on literature and social science books.[104] Later, the *neibu* designation was expanded to cover other controlled items and scarce opportunities. There were "internal sales" (*neibu xiaoshou*), "internal discounts" (*neibu xuejia*), and "internal hiring" (*neibu zhaoshou*). The privilege of seeing an "internal" movie, buying or reading an "internally circulated" (*neibu faxing*) book, or obtaining "internally handled" (*neibu chuli*) goods typified the status orientation of the regime. It is no coincidence that in the 1970s some radical Chinese neo-Marxist critics of the CCP regime characterized the cadre corps of the period as a "privileged class of bureaucratic monopoly," which, under the guise of socialist public ownership, collectively rather than individually controlled economic and political resources.[105] In a typical essay, one such critic wrote:

> Today, many people oppose and hold a grudge against the Cultural Revolution. But there are different motivations: a small group of privileged officials oppose the Cultural Revolution because it damaged their power and positions. They realize that dictatorship does not benefit the interests of the whole privileged stratum. So they want to build an aristocratic regime where political bureaucrats can enjoy privileges according to their status, free from insecurity under a dictator.[106]

To these radical neo-Marxist thinkers, the Thermidorian restoration of the power of the cadres after the Cultural Revolution produced a far more dangerous bureaucratic class than ever before. While class analysis of this sort captured one of the underlying causes of cadre corruption—state monopoly of nearly all economic and political resources—it failed to account for individual corrupt behavior. In this sense, a self-reflection of a senior cadre who joined the revolutionary ranks before 1949 was more cogent:

> Since the first day I joined the revolution, I have always been trained to uphold the principle that the Communists work for the interests of the people; the people are masters, we are their servants. However, years of experience have led me to believe that there are gaps between theory and reality.
>
> Who is the servant? Who is the master? My decades-long career as an official tells me that my direct superior is the master and I am his servant. I am not a servant of the public but a servant of the leaders. Years ago before the Cultural Revolution when I worked in the general office of the municipal government, the goals were "three servings"—serving my supe-

riors, serving my agency, and serving the masses. In fact, serving superiors
was the premier objective. This is true not only of the general staff offices
but also other departments. What decides the fate of the departments is not
the public but superiors who have power. This is absolutely true. When
your superior notices and commends you, you will be successful one way
or another. Otherwise, when you receive blame and give negative impres-
sions, you are nearly doomed. We are supposed to be servants of the public,
but we have actually become the masters of the public.[107]

"Unhealthy Tendencies" in the Party and Society

Zouhoumen became rampant in the initial reconstruction stage of the
Cultural Revolution. In the early 1960s, when *zouhoumen* first emerged
as an informal, illicit way of obtaining consumer goods in short supply,
it was utilized mainly by people with discretion over certain products
for purposes of getting something tangible. By the end of the Cultural
Revolution, however, it had become a routine procedure to get not only
material things such as consumer goods but also other less tangible benefits. One notable practice was the seeking of competitive career opportunities for young people who had borne the brunt of the dislocations
caused by the Cultural Revolution. This practice had become so widespread and involved so many people that the CCP later called it an
"unhealthy tendency" that was endangering the party's legitimacy. In
1972 alone, the CCP Central Committee issued at least three major
directives on the problem of *zouhoumen*.[108] Mao, frail and feeble and in
the last years of his life, was said to have personally issued orders several times to inhibit the practice of *zouhoumen*.[109] In 1974, during the
"Criticizing Lin Biao and Confucius" campaign, a CCP Central
Committee directive was issued in response to "increasing criticism
raised in many units against their top officials who had tried *zouhoumen*
to get their children into the military or college."[110] The directive, based
on Mao's instructions (influenced by the radical leaders in the CCP),
acknowledged that "this issue will implicate several million people,"
and that "there are good people who came in through the back door and
bad people in through the front door."[111] It required that the political
campaign not be side-tracked by anti-*zouhoumen* sentiment. Apparently,

the concerns of the Maoist leaders over official deviance were over-shadowed by more political considerations. These directives and instructions had limited, if any, effects on curbing *zouhoumen*.

BACKDOOR MILITARY RECRUITING

Initially, using the "back door" to obtain scarce opportunity was evidenced in the frenzy to join the army that took place even before the reconstruction stage of the Cultural Revolution. With "politics in command," the stature of the military was elevated to an unprecedented height in the 1960s, after Mao first advocated that "all people should learn from the PLA" in 1964. Mao wore the green PLA uniform when he first appeared on August 18, 1966, to meet the Red Guards. A few weeks later, when he again met with Red Guard representatives, Tian'anmen Square was a sea of green, filled with students in clothing imitative of the green PLA uniform. PLA officers became top leaders in almost all public institutions when regular civilian leadership ceased to function. The military was perceived as the most politically correct segment of Chinese society, and offered the best career opportunities for young people at the time. In the winter of 1967, after two years without annual recruitment, the PLA began recruiting in both urban and rural areas, stirring up a frenzy to join the military. It was so hard to even get a chance for physical exams that every recruiting station was surrounded daily by hundreds of youths dreaming of becoming PLA soldiers. Opportunities to do so became extremely scarce, and the people most likely to get in were those with powerful *guanxi* and able to use the "back door." The most often utilized, and perhaps most effective, type of connection was an "old comrade" or an "old colleague"—typical reliable *guanxi*—of one's parents. It is not surprising that those who had the best chance to be recruited were the children of high-ranking PLA officers. One survey found that of 418 military personnel in the Chengdu Garrison whose parents were high-ranking military officers, 358 (86 percent) entered the PLA during the 1967–79 period when competition to get into the military was at the highest point in PRC history.[112] During this period, a *tiaozi* (a hand-written note) from someone who had a *guanxi* in charge became a popular method of getting things done. The real competition was not over who was most qualified, but

whose father had the best connections. The pervasiveness of this informal and illicit (because of its unfair and off-rule nature) method of getting enlisted was so pervasive that the popular term *houmen bing* (backdoor soldiers)—was coined to describe PLA servicemen who got in
through the back door. Once in the military, the *houmen bing* often had
better chances than others to receive promotions or assignments to better positions in non-combat units.[113]

After 1968, when the policy of sending educated youths to the countryside for "re-education by poor and lower-middle peasants" began
once again to be implemented, getting into the military became an even
more frantically sought-after option—to avoid going to the countryside
or, once there, to get out. This fever lasted until 1977, when getting into
college became a better career opportunity for youths. By then, "backdoor recruiting" had become one of the most widely resented Chinese
social issues. Authorities received a large volume of complaint letters
during the 1967–77 decade. The CCP Central Committee issued several
decrees attempting to stop the practice, calling it a manifestation of
"bourgeois rights." In 1977 alone, Hua Guofeng, then chairman of the
CCP, commented eight times in answer to letters opposing backdoor
military recruiting, warning that "backdoor recruiting seriously jeopardized the prestige of our army and internal unity."[114] The same year,
the Central Military Commission, the highest commanding body of the
PLA, issued an order to "inhibit the current unhealthy tendency of
backdoor recruiting," and the military recruitment for that entire year
was halted. Despite the order, the PLA recruited more than twenty
thousand beyond its original quota in that year. Among the thousands
of extra-plan recruits, 20 percent were found to be unqualified and later
discharged. The decade-long frenzy of joining the army ended on a
rather tragic note: more than 20 youngsters committed suicide after failing to be recruited that year.[115]

Ironically, with other career options open, with more restrictive criteria for military promotion, and with servicemen from rural areas no
longer being discharged to urban areas, the fever lost steam by the end
of the 1970s. Furthermore, since the early 1980s, there has been a
reversed pattern: people tried to avoid being recruited. Military recruitment plans often go unfulfilled. In some areas, the authorities even

applied fines to push the draft. In 1985, for example, 42 percent of draft-age youths were fined in a county in Zhejiang province; even so, in the end the draft was still four people short of the targeted 55 recruits.[116]

Even more ironic, the attraction of more lucrative career opportunities amid the market reforms since the mid-1980s has led more and more servicemen to resort to the back door to be discharged and assigned to better civilian jobs. This has become another area that is prone to illicit dealings.

COLLEGE ADMISSIONS THROUGH THE BACK DOOR

While a military career was gradually losing its appeal to young people, another opportunity opened up with the re-opening of colleges in the early 1970s. The old system of competitive college entrance examinations had been discarded, largely for its alleged bias against "workers and poor and lower-middle peasants." In its place, a purportedly new system of "self application, public nomination, leaders' approval, and school screening" was put into place when colleges resumed operation in 1971, after some five years of virtual shutdown. The new system, intended to favor the previously underprivileged, allocated quotas to different urban, military, and rural units. Its affirmative action aspects of redressing previous unfairness notwithstanding, the new system created fierce competition—not for better exam scores, but for opportunities to be nominated by local officials. In particular, the new system gave incentives and advantages to the officials who in effect controlled the nomination process and to youths who had personal connections with them. In the new system's first year , 60 percent of the students admitted by universities in Beijing had had only a junior high school education and 20 percent had never graduated from primary school.[117] In May 1972, the CCP Central Committee issued a circular warning against possible attempts by local officials to have their children or acquaintances admitted to college through the back door.[118] Still, the practice only got more widespread. In 1974, *People's Daily* published an "application to withdraw from college" from a student who entered through the back door.[119] At the urging of the central government, that year many colleges carried out a mini-campaign targeting backdoor entrance to college. For the first time, the government called *zouhoumen* an "unhealthy tendency," indicating its prevalence.[120] Although there are no existing figures to show how many college students with work experience were admitted between 1972–76 through personal connections and without a fair and open nomination process, there were many such cases according to recollections published in recent years by "sent-down youths" (*zhishi qingnian*).[121] In one, a former "sent-down youth" describes the situation in the commune in which he was located: "College admission was almost totally controlled by the commune and brigade officials. In some places, they had lined their own children up for years to come. One nomination list (in 1975) lined up people to the year 1987."[122]

The extent of this practice was revealed when the CCP Central Committee issued a stern circular titled "Resolutely Prohibiting Through-the-Backdoor College Admissions" on May 1, 1972. According to this document, in some places officials committed serious abuses of power by getting their children unfairly admitted.[123] The issue of backdoor college admissions was politicized and raised by the radicals in the CCP leadership in early 1974; radicals aimed at veteran officials who had regained power after the initial disgrace in the early Cultural Revolution period.[124] Mao himself came out to divert attention and eventually quelled the criticism, which would have implicated a large number of the children of rehabilitated officials.[125] The CCP leadership feared that pursuit of the issue could turn out to be very damaging to the already fragile legitimacy of the post–Cultural Revolution party/state.

By 1976, college admission had become available only to the well-connected. Even before the annual admission drive began, people had already begun giving gifts, hosting dinner parties, and calling on their *guanxi* to prepare for another round of the admission process, which did not require any test scores. *Zouhoumen* in college admissions further heightened the utility of informal and illicit methods in the Chinese society. Most youngsters believed that a good father was better than a good high-school education, for a father with power and connections could get them into college, while education could not. With Deng Xiaoping's personal intervention, the Ministry of Education decided to resume the entrance examinations later that year. Some 11.6 million people took part in the resumed entrance examinations of winter 1977 and summer 1978.[126] Since then, competition through exams has diminished the rationale and opportunities for *zouhoumen* in college admissions.

RETURNING TO THE CITY

College was but one path of escape for millions of urban youths who were in the countryside to receive "re-education by peasants." Only a very small number of these "sent-down youths"[127] would have the chance to go to college. Aside from joining the military, the two most convenient ways to return to the city were to find employment in an urban enterprises (*zhaogong*), or to be "sent back" to the city for medical reasons (*bingdui*). Such opportunities were scarce, and people needed a competitive edge—*houmen*—in order to make it "back." Two features stand out from the many cases: the pervasive use of the backdoor channel and cheating. A widely known open petition letter, signed by over a thousand educated youths in Yun'nan province, characterized the situation this way:

> All of us being sent-down youths, why on earth are our fates so different?
> Children of parents who are in powerful positions are long gone, smiling
> over their good fortune; those who have personal connections quietly
> slipped away, without stirring up any trouble; those who have money
> bought their way out, gone without a trace. Those who are left behind
> are people like us who are from ordinary family background, treated like
> a pile of dumped garbage![128]

Even before 1971, when "sent-down youths" were first allowed to be hired by urban state enterprises and began leaving the countryside, one sure way to get out was to come up with medical reasons that would deem one "unsuitable for rural conditions." Cheating was very common.[129] After 1971, there remained a limited quota on the number of former urban youths sent to the countryside who were allowed to be hired by urban employers. Out of some 18 million urban "sent-down youths," only 1.6 million had been hired away from the countryside by May 1973, many of whom had resorted to *zouhoumen*.[130] The pervasive problem of using *zouhoumen* to return to the city prompted the CCP Central Committee to issue a decree to stop the practice.[131]

Continuous Revolution and Continued Involution

The cadre ranks experienced the most traumatic events in the second decade of Communist rule. Maoist attempts to reverse the trend toward bureaucratization not only failed to produce committed and disciplined cadres, but ended up generating more unintended consequences. While all the mobilizations waged during this period had as one of their objectives attempted to root out corruption and other misconduct among cadre ranks, they nonetheless created additional organizational problems, characterized by growing informal institutions and intensifying informal behavior among cadres. The Great Leap Forward gave rise to the *informalization* of formal institutions (as reflected in dissimulation and formalism). Ensuing political mobilizations such as the Four Cleanup Campaign and the Cultural Revolution, many of which had had eliminating official deviance as one of their major goals, nurtured *informal* institutions and modes of operation (such as the second economy, *zouhoumen*, and *guanxi*) that were the antithesis of formal, regular institutions and norms. The attempted "continuous revolution" resulted in a continued involution of the party organization, which, in turn, encouraged rather than eliminated official deviance.

In this same period, organizational constraints on individual cadres were also the weakest in CCP history, due to the total breakdown of institutionalized rules and regulations. Monitoring mechanisms ceased functioning. Informal relations prevailed, superseding formal and regularized relations in many instances. The restoration of pre–Cultural Revolution institutions did not reduce informal behavioral and relational patterns. It actually intensified them. In writing about the impact of Maoism on Chinese industrial organization, Andrew Walder offers this observation:

> By the death of Mao, therefore, there were these two additional ironic aspects to the Maoist legacy in industry. The subculture of managerial behavior characteristic of over-centralized administrative systems intensified and spread down to the shop level in Chinese factories, creating new kinds of bureaucracy, inflexibility, and waste. And the quasi-legal underside of backdoor deals and petty corruption characteristic of Soviet-style systems—and decried by Maoists as symptomatic of revisionism—

grew to new proportions in China as a direct result of administrative changes made during the Cultural Revolution.[132]

This profile of the industrial sector could be readily used to depict the very staff—party/state cadres—working in various sectors and units.

The proliferation of informal strategies and personal connections was not unique to the Chinese. Striking similarities can be found in former Communist countries when they underwent a neotraditional phase. While things often had to be done through *guanxi* and *houmen* in China, they were done by *pile cunoștiințe și relații* (pull acquaintances and connections) in Romania or by *blat* in the Soviet Union. Similarly, the Soviet *tolkachi* (purchasing expediters) and the Chinese *caigouyuan* were the ones who established the *blat* or *guanxi* networks for enterprises, and they played an important role in filling the gap left by the state plan. In these societies, it was imperative "to make connections" (Romanian, *fac relații*; Chinese, *gao guanxi*) or to "find an acquaintance" (Romanian, *cuncurcareții*; Chinese, *zhao shuren*). In China, when asked to help by one's personal connections, an official would say: "Let me think of some ways to fix it" (*rang wo xiangxiang banfa*); their Romanian counterparts would say, "we shall find a solution" (*găsim noi o solutie*), indicating a willingness to explore the possibility of using *guanxi* and anticipating a reciprocal favor in the future.[133] Both informalization of formal institutions and informal strategies are typical of a post-revolutionary organization undergoing an involutionary process.

In the early years of the Communist regime, officials who engaged in corruption were regarded as either capitalist-class residual elements somehow infiltrated into the party or as revolutionaries who had been contaminated by bad influence from outside the party. In the 1960s, however, this view changed. To the Maoists, corruption was no longer a phenomenon merely associated with the exploiting class. Corruption was now regarded as a symptom of the degeneration of cadre ranks inside the party. The problem came from within, it was reckoned, and affected the legitimacy of the regime. Still, such understanding of cadre corruption was different from that of the post-Mao period. Corruption (*fuhua*) was understood as a result of cadres being tempted and degenerated by power.[134]

The Cultural Revolution was but one of a series of attempts made by the Maoist leadership to reestablish the old revolutionary coherence of the party and its cadres. The Socialist Education Campaign ("Four Cleanups") was launched to regain control over local cadres by the party leadership. But now Mao's determination to stop the trend toward bureaucratization had reached its peak. The party responded to the organizational problem with radical measures that "demanded that bureaucracies be destroyed and replaced by some non-bureaucratic forms of organization."[135] It represented a most critical position regarding bureaucratization held not only by Marx, Trotsky, and Mao (as expressed by reference to the alternate organizational form of the Paris Commune), but also by some Western libertarians, who desire self-governance and full democratic participation. To legitimize the continuing engagement in "political combat" necessitated by the threat-dependent character of a revolutionary party, class struggle in the post-revolutionary periods was written into the party constitution in 1969.[136] Not only were revolutionary values and ideology reinforced, but the recruitment of cadres was reversed back to a pattern of reliance on political activists among workers, peasants, and solders.

The reemergence of party/state organizations and officialdom in the wake of the radical phase of the Cultural Revolution has been used as evidence that Maoists were in fact only opposed to "bureaucratization of content" or Weberian legal-rational authority, but were a "fervent champion of bureaucratization in the first, or the structural sense."[137] According to this revisionist view, the restoration of the bureaucratic institutions, which became so large and resented by the public, happened precisely because Mao intended it. Such an argument ignores the fact that Mao constantly opposed *both* formal and substantive bureaucratization. Many of the methods the CCP adopted, such as *xiafang*, *pingbi*, *jingjian* (trimming and simplifying [the administration]), and *zhengdun* (rectification), were meant to downsize the bureaucracy, reform the bureaucratic structure, and change bureaucratic behavior. The post–Cultural Revolution re-expansion only points out the limits and failures of the most radical remedy.

The Cultural Revolution and the events that preceded it indicate that there were constant and continuing friction and mutual distrust between the party leadership and its cadre corps. As much as the Cultural Revolution brought serious damage to the ruling party, it was neither the beginning nor the end, but part of an ongoing, exacerbated degeneration of the party/state. Many consequences of the Cultural Revolution were unintended, one of the most significant being a profound resurgence and elaboration of pre-revolutionary modes of operation, such as personal networks and patron-clientelism—precisely what the Cultural Revolution campaigns had targeted.[138]

CHAPTER FIVE

The Post-Mao Reforms and the Transformation of Cadres

The reforms that began in 1978 marked a turning point in modern Chinese history. The CCP leadership under Deng Xiaoping realized that the imperative of modernization called for a new type of officialdom whose orientation must not be totally based on revolutionary qualities. The party renounced some of its mobilization modes such as "class struggle," "struggle between socialist and revisionist lines," and "politics in command." Strenuous efforts were made to rationalize the party and state apparatus with more and more procedural-based and merit-based institutions. Routinization and bureaucratization were no longer disdained and avoided, they became welcomed and sought after. But to what extent have these reforms fundamentally changed the way Chinese cadres behave? Has organizational involution continued, or has it been averted? Has the organizational ethos been transformed from that of a neotraditional cadre corps to that of a rational-legal bureaucracy? This chapter addresses these questions by examining the organizational development of the CCP in the reform era, with a focus on persistence and change in the cadres' ethos and mode of operation.

Rebuilding the Party Organization

At the start of reforms, the party organization had survived the volatile years of Maoist rule but had been lastingly damaged. The CCP's legitimacy as the "core leadership over all matters" and its ability to maintain a disciplined cadre corps were seriously impaired. Widespread cadre privileges, usurpation of power, the cultivation and use of personal connections in and out of the party, and factionalism were plaguing the ranks. From the outset of the reforms, the party leadership made the rebuilding of a disciplined, effective organization a top priority. The CCP clearly recognized the danger of popular dissatisfaction and even a direct political challenge to its rule. In a speech to high-ranking officials in the wake of the suppression of the Democracy Wall Movement in late 1979, Deng Xiaoping made the point that "cadre privilege is one reason why we are estranged from the masses. . . . The problem originated at the top, and officials below followed suit. It has also degraded the behavioral modes of the society."[1] Significantly, Deng, like Mao in the 1960s, blamed the problems within the party as a source of the ills outside the party. This approach was a significant departure from earlier (and more "official") views on corruption and indiscipline during the later years of Maoist period, which took an opposite stand—that it was "societal unhealthy tendencies" that influenced the party and caused deviant behavior in the party. But Deng's solutions to party disciplinary problems were quite different from Mao's. Whereas Mao called on people outside to fire at those inside the party, Deng, vigilant against any social opposition, called for "normalization of life inside the party," aimed at reestablishing institutions and norms damaged during the mobilizations of the 1960s.

The dominant drive in organization building in the post-Mao era was to institutionalize and rationalize the party/state structure. By the time Deng Xiaoping ascended to power in 1978 (for the third time in his long career), the party organization faced serious morale and disciplinary problems among its seventeen million cadres, 17 percent of whom had been investigated for possible wrongdoing, political or otherwise. Between 1977 and 1982, the "cadre rehabilitation" drive reevaluated some three million cadres, reinstating 470,000 as CCP members.[2] The disciplinary problems and lack of commitment among party/state officials, which were termed the "problems of party work-style" (*dangfeng wenti*), were believed by the post-Mao leadership to be rooted in the lack of both effective institutions and the rule of law. The initial measures the CCP took to address the issue included establishing or reinstalling formal institutions vital to the effort to prevent further disintegration of the party, resuming the effective deployment of cadres to achieve political and economic objectives, and promulgating rules and regulations aimed at curbing official misconduct.

CONTROL AND SUPERVISORY INSTITUTIONS

Among the institutions that were paramount in organizational rebuilding and were either established or reinstated were the control and supervisory apparatus, bodies such as the party disciplinary commissions, fiscal auditing agencies, supervisory agencies, public procurate, and anti-corruption bureaus. The case of the internal party supervision mechanism—the party disciplinary commission—illustrates how the CCP leadership responded to cadre misconduct and indiscipline over time. The Chinese Communists emulated Bolsheviks in this respect. Lenin's original method of supervisory committee formation was through election by the members of the party congress. The supervisory committees had autonomous power apart from the party committees at the same level, and operated independently of the regular party apparatus.[3] In Chinese Communist terms, this is a typical institutional arrangement of vertical leadership (*tiao tiao*). Under Stalin, the mechanism deteriorated from a body with rank equal to the party committee to a department working under the direction of the latter. The status of the supervisory commission was first written into the party charter in 1927, in the early days of the CCP, with the stipulation that it be a separate body elected by the party congress and not responsible to the party committee at its own level.[4] After the Zunyi Meeting of 1935, at which Mao's role as the party and army leader was confirmed, the CCP ceased to hold regular party congresses. Thus no supervisory commissions were in operation until 1945. The CCP Seventh Party Congress in April 1945 changed the relationship between the party committee and the party supervisory commission from one of equal stature to a leading-led relationship, with the former electing and guiding (*zhidao*) the latter.[5] The party charter revised at the Eighth Party Congress in 1956 reaffirmed the subordinate role of the supervisory commission, which would submit itself to the "direction" (*lingdao*) (not even *zhidao* or guiding) of the party committee at the same level.[6] Therefore, by 1949, the CCP had failed to establish the kind of effective internal party control mechanism that Lenin had envisioned. This supposedly self-supervising body could not function independently, due to its subordination to the party committee.[7] In 1959, during the Great Leap Forward, another control mechanism—the state supervisory apparatus (*guojia jiancha jiguan*)—was declared unnecessary and abolished altogether.[8] Until the 1979 restoration of the internal supervisory system, the party disciplinary inspection commissions (PDICs, which had been dismantled during the Cultural Revolution),[9] there was virtually no regular control mechanism to supervise the behavior of party/state cadres.

Even though these control and supervisory bodies have been functioning since their reinstallation in the late 1970s, their lack of autonomy in investigating and disciplining corruption and other official deviance cases has seriously limited their role. Often their work is subject to intervention from local party and government leaders. Such vulnerability to intervention has, according to one provincial party disciplinary commission head, hindered anti-corruption efforts, resulting in "local corruption protectionism."[10]

FROM CADRES TO CIVIL SERVANTS?

One of the earliest and most important policy initiatives of the administrative and organizational reforms was to abolish lifelong cadre tenure, and introduce methods of appointment by selection or election that were based on ability rather than political loyalty. "Scientific management of cadres" was introduced in the early 1980s, even though it was not quite clear to many what it was to entail. Seminars and conferences were held to discuss administrative reforms, particularly those involving the cadre corps. The very concept of "cadre" (*ganbu*) was debated and challenged by scholars in academic journals and at conferences.[11] Slowly and sometimes regressively, the old nomenclatura system of cadre management was weakened, though not totally eradicated, giving way to a significantly decentralized, diverse, and merit-based system by the late 1980s.[12]

As the reforms progressed, the focus shifted from changing the management of leadership echelons to more fundamentally transforming the existing system of the administrative corps, the cadre system. To replace an overstaffed, incapable cadre corps with a lean, well-educated, yet politically loyal civil service became the main objective of the administrative reforms. At the Thirteenth Party Congress in 1987, it was decided that the dubiously defined corps of *guojia ganbu* (state cadres) should be "rationally disaggregated" (*heli fenjie*). It also announced that the existing uniform cadre managing system should be replaced with a scientific classification system.[13] A new emphasis was to be put on *cai* (ability) instead of *de* (virtue) as the primary criterion of cadre recruitment and promotion. Indeed, the four criteria established by the party to select a new generation of cadres—youth, education, revolutionary loyalty, and professionalization—have underlined the reform of officialdom throughout the first fifteen years of the reforms.[14] Recruiting better-educated and younger people into the official corps was a great success, particularly in urban state agencies and certain other units.

The increasing recruitment of better-educated people into officialdom is not mere rhetoric. Although national figures are not available, it is safe to assume that an increasing number of officials have received at least a high-school education. The promulgation of the "Temporary Provisions for State Civil Servants" in 1993, which mandates recruitment of certain levels of government staff through an open and competitive process, has brought about a gradual transformation of cadres into state civil servants (*guojia gongwuyuan*). New recruits must pass civil service exams in order to enter all central ministries and provincial bureaus in 28 provinces.[15] Some locally designed examinations have also been instituted for the recruitment of local officials. The highest-ranking officials recruited through open examinations so far have been deputy bureau chiefs at the provincial level.[16] However, the entry-through-exam, or open competition, process still remains limited. Since 1994, only 1,722 people have been hired by central ministries through civil service examinations.[17]

Exit from a job is supposed to be made "scientific" also. Under the cadre system, unless an official had been found politically liable or guilty of certain administrative and criminal offenses, he or she could keep the job for life. Beginning in 1994, many local governments have implemented regular annual evaluations of civil servants. The new system allows government agencies to fire personnel whom they find incompetent and also allows personnel to resign from government positions. This, too, has been a slow process. Nationwide, only 5,500 people were fired and 16,000 resigned from government jobs between 1994 and 1997.[18] In Beijing, only 98 out of the 90,000 civil servants were removed from their positions in the annual evaluations since 1994 due to incompetence or malfeasance.[19] In Shenzhen, 34 civil servants resigned from government agencies in 1997, mainly to seek other career opportunities.[20]

The planned transformation of public officials into civil servants does not address the issue of political loyalty. The distinction between government and party functionaries is reflected in the fact that only government administrative employees, not staffers and officials of the party organizations, are classified as civil servants. But such a distinction is blurred because government and party organization employees are both paid by the state, and because government officials often serve in party posts as well. More important, there is not yet any evidence that these changes are making a significant impact on the behavior of public agents, who, as later discussion will show, still cling to many neotraditional modes of operation.

EXPANSION OF THE STATE

Without transforming the functions of the state, the administrative reforms (some of which were called "political reforms" by the government), although aimed at downsizing over-staffed governmental agencies and enhancing efficiency, have resulted only in more party/state expansion. This expansion can be seen from the notable increase of permanent offices. Between 1984 and 1991 (during which time there were two major administrative restructurings), not only did the number of government offices not decrease, it actually grew. During this period, some 50,000 new "section-level" offices were created or upgraded, with 9,000 additions every year.[21] Since the reforms began in 1978, the size of the government continues to grow at a faster pace than other sectors (see Table 5.1).

Marc Blecher and Vivienne Shue found in their study of Shulu county, for example, that since the mid-1980s, a series of government offices were set up at the township level, including an economic management station, a legal service office, a family planning work station, a finance office, a land management office, and an urban construction leading group.[22] Though names may vary in different places, township

TABLE 5.1

Chinese Government Personnel, 1978–1996

Year	Number of people (thousands)	Increase (%)	% of state sector	Employment increase, non-state sector (%)	Total labor force increase (%)
1978	4,670	—	6.2%	—	1.90%
1979	5,050	8.14%	6.6	2.10%	2.17
1980	5,270	4.36	6.6	3.25	3.26
1981	5,560	5.50	6.6	3.19	3.22
1982	6,110	9.89	7.0	3.51	3.60
1983	6,460	5.73	7.4	2.48	2.52
1984	7,430	15.00	8.6	3.63	3.80
1985	7,990	7.54	8.9	3.41	3.48
1986	8,730	9.26	9.4	2.72	2.83
1987	9,250	5.96	9.6	2.87	2.93
1988	9,710	4.97	9.7	2.90	2.94
1989	10,220	5.25	10.1	1.77	1.83
1990	10,790	5.58	10.4	2.49	2.55
1991	11,360	5.28	10.7	15.80	2.86
1992	11,480	10.50	10.5	1.21	1.84
1993	10,300	−10.28	9.4	1.50	1.32
1994	10,330	0.29	9.5	1.28	2.04
1995	10,420	0.87	9.5	1.21	1.20
1996	10,930	4.89	10.0	1.27	1.33

SOURCE: Based on data from *Chinese Statistical Yearbook, Chinese Labor Statistical Yearbook,* 1978–1998. See also Hu Jiayong, "Woguo zhengfu guimo."

governments are also outfitted with many branch offices (*paichu jigou*) of county administration, the so-called "seven bureaus and eight stations" (*qisuo bazhan*) (consisting of the industry and commerce administration, national tax bureau, local tax bureau, public security bureau, land management bureau, environmental protection agency, post office, grain station, cotton station, power management station, industrial management station, road management, farm machinery station, veterinarian station, and water management station). These offices, plus local supply and retail cooperatives, credit cooperatives, and the courts, make township government structure more complex and differentiated than it was in the Maoist period. According to a recent survey of township government in Henan province, a typical township government has more than 30 functional agencies in addition to the party committee, people's congress, and administration.[23]

We may call this "vertical expansion," namely, an increase in the number of functional or regulatory agencies at the local level as a result of the newly developed regulatory functions of the state. It is "vertical" because such units are created to correspond to similar departments, bureaus, or offices at higher levels. At the township level, these units are usually under the auspices of quasi-independent functional agencies of the county, and are themselves quasi-independent—that is, not totally responsible to nor responsive to township authorities.

In addition, another expansion also took place—a staffing increase in each government office. Over the past two decades, the number of state-paid officials actually increased in many places. The minister of labor and personnel revealed that in 1985 the number of cadres on the government payroll increased 40.1 percent from 1980, a net increase of some 7.6 million. Among them, cadres in administrative agencies increased 49.3 percent, cadres in non-enterprise units increased 39.3 percent and public enterprise managers increased 36.9 percent.[24] Since then, the growth rate of the administrative staff has slowed. Still, each year before 1990, some one million new recruits were hired by government agencies and non-production units.[25] In 1951, the ratio of officials to other employees in public units was roughly 1:600. It had increased to 1:36 in 1991.[26] Nationwide, despite downsizing efforts in the late 1990s, the bureaucracy has continued to grow, with a total of 36 million public personnel on the government payroll, including some 11 million currently working in administrative agencies.[27] When the reforms began in 1978, the personnel on the government payroll represented 2.1 percent of the total population. By the end of 1996, they accounted for 3.0 percent. While the population increased 27.1 percent during the same period, the number of people on the government payroll grew by 82.3 percent.[28]

In the rural areas, post-Mao reforms and reorganization had some enduring impacts, perhaps more so than in urban areas, due to the more drastic changes in rural administrative systems. The irony is that, while state control over the rural economy was relaxed as a result of decollectivization and farm product market reform, the number of officials on the state payroll actually increased in many places. The number of cadres from the township level and up increased at a faster pace than when the commune system was still in place, in some areas by as much as 50 percent in the first decade of reform.[29] In the 1960s, for example, there was an average of a dozen "non-production" (*tuochan*) officials in each commune (now township) in one rural county near Beijing. By 1992, over 160 such cadres worked in the township agencies, many of them wearing uniforms as law enforcement or regulatory agents.[30] According to a Ministry of Civil Affairs report, in Kaiyuan county, Liaoning province, a similar level of government had fewer than ten cadres during the pre-collectivization period (1949–56).[31] Today, there are over four million officials with the rank of *ke* or higher. At the township level, in particular, administrative downsizing has never worked. The current 800,000 townships maintain a sizable body of officials. During the commune era (1958–83), usually there were some twenty cadres working under the principle of unified leadership at the commune level. By 1991, by contrast, the number of cadres in the township government proper (excluding functional agencies) had increased to 70 or so.[32] By a recent account, among the 3,202 townships in Hebei province, most township governments have between 50 and 80 (in some cases up to 180) staffers, despite an average population in each township of less than 20,000.[33] Out of all these "officials," only 850 have actual positions. The rest are all "shadow heads" who do not function administratively but nonetheless are given ranks and titles.[34] Administrative reform has actually resulted in further expansion of an already bloated state administrative staff corps.

Changing and Persisting Organizational Ethos

In addition to the multiple efforts to institutionalize formal party/state structures, many rules and norms aimed at changing existing neotraditional organizational ethos and preventing official deviance were formulated, reformulated, and reiterated from the very beginning of reform. In just the first two years of reform, the party/state issued the following rules in an attempt to establish organizational norms and code of conduct for post-Mao officialdom:

> Central PDIC decree prohibiting accepting gifts from foreigners (June 8, 1979, the first decree after the Central PDIC was re-established);
>
> Central PDIC decree warning against attempts to intervene in college graduate assignments (July 3, 1979);
>
> Central PDIC directive prohibiting the unhealthy tendency to cadre dining and wining at the costs of peasants (August 31, 1979);
>
> Central Committee directive to guarantee the implementation of the Penal Code and Criminal Procedure Law in the spirit of the rule of law (September 9, 1979);
>
> Central Committee and State Council announcement of rules on the treatment (privileges) of high-ranking officials (November 13, 1979);
>
> Central PDIC decree prohibiting cadres from "trial use" of products by public enterprises (November 22, 1979);
>
> Central Committee and State Council directive opposing squandering of public funds (January 24, 1980);
>
> Central Committee "Norms on Inner-Party Political Life" (February 23, 1980);
>
> PDIC decree prohibiting unhealthy tendencies in hosting officials (June 25, 1980);
>
> Central Committee directive banning gifts in foreigner-related activities (August 16, 1980).[35]

Also during the same period, the official *People's Daily* published editorials reflecting the views of the Communist party, with headlines such as "Resolutely Oppose Privilege Seeking";[36] "On Violation of Law and Rules by Children of High-Ranking Officials";[37] "High-Ranking Officials Must Be Restrained";[38] "Strict Adherence to Fiscal Discipline Is an Important Guarantee of Four Modernizations";[39] and "Strengthen the Party's Inspection on Economic Discipline."[40] These rules and norms, issued with high frequency, indicate both the existence of widespread problems and the concerns of the regime about decline in cadre integrity and the effectiveness of organizational norms. Ironically, however, though these rules and norms were directed at informal modes of operation, they were made and promulgated via decrees and announcements. As such, they were often regarded by cadres, learning from past experience, as ad hoc, less stringent, and replaceable.

Later organizational development in the early 1980s proved how difficult it was to change informal modes among cadres, the "unhealthy tendencies in the party" or "problems of party work style" as they were called at the time, which were increasingly at odds with organizational goals and norms. In this section, I examine the informal constructs that existed and grew within the party/state. Ultimately, what are officially regarded as "problems of party workstyle" are problems of organizational ethos and cadres' modes of operations. Although a great deal of administrative restructuring and streamlining has been implemented during the two decades of reform, concurrently informal modes and relations have developed and become increasingly significant. Many new institutions have been set up, new laws and regulations promulgated, and new policies implemented. Despite these changes, however, the reform regime has not been able to develop an organizational ethos of modern bureaucracy, or a rational-legal orientation. Instead, organizational involution seems to have continued as the operational mode of members of the party/state organization, and the relations developed remain neotraditional. Agents of the state and members of society often opt for informal, personal ways of coping with formal institutions.[41]

DEPLOYABLE AGENTS NO MORE

After the Cultural Revolution, a great number of cadres, including "emancipated" veteran officials, had to be reassigned to new positions, after some years of idleness or manual labor in the "May Seventh cadre schools." By early 1980, 2.9 million people had been rehabilitated, many of whom had been officials before the Cultural Revolution.[42] One of the first problems the Communist party confronted was that cadres refused their new assignments. The ability to deploy cadres was once a distinctive characteristic of Communist parties. In a detailed study of the post-revolutionary elite in China, Hong Yung Lee has noted one remarkable aspect of the Cultural Revolution: that, despite ten years of chaos and purges, the majority of the elite managed to regain political power.[43] Many rehabilitated officials became prominent reformers, carrying out sweeping reforms. Yet the rehabilitation of cadres at various levels also had other effects, including cadre resistance to authority. This is particularly salient in light of the new requirements for officialdom: to be younger and better educated. Newly promoted officials have a competitive advantage over senior cadres. A *People's Daily* commentary reveals such a threat to the party's well-being:

> The phenomenon of disobeying assignments by the organization and insisting on personal preferences still exists in many areas. These comrades often make excuses of "unsuitable areas," "unfit posts," "health problems," or this difficulty, or that problem, in order to bargain with the organization. Some cadres want their job assignments to be satisfactory not only to themselves but also to their families. Otherwise, they would allow their family members to make unreasonable demands on the organization. If they can achieve their own objectives, they would refuse to report to work for one or more years. Such tendencies have obstructed the discipline of our organization and weakened the combat capacity of the party.[44]

In one province, 361 cadres of various ranks refused to accept job reassignments after the Cultural Revolution, and stayed idle for up to three years.[45]

In the early years of the post–Cultural Revolution period, it was common for family members to intervene in the job-assignment decision-making process. Such intervention occurred most frequently among mid-level cadres whose positions were above division chief (*chuzhang*). In many instances, if family members, usually spouses, found new job assignments undesirable, they would go to the party organization department and use their old connections to exert pressure on those who had been their subordinates. A case cited by the COD is typical: during a unit leadership reshuffle in 1980, a senior official expressed his intention to retire from his formal position to become an adviser. The party committee of his unit accepted his request and was ready to select his successor. However, once the news of his planned retirement reached his home, his decision was not welcomed by his family. He changed his mind and declared to the party committee that his earlier decision "did not count." In order to exert pressure on the party committee, he mobilized his wife to visit each member of the com-mittee. The party committee was put under heavy pressure and became divided due to the wife's lobbying. It was only after intervention from higher authorities that an agreement was reached to hold to the original retirement decision.[46]

In rural areas, the CCP leadership found that party members did not live up to their roles and responsibilities. A 1986 investigation found that, among 1,949 party members in Beijing's suburban counties, 36 per-cent were up to the "model role of the vanguard"; 52 percent "basically act as party members but failed to stand out as good models for the masses"; 11 percent were "problematic," "not active," or "failed to ful-fill the role of Party members"; and some 2 percent were "violators of discipline and the law."[47] The number of party members had also declined. In 1989, for example, in a county with a population of 120,000, only 4,200 people applied to join the CCP, among whom only 19 were peasants.[48] A majority of CCP members in rural areas had joined before the 1970s.[49] Perhaps not since before the land reforms of the late 1940s and early 1950s had the power of the party/state grown so weak, and control of grassroots organizations and cadres so difficult. In some vil-lages, there was no new party recruitment throughout the entire decade after 1979. In one village, there were only three veteran party members, who were all over sixty. A joke went around that village: "(among) three party members, (there are) two factions, and one (non-party member) common folk runs the show."[50] Some party members even turned to religious faiths such as Christianity.

ADMINISTRATIVE RANK-SEEKING

The organizational ethos of the Maoist era had not been entirely trans-formed in the market reform era. Nor were many informal practices abandoned. One phenomenon long associated with Communist regimes is the status-oriented political and administrative hierarchy.[51] In a bureaucracy under capitalism, rent-seeking is common, whereas in a Leninist cadre organization under state socialism rank-seeking prevails. Under market transition, however, a neotraditional officialdom, as a result of organizational involution, participates both in rank-seeking and rent-seeking.

In post-1949 China, the hierarchical status of personnel and units is tied to certain treatment (*daiyu*) and privileges cadres and units receive. The higher the rank, the better the treatment, and the more perquisites and privileges. Thus, ranking in the official hierarchy is crucial. It determines not only political privileges, such as who can read what internal circular from which level of party/state organs, but also a variety of material perquisites. For example, when a CCP Central Committee circular was issued, it would designate a readership that consisted of certain ranks; readership often reflected the degree of secrecy. The higher the rank of the unit, the more information on policy and internal party leadership decisions was made available. A cadre's rank was determined, in part, by the rank of the work unit with which he/she was affiliated. A manager of a "bureau-rank" enterprise could not have a rank higher than a bureau chief. The saying, "Among cadres, rank is all that matters," captures this feature. Indeed, according to the COD, rank became, for public units, the basis of budget appropriations, material allocations, administrative structure, personnel assignments, and document readership. For individual cadres, it was the basis for a host of perquisites: access to classified internal circulars (which enhanced information about leadership's intentions, thus reducing uncertainty), attendance at meetings at certain levels, the use of office supplies, transportation privileges, business travel per diems, reception protocols, salaries, housing, medical care, scarce consumer goods, reunion of separated couples,[52] acquisition of urban residency for spouses,[53] funeral arrangements, widow's pension standards, and even postmortem access to columbariums.[54] The consequence was a pervasive "apparatus-*ization*" (*jiguan hua*) of non-production units and "administrat-*ization*" (*xingzheng hua*) of industrial enterprises, as well as fierce competition for higher rank in the official hierarchy among individual cadres. For example, in the so-called "mass organizations" such as labor unions, women's groups, and religious groups, there were department-ranked (*chuji*) Muslim imams, section-ranked (*keji*) Buddhist monks, and the like.[55]

Status-consciousness and rank-seeking were not unique to the post-Mao period. CCP leadership, and Mao in particular, expressed concern for the growing bureaucratization of the party when the Soviet model became less attractive in the late 1950s. Mao had attempted to eliminate rank-consciousness by reinstalling the free supply system; Liu Shaoqi made the point before the Four Cleanup Campaign that "if the rank system which we inherited from feudal regimes begins to blossom, we must eradicate it";[56] and the political campaigns launched thereafter, including the Cultural Revolution, all had mitigating or eliminating rank-seeking as one of their objectives. Yet official rank became even more important than before the reforms and was actively sought after by both units and by individual cadres. In a remote rural county of Hunan province, there were some 180 administrative units or enterprises with "deputy-section-chief rank" (*fu keji*) or above in the early 1990s, an increase of 68 percent from before the 1985–86 administrative restructuring.[57] As the ranks of cadres are comparable to those of their units, among the 4,659 government officials in the same county, 1,458 held deputy-section-chief rank or higher; 41 percent of them did not have genuine positions.[58] When asked to compare rank-seeking in the Maoist and post-Mao periods, a retired mid-level official made this observation in an interview: "Certainly we understood the significance of cadre rank. There were cases where officials squabbled over which rank they should receive when a few administrative ranks were accessed.[59] But people did not feel it was as imperative nor were they as desperate as today. Now cadres go out of their way to get a higher rank."[60]

More recently, the administrative ranking practice was formally replaced with transitional measures—after 1996, non-production units (*shiye danwei*) were no longer given designated administrative ranks, but heads of a given unit would still be assigned an administrative rank.[61] The effects of such reforms have been slow and limited. Administrative rank remains significant today. Years after the industrial reforms began, most large and mid-sized state-owned enterprises still maintain certain designated administrative ranks.

FORMALISM AND DISSIMULATION

Some of the informal cadre strategies that existed well before the reforms have shown remarkable continuity and tenacity. One of them is dissimulation, as manifested in such practices as false reporting, deceiving superiors, staging shows (*zou guochang*), and covering up misconduct and errors. This kind of behavior is a far cry from the tradition of "seeking truth from facts" that the CCP has always boasted of. In 1986, Hu Yaobang, then the party secretary general, commenting on the attempts to cover up wrongdoing by a local party committee, noted the extent of the problem: "Now cheating, deception, and cover-ups between party organizations at one level and another, and between party members, have become terribly pervasive in some localities."[62]

An internal publication of the COD admitted that, despite years of tireless efforts to cure this chronic disease, dissimulation had only become more common among party members, especially high-ranking officials. It said that those who cheated "not only got away unpunished, they actually benefited from such acts, getting promoted."[63] At a 1996 National People's Congress meeting several deputies raised the issue of the prevalence of *fukuafeng* (the tendency to exaggerate and show off) among public officials, more than three decades after the problem was first noted in the wake of the Great Leap Forward. Similar concerns were voiced again at a Chinese People's Political Consultative Committee meeting in March 1998.[64]

Unreliable statistics were once a common phenomenon among state socialist systems.[65] Two decades into the reform, "surgery of numbers" still remains a widespread practice among local Chinese leaders. Officials often have several ways of presenting statistics—when demanding levies and taxes, they give one set of figures; when the media ask for data, another set is provided.[66] Some of these tailored statistics have as much as a 20 percent differential from the actual figures.[67] Many officials maintain three different sets of statistics—one for reporting good news, one for complaining about bad conditions, and another for a reality check. One provincial leader offered *four* different versions of the province's 1993 grain output on different occasions: the first time, a "drastic reduction" was reported; the second time and third time, it was said to have "decreased somewhat"; the fourth time, the grain output was said to have "maintained the level of the previous year." Later, in a local television report, the province had achieved a record-high grain yield.[68] Some township and village enterprises have reported millions of *yuan* in profits while in reality taking losses worth hundreds of thousands of *yuan*.[69]

In a Communist organization and a command economic system, all levels of organizational hierarchies are responsible and responsive only to their superiors. When self-disciplinary and monitoring mechanisms weaken, dissimulation becomes an intrinsic part of the operational mode of officials. As long as the numbers satisfy those at a higher level, no heads roll and chances for promotion increase. Thus, as a scholar of state socialism has pointed out, "socialism compels compliance to its rituals of affirmation" and "becomes an elaborate game of mutual pretense which everyone sees through but everyone is compelled to play."[70] The Janus-faced behavior is a product of a regime that requires utmost loyalty and demonstration of performance.

Why do such practices persist after all the administrative and economic reforms? The answer lies in the typical reaction of a neotraditional organization continuing on an involutionary path: new rules and procedures are often turned into something familiar that bears the imprint of yesteryear. Statistical falsification, for example, arises partly from the pressure from above to reach certain standards, particularly in economic growth. To be sure, this is not a mere copy of the socialist competition of the Maoist era, but a result of administrative reforms intended to link officials' performance with socio-economic development. Officials are no longer monitored or tested by a superior's subjective standards. They are now subject to what is known as "advanced managerial experience" learned from the West, procedures called "responsibility and standard fulfillment evaluation." Officials must fulfill certain set standards for their work, often with written contracts, in order to be evaluated and promoted. With such "modern," meritocratic procedures, it is believed, cadre evaluation and promotion are to be based on objective standards, rather than the personal discretion of their supervisors. In rural areas, a most common and important criterion by which cadres are evaluated is level of local economic development. Some concrete criteria are applied: whether all villages have electricity; whether paved roads are connected to villages; whether all children of school age are able to attend schools—the list can go on and on. If, for example, a township is able to generate a certain amount of GDP from local township and village enterprises (often the standard is 100 million *yuan* annually), local leaders are likely to be promoted to higher rank or rewarded with bonuses.[71] Local officials thus face mounting pressures as well as economic incentives to show evidence of achievements under their leadership, even if it means they must inflate statistics, not unlike during the Great Leap Forward. Little wonder that the relationship between officials and statistics is often described as "officials produce numbers and numbers make officials" (*ganbu chu shuzi, shuzi chu ganbu*).

Another source of pressure prompting local officials to attempt to cheat higher authorities recalls the Great Leap Forward even more closely: *pingbi,* or competition for glory and praise. Though the labeling has changed—"townships with strong economy," "star enterprises," or "well-to-do counties" have replaced "red flags" and "satellites"—the basic thrust remains remarkably similar. In one rural township in Sichuan province, local officials over-reported per capita income in 1997 by more than 100 percent in order to be designated as a "township with a strong economy." The way it was done was especially appalling: grain output was over-reported by 43 percent; the navel orange output (a local specialty) was also exaggerated. But, the rest of the purported income came from the sale of blood from farmers, who had been told by the township director that blood extraction would benefit their health.[72]

The pursuit of lofty goals is not done simply for the personal advancement of officials. The ethos of an organization rooted in a goal culture provides motives for units to compete for formal recognition and glory. In 1998, under pressure from Beijing, governments at various levels had to cancel more than 22,000 celebratory or ceremonial activities while many others were held.[73] The fact that dissimulation and formalism continue to be common practices among Chinese officials indicates that the regime still retains significant elements of the mobilization mode and that the pre-reform command economy ethos is still influential. More significant, it shows that at least some aspects of the organizational involution process have thus far survived the reforms.

THE RESHAPING OF A RESIDUAL MOBILIZATION MODE

The thriving ethos of dissimulation among officials reflects a much broader phenomenon in Chinese political life. Soon after Deng Xiaoping ascended to the leadership of the CCP, much of the Maoist mobilization mode—"storming methods of large-scale mass campaigns of class warfare"—was renounced, and much attention was given to institutionalization and rationalization of the party's organization and operations. However, despite the reforms of the last two decades, changes in the way the Chinese officialdom handles policy tasks and routine functions have been limited. Many practices that existed under the mobilization regime either remain or are being reshaped in some distinct form as an unintended result of institutionalization efforts. The political campaign method has not been completely given up. As I pointed out earlier, even though large-scale campaigns are rare in the 1990s, campaign-style mobilizations, including anti-corruption drives, are still used from time to time. Occasionally, full-fledged nationwide campaigns are launched to achieve certain important objectives. One example is the sweeping campaign against the semi-religious Falungong movement in the summer of 1999. In this campaign, Maoist tactics such as confession, unit-organized meetings that denounced deviant practices, group detention for self-cleansing, and an intensive propaganda campaign were used.[74]

One inherited practice is the use of *wenjian* (documents or circulars); they contain *policies* that can be easily bent to suit the needs of the people who are to execute them rather than statutory regulations, containing rules and procedures. The party and its leaders, rather than functional agencies, still come out from time to time to steer the economy in the name of macro-control.[75] Some Chinese commentators have dubbed an economy operated in such a way as an "economy ruled by decrees."[76] With the greater decentralization of power, policy circulars come from all levels of administration. This practice has led to a situation in which more and more decrees, directives, and ordinances are issued, but they become less and less effective. Meanwhile, the jurisdiction of the decrees becomes narrower and more limited, facilitating regionalism and engendering conflicting rules.[77] Bureaucratic decrees and circulars are partly responsible for the growth in informal levies and charges imposed on rural farmers, rural industries, urban enterprises, and other businesses. Local government departments impose and collect these levies through issuing decrees. In one small county in Hubei province, for instance, an inspection in July 1997 discovered 35 decrees that illicitly imposed charges on farmers that were issued by various county agencies.[78]

The preoccupation with "core tasks" (*zhongxin gongzuo*) remains another important feature of the functioning of the Chinese party/state. Although such a preoccupation is no longer the same as in the Maoist period, when "core tasks" were nothing short of survival-dependent "combat tasks,"[79] it still plays a significant part in government's routine functions, often couched in "modern" terms. While "core tasks" may still override and disrupt routines,[80] they have nonetheless become more ritualized and routinized. The most salient example of this development in recent years has been *dabiao* (reaching certain standards or planned targets) and *shengji* (upgrading) activities. *Dabiao* as a method of competition is a residue from the pre-reform mobilization regime. What makes such a phenomenon significant today is its blend of revolutionary rituals with market utility. To meet quotas and achieve set targets or to upgrade to better classifications and an enhanced stature now becomes an important criterion for measuring bureaucratic competence, tied not only to personnel advancement but also to a government agency's performance. In some places, monetary awards or bonuses were given to reward local officials who can get more funds or investment. Hence these policies reward, both politically and monetarily, officials whose behavior tends to be flamboyant and arbitrary.

Officials are not the only ones who feel the impact of such a reshaped mobilization mode. Efforts to reach certain standards or to upgrade existing facilities often require local funding or, in the case of failure to meet certain standards, monetary penalties of residents—both of which resulting in peasant payments in rural areas. This has been a major source of the growing burden on the peasants in recent years.[81] According to one official report, there have been as many as forty different kinds of *dabiao* activities in the countryside that required peasants to pay for them in one way or another, among them militia training camp *dabiao*; rural school building *dabiao*; senior home construction *dabiao*; elimination of rodents *dabiao*; newspaper subscription *dabiao*; and insurance purchase *dabiao*.[82] In 1991 alone, there were 619 various kinds of *dabiao*, competition, and inspection activities in Shandong province.[83] It is no coincidence that in an "Urgent Decree on Reducing the Burden of Peasants" (March 19, 1993), the CCP Central Committee and the State Council ordered all *dabiao* activities that required payments by peasants to be eliminated.[84] The effectiveness of this decree remains questionable, however, as long as such practices as "core tasks" and competition to achieve certain set goals persist. In many places, *dabiao* activities continue as usual. In at least one case, *dabiao* has led to the suicide of a farmer who could not afford to pay his local "reaching rural electrification standard fund."[85] Indeed, at the meeting of the National People's Congress in March 1996, Vice Premier Zhu Rongji blamed *dabiao* activities as one of the sources of the "bouncing back" (*fantan*) of financial burdens onto peasants.[86]

The residual influence of the mobilization regime also hinders attempts to rationalize the government structure. A given government organ often takes up newly designated "core tasks," creating new ad hoc offices to handle them. These offices often become semi-permanent (because of the ineffectiveness of the policy or an inability to implement it), necessitating new staff to operate them. A 1990 investigation of township governments in Pinggu, a suburban county near Beijing, found that half of the staff's workload was devoted to "core tasks." In this township, the newly implemented annual evaluation of cadres had three criteria: functional work (43 percent), core tasks (43 percent), and *dangwei zhangwo* (that is, discretionary assessment by the party committee) (14 percent).[87] In the same township, eight different such ad hoc offices were set up in just one year starting in 1989. Examples of these offices included the "leadership group for raising educational funds," the "leadership group for village council elections," the "command post for anti-riots and improving public security," and, most astonishingly, the "office for supplies to the Asian Games."[88]

When a nagging problem persists and policies to address it are rendered ineffective, core tasks often become part of the routine, and the office created to deal with them becomes semi-permanent. One example is the "office in charge of reducing peasant burdens" set up from the State Council on down in the government. The peasant burden problem (i.e., the imposition by local government agencies of numerous levies, fees, and other charges on peasants) has been on the core task list ever since the late 1980s, but it remains unsolved. Reducing peasant burdens thus has become a routine effort. Ironically, one of the main reasons for such exactions by local government is a bloated government and its costs. To address the problem, which apparently requires urgent and resolute attention, an office especially devoted to solving the problem may itself be a source of increasing financial costs of government.

Guanxi *in the Market Reform*

Unlike the phenomenon of special material treatment and official privileges, the importance of which has gradually diminished (though not disappeared) with market reform and with the increasing availability of consumer products, *guanxi*, as a mode of informal social exchange and relationship, has not only survived the changes but become more refined and complicated than it was in the late Maoist era.[89] A senior CCP official, who had once been in charge of the COD, contended in the mid-1980s that bureaucratism, usurpation of office for private interests, *guanxi* networks, and money fetishism were the four major "epidemics" currently plaguing the party. They were "the main aspects among all the unhealthy tendencies from which many other deviances derive."[90] In many respects, the widespread practice of building and using *guanxi* and the flourishing *guanxi* networks were a continuation and refinement of the earlier *zouhoumen* practice. If *zouhoumen* was practiced as a response to shortages (consumer goods or otherwise) and needed *guanxi*, the practice in the 1980s was more proactive, open, and widely exercised. By the early 1980s, *guanxi* was more openly used not only by individuals but also by units. In July 1980, the Central PDIC issued a directive to denounce the "unhealthy tendency of *guanxihu*," which it assailed as a disguised bribery relationship.[91] The commission required party organizations at all levels to curb the practice of *guanxihu* (connected persons or units). Any individuals or units who were found guilty of this practice would be subject to punishment.[92] As an indication of the failure of this and other similar efforts, the vocabulary used to describe this informal strategy evolved and the term *guanxihu* was replaced by *guanxiwang* (web of connections) and *guanxixue* (the art of *guanxi*) by the late 1980s.[93]

A county party organization department head has distinguished four categories of *guanxi* relationships: (1) links of kinship with relatives; (2) links with ex-colleagues, old friends, or acquaintances; (3) factional ties left over from the Cultural Revolution; (4) those involving exchange of money or materials. These relationships often intertwine and knit into a web in which many cadres are connected.[94] Although personal networks had never been really eliminated, even during the most radical revolutionary transformation periods, the use of connections in the post-Mao reform era is more complicated, entrenched, and powerful than before. Connections have become a necessary method of circumventing formal rules, and they are used not only by individuals for personal purposes but also by *danwei* of all kinds to protect their vested interests. In an interview, a factory manager in a small rural township discussed the pervasiveness of *guanxi*: "Factories of our size and type often have to stash aside a certain amount of money each year to spend on developing connections. Without good *guanxi*, you won't get too far. Sometimes we need materials which are hard to obtain, sometimes we need to be shielded from more inspections and fines for not meeting standards. These all require some work in cultivating good relations with various parties."[95]

Connections are instrumental in securing bank loans, securing construction contracts, and avoiding quality inspections, among other things. The significance of *guanxi* can be seen in an employment advertisement by a company in Zhengzhou. The company, which was hiring 200 public relations and sales persons, openly indicated its preference for the children or other relatives of high-ranking officials, high-level managers, and officials serving on boards of directors of other firms.[96] A similar phenomenon is found in foreign joint ventures. *Guanxi* ties can help managers of joint ventures circumvent bureaucratic control.[97] Using connections can also get someone off the hook when he or she faces criminal or disciplinary charges in an anti-corruption drive. Such was not the case in previous anti-corruption campaigns, especially those of the 1950s. During the Three Anti Campaign of 1952, no one would come out to twist arms for those who were found guilty of corruption. There was no "back-stage boss" to support them. Today, however, corrupt officials not only often have a vast web of *guanxi* they can count on to achieve their goals, they have patrons who may offer protection even after they are found guilty.[98] According to employees of party and state control agencies, in almost every case investigated or prosecuted, people have tried to intercede for those under investigation or after they were disciplined.[99] One survey (N = 664) found that when peasants were asked whether in actual life personal indebtedness (*renqing*) stood higher than the laws of the state, 20.6 percent of respondents answered positively, while 34.7 percent chose to answer "not quite so."[100]

The large part played by connections in an economy being transformed from central planning to markets distorts the process of transition. Some Chinese scholars have characterized China's economy as one of "thirty percent power, thirty percent *guanxi*, forty percent market."[101] Some commentators simply call China a "*guanxi* economy"[102] or a "*renqing* economy."[103]

Officials may blame their environment and external factors for their engaging in *guanxi* and related informal relations and deviant behavior. A high-ranking official in a mid-sized city spoke candidly with the author about *zouhoumen*:

> You ask me if I cultivate and use *guanxi*. To tell you frankly, I don't have
> to go through the back door: the front door is enough. I have been working
> in this city for over twenty years. I know one or two important people. It is
> easy for me to have things done, openly, not furtively. Here is an example:
> my grandson took the high school entrance exams some years ago. Somehow Old Wang of the education bureau got to know about it and offered to
> help him pass. I was criticized by some people for abusing power, but I was
> not aware of the thing at all. . . . You can't blame leaders for *laguanxi* and
> *zouhoumen*. It is often the fault of those who work under the leaders.[104]

What he did not say, however, is the reason behind such actions by his subordinates. In a system where loyalty to and good relationships with one's superiors are vitally important, actions by Old Wangs should be seen as rational and shrewd because of possible future payoffs. Another informant, the director of a provincial bureau of commerce, commented on how leading officials get involved in personal networks: "Nowadays some people seem to always pick on leading cadres. Once any flaw is found, they'll allege that it is an unhealthy tendency. I am outraged by this. Why only picking on leading cadres? They are also human beings who have relatives and friends. They must consider *qing-mian* (affection), too."[105]

He did not shy away from his own experience:

> I don't care what others say. I have set some limits. The higher you go, the more people come to you for help. *Laguanxi* and *zouhoumen* cannot be avoided. One can make some connections and go through the back door, but one needs to be aware of limits. The back door should not be open too wide and allow too many connections. Absolutely no illegal stuff. Many people gave me gifts. I accepted all of them, never refusing them, so long as they didn't give me hundreds of thousands in cash. I accept gifts for the sake of revolutionary work, not for my own private gain.[106]

While some officials blame outside influences that force them to conform in *guanxi* relationships, others bluntly acknowledge the rationality of such actions. The director of a county bureau of material supplies admitted in an interview:

> When you are in this position, you can't avoid *laguanxi* even if you want to. They would knock on your door and befriend you. To tell you the truth, I did not do anything illicit before. Now I have seen it all. Those whose ranks are higher than mine dare do this kind of stuff, so what do I have to fear? Everybody believes people working in this profession do it all the time. Well, since we already have such a reputation, why not actually do it? Besides, I know I won't be in this position forever. Don't you know the saying that *you quan buyong guoqi zuofei* (power will be invalid if you don't use it now)? When it becomes invalid, you won't be able to use it even if you want to.
>
> A saying goes: "give others some convenience, you yourself will find convenience later." I want to make more *guanxi* while I am in power so that when I leave, I will not be too badly off. Look at those retired cadres. Nobody wants to deal with them any more. They cannot even get things done. It's a real lesson.[107]

At a provincial people's congress meeting, the party secretary of Hebei province declared, with much frustration, that because so many people had tried to twist the arms of high-ranking officials by using various forms of *guanxi*, he had decided to refuse to receive visitors who would come to his office or home to seek official positions (*yao guan*).

He blasted those who try to find patrons (*zhao kaoshan*), who seek, buy, and sell official positions, who collude to form factions and cliques, and who weave networks of nepotistic relations.[108]

To be sure, not all *guanxi* or informal relationships are corrupt or illicit. Informal relationships and informal means do, however, encourage deviance. What we find here is that, in organizational terms, informal relationships and means have gained ground as dominant relational and action modes vis-à-vis formal relationships and means. Intertwined with other forms of informal and primary relations, such as familial and lineage ties—and the latter have already undergone a rapid renaissance, despite years of social transformation in urban and rural China—they further weaken formal organizational ties that the party has always intended to maintain.

Urban Cadres and Nepotism

One of the most noticeable yet rarely discussed phenomena in government agencies and public units of the reform era is nepotism. Scholarly analyses of post-1949 Chinese socio-organizational relations involving Communist cadres have pointed to the predominance of patron-clientelism.[109] While patron-clientelism has existed throughout the post-1949 period, cadre nepotism, related to yet distinct from patron-clientelism, is a relatively new form of informal relations in the post-Mao period. A publicized circular of the CCP Central Committee indicates the scope of the problem of *renren weiqin* (recognizing people by familial or lineage ties) in the party's organizational work:

> There are some problems in our current work of cadre selection and appointment. The most salient ones include: (1) some leading cadres select people according to their own personal standards or to their own needs and interests, or out of feudal kinship values, violating the principles of the party and discipline of the organization; (2) some use "*zouhoumen*" through various means to select or promote their own relatives and friends; (3) some abuse their official power to engage in illicit exchanges; (4) some scramble hard to increase the rank and treatment (*daiyu*) of their units or sectors (*xitong*), disregarding policies and regulations; (5) some comrades who are in charge of organizational work misperform their duties.[110]

Working alongside people with whom one shares direct family or lineage ties is not an isolated phenomenon. It occurs in central ministries as well as in local government agencies, in the military as well as in educational institutions. A popular satire epitomizes this serious state of affairs: "pop-son bureaus, hubby-wife sections, son pours water for dad, grandson drives for granny, spouses share the same desk in an office." In the Ministry of Justice, 20 percent of the 500 staff members were related in one way or another.[111] Before the implementation of a set of "temporary rules on avoidance among state officials" in 1996, 10 percent of the nation's 20,000 customs agents had relatives working in the same agencies.[112] Among the 850 personnel of the State Bureau of Statistics, 15 percent (or 130 people) had kin working in the same bureau.[113] In the county government agencies in a remote northern province, 68 of 148 cadres who held important positions had relatives working in the same agencies. In this case, 27 children worked with their parents, four couples shared the same offices, and 23 people had their cousins, uncles, brothers-in-law, or godchildren (*gan erzi* or *gan nü'er*) working in the same county agencies.[114] In the same province, a prefecture court had 84 cadres, seventeen of whom were related in one way or another. One deputy chief judge and his wife and daughter all worked under one roof.[115] According to another investigation of seven urban work units, out of 1,499 cadres and workers there were 87 couples (including 2 county-level and 14 section-level officials, and 71 general staff), 141 people with parent-children ties, 26 siblings, 85 who were related through in-law relations; 25 families had three or more people working together in the same unit. Seventy-nine people had relatives working in one of the seven units. Thus, over half (56.7 percent) of the officials and staff workers were related to one or more staff members in some way.[116]

An investigation revealed that this "inbreeding" was not limited to state agencies. Of the fourteen state-owned enterprises investigated, the number of employees grew from 2,154 in 1983 to 4,006 in 1989, an 86 percent increase. During this six-year span, the number of employees who were related directly or indirectly increased 4.75 times, from 251 to 1,422. The percentage of related employees increased from 11.6 percent to 33 percent of the total number of employees. Among these lineage relations, nuclear familial relatives (spouses, parent-children, and siblings) constituted 92 percent.[117] The most startling case was of a local supply and marketing cooperative in Hunan province, where 302 or 75 percent of its 409 employees had some kind of familial relationship.[118] In the nation's supposedly most modern institution—the military—the problem also exists. At one PLA air force division headquarters, eight out of twelve division-rank officers were either related among themselves or to someone else in the same division.[119]

It was estimated that, nationwide, 10 percent of the cadres in local administrative agencies had relatives working in the same agency, and in some places as many as 30 percent by the late 1980s.[120] Cadre inbreeding in the workplace often imperils formal organization and relationships. In some cases, people with kinship ties managed to thwart corruption investigations at the unit level.[121]

Similar phenomena can be found in other former Communist regimes. It has been observed that in the Soviet Union, one of the most pervasive forms of corruption was "protectionism," or cronyism and patronage,[122] which, according to Soviet sociologists, was no less venal than bribery and should have been codified as a criminal offense.[123] The problem was purported to be a "legal deficiency," because, as Soviet Georgian investigator Menadze commented, "legal science did not pay, in fact, enough attention directly to protectionism. It is remarkable that there is no such term in the law dictionary."[124] In a letter to the editor in one of the major newspapers, a Hungarian farmer wrote: "In our village things developed so that the head administrator is the president's daughter, and the second administrator is the daughter of the president's wife's cousin. The Control Committee's president is the husband of a cousin of the president's wife. The warehouse head is the cousin of the president, a brigade leader is also a relative of the president's wife."[125]

Such a case, extreme as it may be, was not an isolated incident. "Miskoism," as one Hungarian author called nepotism in Hungary, "evolved into a kind of network of favoritism and reciprocity,"[126] and it had become embedded in the Communist regime. Note the parallels between Miskoism and a Chinese case from the 1980s:

> Li Huihai, the director of the county foreign trade bureau who joined
> the party in 1952, has skillfully knitted a network of personal relations,
> which penetrated more than 80 units and involved over 200 people. Many

of his relatives were put into positions in various county agencies. His brother was the deputy director of the agriculture bureau. A relative of his was promoted from driver to vice president of a county plant. Another relative was supposedly unfit for legal work. Yet he, with the help of Li, left the procurate for the bureau of justice, and joined the party six months later.[127]

Although there had been some local efforts to remedy the problem,[128] a national regulation on avoidance of conflict-of-interest and promotion of job rotation came into effect only in June 1996. The regulation—in the form of "temporary measures" (*zhanxing banfa*)—promulgated by the Ministry of Personnel stated that "civil servants" must not work in the same unit as, or deal with matters concerning, anyone related by family ties.[129] Even so, only a few localities have begun limited implementation of the regulation since the announcement. In Beijing, for example, a pilot program was launched in 1996 in the taxation bureaus, where 431 pairs of personnel were found to have close family ties (i.e., spouses, parents, or siblings); they were to be transferred to other units.[130] Even in the central ministries, however, only 77 percent of the personnel to whom the avoidance clause should apply have transferred or been transferred to other departments.[131]

Throughout the history of the CCP there was no lack of anti-localism and anti-sectarianism efforts on the part of the party. Since it came to power, the CCP has not let up its vigilance against potential forging of primary relations at the cost of organizational ties among its cadres. There were de facto practices of posting non-natives to key positions after 1949, when many wartime army cadres were put into administrative posts throughout the country. In provinces in southern China, northerners who had marched south with the People's Liberation Army during the final battles with the KMT occupied most of the high- and middle-level positions. The resulting friction between local officials and those from the north, who often did not speak the local dialects, became a prominent issue during the Hundred Flowers Campaign in 1956–57. Severe attacks on "localism"[132] was one of the themes in the anti-bureaucratism thrust of the late 1950s.[133] Yet, despite all this, the phenomenon of cadre inbreeding and workplace nepotism "has made rules and procedures nothing but shallow skeletons, obstructing scientific management. It also has further complicated personal relations. Routine and normal operation of intra-party and intra-unit affairs could not be carried out smoothly."[134] Such an "internal elaboration" of relations represents a typical pattern of involution: while more rational, impersonal forms—organizational streamlining, recruitment of capable people, and the like—were imposed during several rounds of administrative reforms, personal networks have also grown. They have evolved into a dense web of finely spun rights and responsibilities. The consequence is often foot-dragging, inability to make decisions, and ineffectiveness in censuring misconduct of members.

Several factors explain why, under the Communist party/state, nepotism has grown within the heart of its own organizations despite its wariness. First, under the state socialist system, new personnel usually expected their work units to take care of the job assignment of their spouses as well. In a unique arrangement, discharged servicemen and their families were to be assigned jobs by a work unit or its affiliates. This policy, made in the mid-1980s in the wake of a major military reduction of one million servicemen, was aimed at absorbing a large number of former military officers, many of whom were from rural areas.[135]

Second, in the late 1970s, a practice called *dingti* (replacement of retired workers or cadres with their children or other relatives) became common. In addition, the policy of "internal recruitment" (*neizhao*)— hiring of children of employees from inside industrial and commercial units or administrative agencies—was also endorsed.[136] Thus, the old ties of personal networks were carried over from one generation to another, further complicating human relations within work units.

Third, a number of policy developments intended to remedy the disruptive consequences of the Cultural Revolution turned out to be partially responsible for this phenomenon. These include reuniting separated couples who had worked in different places,[137] returning urban youths who had been sent down to the countryside,[138] restoring many agencies dismantled during the chaotic years, and reinstating discharged officials. As a 1982 State Council directive indicates, the most widespread "unhealthy tendency" during the early post-Mao years showed up in government agencies, where abuse of power to help place relatives or other connections was commonplace.[139]

But even more fundamental to the problem is the CCP's understanding of the impact of the revolution on old primary relations. The Maoist discourse on human nature resembles Confucian discourse in the notion that, properly cultivated, humans can be *homo moralis*. The way that institution building in general and personnel management in particular have developed reflects such Confucian and Maoist beliefs. As one study points out, nepotism began to reemerge in China in the late 1950s. The party did not give it enough attention, however, believing that increasing Communist morality and consciousness would naturally lead people to subordinate their familial and kinship interests to those of the nation.[140] Perhaps it was not that the party failed to realize that revolutionary comradeship had not yet permanently replaced the old familial ties; rather, the Maoist belief in internal transformation, rather than external control, may have led to a frontal assault on residual elements in people's consciousness (e.g., the Socialist Education Campaign and the Cultural Revolution). Regulations and rules, such as the law of avoidance, which Chinese administrative scientists boast of as having originated in the traditional Chinese bureaucratic system,[141] were thus not regarded as vital measures to prevent or mitigate this trend.

One of the tenets of such a law was locality avoidance, that is, to avoid appointing officials who were from the same locality where they were posted. In such instances, traditional court-appointed officials were prevented from having daily contacts with relatives, who in China usually resided in the same locality. After the Communist revolution, this practice was abandoned along with other principles of avoidance, such as avoidance of relatives working in the same state agency. The hope, then, was that once the law of avoidance was reestablished as a rule in administrative reform, the problem of nepotism would be mitigated.[142]

Reemergence of Lineages and Rural Cadres

If in recent years nepotism in the form of "cadre inbreeding" has been mainly an urban phenomenon found in government agencies and state enterprises, in the countryside it has primarily reappeared in the revival of lineage and patriarchal clan organizations (which in some areas have even permeated local party organizations). Amidst the rural economic and social transformations after 1949, formal patriarchal clan and lineage organizations were eliminated. Clan organizations and activities, seen as pre-revolutionary traditional institutions, were suppressed by the government. But the most serious destruction of lineage ties and organizations took place during the Cultural Revolution, when many lineage genealogies and ancestor halls were destroyed or used for other political or social purposes.[143] Since the end of the Cultural Revolution, particularly during the early reform era, clans and lineage groups have revived in villages, particularly in the southern provinces, where kinship and clan ties traditionally were stronger than in northern China. Ancestor halls that were destroyed or used for other purposes during the Cultural Revolution and the clan organizations, which were abolished even earlier, during the collectivization of the 1950s, have been rebuilt in many places. Kinship and clan pedigrees were re-established and updated.

The reemergence of clan organizations and the unofficial authority of clan leaders is not a simple revival of pre-revolutionary customs, however. In many ways it is more neotraditional than traditional. The formal organization and authority of the party were not replaced by the informal clan organizations. They actually cross-penetrate, and sometimes reinforce, each other. For example, in Yueyang prefecture, Hunan province, one-third of the villages reorganized clan groups, and many clan chiefs became village or even township heads.[144] In Nanchang county, Jiangxi province, several hundred thousand kinsmen paid dues to join in the updating of clan or lineage pedigrees in 1988.[145] In Linhu county, Hunan province, out of 273 villages, 230 have established clan organizations such as "*qingming* committees"[146] and "kin committees," and 574 people were selected by kinsmen to become their clan or lineage heads. Among them, 38 percent were CCP members and/or officials.[147] The dependent relationships in the revived clans have been strengthened through the power of rituals, rules, and economic activities.

One of the most significant effects of this development is that the authority of the patriarchal clan and kinship organizations has changed the dynamic of the relationship between the party/state and peasants, as well as affecting the behavior of rural cadres. In Yueyang prefecture alone, from 1988 to 1990 there were over 600 armed brawls between rival clans, involving more than half of the villages in the prefecture.[148] The most violent case took place in February 1990 in Tiantai county, Zhejiang province: there, 5,000 people were involved in a 43-village, seven-township, eight-clan, two-way bloody armed battle.[149] Many such violent clan clashes were organized and instigated by party members and village officials, who were simultaneously village heads or township directors and clan chiefs.[150] In Wugang county, Zhejiang province, a "Li kinship committee" in one village stipulated that the jurisdiction of the village party branch was limited to managing only production activities; any civil and legal matters that involved the Li clan were to be taken care of by the kinship committee.[151] Some village officials served concurrently as clan chiefs and refused to follow state policies unless they advanced clan interests.[152] State power has been seriously challenged by the growing power of the clans, both overtly and indirectly. In many instances, clan organizations protected criminal suspects who were clan members and even beat up law enforcement personnel when they tried to detain suspects.[153] In these areas, clan ties have often been more important than state rules. A popular peasant saying goes, "It is better to rely on the clan than the government; it's better to go to the clan head than to the township head."

The reappearance of "strongmen" in rural China is powerful testimony to the neo-traditionalization of authority relations that characterizes the involutionary development of the regime. Regime organization is permeated by clan organizations. Not only do clan heads become village chiefs, but in some cases party secretaries or village chiefs take over as clan heads.[154] The patterns of relationships among rural party organizations permeated by clan and kinship groups are basically particularistic and dependent. When the head of township administration nominated village officials or promoted someone to state-paid positions, he tends to favor his own kinsmen or protect them when they got into trouble with state laws.[155] In one survey, over 80 percent of the people polled said cadres were working for the cadres' own interests or the interests of their clans. Only 21 percent said they believed cadres worked for the general interests of the villagers.[156]

It is no coincidence that while clan and kinship organizations rose to prominence, grassroots party authorities were weakened, in some places even paralyzed. An investigation of 2,400 party branch organizations in Hebei province conducted in 1986 found that, in capacity and activity, 35 percent of the organizations were considered "good" or "fair," 45 percent were "mediocre," and 20 percent were "paralyzed" or "semi-paralyzed."[157] A similar nationwide investigation of 47 counties conducted three years later showed almost identical results: among 504 villages investigated, only 30 percent were operating well, while 50 percent remained mediocre and 20 percent were either partially or totally paralyzed.[158] The same investigation found some areas in which "dysfunctional" village party branches constituted as many as half of the total grassroots organizations. The report estimated that there were 180,000 such "paralyzed" organizations in the rural areas, which had jurisdiction over a total population of some one hundred million people. A county party secretary admitted that rural party cells were rife with internal strife. At least one-third of these branches, partly or wholly paralyzed, are incapable of assuming an effective leading role.

By no means, however, were formal laws and regulations openly pushed aside and violated. More often than not, the challenge to state power was more subtle. The activities of clan organizations often expanded under the guise and protection of legitimate rules. In the 1989 election of township officials, for instance, different clan groups mobilized to elect their own candidates to posts in Tiantai county in Zhejiang province.[159] There were also instances where the requirements of the state (such as taxation, grain contract fulfillment, and population control) had to be met with the help of clan organizations, particularly their leaders. At the same time, the revival of clan organizations and lineage relations facilitated official deviance, including corruption among cadres. In one instance, a village party secretary was found to have embezzled 2,900 *yuan* from public funds, but the authorities did not lodge any disciplinary or legal action against him because he had kinsmen working in the township government.[160]

It appears that the state has reacted cautiously to the subtle challenges posed by the neo-traditionalization of rural society. A town in Hunan province had in its official record book some 290 village councils in 1985, established as a part of reforming local governance. However, in 1989, new statistics showed that there were over 500 village councils. It turned out that the additional 200 or so councils were set up mainly by lineage clans, despite those that already existed. In villages where there is but a single family surname and a single lineage, there is only one council, but in villages with more than one lineage, sometimes there are three or four councils, which all elect "village heads."[161] Village elections implemented since 1988 have done little to change the dominance of rural lineage groups in some southern provinces. A recent investigation found that many village council elections were influenced by clan leaders.[162]

The End of Involution?

With the passing of Mao and beginning of reform, the party/state entered a new historical stage. The objectives of the reform regime are clear: to transform the old economic system in order to achieve economic development and to maintain its political authority. Crucial to achieving such goals is an effective, disciplined official corps. The party organization and public administration that survived Mao's "continuous revolution" hardly met such criteria when reforms began in the late 1970s. Organization building took place, with the emphasis on institutionalization and enhancing the efficacy of formal rules and codes of conduct. Wary of the cadre corruption and widespread official deviance, the CCP leadership intended to avert the involution in the party organization by recasting its organizational ethos.

As a reforming regime, however, the party did not completely give up what it knew the best: mass mobilization, with core tasks overriding routines. The decade of the 1980s actually began with a major crackdown on economic crimes and ended with an anti-corruption campaign as result of the 1989 popular protests. How successful were the efforts to apply old tricks to curb corruption and other misconduct? Apparently successes have been quite limited. As we will discuss in Chapter 6, corruption has become more pervasive. A simple explanation of the failure to inhibit worsening corruption among officials would be that reforms and marketization also brought greater opportunities for illicit activities and strengthened the influence of the materialism innate in a market economy. However, the question still remains: why is a cohesive, strong organization, as the CCP was once billed, not able to resist such materialist temptations and maintain organizational discipline? The answer lies in the decline of the coherence and discipline of the regime organization, which explains why the misconduct of individual agents of the party/state has gotten so out of control.

The findings herein suggest that the organizational involution of the party has continued. To be sure, there has been a strong thrust to rationalize the government in order to enable it to lead a successful transition. The tendency for Chinese officialdom to continue many of its neotraditional practices persists, however. The capacity of the party organization to maintain committed and disciplined agents is still seriously impaired. It is unable to resist being penetrated by informal groups such as rural clans and the Falungong sect, whose organizational capacity, ironically, has overshadowed that of the CCP.[163] The gradual changes in the functions of the government in the economy and society have made substantial inroads in cadres' behavior. Nevertheless, however many changes there may have been, the post-Mao period has seen not only a continuing boom in informal relations and operational modes among cadres but also a new development—to wit, the *informalization* of formal institutions and rules. Informalization fills the gaps created by the inadequacies of formal institutions, as we have seen in the cases of *guanxi* networks, *zouguochang*, and the revival of lineage groups.

CHAPTER SIX

The Economic Transition and Cadre Corruption

Corruption in contemporary China is often seen as a function of changing political economy, particularly the transition from state socialism to a market economy. Such an assumption is not wrong. As the reforms unfolded and widened, more opportunities for public officials to seek private gain by abusing the office emerge. The organizational roots of the corruption problem, however, should be also taken into account. What has changed from the pre-reform period is that new opportunities for corruption (mainly in its economic forms) presented themselves to an officialdom inundated with informal relationships and accustomed to informal strategies. At the same time as the ability of the organization to maintain a committed and disciplined officialdom was diminishing, the temptations afforded by the emerging economic structure grew stronger.

Precisely because of these new opportunities, Communist cadres have not been as resistant to reforms as they were expected to be. They were quick to adapt to the changing game of the new politico-economic structure. Though rank no longer brought with it perquisites only a few could enjoy, public power provided chances for lucrative rents or transactional profits for rank-and-file officials. Corruption has changed its patterns, amounts involved, and locale. All the while, something remains little changed: the new transactional, market-based corruption still takes place in a neotraditional, rather than bureaucratic, organizational setting.

From the very beginning of the reforms, the problem of corruption was recognized as a serious challenge to the regime. In a 1982 "Resolution on Cracking Down on Serious Criminal Activities in the Economic Arena,"[1] the CCP Central Committee and the State Council openly admitted the severity of the corruption that had arisen since the beginning of the reforms:

> There are many ills existing in our economic and political life. What's especially unsettling is the fact that in the last two or three years, activities such as smuggling, embezzlement, bribery, profiteering, and theft of state properties have increased dramatically. In some places, the situation is quite grave. These criminal activities, seriously detrimental to the economy, are often conducted by a few people working in state agencies and other work units in collaboration with criminal elements in society. Sometimes they are done under the guise of serving the state and collectives. Some are even supported by leading officials. The problem is far more serious than in the 1952 Three Anti Campaign.[2]

Significantly, this is an official depiction of the situation in the early years of the reform. With the advent of more market-oriented economic reforms since then, official corruption has become more pervasive than ever before, both quantitatively (in terms of the amount of money involved and the number of cases investigated and prosecuted) and qualitatively (in terms of the types of corruption and the actors involved). Almost every reform policy was subject to distortion for personal or group benefit. This same situation had arisen in the earlier cases of price reform, housing reform, administrative reform, as well as more recent fiscal, regulatory, and enterprise reforms. When the policy of reforming local state-owned enterprise was first implemented on a trial basis in the early 1990s, for example, the officials of a county chemical plant in Hebei province took advantage of the new policy of employee share-holding by taking out low-interest loans from state-run banks and investing them as personal shares—a practice nicknamed "taking power shares" (*ru quanli gu*). Ordinarily, banks would not have lent to private investors without collateral. Among those who pocketed tidy profits in this fashion were both the factory director and the party secretary. An official in the county bureau of chemical industry even took a loan from his own plant to "invest" as private shares.[3] The county officials had been so corrupt in this case that Jiang Zemin, the party secretary general, was prompted to comment that "if this is indeed true, then we Communists are destroying ourselves."[4] The

Communist party is keenly aware that this case is not isolated —as are the Chinese people.

Changing Patterns of Corruption

As the old economic system is replaced by an emerging market economy, economic corruption has replaced non-economic corruption as the dominant form. This is not to say that official deviance rooted in the pre-reform mobilization regime no longer exists. On the contrary, what characterizes official deviance (including corruption) today is the persistence of certain old patterns and the emergence of certain new ones. In the last two decades, the underlining pattern of corruption has gradually changed from "whom one knows" (prebendalism based on *guanxi*), to "what one controls" (graft based on one's discretion over resources) and "how much one pays" (rent-seeking based on market logic). The locale where corruption is most likely to take place also has changed. Early on in the initial stage of the reforms, corruption tended to occur in state-owned industrial and commercial enterprises. Later, it moved to administrative units that controlled resources that either were experiencing shortage or were a monopoly. More recently, corruption has crept into regulatory and law enforcement agencies. The police, judges, prosecutors, tax agents, and business and market regulators have become more susceptible to corruption in the form of graft and rent-seeking.[5] The actors involved in official corruption have also changed. At first, corruption in the form of graft was most common among managers, supply and sales agents, and accountants in the state sector. Later, officials and staff of public units who had monopoly control over resources or services such as production materials (for example, officials in electricity, telephone, and railroad bureaus as well as banks) were the ones who tended to commit graft. Although corruption in China shares many common features with that in other countries (such as bribery, kickbacks, embezzlement, and peculation), it also has some unique patterns. In this chapter, I will highlight some of the most significant patterns including housing irregularities, public offices for sale, and various forms of administrative rent-seeking, all of which involve abuse of power by public officials. More significant, however, corruption in China is committed not just by individual officials and public employees, but also by government agencies and other public units. Arguably, the defining feature of official corruption in the reform period may be the widespread rent-seeking activities of public organizations.

HOUSING IRREGULARITIES

The construction industry and public housing authorities are hotbeds of corruption in many countries. This was also true of China, but with a twist. Among the host of "unhealthy tendencies" early in the post–Cultural Revolution period were housing irregularities—officials built private residences with public funds and materials, or abused their power in order to occupy better apartments allocated by the government. Such housing irregularities among officials are a typical prebendal form of corruption. In socialist China, theoretically at least, all urban land belongs to the state. Until the most recent housing reform in 1998, the state has been the main provider of housing, either through allocation by housing agencies or by individual work units. After some three decades of state socialism, there were few private residential properties in urban areas by the time the reforms commenced.[6] Most housing was provided by the state, and it remained scarce for a long time. For most working couples, getting a comfortable living space for themselves and for their children thus was the ultimate goal, and they sometimes resorted to illicit means.

Housing irregularities first appeared among privilege-seeking cadres maneuvering within the boundaries of legitimate treatment comparable to their status within bureaucratic ranks. Officials who had power or connections not only tried to obtain larger, better apartments, but they got them sooner. The regime tried to crack down on this practice because it caused widespread dissatisfaction among ordinary people who had waited years to get apartments. But the problem only got worse, evolving from a category of privilege to one of usurpation of administrative power. Officials even attempted to build houses for themselves at government expense.

In the decade of the 1980s, there were three "waves" of private housing construction at public expense, in 1980, 1985, and 1988. Each swept wider than before. In Jiangxi province, 2,246 local cadres above the *ke* rank engaged in building private homes between 1979 and 1983. Between 1986 and 1988, the number increased to 4,527, out of 11,055 state administrative staff of all kinds in the same province.[7] In a small town-turned-city, 295 officials engaged in building private housing; it amounted to 37 percent of all the housing built in the city. These private residences required some 300 tons of steel, an item that was strictly controlled and in constant shortage. In the end, the government treasury had a debit of 3 million *yuan* "borrowed" by these officials to build private housing.[8] In another county of Hebei province, 815 officials and others were involved in building private housing in the county seat from 1982 to 1989. Among them were 14 county-level officials, 164 bureau or section chiefs, and 380 staff.[9] In Hunan province, some 20,000 officials of various levels illegally built private residences in 1987–89 alone,[10] as did 428 of county rank or above and 1,799 *ke* rank cadres in Guizhou province.[11] Common housing irregularities included: (1) "mother-son construction"—building private homes when the *danwei* has other construction under way by bribing the contractor to raise the cost of the *danwei* "mother" building; (2) construction at public expense—openly abusing power by building private homes with public funds and occupying public land; (3) obtaining housing space exceeding the regulations for public housing assignments.[12] Controlling housing irregularities among party/state officials was one of the four main targets of an anti-corruption drive soon after the 1989 crackdown on mass demonstrations.[13]

With the onset of urban housing reforms in major cities beginning in the late 1980s, more and more housing became available for private citizens to purchase. Availability of housing has not, however, eliminated irregularities. According to the Central Party Disciplinary Inspection Commission, some 586,000 officials of *ke* (section) rank or higher were found to have violated disciplinary rules regarding housing during the period between 1993 and 1997.[14] During my interviews in 1994, housing irregularities were among the most frequently raised complaints about the "unhealthy tendencies" of the leaders of public units.

ADMINISTRATIVE RENT-SEEKING

With the emerging market economic system and the changing role of the Chinese state from that of redistributor of resources to regulator of the economy, there have been changes in the pattern of corruption and other deviances. While both economic and non-economic types of corruption still exist and prebendalism and graft remain significant forms, rent-seeking has become the predominant form of official corruption. In the early stages of the reforms, when state power still remained mainly redistributive, corruption generally took place in the form of what may be called "procreative" rent-seeking, as exemplified by the cases in which official firms benefited from their control of or access to monopolies of materials and goods in great demand. Later, when the redistributive power of the state decreased, more often venal actions took the form of "punitive" rent-seeking or official extortion such as illegitimate levies, forced donations, fines, and other payments under various pretexts. This form of corruption derived mainly from abuse of the regulatory power of the state. In both forms, government agencies and public units with monopoly of resources or products created rent opportunities. According to one estimate, every year more than 10 billion *yuan* worth of rents of various kinds is collected by officials and agencies endowed with regulatory power or monopoly.[15]

The banking and finance sector. One of the most notable developments in the patterns of corruption in the reform period is the increase in economic crimes committed by officials in banking and financial institutions. Because banks are still predominantly owned by the state and most credit activities have been dictated by government policies, many major cases involving huge sums were in this sector. As a result of banking reform, the discretionary power of bank and government financial officials has increased significantly in the last decade. In many places, credit agents of state-owned banks were authorized to approve loans of up to 150,000 *yuan* to collective enterprises or private businesses. High economic growth has often led to a shortage of capital for industry and other businesses. Periodic credit tightening by the government has added to the scarcity of funds and further magnified the power of local bank and financial officials. In order to elude the macro-economic policies of the central government, local businesses (both state-owned and private) adopted informal methods, including offering bribes in order to secure bank loans. In recent years, not only has the number of bribery cases involving banks and financial officials increased dramatically, but the amount of money involved has also sky-rocketed.[16] In one case, a farmer-turned-businessman in Hebei province bribed some 80 officials in 40 different financial agencies in order to obtain 286 million *yuan* in loans. Thirteen of the officials implicated in the case were indicted for taking bribes.[17] In another case, a young director of a municipal branch of the Construction Bank accepted 1.6 million *yuan* in bribes in exchange for bank loans.[18] A seafood company owner spent more than 400 million *yuan* to bribe 26 officials of various banks in Rudong county, Jiangsu province. In the most serious embezzlement case since the founding of the People's Republic, two officers of the Bank of China branch in Zhongshan, Guangdong province, embezzled over 390 million *yuan*, in addition to misappropriating 800 million *yuan*.[19]

Tax agents. In China, due to the lack of sales and income tax monitoring or an effective audit system, state taxation authorities employ a large number of tax agents to collect taxes *directly* and *personally* instead of via paperwork. Thus the process of reporting and assessing taxes is very arbitrary and highly prone to corruption. Tax agents are notorious for their abuse of power, which mostly takes two forms, tax evasion forfeits and outright demands for bribes in exchange for tax reduction or exemption. Evasion penalties, unlike regular tax revenues, can be legitimately retained (in certain proportions) by the local tax agency in charge.[20] Tax agents then may also find loopholes to keep the forfeits illicitly. They may also treat people differently. One popular saying has it that "official taxation treats acquaintances (*shuren*)[21] with lower levies, strangers with higher levies, and *guanxihu* with no levy."[22] Because of corruption among tax agents, the state has experienced a growing tax revenue loss in recent years. It is estimated that 1,300 million *yuan* was lost in 1983, 6 billion *yuan* in 1985, and 15 billion *yuan* in 1987.[23] One tax agent put it frankly: "In our profession, those who obey the law and try to be altruistic die either from hard work or poverty. Yet if one just taps a little bit of the power in his hand, it is absolutely certain that money will roll in. It is very proper to use 'those who are daring get fat, and those who are not, get starved' to depict our profession."[24]

Law enforcement officers. As corruption spread to more of the sectors of public administration, it eventually found its way into the very agencies mandated to combat corruption, including anti-corruption bureaus. Before 1986, graft cases were relatively rare in law enforcement agencies. Since then, an increasing number of officials from law enforcement agencies including public security, procurate, courts, and customs have been found to have engaged in either graft or rent-seeking activities.[25] "Judicial corruption" (*sifa fubai*) has become a main target of anti-corruption efforts in recent years.[26] In 1996, corruption cases involving law enforcement officers increased by 23 percent over the previous year.[27] In the first ten months of 1997, 7,208 corruption cases involving law enforcement officers were prosecuted nationwide. Of these cases, 1,303 involved mid- or high-ranking officials in law enforcement agencies.[28] In 1998, in addition to ordering law enforcement agencies to divest from business, nearly 10,000 agencies were reviewed. As a result, the leadership ranks of 1,339 agencies were reshuffled and 2,270 lead officials removed for various forms of misconduct (mostly corruption).[29] The most common form of judicial corruption is abuse of the office, which includes extortion, leaking information to suspects, and falsifying evidence.[30] Anti-corruption bureaus, which were established in the early 1990s, are themselves not free from corruption. In Hebei province, a deputy director of the anti-corruption bureau was expelled from the party and indicted for forcing a businessman who had accused an official of accepting bribes to commit suicide. Instead of investigating the official (who, incidentally, had helped the deputy director obtain housing and find a job for his wife), the deputy director accused the businessman of bribery. After long hours of detention and physical abuse, the businessman committed suicide.[31] Though the reforms have changed the way law enforcement officers behave, some practices recall those of pre-revolution law enforcement officers. Not only do they offer protection for illegal operations such as gambling parlors, prostitution, and smuggling, they also demand "three sames" (*santong*, i.e., to eat, live, and travel the same as people involved in the case) and pursue "three kinds of cases" (i.e., cases involving money, *guanxi*, and *renqing*). A popular saying reflects how pervasive corruption is among the law enforcement officers: "anti-corruption bureau, traffic police, they are all the same as pimps and gangsters."[32]

Corruption has also permeated the judicial agencies. As in other government agencies, lack of sufficient budgetary funding provided one of the incentives for agencies to seek revenues through less legitimate channels. Some courts have collected commissions for enforcing debt payments. Others have operated profit-making companies. Some law enforcement agencies have even imposed revenue quotas on internal subdivisions.[33] In 1998, all law enforcement agencies, along with PLA units, were ordered to divest themselves of business concerns.

Of all the law enforcement agencies, the public security bureau (i.e., the police), is the most beleaguered by corruption. This situation is especially significant because of the stature of the police apparatus in the Chinese state hierarchy. Although the police were used less as a political tool in internal party strife than in, say, the former Soviet Union, they have nonetheless been a powerful force in the daily life of the PRC. In the decades of reform, the police, both as an institution and as individuals, have found new ways to turn law enforcement authority into tangible gains. For instance, the control of residence registration has become a source of considerable income as urban residency became a marketable commodity. Police officers in charge of residency registration are among the richest government employees.[34]

Officials in charge of enforcing family planning regulations. In rural areas, state power over birth control/family planning is in the hands of township officials, who, after decollectivization, retained fewer powers, one of which is family planning. A common way that they abuse their authority is to sell second-child permits or "sterilization certificates" to peasants who want to evade the one-child-only regulations.[35] In one case, a township official began selling sterilization certificates to individual women who came to the family planning clinic for sterilization. Later, the "family planning service station" under his control became a counterfeit certificate producer and wholesaler. Hundreds of counterfeit certificates found their way into seven counties in two provinces.[36] There are also cases in which cadres in charge of family planning encouraged peasants to have more than one child as long as they were willing to pay the fines, which eventually were divided up among the cadres in the family planning office.[37]

Rent-seeking practices are not confined to these types of government agents. The military, supposedly the most disciplined sector, is also subject to them. A "fake discharged servicemen" case once shocked the people of a province for its flagrancy and the boldness of the officials involved. In April 1993, the government agency in charge of arranging work for discharged servicemen in Jinxi city, Liaoning province, sent some 400 "former servicemen" to a large oil refinery. After a careful screening, the managers of the factory discovered that of the 400 people sent with their full dossiers, 292 had never served in the military. All of the dossiers contained doctored records of military service. Some even contained certificates of commendation and records of party membership. The factory found out that some employees previously fired by the factory and some children of their own workers were among the so-called discharged servicemen. Later investigation revealed that not only were government officials involved, but more than two dozen military units and 300 officers had been responsible for providing the fake certificates and forms. The "fake soldier business" had a sliding scale— 10,000 *yuan* for a fake male soldier and 15,000 for a female.[38]

SELLING PUBLIC OFFICES

Selling official positions for money is nothing new. In traditional China, it was a common and at times legitimate means by which local magistrates raised money. After 1949, however, the practice was completely eliminated. With a tightly controlled organization, the CCP determined all assignments to official positions. But with the increasing influence of money in political and administrative processes, selling and buying official positions reemerged in the 1990s, despite years of anti-corruption efforts. In a well-publicized case, a county party secretary in Jiangxi province accepted money in exchange for appointing or promoting cadres to higher official positions. In his three years as the head of one of the poorest counties in the province, he sold positions to 45 lower-rank cadres from 18 of 38 townships who bribed him.[39] Almost all of the bribe money originally came from public sources, a testimony to the neotraditional nature of such an act. In another case in Guangdong province, a young businessman bought his way into the Communist party and the district government, becoming a party member and a director of the legal affairs commission of the district government—all in a few months. The district officials who had been entertained often by the businessman and accepted his "gifts" had not only offered official positions to him but had appointed one of his relatives "anti-corruption agent."[40]

What makes this form of corruption analytically interesting is that it is a resurgence of a historical phenomenon, and yet it is also dictated by contemporary impersonal market logic. Whereas in traditional societies, local gentry or lower-rank officials bought official positions with their own money, today Communist cadres acting in the marketplace often have their expenditures for bribes reimbursed by their agencies under various pretexts. This case is by no means unique. Jiang Zemin, speaking at a meeting celebrating the seventy-fifth anniversary of the CCP in July 1996, declared that selling, buying, and swindling official positions has become an "ugly trend" (*waifeng*).[41] The director of the COD has assailed the selling and buying of official positions, though in theory the selection of public officials is supposed to be made through an open process of rigorous examination and screening.[42] In 1996, an array of cases involving the selling and buying of official positions was exposed. Many of the officials involved were county and township party secretaries; the highest was mayor of a city in Shandong province who, according to local residents, had "turned cadre promotion and appointment into his personal *disan chanye* (service business)." [43]

Organizational Corruption

Rent-seeking and graft exist in many societies. What characterizes such activities in contemporary China under reform is the widespread rent-seeking activities by government agencies and public units. It is not uncommon for a policeman in the United States to be found guilty of extortion or of accepting bribes. What is rare is for police departments to run their own businesses (some of which involve prostitution and drugs) and to extort payments as a unit. Corruption in the post-Mao reform period has become more pervasive, as evidenced in the fact that official corruption takes place both the individual level and the organizational level—that is, illicit actions are taken not by a single individual or by collusion among individuals, but by a public agency to achieve material gains for the agency as a whole through the use of its power. Ever since the mid-1980s, the government has targeted organizational misconduct in its anti-corruption efforts.[44] However, significant as it is, organizational corruption is also the least studied and least understood pattern of corruption. No studies of Chinese corruption published in the West have examined it.

For an action to be conceived as organizational corruption, the following criteria must be met: first, it involves the (ab)use of state power, whether regulatory, distributive, or enforcement; second, it is conducted for the benefit of private interests disguised as "minor public" (*xiaogong*)[45]—a local part of the larger public (interest) domain—for whom public funds are spent for such purposes as purchasing cars, building houses, and wining and dining; third, it is in violation of official rules and is often concealed from open auditing and scrutiny. Some actions maybe outright *illegal*—such as demanding levies that violate laws or official regulations; others may be *alegal*—if no clear legal statutes exist regulating certain "innovative" actions—or *rule-violating*, when no laws are breached but administrative rules such as budget procedures, revenue regulations, spending controls, and accounting procedures are violated. These rules and procedures concern "financial and fiscal discipline" in China.

Organizational corruption is different both from corrupt acts by individuals and from corruption by collusion among individuals (i.e., "collective graft," or *jiti tanwu*) in that (1) the conduct is not by a single individual; (2) the action is department-based[46] and conducted in the name of an official unit equipped with legitimate discretion; and (3) the extracted funds or materials are retained, theoretically, for *all* the members of the unit concerned. While both types involve a group of people rather than a single individual and both abuse public office, collective graft usually does not benefit the whole unit, but a group within a unit or a collusion of people from various units. There are ample cases of collective graft in China, which sometimes involve over a hundred people.[47] However, it is organizational corruption that typifies new patterns of corruption during the economic transition in China.

OFFICIAL PROFITEERING

An early pattern of organizational corruption during the reform period was *guandao,* or "official profiteering," a phenomenon that was not regarded as corruption by the legal standards of the time. Taking advantage of the new policy of encouraging economic entrepreneurship, a large number of state agencies, enterprises, or non-production organizations rushed to set up companies to engage in profit-making activities.[48] The prototype of this kind of firm first appeared in the late 1970s and early 1980s under the name of "labor service firm" (*laodong fuwu gongsi*). These were profit-making bodies affiliated with enterprises or, more often, with state agencies and other non-production units. They were initially set up to absorb surplus labor and create job opportunities for returned youths from the countryside, unemployed high school graduates, and other potentially unemployed personnel affiliated with the same unit. Another type of official firms were direct offshoots of state administrative agencies that had economic power operating under a corporate name or were financed by agencies. These companies were dubbed "official firms" (*guanban gongsi*) because their capital, production facilities, personnel, and transportation vehicles were all taken from the state at no cost. Or, in some cases, they were simply a part of a government agency's operations, with the administrative and commercial roles of the staff indistinguishable. In 1985, there were already, according to one source, some 300,000 registered companies, among which 20,000 were "official firms,"[49] and the number grew rapidly thereafter. According to official statistics, by the end of 1988, the year of a new round of "rectification of companies," 24,187 registered firms (or 8.2 percent of the total number of registered companies) were directly financed or operated by government agencies or party organizations,[50] and some 700 companies were affiliated with various central ministries.[51]

Official profiteering, a typical rent-seeking activity, caused considerable public discontent and anger, due to its unfair and corrupt nature, fueling the eruption of mass demonstrations during the Beijing Spring of 1989. Similarly, official firms also received criticism for their profiteering activities. Since many of them are affiliated with non-production, non-profit units—most likely government agencies—and because they often enjoy privileged access to policy makers, government policies toward them have been somewhat ambiguous, if not contradictory, depending largely on the political and ideological climate. The outrage of the public and the hostility of the government over these official firms has two main sources: first, their main business activities are commercial rather than productive (hence *dao*, or speculation, profiteering), and second, their profitability stems from control of or access to generally scarce materials and products. The first feature sets them apart from the officially sponsored (i.e., financed) firms that have facilitated economic growth in newly industrializing economies such as South Korea and Taiwan. The market reforms, limited as they were, offered an opportunity for these firms to speculate, given the increasingly relaxed price controls by the state. The "dual-track" pricing system—the legitimate coexistence of state-imposed prices and market-dictated prices— enabled individuals or organizations with access to and control of scarce products or materials to make money from lower state prices and higher market prices. The official firms had a significant edge over non-official business firms with respect to their access to controlled materials, products, and commodities, which were in short supply. Indeed, throughout the 1980s, after the urban reforms began in 1984, the underlying cause of corruption was the dual-track pricing system. A typical *guandao* process in an official firm resembled that of a firm affiliated with a larger state department store: the firm (not the store itself) bought a shipment of polyester at 12.77 *yuan* per meter and sold it to the department store at 14.7 *yuan* per meter. The store later sold the fabric to another client at an even higher price. In the end, when the fabric was finally sold on the open market, the price was 28 *yuan* per meter.[52]

Sensing the increase in illegal activities by official firms, the government has tried to either crack down on or streamline these firms. After all, non-economic units (*shiye danwei*) are not supposed to be directly engaged in any economic activities. However, as markets proliferated, more and more of these types of for-profit firms have appeared. The earliest efforts to control official involvement in business included a central government decision announced in December 1984 that prohibited party/state organizations from engaging in business activities.[53] The first major publicized and prosecuted case of official profiteering was reported in the *People's Daily* in August 1985. The provincial government and party committee of Hainan were found to have engaged in speculation in imported cars, television sets, and VCRs. High-ranking officials, including a deputy governor, were reprimanded.[54] In the game of official profiteering, as in many similar rent-seeking situations, both the state and consumers are the big losers, and state agencies and their staff the big winners. In one case, China's major food import-export company, China Cereals, Foodstuffs, and Oils Import and Export Corporation, imported 291 million kilos of bananas in the summer of 1987. When the shipment arrived in Shanghai, its local branch firm sold it to a labor service firm belonging to one of its affiliates. Then the mother company in Beijing bought the bananas at a higher price *and* gave them to two of its own wholesale companies, which sold the fruit eventually to retail stores.[55] Thus, in the end, the mother company, which was a state-run entity, funneled profits to collectively operated firms. Ultimately, their control over scarce goods gave the official firm a great advantage in the still-distorted marketplace.

Practices changed as products became more abundant and official firms no longer had an advantage in exploiting price differentials. Service became a new source of revenue. After 1992, when official firms were legitimized, government agencies attempted to set up their own profit-making entities, be they a "consulting firm," "service firm," or "service center." In Shanghai, for example, the municipal bureau of finance set up a firm to sell merchandise under the government's "restricted social group purchasing" regulations. According to these regulations, designed to control the expenditures of public units, a unit has to obtain approval from the authorities—in most cases, the bureau of finance—to purchase certain restricted items. So unless the purchasing unit buys items from this particular firm, it can not obtain official approval for purchases. The profits made by this firm eventually went into the pockets of the staff of the finance bureau.[56]

In another example of official profiteering, to apply for a passport, people ordinarily run into months of agonizing delays and endless red tape caused by the Office of Border Entrance and Exit Control in the public security apparatus. One way to address that is to find a *guanxi* and expedite the process. However, not everyone has connections to the agency. Nowadays there is a new solution: you pay a price and you get your money's worth. Public security bureaus operate a service just to make life easier (for both the applicants and themselves). The more one pays, the faster one can get one's passport.[57] In the banking sector, some state-run bank branches have set up their own "consulting firms" to provide "advice" to customers who need loans. The common advice, of course, is to seek a consultant's advice before approaching credit agents. The catch: one has to pay a fee to these consultants, who are actually bank insiders. According to one account, there were at one time over 500 such firms nationwide.[58]

Following the 1989 mass demonstrations against official corruption, the government decided to set up a special coordinating office to oversee its efforts to "rectify official companies." By February 1990, 91,960 cases involving official companies had been investigated and the perpetrators disciplined. Among them, 4,118 were related to central ministries.[59] After a few rounds of shutting down "agency-run firms" produced few results, the government silently accepted the status quo. In 1992, in its efforts to downsize administrative organs and staff members and find new jobs for them, the government acquiesced to loosening restrictions on official firms and business activities of not-for-profit public agencies; more cadres were encouraged to "take a plunge into the sea (of the marketplace)." In 1993, the government once again tried to rectify official firms, ordering that all "economic entities" set up or operated by government agencies be "de-linked" (*tuogou*) from these agencies. While some ties were broken, many of these firms still retain relations with their mother agencies in various forms. At the Fifteenth Party Congress in 1997, the CCP Central Committee reiterated its intention to continue enforcing divestment of government agencies from businesses.[60] According to an official report, by the end of 1998 all law enforcement agencies and military units had divested from businesses they once ran: 19,241 companies were closed, 6,419 were transferred to local government or state asset administration, and 5,557 were delinked from the agencies or army units.[61]

ORGANIZATIONAL RENT-SEEKING

With the liberalization of prices and gradual emergence of a market economy, both the dual-track pricing and official monopolies over many commodities and products became irrelevant by the mid-1990s. There has been a decrease in instances of official profiteering in recent years. However, as the role of the state changes, government agencies and other public units with either redistributive or regulatory power have adapted to the emerging marketplace. One proclaimed objective of the Chinese reforms is to reduce the intervention of the state in economic affairs and to let the market run its course, especially at the micro level. The state is thus to play a role of regulator, maintaining order in the marketplace and reducing transaction costs. Reactions from the officialdom involved not simply resistance, as had been expected once the reforms had reduced the power of the bureaucracy in redistributing social resources. Rather, the more salient strategy adopted by officials has been *distortion*—exploiting the new opportunities, individually or collectively, to maximize their own interests. New forms of organizational corruption have thus emerged. Since the mid-1980s, a new phenomenon in the growing array of deviance has spun out of control—organizational rent-seeking—that is, irregular and illicit behavior by various state agencies that exploit their monopoly or regulatory power to enrich the unit. Chen Zuolin, a deputy chairman of the Central PDIC, offered a definition of what is known as *hangye buzheng zhifeng* (unhealthy vocational tendencies): " . . . behavior which is aimed at utilizing special authority for individual or small group interests at the cost of the interests of the public and other people. It is a reflection of feudal guildism and bourgeois egoism under new conditions."[62]

Organizational rent-seeking is found in many public agencies and involves many people, from the agencies that have control over materials and funds to those that have neither (*qingshui yamen*), from leading officials on down. It often takes place in legitimate forms based on regulatory authority, in the name of the reform and revitalization of the economy.[63] It differs from earlier forms of organizational corruption such as official firms and official profiteering. Although it also involves public units and abuses of state power, these units are not directly engaged in business transactions as is the case with official speculation and official companies. What makes it difficult to control is another of its attributes: it usually involves a public unit or a group of state agents rather than individuals, and benefits are shared by a collective. Furthermore, these rent-seekers do not directly violate the law, but violate so-called fiscal discipline—the rules that regulate public funds.

RETREATING STATE? EXPANDING STATE?

While in theory the state is withdrawing from meddling in the economy and social life, in reality the fast-growing functionalization of government agencies has made it a more interventionist regulator than ever before, providing opportunities for the otherwise poor, get-rich-last state agents (because of their fixed low salaries) to catch up fast. The number of government regulatory agencies, many of whose staff wear uniforms and function as law enforcement agents, has been on the rise over the last decade. One report counts the number of uniformed agencies in Zhejiang province at over 30, including public security, tax, business regulation, traffic, environmental protection, municipal management, tobacco licensing, public health officials, and many more.[64] All uniforms were paid for by the units, which in turn charged the cost to the administrative budget appropriation from the state. In Jiangsu province, spending on uniforms in 1989–91 was more than 100 million *yuan*, creating a serious strain on the government budget and ultimately a heavy burden on taxpayers. [65] The problem is so pervasive that even the government of one small rural township has dozens of state-paid cadres in various functional agencies dressed in uniforms. Officials in other agencies having nothing whatsoever to do with regulatory or law enforcement functions receive a "uniform allowance," too, in order to make everyone happy.[66]

Government agencies strove to make money, particularly after the reforms picked up pace following Deng Xiaoping's early 1992 visit to the southern provinces, in which he incited renewed enthusiasm from reformers for further change. New methods of generating revenues were created, even by agencies without any direct regulatory power, through such activities as *pingbi*,[67] *jiancha* (inspection), *kaohe* (emanation and check), and *yanshou* (evaluation and acceptance). Although not all of these activities were utilized by agencies to extract payments, many enterprises in both the state and the private sectors felt pressure to ward off these illicit intrusions from state administrative agencies.

Organizational corruption can take less subtle, even outright venal, forms. Taking bribes, for instance, is a punishable economic crime according to a 1988 legal statute.[68] Let us look at a typical pattern of how a *danwei* can use bribery to benefit its staff. A county pesticide factory approached the director and deputy director of the county's economic commission about renewing its license to continue the production of its below-standard products. The pesticide factory promised the commission an annual "office expense subsidy" of 20,000 *yuan*. The commission then issued an official approval to the factory to allow it to continue production, in exchange for 40,000 *yuan* up front as the subsidy for the 1986–87 fiscal year. From 1987 to 1989, the factory produced a large quantity of low-quality pesticide that caused tremendous damage to the peasants who bought the product. In this particular case, the directors were prosecuted for the crime of "bribery by public unit."[69]

Some of the most widespread (and most resented) illicit practices of state agencies are the so-called *san luan* (three unruly actions)—i.e., illicitly levying fines (*luan fakuan*), imposing fees (*luan shoufei*), and apportioning forced donations (*luan tanpai*). To be sure, the government does allow some levies or fee charges. However, facing the mounting pressure of fiscal shortages, local government agencies resort to extra-budgetary (*yusuan wai*) or self-raised (*zichou*) revenues generated through *jizi* (fund raising), *shoufei* (charging fees), or *jijin* (endowments). Ordinarily, the government either sanctions these methods as legitimate, or acquiesces in them. From the point of view of central revenue-making, however, they are typically regarded as illegitimate but not illegal, or as something inherited from the pre-reform past and not easy to change.[70]

In practice, these methods are often used to levy excessive and irregular charges on local populations and enterprises. To escape regular budgetary control, public units often try to raise extra-budgetary revenues or transfer budgetary revenues into extra-budgetary revenues, which violates the Budget Law. Certain services provided with a fee should be part of normal functions and free of charge. Furthermore, most of the charges in question are imposed without clear mandates by laws or rules. Although not all extra-budgetary funds are illegitimate, lack of proper financial monitoring often provided ample opportunities for abuse and waste. Sometimes, government agencies and public units simply raise funds for public projects or social services without any regular budgetary procedure. Through these involuntary donations from local enterprises and non-enterprise units, government agencies are able to enrich themselves. As early as 1983, the central government issued a decree to "resolutely stop the practice of apportionment imposed on units and individuals in the name of fund raising."[71] The practice spread.

What kinds of sums are involved in these extra-budgetary funds? The annual fiscal statistical reports issued by the Ministry of Finance do contain certain figures, but it is a widely accepted fact that the real amounts are much higher. On the occasions when a joint effort was made by several government ministries to investigate these funds, startling figures emerged. According to one such national investigation, extra-budgetary funds amounted to 38.43 billion *yuan* in 1995. Of this sum, 15 billion fell into the category of "administrative fees," 17 billion were "various funds raised by local governments," and 2.4 billion were "supplementary charges."[72]

Unconstrained and arbitrary financial charges by government agencies have generated growing discontent, particularly in rural areas where peasant tax revolts, violence, suicides, and other disturbances have been increasingly reported since 1993.[73]

Nationwide, efforts have been made to investigate and clean up "illicit impositions." One report in 1992 found that in eleven provinces and cities (including Shanghai and Tianjin), 89,000 various fees were imposed, of which 53,000 were neither legal nor authorized ones; there were 13,000 imposed penalties, 12,000 of which violated local or national regulations. The same report revealed that only 10,700 of these items were eventually eliminated. All told, an estimated 10 billion *yuan* in illegitimate fees, fines, and apportionments was taken in, but by 1991 only 4.5 billion *yuan* worth had been eliminated.[74] In another city, more than 600 various public units imposed charges and apportionments.[75]

In rural areas, charges and levies have been growing since the early 1980s. Although the government was alarmed at this problem and, as early as 1985, stipulated that charges (excluding taxes) on peasants could total no more than 5 percent of their annual income,[76] the actual burden on peasants is much heavier. According to the Ministry of Agriculture, nationwide there were some 150 items of payment in 1993.[77] In 1991, fees, fines, project contributions, and apportionments (*tanpai*) amounted to a national average of 2.5 percent of an individual peasant's annual income.[78] Almost every service rendered by the government in the countryside requires a fee. In interviews with peasants, one of the most frequent complaints about the heavy payments concerned this kind of service charge. They sarcastically called it "no services without fees."

In some places, the financial burden on peasants is even heavier.[79] In some villages in Yuci city, Shanxi province, people had to pay as much as 13.98 percent of their income to various agencies in 1992. In Bo'ai county, Henan province, peasants made 136 kinds of financial payments, or 15.1 percent of their annual income in 1991. A large proportion of the payments went to government agencies at the county and township levels, including finance, land management, town planning, water conservation, farm machinery, public health, veterinary services, seed services, forestry, family planning, civil affairs, courts, police, culture, postal service, power generation, and environmental protection. In other words, in Bo'ai county all essential public services provided to peasants were fee-based, and almost no governmental service was free. Besides the fees and charges for governmental services, peasants in this county also had to pay eleven types of forced contributions and fund raising.[80]

Further evidence of state agencies illicitly preying on the state, businesses, and private citizens can be found. There is a huge discrepancy between the increasingly heavy burden of levies borne by individual entrepreneurs or enterprises and the decreased actual revenues of the state treasury. A 1992 report from the State Tax Bureau indicates that, of the 30 or so levies commonly imposed in China, only a few are solidly grounded in the taxation laws. The rest are all levied according to an assortment of local and agency "ordinances," "regulations," or "pilot procedures." At the same time, the state loses an estimated 100 billion *yuan* in tax revenues each year due to tax evasion and under-reporting of profits.[81] To stop this increasingly widespread problem, which has defied numerous efforts to curtail it, in July 1997 the central government issued new regulations regarding levies, charges, and apportionments on businesses, and it designated "enterprise burden reduction" as a core task.[82] In the two months that followed the launching of this campaign, 2,877 different charges were invalidated nationwide, amounting to 15 billion *yuan*.[83] Without a fundamental reconstruction of the existing government-business relationship and a reform of the public financial system, however, it is highly doubtful that these efforts will succeed.

IRREGULAR USE OF REGULATORY POWER

Not only do traditional law enforcement agencies such as the public security bureau, state administration of industry and commerce (SAIC), public health bureau, price bureau, and bureau of road management continue to grow and wield more power. New agencies such as state property administration, state land administration, industrial standards and quality, intellectual property rights protection, family planning, and financial discipline inspection have also mushroomed. In addition, sectors with business monopolies such as telecommunications, public utilities, and railroads have joined the scramble to generate revenues by adding their own charges.

Fines have become a source of funds for regulatory and law enforcement agencies. According to a report by the SAIC, there was an increase of more than 10 percent in fines and confiscations by the SAIC system nationwide in 1993; they reached a whopping 800 million *yuan*. Of course, this figure reflects only the revenues reported to the central bureau.[84] Despite numerous central government regulations regarding these revenues, agencies continue to ignore the rules. Only recently did the central government decide that law enforcement and regulatory agencies have power to assess and impose, but not to collect, fines. Banks will act as collecting agents. By separating assessment and collection, the government hopes that local agencies will stop abusing their power and impounding revenues.[85] The new measure has so far yielded limited results in curbing irregularities, especially in areas where fiscal conditions remain bleak, however.[86]

A portion of, or sometimes all of, the revenues from fines are impounded by an agency with regulatory authority for the benefit of its own members without turning them over to the state treasury. Table 6.1 gives an example of how money is spent by agencies in one prefecture. Frequently, the money collected as fines goes to individuals in an agency; sometimes agents assess fines at will and take bribes from the intimidated units or persons to reduce fines. Thus, organizational corruption and personal corruption are intertwined.[87] An investigation by the municipal audit bureau of Dalian found that the penalty money collected by a neighborhood commission for public health, which was in charge of neighborhood sanitary conditions, was divided between the neighborhood governance body, which took 60 percent, and the committee itself, which kept 40 percent. The income of the neighborhood governance body was, in fact, divided among the sanitary inspectors themselves.[88] The income from what some Chinese scholars call "marginal" (e.g., subsidies or materials for uniforms) and "hidden" sources (e.g., fines and confiscations) has become a major part of the staff's regular income in some state agencies. An investigation of the personal income of the agencies of average cities shows that, while all are state agencies, some have much higher incomes than others. The agencies with the highest incomes are the financial and post/telecommunications agencies, followed by business regulation, tax, police, and urban development administration (which controls urban land use and building permits) offices. The agencies with no "marginal" or "hidden" sources, such as departments of party committees and municipal governments, have the lowest incomes.[89]

The normal and regular use of regulatory power by government agencies is not the issue here. What is to be regarded as corruption is an irregular, and indeed often arbitrary, wielding of power that is predatory in nature. A good example is illicit road tolls and charges. Roadways became a source of revenue for those government agencies in charge of road management, public health, taxation, tobacco, and the salt monopoly. In the name of highway safety, disease control, and prevention of tax evasion and salt or cigarette smuggling, these agencies became quite efficient at imposing fines, fees, or other charges along roadways. In one small county of Hubei province, sixteen different agencies simultaneously had checkpoints; they charged among them some 30 fees along the two main inter-provincial highways.[90] In some places, toll posts and checkpoints were set up on an average of every 3.2 kilometers. According to one report, in 1995 alone, 6,745 checkpoints or toll posts nationwide were dismantled, a 50 percent reduction from the previous year.[91] However, the problem has not been totally eliminated. Travel on China's highways and roads can be a costly experience.

In seeking administrative rents, government bureaus literally can act as entrepreneurs in the marketplace as they exploit the power vested in a state organ. In an astonishing case, public security bureaus from several provinces set up street stalls in Shenzhen, the boomtown in Guangdong province; the stalls sold restricted "border zone entry passes," which enabled holders to enter restricted areas bordering Hong Kong. The applicants had to pay a service charge of 30 to 80 *yuan*, depending on the length of the validation period. What is unique about this case is that not only were public agencies from other jurisdictions disregarding the local authorities; in addition, they in fact initially competed to attract clients by cutting prices and later made an agreement dividing up territories with unified prices, not unlike for-profit firms acting in the marketplace. Warnings and intervention from the local municipal government were completely ignored.[92]

In addition to state agencies' exacting money from individuals and businesses, there was also a collusive and mutually beneficial relationship between state agencies and the enterprises that these agencies supposedly supervise or control. Patron-clientelism of this sort may deviate from the norms of the state and have damaging consequences.[93] One manifestation of such a relationship is the practice of assessment and designation of a product as an "excellent quality item" by a state agency. The practice was first introduced in the late 1970s as a way of enhancing the quality of consumer and industrial products. Customers would look for "excellent quality" labels issued by the Ministry of Light Industry. But such assessments were discredited when each province, county, and even district began to issue its own "excellent quality" label. Managers conceded that by spending some money and establishing cordial *guanxi*,

TABLE 6.1

Disposal of Revenue from Fines by Government Agencies
in Xiaogan Prefecture, Hubei Province, 1989–1990

Usage	Amount (*thousand* yuan)
Total income from monetary penalties[a]	11,406
Building, purchasing, and renting of apartments	1,580
Purchase of automobiles	1,192
Salaries, subsidies, and bonuses	1,042
Uniforms	134
Receptions and banquets	435

SOURCE: Jia and Su, *Heimao baimao.*
[a]Includes both illegitimate fines (2.24 million *yuan*) and locally impounded portions of tax and penalty revenue that should have been turned over to the state treasury (9.18 million *yuan*), which amounts to 60 percent of the total penalties collected.

it was not difficult to obtain such a designation. They pointed to the fact that nowadays the so-called product assessment meeting (*chanpin jiandinghui*) is usually a time for the enterprise to spend large amounts of money to invite "experts" and "leaders" to attend. "You do not bribe them, of course," said one informant, a factory manager, sarcastically, "you only ask them to take some 'souvenirs' with them after they attend the meeting in a summer resort or a tourist city." The result, naturally, was a dazzling array of consumer products labeled as "national high quality" (*guo you*), "ministry-designated high quality" (*bu you*), "province-designated high quality" (*sheng you*), or "county-designated high quality" (*xian you*), the real qualities of which were highly dubious.

Government agencies that are supposedly not-for-profit have also exploited other ways to extract revenues for their own benefit. As a result of the limited liberalization policy of the last decade, the number of non-official societal groups (*shetuan*) under the names of "associations" or "societies" registered with the government has increased. What is significant about this development is not only the semi-autonomous character of such groups, which some Western scholars have cited as evidence of an emerging civil society,[94] but the methods by which these entities became lucrative money-making vehicles. In

TABLE 6.2

Disposal of Impounded (*jieliu*) and Diverted (*nuoyong*) Funds
by Government Agencies, 1989

Usage	Amount (million yuan)
Unapproved construction	422.8
Purchase of automobiles and other luxury items	576.7
Bonus and materials to individuals	334.6
Gifts and banquets	835.0
Money possessed illicitly by individuals (*siren zhanyong*)[a]	470.4
Graft and theft	104.5

SOURCE: Caizhengbu and Jianchabu, *Caizheng jiancha gongzuo wenjian ziliao xuanbian.*
[a]Refers to cases in which individuals "borrowed" from public funds, often for private business, but never paid back monies.

reality, they are anything but unofficial and autonomous groups representing social interests. Associations of one sort at the national level often have counterparts at the provincial, prefecture, and county level, and all the way down to the district level, similar to the way Chinese administrative organs are set up. The problem is that they all charge a membership or sponsor fee. The members or sponsors, usually enterprises and other production or service units, are involuntarily dragged into the group. Indeed, many of these associations or societies are in fact "attached" (*guakao*) to a state agency, and they often have senior officials on their boards.[95] In Chongqing, recent statistics list 12,000 or so "social groups." Twenty-seven municipal-level officials serve on the boards of 70 municipal-level groups (among 280 such groups), with one person serving on eight corporate boards. In addition, some 550 mid-ranked city officials serve in 3,742 various associations. The highest-paid official received 5,000 *yuan* per year as compensation. In turn, the associations could use the names of officials to raise more donations and fees from enterprises. In the same city, an iron and steel plant had to pay 270,000 *yuan* each year in various association fees.[96] One sarcastic comment vividly captured the irony of *gaohuo* (revitalize or make enterprises profitable and efficient): "The objective of the reform is to revitalize enterprises, but now what is being revitalized is the government. Enterprises are being devitalized."[97]

SMALL COFFERS

Revenues raised by public units through various means go into the pockets of the staff often via the "small treasury" (*xiaojinku*)—illegitimate slush funds. These secret, illegitimate accounts are kept by government agencies, state-owned enterprises, and other public units in addition to their regular auditable accounts. Common methods used to create such piggy banks include concealing receipt records, maintaining bank accounts under personal names, retaining extra-budgetary revenues, under-reporting profits, and retaining cash income. The accounts are usually at the discretion of unit leaders, who use bookkeepers whom they trust. The problem of public units keeping unreported accounts has been always existed, albeit to varying degrees at different times. For example, in a 1954 report by the Ministry of Supervision it was revealed that in 1954 some units kept a total of 20.8 million *yuan* in "black coffer" funds in addition to unreported materials.[98] Throughout the history of the PRC, the government has often tried to crack down on what were called "actions that violate financial discipline" (*weifan caijin jilü*) on the part of public units. This type of violation has perplexed the government because of its "gray" or marginal nature: although it violates "fiscal discipline," no regulatory provisions officially define it as illegal. In addition, use of these accounts involves a collective, *pro bono publico,* rather than an individual. On the surface at least, its purpose is not for "private gain." Although not all slush funds are used for private purposes, they are nonetheless a major source of abuse, waste, and irregularities. In one small city, funds in the "small coffers" were discovered to be 2,629,200 *yuan* in the fiscal year 1988–89 alone. Of this amount, only 322,400 *yuan,* or 13.7 percent, was spent on collective purposes. The rest was spent on deviant activities—orgies of eating and drinking, gifts and bribes, smuggling, private embezzlement, and the like.[99] In 1990, revenues earned from the "three unruly actions" and illicitly retained by the law enforcement agencies of Hebei province amounted to 32,913,400 *yuan.*[100] The State Statistics Bureau estimated that each year at least 3.3 billion *yuan* was lost through the three unruly practices. Actual figures may be several times higher.[101] Nationwide, the hidden funds in the small coffers have grown to an enormous amount; but, due to its secret nature, it defies any accurate account. According to a 1996 national inspection, of the 10.2 billion *yuan* expenditures by public units that had violated fiscal regulations, 400 million came from small coffers.[102] The records of the public procurate of another city show that among the 56 embezzlement cases it investigated and prosecuted in the first six months of 1990, six involved small coffers.[103]

When the State Audit Bureau first audited 66,200 public units nationwide in 1985, it found 10 billion *yuan* in problematic accounts, 76 percent of which were revenues illicitly retained by these units.[104] So far, the largest single small coffer uncovered belongs to the State Bureau of Grain Reserve and amounted at 360 million *yuan* in 1998.[105] According to reports based on Ministry of Finance figures, the illicit funds that "violated financial discipline" that were uncovered during annual nationwide general inspections during the period of 1985–93 amount to a staggering 100.6 billion *yuan*. This sum does not of course include undiscovered funds, which were estimated to be far more than the amounts discovered.[106] One estimate is that in China's current bank deposits, there are several hundred billion *yuan* in savings in the names of private citizens (many are pseudonyms) that actually belong to public units.[107]

A NAGGING PROBLEM

To be sure, the Chinese government has not been ignoring the problem of organizational corruption. The State Council issued eight different "prohibition" decrees from 1982 to 1989. In 1991, it convened a special meeting to discuss how to address the problem, which Vice Premier Zou Jiahua called a "public enemy of our nation's economic life."[108]

Despite efforts by the government at various levels, illicit money-making activities of administrative and non-profit organizations continue in China. As one factory manager put it, "Government power has become departmentalized (*bumenhua*), departmental power personalized (*gerenhua*), and personal power privatized (*siyouhua*). It has become a decaying disease in some state agencies and one hard to cure."[109]

Why are such practices so entrenched? The manager of a large state steel corporation suggested one possible explanation for such a prevalent problem:

> Ours is a large enterprise that receives many instructions from both vertical (*tiaotiao*) and local (*kuaikuai*) superiors. Since 1987, we have received 18 directives, containing 202 clauses, from the central and provincial government alone. If adding documents from the vertical leadership, we may have received several hundred policy directives. It is not uncommon to have contradicting policies. Any regulatory agency can easily come up with some policy clause to pick on us. Last year (1990), one agency accused our company of having exceeded the number of staff working in the labor union, and fined us 100,000 *yuan*. As a matter of fact, we had strictly followed the provisions of the labor union law of the 1950s and had been doing so for decades. Now they insisted that we had violated current policy. What they really wanted was money. Now we have learned to deal with it better. Whoever comes, we cannot let them leave empty handed. Fines are fine with us so long as the enterprise can still bear it. After all, all the money belongs to the state.[110]

Factors that directly affect rent-seeking behavior by government units include the lack of hard budgetary constraints and insufficient budgetary appropriations for government units, the continuing expansion of bureaucracy, and the murky nature of such rent-seeking behavior by units.

A major contributing factor is the informalization of government funding. Many government agencies, especially those at the lower levels, have resorted to the informal strategy of "raising some, borrowing some, moving around some, mortgaging some, accepting some." In addition to budgeted revenues and expenditures, there are also revenues and spending that are outside of regular budgetary control. In urban areas, these are known as "extra-budgetary funds," and they originated in the late 1950s when the rapid industrialization under central planning called for more local initiatives. With the policy known as "walking on two legs," the central government allowed local governments to retain a certain amount of revenue outside of the budget in order to encourage their participation in economic development.[111] The original intention was to supplement regular revenues; later, however, the extra-budgetary funds problem took on a life of its own, and its share in the national economy kept growing. As an established and common fiscal category (more so among urban units), it has been a focus of fiscal reforms in the last decade.

The collection and disposal of extra-budget revenues are in the hands of government agencies. The revenues are not transferable but are to be used only for the specific purposes for which they were collected. In theory, they are subject to fiscal regulations and laws. In reality, however, enforcement has proved difficult despite annual "general inspections of fiscal and financial discipline." There are few constraints on the collection, management, and expenditure of off-budget funds. Not only do the funds undermine the fiscal policies of the central government, but many fiscal irregularities and a great deal of corruption derive from them.[112]

Until recently, organizational corruption remained a fuzzy area in which neither legal statutes nor administrative rules could effectively gauge the venality involved. Organizational corruption was once regarded simply as a violation of financial discipline, and required only repayment or return of illicit funds. The penalty for violation was often decided based on its degree of "seriousness." Existing legal statutes stipulate that public units can be prosecuted as "legal persons" for graft, peculation of public funds, bribery, secret overseas bank accounts, and possession of large sums with untraceable sources.[113] However, in practice, there are difficulties in prosecuting cases of organizational corruption. Unlike "collective graft," it is hard to determine if a public unit as a whole is implicated. Although in theory public units can be found guilty of giving or receiving bribes, it is not entirely clear whether these constitute prosecutable transgressions. The most common form of organizational corruption—administrative rent-seeking—is entirely beyond the criminal justice system. The only formal remedies are regulations and administrative rules.[114] Moreover, the purpose of illicit revenue-raising may not always be purely private—that is, on the surface at least, some of the funds go into "public goods," such as improving the lives of unit members or the construction of housing. A new amendment to the Penal Code has made it a crime for "state organs, state-owned companies and enterprises, public nonprofit units, and citizen groups to illicitly divide up a large amount of confiscation and penalty revenues and other public assets among members." This newly designated criminal offense—"illicit division of state assets"[115] (*sifen guoyou caichan zui*)—was created to prevent the kind of organizational corruption that I have addressed. Despite this legal provision, there remain some practical difficulties for enforcement. For this crime to be established, a public unit, not a collusion of individuals, has to be the party that commits the offense, yet penalties apply only to persons in charge directly or indirectly. Further, for an action to be prosecuted as "crime of illicit division of state assets," "a large amount" of funds must be involved. This leaves a lot of leeway as to how much money is "a large amount." So far, there have been no reports of any cases of the prosecution of any public units for such a crime.

Deeper causes of organizational corruption, however, lie in the distortion of the role of the state in a state socialist system under drastic reform, and in the lack of fundamental change in the deeply embedded neotraditional mentality and organizational ethos whose roots are in the pre-reform era. Here the link between organizational involution and corruption could not be more salient. The "bigger and faster" mentality and "showing off by whatever means" (*biaoxian*) ethos of the Maoist era and the competitive pressure that these two gave rise to between territorial units have by no means disappeared from the minds of officials in the reform era.[116] Officials, moreover, widely believe that displays of visible progress—the construction of impressive and expensive party and government compounds, local bridges, roadways, or guest houses— added to their status and prestige, exacerbating the tendency to spend. Terms such as "tributary projects" (*xianli gongcheng*) or "leader's projects" (*shouzhang gongcheng*) are still being used. Government policies add to this competitive pressure and encourage the competition that has always been a source of dissemination and distortion of information in command economies. The practice of *dabiao* is an example of how the "goal culture" of the Maoist era has not only survived the changes but adopted a new rule-oriented form. Instead of appointment and promotion of cadres by superiors' evaluation (*kaocha*) without standard procedures, now examinations and performance evaluations with set standards (*kaohe*) are applied. In a mobilization regime, routine rules and procedures are disregarded and overshadowed by goals and ends. In a neotraditional regime, officials are judged by their goal-oriented performance, but with rule-oriented requirements. The fact that provincial governments still designate a county "well-to-do" through a systematic evaluation (*yanshou*) indicates, ironically, that the pressure to be unrealistic about developmental goals comes from the very authorities who try to stop predatory practices by government agencies.[117]

Organizational Involution and Anti-Corruption Efforts

SERIOUS EFFORTS, LIMITED RESULTS

Despite the anti-corruption efforts (which are genuine and based on a sense of urgency), the government has failed to stomp out corruption. Indeed, it has become more pervasive than ever. The amount of money involved in corruption cases has steadily increased: the 1995 corruption case involving Beijing's vice-mayor involved 18.3 billion *yuan* in embezzlement and peculation of public funds.[118] Moreover, the officials found guilty of corruption come from higher and higher ranks. Before 1986, not a single official at the provincial or ministerial level was investigated and prosecuted for corruption.[119] Between 1992 and 1997, however, 78 provincial and ministry-level officials were prosecuted for corruption, the most senior being a member of the CCP Politburo.[120] (See Table 6.3.) In a recent case, a deputy governor of Jiangxi province was stripped of all government positions, indicted, and sentenced to death in December 1999 for bribery and extortion.[121]

The limited results of the anti-corruption efforts can also be seen in the public opinion polls. According to a poll conducted in 1995 among urban workers by the Public Opinion Institute at People's University, the most pressing issue was to "clean government and combat corruption," whereas it had ranked sixth in 1993 (with "prices" being number one).[122] In a series of surveys conducted in Shanxi province between 1995 and 1997, corruption was ranked the most serious problem for three consecutive years. In 1997, 65 percent of the respondents regarded corruption as the number-one issue, a thirteen point increase from 1996.[123] The same surveys found that in 1997 only 20 percent of those

TABLE 6.3

Corruption Cases, 1992–1998

Citizen reports of corruption received by PDICs	75,500,000[a]
reports of corruption by high-ranking officials	930,000[a]
Cases brought up by PDICs and supervisory apparatus	873,000
Cases closed	790,000
Cadres who received disciplinary and administrative actions	789,300
expelled from the party	121,500[a]
expelled from the party and received criminal penalties	37,492[a]
officials of county/department rank	24,265
officials of bureau rank	1,977
officials of province/ministry rank	84

SOURCE: The Central PDIC, see *RMRB,* September 24, 1997; January 14, 1999.
[a]1998 figures not included.

polled thought the efforts to contain corruption were "very good" or "good," while 51 percent said they were "fair" and 29 percent "not good."[124] Internationally, as China's integration into the world economy increases, more foreigners find it to be a place where corruption is endemic. In a survey of businesspeople around the world in 1995, China was ranked the second worst place to do business because of corruption, after Indonesia.[125] In 1997, a larger survey on corruption in 52 major countries found China was perceived to have one of the highest corruption rates, ranking twelfth overall.[126] Another survey on corruption in Asian countries rated China as the third most corrupt country in Asia in 1997, next to Indonesia and India. Respondents in the survey "seemed to feel that the problem of corruption has worsened marginally in both India and China compared with one year ago."[127]

NEOTRADITIONALISM AND ANTI-CORRUPTION

The failed anti-corruption efforts of the last two decades indicate that the reforms, often touted as the "second revolution," have not totally averted involutionary development and have not changed the neotraditional nature of the Chinese regime. Gradualism and piecemeal reforms in administrative and political systems have resulted in a continuation of an organizational involution characterized by neotraditionlist traits; there has been an elaboration of some preexisting patterns of the mobilization regime and a revival of some traditional modes of operation, even as more rational-legal forms and rules are adopted in the name of streamlining and reform.

Perhaps the most telling indication of the continuation of neotraditionalism is the ritualization of anti-corruption efforts. The pervasiveness of corruption in China has certainly not been due to a lack of determination or effort on the part of the party/state leadership. Numerous anti-corruption, "clean government" laws and regulations have been promulgated since the late 1970s. In 1997 alone, six new national anti-corruption laws and disciplinary regulations were promulgated.[128] There are also numerous local anti-corruption rules.

Campaign-style mass mobilization continued to be a method of choice by the CCP leadership until recently despite its diminishing effectiveness. Since the beginning of the reforms in 1979, particularly since the CCP's 1982 "Resolution on Crackdown of Economic Crimes," anti-corruption campaigns have abounded. Practically every two years there would be a new campaign: in 1980–81 (the "Campaign to Curb Official Privileges and Unhealthy Tendencies in the Party"), in 1982 (the "Campaign to Resolutely Crack Down on Economic Crimes"), in 1983 (the "Campaign to Eradicate Housing Irregularities by Officials"), in 1984–85 (the "Campaign to Stop Officials from Engaging in Commercial Activities"),[129] in 1986–87 (the "Campaign of Punishing Violations of Laws and Discipline of the Party and the State"), and in 1988–89 (the "Campaign to Build a Clean Government and Curb Corruption"). In the 1990s, new anti-corruption campaigns were launched in 1991, 1994, and 1996. In each of these campaigns, more anti-corruption measures were taken and ordinances passed, but the problem remained. After the many anti-corruption campaigns since the early 1980s, the party leadership seems finally to have realized that the mass mobilization style of addressing the problem of bureaucracy has lost its efficacy. Since 1993, the State Council has convened annual anti-corruption meetings designating certain tasks for the year. But after 1995, the emphasis was switched to institutional methods rather than ad hoc mass campaigns. Still, the campaign strategy has not been totally given up. Most recently in 1999, another drive to curb corruption among officials was launched under the name of "three emphases" (*sanjiang*), during which all officials must go through stages of self-evaluation followed by evaluation and revelation by others.[130]

New measures and institutions—some emulating models from other countries and others innovative—have been adopted to combat corruption. Since the mid-1980s, there have been dozens of published handbooks (*shouce*), case studies (*anli yanjiu*), guidelines (*zhinan*), compilations of laws and regulations (*fagui huibian*). From 1990 to 1996, new regulations were promulgated regarding the declaration of income by public officials, registration of gifts received by officials,[131] and avoidance of close relatives working in the same unit. The Supreme People's Procurate set up a 50-member "special case investigation task-force" mandated to investigate corruption cases involving high-ranking officials.[132] Some provinces and cities established "anti-corruption and clean-government funds" and appointed "good-governance citizen inquirers."[133] The central government also dispatched special anti-corruption inspectors to various localities.[134]

A large number of anti-corruption agencies have been established over the last two decades. At the start of the reforms, the procurate system resumed functioning in 1978, and the internal disciplinary body of the Communist party, the PDIC system, was re-established in 1979. In 1987, the supervisory agencies were reinstituted. All three systems have their own investigative and regulatory powers: the party disciplinary commissions deal with cases of violations of organizational rules and discipline involving party members, the supervisory agencies handle cases of violations of administrative regulations involving administrative staff of public units, and the procurate cases involve anyone, including party members and state workers, who violates laws.[135] In addition, other anti-corruption-related bodies have been established in the past two decades: the audit bureaus (in charge of public unit auditing), the centers for reporting corruption (*jubao zhongxin*, where citizens can anonymously report any suspicion of corruption), the "office of correcting unhealthy vocational tendencies" (which is in charge of combating abuses by government agencies),[136] the "office of general inspection of financial and fiscal discipline" (which conducts annual inspections on collection and disposal of extra-budgetary funds),[137] and specially appointed non-official corruption monitors (*teyao jianchayuan*),[138] involved in reporting or investigating corruption cases of various sorts. More recently, "bureaus of anti-graft and bribery" (*fan tanwu huilu ju*) were established within the procurate, in charge of investigating and prosecuting grafts at various levels. In 1989, China's first anti-graft and bribery bureau was established in Guangdong province. Then, in November 1995, the Central Bureau, under the auspices of the Supreme People's Procurate, was established. By late 1996, there were over 1,500 such agencies, operating in 26 of China's 30 provinces.[139] The PRC can boast having more special anti-corruption/disciplinary agencies than any other country in the world.

In addition to these institutions and regulations, the government also constantly reiterates its rules and regulations and uses a quasi-campaign style of general inspection (*da jiancha*) to check on their execution. Despite all these measures, however, violators either disregard them or, as is often the case, utilize the laws and rules to their own advantage, in effect subverting them. One of the most important inspections is the "general inspection of financial and fiscal discipline." Each year since 1985, almost like a "rite" (as an agent in a local business licensing agency described it), the government launches such an inspection and uncovers millions of *yuan*, while millions more escape inspection. The problem not only persists, it has become even more aggravated. An instance is the corrupt practice of building private residences and wining and dining with public funds (*gongkuan qingke*). As corruption pervaded law enforcement and regulatory agencies, the government implemented, beginning in 1993, national inspections of these agencies. Between 1993 and 1995, 15,900 such inspections were launched and 31,800 cases of violation of rules were investigated.[140] Anti-corruption efforts have thus been ritualized without substantive effect. Furthermore, not only have anti-corruption institutions and other measures been rendered ineffective, distortions resulting from ritualized attempts to clean up the cadre ranks have also, ironically, created new opportunities for wrongdoing. Under the pretext of promoting clean and efficient governance, government agencies or individual officials resorted to legitimate practices like *pingbi* (competition), *jiancha* (inspection), *kaohe* (examination), and *yanshou* (evaluation) but use them to collect more funds or to be entertained more often.

The limited results of the anti-corruption campaigns and institutions have led some people to believe either that the leadership lacks the resolve to punish all who committed corruption, including high-ranking officials, or that leaders are intentionally lax toward officials as a "side payment" meant to give them a personal stake in reform.[141] Neither of these views finds much empirical support. The problem points out the defects that lie in a regime that has undergone an involutionary development. There has not been a lack of leadership resolve to root out corruption, nor has there been any shortage of detailed, technical, even hairsplitting regulations regarding corruption. But while anti-corruption measures become more and more technical and detailed, and the law/discipline enforcement apparatus becomes better trained, corruption continues, showing up in new forms and patterns. Meanwhile, people continue to find ways—many of them traditional and informal—to cope. Frustrated by the ineffectiveness of its decrees and by its inability to implement its policies or regulations, the CCP leadership has resorted to special decrees to enforce earlier decrees. For example, in December 1984, the government announced its decision to ban government agencies from running money-making companies. The ban did not work. A few months later, to reiterate the ban, the Central PDIC issued a "Decree on 'Orders Must Be Followed and Prohibition Must Work.'"[142] Notably, this decree particularly assailed the phenomenon of "where there is an order, there is no implementation; where there is a ban, there still is the prohibited practice" (*youling buxing, youjin buzhi*). It clearly indicated that the effectiveness of rules and orders from the party had been seriously compromised by the mid-1980s. The decree added that another common phenomenon—"where there is a policy from higher authorities, there is a counter-policy from local authorities" (*shangyou zhengce, xiayou duice*)—had further weakened party/state authority.

In one further indication of entrenched neotraditionalism, local leaders have engaged in what the chief of the Hunan provincial PDIC calls "corruption protectionism," that is, efforts by leaders to thwart corruption investigations involving staff of their own agencies.[143] As anti-corruption agencies have found out, corrupt officials often escape investigation and persecution thanks to the shelter offered by local leaders. In some major corruption cases that involved high-ranking officials, special investigative groups from the central government had to be formed in order to avoid local resistance and lack of cooperation.[144] With the administrative system set up so that vertical and horizontal leaderships are often at odds, even anti-corruption agencies find it hard to investigate corruption at lower levels of government. The goals of effectively controlling corruption remain as elusive today as twenty years ago, when the CCP launched the ambitious reform programs.

CHAPTER SEVEN

Conclusion

I started out with the general assertion that we cannot possibly under-stand adequately many central aspects of official corruption in Communist polities merely by looking into the phenomena themselves. A cogent explanatory thesis has to come from an analysis of the broader social and political context in which corruption occurs. I have focused on the regime organization, which has greatly shaped the course of development of Chinese history in the last half a century and more. One of the fundamental causes of official deviance, including corruption, has been the changes in the organization's capability to maintain com-mitted, coherent, and deployable cadres over the fifty years since the CCP came to power. Such changes are described as a process of organi-zational involution, which has had a profound impact on the attitudes and behavior of the elite.

Ultimately, I regard the regime organization as an institution that, through an intentional or unintentional creation of values and norms, exerts influence by imposing incentives and constraints on individual cadres. Official deviance is, then, an outcome of choices made by indi-viduals acting within certain structurally provided confines, though it may be referred to and judged by the organization as deviant and aber-rant. What I have tried to suggest in this study of organizational devel-opment and official deviance is one possible, but not necessarily sole, cause of official corruption in a Communist regime. Asserting a possible causation does not mean that other sufficient causes cannot exist beside it. When I claim that the roots of cadre corruption in post-1949 China lie in the organizational involution of the ruling party, I do not intend to exclude every other possibility with regard to the causal relationship asserted here. In the course of five decades of Communist rule, as I acknowledge, corruption did tend to occur when a combination of factors were at work.

Rather than diagnosing corruption as a malaise of a transitional society, present when an imperfect market dictates the behavior of officials with redistributive power, I show that corruption in the PRC under its Communist regime resulted from policies, institutions, and norms underlain by a process of involutionary development of the regime organization; this development was due largely to its failure to adapt to a changing environment in the post-revolutionary period. As I stated at the outset of this study, this is not a narrowly defined corruption study per se. It is meant also to address—through the analysis of changing patterns of elite corruption in the PRC since 1949—some of the broader issues of theoretical significance. In my discussions of official corruption, some general themes have also emerged: the developmental trajectory of the post-revolution Chinese party/state, the dynamics between leaders and staff in a Communist regime, the changing role of the state in market reforms, and a characterization of the contemporary Chinese administrative elite.

Organizational Involution of a Revolutionary Party

Although official corruption in China has taken on various patterns and had various sorts of causes in different periods, one underlying cause can be charted throughout the five decades of political development in the PRC—an involution of the regime organization and its officialdom.

Building upon the pioneering contribution of Kenneth Jowitt on Communist neotraditionalism and the efforts on the part of China scholars to re-examine the state-building process, I propose the thesis of organizational involution of the Chinese Communist regime, which has affected the behavior of officials and of the party/state capacity of control over its agents. I suggest that:

1. The failure of the state to transform Chinese society or the persistence of societal values is not necessarily what has caused the involutionary development; it may have arisen from the institutions, policies, and norms the regime has adopted.

2. These new institutions, policies, and norms, which were intended to create a new type of "socialist man," have prompted cadres, as well as ordinary citizens, to seek effective coping strategies. They have formulated a set of informal rules of the game that deviate from, and sometimes are distinct from, those of the official order.

3. Involution is not predetermined for a political regime. Many unintended consequences have been at work. As an analytical type, it indicates a distinctive developmental path.

4. Involution is not a static feature of any given regime but a dynamic process. It happens when a revolutionary movement refuses to become bureaucratized and yet is unable to continue to integrate the organization by means of revolutionary modes such as mass mobilization, core-task creation, moral inspiration, and ideological indoctrination. However, involution's features and effects become salient and prevalent only when there is an attempt to depoliticize and modernize the administrative apparatus (i.e., denunciation of revolutionary modes, and the installation of modern rational-legal institutions, rules and procedures). Official deviance, which has always been present, became qualitatively more perverse and quantitatively more pervasive.

The post-revolutionary regime organization in China did not evolve into the Weberian image of modern bureaucracy, even after the end of the Maoist "institutionalized revolution."[1] Instead, it embarked on an involutionary path. While each stage of this development shared some common denominators with others, they had their distinctive characteristics—a particular example being the unintended consequences of the leadership's strategic choices apropos cadre behavior. Clearly, the issue of regime building—or of solving the problem of the "bureaucratic dilemma," as Harry Harding phrases it—has been always a priority in the agenda of the CCP leadership.[2] Nevertheless, the history of the past five decades indicates that the problem is far from solved. The Chinese Communist leadership has resorted to two basic approaches to addressing the question of organization building and the maintenance of the cadre corps: politicization and depoliticization of the bureaucracy (but not bureaucratization). These methods represent two different goals of organizational development at different times—continuous revolution and modernization. The politicization method during the Maoist period failed because the regime, guided by a Maoist understanding of the bureaucratic problem, failed to meet the challenge of post-revolutionary routinization of a revolutionary movement and negatively affected its organizational integrity.[3] The Communist "deployable agents" depicted by Selznick, who wanted but could not obtain security and were subjected to arbitrary "virtuocratic" criteria by their superiors, turned into "uncontrollable principals" operating within their own "independent kingdoms" with resources that were more political than economic. The revolutionary impulse of politicization of the bureaucracy had an impact mostly under the radical Maoist leadership, which demanded simultaneously a revolutionary transformation of social relations and the people's consciousness as well as rapid economic development. As this study shows, the beginning of organizational involution of the CCP can be traced back to the Anti-Rightist Campaign and the Great Leap Forward, when the politicization of the cadre ranks began to affect how officials operated. Later, Maoist attempts to solve the "problem of bureaucracy" and to avert the danger of what was perceived as degeneration of the party caused by bureaucratization reached their peak in the Cultural Revolution. However, not only did involution fail to be thwarted, it actually accelerated in the early years following the chaos and became entrenched. The anti-bureaucratization impulse has not, as some China scholars argued, inhibited the dissociation of a professional vocational ethic from the Maoist political ethic or forestalled the stratification of a bureaucratic elite separated from the masses.[4]

The depoliticization approach adopted in the post-Mao era has yet to produce fundamental changes in re-integrating the party/state organization, mainly because, instead of formulating a new organizational integrity à la Weberian bureaucratization, the regime has mainly attempted to depoliticize the overly ideology-driven process of cadre selection and to restructure administrative institutions. There have been some efforts to establish a civil service system, converting state officials—but not party cadres—into civil servants who are expected to uphold high professional standards but whose political allegiance to the party is not to be changed. To be sure, this institutionalization and bureaucratization thrust gained momentum in the post-Mao transition and has become increasingly dominant in the strategic choices of the leadership. Conscious efforts have been made to improve the rule of law and to make public officials more accountable. Laws, administrative rules, and other procedures have been promulgated in the last two decades or so. However, many existing modes of operation among officials that originated in the Maoist era and are at odds with the organizational ethos desired by the regime (such as statistical fabrications, small coffers of off-budget revenue, formalism, and *guanxi* networks) remain prevalent among public officials, as has been the case in other former Communist officialdoms undergoing post-Communist transition.[5] It is in this sense that we speak of a continuation of an organizational involution in the regime that has substantially *grown* (in number of formal rules, structures, and size) but only marginally *developed* (in its capacity to maintain committed and effective agents and assure the organization's stability and efficiency).

The organizational involution of the Communist party is a historical development. But it is not the simple recurrent phenomenon in Chinese history that some scholars have asserted it is,[6] nor is it a sociological pattern embedded in Chinese culture.[7] Rather, it is a novel, generic process of its own. Such a development reveals the tension and conflict among different modes of relations and authority within and without the party organization, between formal institutions (policies, ideological doctrines, organizational rules, etc.) and informal modes of operation. The consequences of organizational involution suggest that neotraditional modes continue to dominate. It is important to make this distinction because involution seen as a consequence of cultural embeddedness (as in some scholarship) implies the inability and failure of the Communist regime to transform old relationships, whereas my argument is that the new institutions, policies, and norms have played a major role in motivating cadres to pursue neotraditional modes of action. In the Maoist era, it was precisely the conscious choice of anti-routinization and anti-bureaucratization strategies, purported to fulfill the goal of "continuous revolution" under socialism, that was responsible for the involution. The cadres' resistance to revolutionary integrative instruments (doctrines, discipline, rules, etc.) and the leadership's rejection of bureaucratic routinization did not stem merely from the extra-organizational cultural patterns of society. It was also, and mainly, a paradox that the

regime created for itself, that is, these new institutions and norms reinforced traditional patterns rather than sustaining norms of a new type.
In addition, revolutionary values were too precarious to successfully
transcend, transform, or, more important, maintain the rank and file as
loyal and deployable agents. This pattern of involution has not produced "party technocrats" who are procedural- and rule-oriented,[8] but
rather neotraditional quasi-bureaucrats[9] who approximate pre-revolution local officials. They have failed to put the interests of the regime
above those of more intimate secondary and primary groups. In this
way, corruption by officials became a routine phenomenon.

The Chinese Communist movement, which began as a revolutionary movement prized as an "organizational weapon," never was of a
purely charismatic type. It included what Jowitt calls an "amalgam" of
charismatic, traditional, and even modern features. From the very outset, as my discussion of the Yan'an production campaign shows, the
revolutionary characteristics of the Chinese Communist party were
challenged from within. Economic considerations of surviving in a
backward and hostile environment during wartime played a significant role in the CCP's organizational development, making it susceptible to mundane and ordinary influences by society despite its purported "extraordinary" qualities. The rectification and anti-corruption
campaigns of this period reflected the determination of the party leadership to fight off traditional-based tendencies such as factionalism,
cronyism, and patronage as well as rational-based individualism and
materialism within the party in order to build a more effective organization. Even before the Communist victory in 1949, the task of maintaining a revolutionary Communist organization was already a formidable one.

In the past half century, there have been numerous theories of
Communist politics, some of which were adopted by students of contemporary China. The once-dominant totalitarian theory gave way to
more sophisticated neo-Weberian "devolutionary" theories, which predicted that, inevitably, the "extraordinary" quality of revolutionary
movements would be transformed into "ordinary" traditional or rational
ordering.[10] Whereas early writings along this line hypothesized a future
bureaucratization of revolutionary regimes,[11] more recent scholarship,

represented by the theory of neotraditionalism,[12] emphasizes the other "ordinary" path—a routinization toward traditional patterns. More and more scholars in comparative communism, especially China scholars, look back to pre-revolutionary politics and society for possible explanations of the seemingly failed revolution. Some see the continuity of traditional relations and forms as highlighting the recurring patterns that were similar to pre-revolution China,[13] while others argue that the "traditional orientations are in fact *re-created* in the present, not despite the new institutions but because of them."[14] Both views have merit. Still, we have much to learn about the nature and change of Chinese regime-building[15] over the past fifty years.

The involutionary change of the Chinese Communist party testifies to the failure of both the totalitarian and modernization (convergence) arguments to account for the demise of Communist regimes. My analysis also rejects the argument of cultural relativists who see the past decades of Communist rule as nothing but another cycle in the long turbulent history of Confucian China. To them, change is more superficial than substantial, and continuity more essential than nominal.

In the discourse on continuity between the pre- and post-revolutionary politico-economic structures, the power of the administrative elite occupies a central place. A great deal has been written about the resemblance of the Communist cadres to the traditional gentry elite.[16] There are indeed many striking continuities shown by these works. However, as Philip Huang correctly points out, "the discontinuities are even more striking . . . in both theory and practice."[17] These discontinuities are not merely quantitative, as reflected in the ever-expanding organizations of the Communist party/state. They are also qualitative.

Others portray continuities that show "surprisingly little has changed in human relations and understanding in spite of the war against landlords, private property, and the market, in spite of mass campaigns and catastrophes."[18] The reason they suggest for lack of change is that

> the irrationality and experienced immorality of certain state actions led villagers to turn ever more to traditional norms and forms. . . . An unintended consequence of the state's war on village culture and the peasant household economy was that villagers, expropriated of so much they

treasured, clung more tightly to surviving, virtually sacred, household resources, from home to the lineage to the marriage bond. These embattled traditions burrowed deeper . . . families turned inward to preserve what they cherished.[19]

This apt observation on why involution took place is in line with arguments made here in this study. My subjects are not villages and peasants, however, but the party organization and cadres.

Cadre Corruption in Post-1949 China

Many have assumed that China's profound economic reforms and limited political liberalization have increased the opportunities for cadre corruption. Much of the scholarship on corruption in the PRC deals solely with the post-Mao period, implying that corruption is a problem associated with the reforms and rapid economic changes.[20] However, as our inquiry shows, it had existed long before the post-Mao reforms began in the late 1970s, albeit in different forms. Thus, the advent of the market and the reform of China's administrative structures are not the fundamental causes of cadre corruption. Does this statement mean, then, in the words of some scholars, that "neither corruption nor patrimonialism is more prevalent in post-Mao China than it was during previous decades"?[21] It is true that corruption by cadres existed in the Maoist era. It is also true that the characteristics of Communist organization created the extensive networks of informal relationships and operational modes from which corruption derives. However, corruption, even informal relationships, has manifested itself in different forms and has been affected by various factors at given times over the last fifty years. Although it is nearly impossible to quantify, it seems fair to suggest that corruption in the post-Mao period (especially in its economic form) is more pervasive, serious, and regime-threatening than in previous periods. In this study, I have examined official deviance in different historical periods after the CCP became the ruling party in 1949. In each of these periods, official deviance and corruption occurred due to a set of short-term and long-term factors. There were, however, some consistent and salient patterns of corruption in PRC history that warrant our attention.

First, official deviance and corruption have taken place at both the individual and the unit level. In the social science literature on corruption, the focus tends to be on illicit action by individuals. This study shows, however, that both in the early period of the People's Republic and in the reform period, Chinese public units have frequently engaged in illicit practices. These practices had much to do with the *danwei* system, which grew out of the communist wartime institutions of free supply and self-sufficient production by units.

It is not readily clear whether corruption by a public unit such as a government agency or an enterprise in the state sector is uniquely Chinese. More research is needed to learn whether a similar phenomenon exists in other countries. What is clear, though, is that organizational corruption is different from both the individual and the collective corruption defined in Chinese legal codes.[22] The latter are conducted by a collusion of individuals from various government agencies or public organizations, or from inside one unit (but not aimed at enhancing the benefits of all members of the unit). This pattern is not uncommon in developing countries.[23]

Second, from the trajectory of corruption in China in the last fifty years or so, we can identify two distinctive types of corruption: *nonstructural* and *structural*. The non-structural category is found in all societies and examples of it can be clearly defined as "illegal" and "criminal"—mainly in the form of graft: embezzlement, extortion, bribery, and so on. Structural corruption, on the other hand, arises from certain political and economic structures. Existing studies of corruption in the Chinese and similar systems often do not distinguish between these two types. But most significant, they ignore seemingly marginal and less rigorously (i.e., legally) defined cases that have been described as "deviance," "irregularity," "impropriety," "malfeasance," "misconduct," "malpractice," or "violation of discipline." This last category typifies the corruption problem in Communist regimes in general. The conceptualization of corruption, as I have suggested early in this book, has to be broadened to include these forms. While the prevention of non-structural corruption may not require structural changes, the prevention and elimination of structural corruption do entail structural reforms. For this reason alone, it is difficult to root out structural corruption without making changes in the broader political and economic systems.[24]

Besides the *conception* of corruption, there is also the issue of *perception* of corruption. In China, corruption is perceived in very broad terms. A wide range of behaviors belong to what I call "official deviance." They may or may not be defined as corruption in other systems. The boundaries of perception of corruption are pertinent to the boundaries of the public sphere. Like all other Communist states, the public (i.e., official) sphere in China is very large. It embodies an enormous number of state agents known as cadres. The state, through its agents, controls and allocates large quantities of political and economic resources. It is thus no surprise that China has constant problems of waste and squandered public funds, and that using public funds for wining and dining has been one of the most pervasive forms of official deviance, much of which falls into the category of structural corruption.

Third, a notable pattern of corruption in post-1949 China is the *auto-corruption* type of illicit action, a category that includes both rent-seeking by public officials and prebendalism such as embezzlement, misappropriation, malfeasance, privilege, and extortion, as opposed to the *transaction* (bribery) type, which usually involves two or more parties. Auto-corruption is particularly a feature of the pre-reform periods. It is typically found in non-market systems, where transactional exchanges are minimal. In non-market systems, the rule of the game is "power for money," whereas in market systems corruption is common in transactional types and the rule of the game is "money for power." In acts of auto-corruption, attainment of materials and monetary gains is not determined by the market but by power and status. The power of office is what ultimately tips the balance.

Fourth, corruption is not an isolated phenomenon. In an involutionary polity, corruption is closely related to the involution of relational patterns and the operational modes of the organizational and social environment. The phenomenon of "official inbreeding" in Chinese urban units, the reemergence of lineage organizations in rural villages (sometimes led by party members), the entrenched *guanxi* networks, and, most recently, the penetration of the regime organization by cult-like groups demonstrate how the regime has involuted into a polity dominated by neotraditional patterns. These patterns not only provide channels and mechanisms for political and economic corruption, they themselves are corrupt actions that deviate from officially prescribed norms.[25] In this sense, what China has been experiencing is a continuation of what James Scott has called the "parochial" form of corruption, commonly found in third world developing countries where ties of kinship, affection, and personal connections determine access to the favors of power-holders.[26] At the same time, with increasing market dominance of the PRC's economy, China in recent years has been confronted with more "market" forms of corruption, which, according to Scott, are characterized by an impersonal process whereby influence is accorded those who can "pay" the most, regardless of who they are. The increasing official rent-seeking form of corruption is a reflection of this development. The dominant pattern, though, still remains a parochial one.

Finally, the existence of auto-corruption does not mean there has been no transaction type of corruption. In China under state socialism, there were more subtle forms of bribery, one of which was wheeling and dealing in which one side gave bribes and the other accepted them, especially in the post-Mao reform period. The reforms since 1979 have opened up more opportunities for corruption. Besides longstanding forms of auto-corruption, there has been a growth in transaction-type corruption. However, what makes the pattern of corruption in contemporary China different from those commonly found in mature market systems are the prevailing personal networks in which the transactions, reciprocal and instrumental, are established.

Chinese Corruption in Comparative Perspective

Is the organizational involution of China's ruling party unique? How common are the Chinese patterns of official corruption? Some brief comparisons can be made between corruption in China and that in former Communist regimes, developing countries, and traditional Chinese societies. Despite the many idiosyncrasies that are result of each country's past, striking similarities in patterns of official deviance, including corruption, exist (or existed) in all of these societies. One can point to the patterns of corruption, prevalent informal relations and strategies, and "feudalization" of apparatchiks to argue that similar involution processes may have taken place in other former Communist regimes.

REGARDING CORRUPTION

Corruption under a command economic system was understood in all Communist regimes to occur "in the conditions of growing bureaucracy, when bureaucrats are out of touch with the people and are changing into [a] privileged section which is above the masses."[27] However, the official Chinese understanding of corruption and bureaucracy is somewhat different from that of the Soviets, who viewed the bureaucratic problem as neither a political threat nor a subject of social science discourse but an *administrative illness*, in the same category as other such illnesses: "sectarianism," "careerism," "formalism," and "excessive centralism."[28] In the Soviet Union and Romania, as in China, the term "bureaucrat" (in Russian *biurokratii*, Romanian *birocraţie*, in Chinese *guanliao*) in official use is usually an epithet denoting the political pathology called "bureaucratism" (in Romanian *birocratismul*, in Chinese *guanliao zhuyi*). Popular understanding of bureaucracy was that it is something inefficient and inflexible, out of touch with, and unable to solve, problems in reality. It would not come as a surprise that a Romanian émigré marvels at how *little bureaucracy there is* in Switzerland and how bureaucratic it was in Romania under communism, so much so that he had to use personal relations to achieve the most mundane goals.[29] To Romanians before the fall of the Ceausescu regime, as to the Chinese, the notion of an efficient and reliable Weberian type of bureaucracy seemed to be hopelessly contradictory. An interesting question, therefore, is whether Romania was an oppressive bureaucratic Leviathan as people, including some scholars, believed. Even today, with the repressive Communist regime under Ceausescu long gone, such a question remains valid for a better understanding of a society before and after the collapse of the former regime. It seems clear that Romania and other Communist regimes in Eastern Europe were not *bureaucratic* in the Weberian sense, and official deviance and other informal social relations were fostered and became overwhelming essentially because of what some scholars call "*de*bureau-cratization,"[30] a situation described as "neotraditionalization" by Jowitt.

INFORMAL RELATIONS AND STRATEGIES

Informal relations and modes of operation were common in the former Communist regimes in Eastern Europe and the Soviet Union. For example, playing to a superior's liking with a demonstration of performance, even if it meant to cheat, was unavoidable for those who wanted to enter and climb the cadre hierarchy. In Hungary, such an informal strategy was known as *cigánykodás*—worming oneself into the good graces of the leadership through ingratiation, double-facedness, betraying fellow workers, and fabricating. It was prevalent in the Hungarian countryside in the 1950–80 era.[31] In the Soviet Union, the equivalent of the Chinese practice of *fukua*, a form of malfeasance under a centralized planned economy known as *pripiski*, or falsified reporting and statistics padding, was commonplace.[32] As in the PRC, in the Soviet Union where there were economic and social-engineering plans, there were extra-plan activities; where there were formal policies (*zhengce*) from the top down, there were informal countermeasures (*duice*) and distortions from the bottom up. Studies of the Soviet bureaucracy found that there were two separate worlds of elite belief and behavior. In a psychological study of Soviet corruption, Jeffrey Klugman noted that on the one hand there was a lack of psychological autonomy among the elite and a dependent, controlling relationship between the regime and its cadres that echoed the pattern of parental discipline via withdrawal of "goodies";[33] on the other hand, the individual had "a role and self-identity in official Russia, but also a hidden unofficial existence and identity."[34] Such a split between "official individuality" institutionalized via medals and titles, and the private person, who experienced "inner emigration" invisible to the state, characterizes the failure of the Communist goal of producing "the New Soviet Man," whose private world would have been absorbed by the public, and where "elite membership ideally enlists the whole of a person's identity."[35]

In almost all the studies of Communist regimes, the bureaucratization of these societies is taken at face value, as if the very presence of large-scale Communist organizations is proof that socialist societies actually function bureaucratically.[36] In the late years of the Communist regimes in Eastern Europe and Russia, as in post-Mao China, there was no lack of formal "bureaucratization" of the system in terms of the laws and institutions that were in place. In all these countries, "socialist legality" was very much a façade of everyday life. Just as in China, a variety of control and disciplinary mechanisms were supposed to eliminate administrative malfeasance and corruption. In the Soviet Union, there were no less than half a dozen control and discipline-monitoring organs, both of the state and the party, in the form of a ministry or commission, at any given time.[37] In Hungary, even at the grassroots level, there were control committees, disciplinary committees, and complaint and grievance committees, all of which were powerful bodies. Local officials often manipulated the committees by nominating and appointing their protégés or simply ignoring the rulings of the committees.[38] As one Hungarian farmer who commented on the local disciplinary committee put it, it was merely a "formality," that "they baptize it so it will have a name."[39]

Yet alongside this ostensibly bureaucratic façade there existed throughout Eastern Europe unmistakable evidence of personalistic, anti-bureaucratic forms of social organization. As Steven Sampson noted, "the paradox of Eastern Europe is this remarkable coexistence of rigid, bureaucratic structure with flexible, personalistic social relations."[40] How do we account for the presence of so much non-bureaucratic behavior in societies that appear to be so bureaucratized? The answers do not lie in the informal ways to "fill gaps" that inefficient bureaucracy could not handle,[41] nor was it in an inheritance from the peasant past's resistance to modernizing forces, as the Communist regimes once suggested. The answer is very close to the argument Sampson offered: "Instead of creeping bureaucratization, there is a creeping 'Georgianization' of Soviet-type societies in which friends, networks, patrons and payments are facts of life for both the ordinary citizen and the elite."[42] The Georgianization—what Jowitt called neotraditionalization—was a result of the organizational involution of the ruling Communist parties.

FROM APPARATCHIKS TO ENTREPRENEURCHIKS

In countries like Poland and Hungary, where private enterprises were drastically limited but not totally abolished, reforms of the administrative system often resulted in reductions in the number of apparatchiks and other administrative personnel in state agencies, who later became entrepreneurs. This process happened in Poland as early as the late 1950s.[43] The party quietly supported such new careers, partly because it helped to reduce the discontent of the apparatchiks who had lost their jobs.[44] The phenomenon of much larger-scale, "revolving door" style government officials getting into business came later in the 1970s in Poland. More profound, though, were the privileges enjoyed by elites while they were in office. The decade of the 1970s saw a "feudalization" of the system (i.e., prebendalism); power was a direct source of wealth and prizes, and booty and tribute were given in kind. In a system that some scholars called "legalized corruption," a network of internal hospitals, clinics, health resorts, better housing, and special shops was available only to the circles of officials.[45] The 1980 Solidarity strikes helped to put an end to this system of privileges. The reforms implemented thereafter changed the patterns of corrupt practices of the Polish apparatchiks. Under the officially endorsed slogan "Enrichissez-vous!" there appeared in Poland a new phenomenon of "the endowment of the nomenklatura": the nomenklatura assumed positions in newly established semi-private companies that were created by state agencies, taking advantage of liberal policies toward private business.[46] For example, a company called Agrotechnika was established by the Peasant Youth Union, which held a majority of the shares. The rest of the shares belonged to leaders of the union. In such companies, officials-turned-business executives extensively used their personal connections with political power, which they had cultivated previously, and took advantage of having overlapping personnel with state agencies. Another common practice was to place state/party officials on boards of trustees of companies. Even after the collapse of the Communist regimes, many people in these countries still feel at a disadvantage with bureaucrats-turned-entrepreneurs because of their unequal access to the bureaucracy. In Moscow, disgraced officials from the old regime—

known as *korruptsia*—have become power brokers again, thanks to their contacts and experiences in the old government.[47]

In Vietnam, where the private sector was insignificant before the reforms, which remarkably resemble the Chinese reforms since the mid-1980s, the "commercialization" of party/state apparachiks came much later. In Vietnam, a country under slow and controlled transition to a "socialist market economy," corruption resembles that in China. There seems to have been a similar organizational involution of the ruling Communist party, which, according to a Vietnamese, "is like a box: It looks impressive from the outside, makes a good sound if you tap it. But if you open the lid, you'll see there is nothing inside."[48] As one long-time observer of Vietnamese reforms points out, the country has not so much gone from plan to market, but from plan to clan.[49] As in China, under the rule of an involuted party organization, public office became a source of benefits not only for the cadre him- or herself, but for all the relatives. Here, too, organizational corruption found its best breeding ground in a regime under the market reforms. Vietnamese military, police, and other law enforcement agencies also grabbed the opportunities afforded by the reforms to enter lucrative business. For instance, the army operated 35 joint ventures with more than $335 million of foreign investment by the end of 1996. The Interior Ministry earns money from a number of businesses, including a $500 million joint venture with a Taiwanese firm to build a hotel and office building on the site of a Ho Chi Minh City jail that once housed political prisoners.[50]

Before the worldwide Communist regime transition took place, there had been a popular assumption that once the market was in force and the central planning mechanisms dismantled, the power and careers of the gigantic corps of Communist cadres would be seriously threatened and thus strong resistance to any transformation should be expected. But that has not quite been the case. In almost all the Communist countries under transition, public officials quickly adapted to the new incipient capitalism. By the time the transition began, the officialdom in these countries had been transformed from revolutionary cadres to "feudal nobles" enjoying a "legitimized corruption" of privileges. They were soon to become "new-age entrepreneurs," empowered with pre-transition connections and privileges. Many found themselves in the market with experience of being insiders with extensive government contacts. Some took state agencies with them, transforming them into independent "corporations." Others ended up on the boards of private companies.[51] People have realized that corruption could not be eliminated even after regime change because there still remains a "corruption mentality"—values, attitudes, and patterns of behavior developed and consolidated during the long years of Communist rule. The core of human relations in the Communist regime—disregard for law, amoral familialism, suspicious and hostile attitudes toward official institutions, the continuation of nepotism, favoritism, patron-client relationships, and "dirty friendships"—has outlived the conditions and factors that had nurtured it. Feudalization continues in many of the post-Communist polities.[52]

CORRUPTION IN DEVELOPING COUNTRIES

The organizational involution thesis also shares many concerns and assumptions of the neo-patrimonialism model that dominates studies of political corruption in third world countries. In the neo-patrimonialist framework, politics in third world countries is highlighted by "the privatization of public affairs," where corruption defines daily practice.[53] Pre-modern forms of organization, it has been argued, may survive into the modern era even though the traditionalist legitimation that once underpinned them is disintegrating. Patrimonialism is one such form.[54] To some extent, a common denominator both in developing countries and in former Communist societies is that patrimonialism in its modern form has been encouraged by the expansion of state activity in the economy whether capitalist and socialist. One of the significant aspects of the patrimonial state is the close link between office and economic benefits for the office holder—the prevailing prebendalism. In an involuted organization such as the Chinese Communist party, prebendalism, which is called in Chinese *guan ben wei*, has been a major form of corruption, as it had been in the pre-revolution imperial Chinese state. In many third world states, one such being Nigeria, offices of the state are used for the "personal benefit of office-holders as well as their reference or support groups . . . [while the] statutory purposes of such offices become a matter of secondary concern."[55] An important pattern of corruption shared by both Communist and third world regimes is the *self-enrichment* of incumbents of offices, including the rather unusual phenomenon of the "collective endowment" of bureaucrats in Communist regimes.[56] This feature sets them apart from the "market" type of corruption often found in developed capitalist countries, where politicians or bureaucrats—most likely the former— are engaged in *reciprocal* corrupt exchange with people in the private sector.[57] As I pointed out earlier in this study, auto-corruption is a significant form of illicit action by officials in developing and Communist regimes, rather than a transactional type of corruption.

Despite the similarities, there are also significant differences between the Chinese regime and third world states. While both share some generic features of what Myrdal called "soft states," which have "a general lack of social discipline . . . signified by deficiencies in their legislation and, in particular, in law observance and enforcement, lack of obedience to rules and directives handed down to public officials on various levels,"[58] societal forces in developing countries permeate and influence public administration rather than the other way around. In these countries, the political game consists primarily of a struggle among various social forces for control of the state apparatus and for the resources that this control will yield. This activity, in its extreme forms, can result in virtual privatization of the state by powerful elite factions.[59] The continued importance of ethnic and other primordial attachments gives further thrust to the desire for personal intervention in dealing with public servants. In these societies, personalism survives from earlier modes of social organization based on kinship, clan, and the like.

In China, the neotraditional officialdom is a result of organizational change rather than any simple continuity of the *ancien régime*. The Chinese Communist party, like other Communist regimes, had once built a coherent revolutionary organization with a distinctive ethos, discipline, and capacity. The party afforded a small group of core leaders the "organizational weapon" it needed to win the "revolutionary breakthrough."[60] Administrative elites in many developing countries, as "Westernized" and "modern" as their administrative institutions supposedly were, have never fully integrated relations of legal-rational authority and have been permeated by fragmented social and ethnic groups. Robert Price described this situation as a *malintegration* of bureaucracy, and he argues that it is the cause of corruption in these countries.[61] In Communist countries, a *disintegration* occurred—a formerly strong organization became weakened not because of threats from outside but threats from inside. In other words, the state in developing countries is "soft" because it is captured by strong societal forces, whereas the Communist state became "soft" because it has been captured by its own agents, who distort policies and resist control from above.[62] This distinction is also why the focus of attention in this study has been regime organization, where the forces of involution are generated from within. Lenin created and strengthened the party organization in order to fence off corrupt influence from the masses. The party was intended to be an organization of the virtuous. In the case of the former Soviet Union, Gorbachev realized that the source of corruption was the party itself, and that the "virtuous" had become so corrupt that they could not reform themselves in good time. In the end, this corruption brought about the collapse of the Soviet system and the rise of an even more corrupt transitional regime.

In countries in which a powerful state dominates society and regulates a vast scope of socioeconomic life, corruption usually takes place at the stage at which policies are implemented, rather than at the policy-making stage as in many Western democracies. Robin Theobald, in his analysis of corruption in both developed and underdeveloped societies, likens the formal structure of modern bureaucracy to a "steel net." Like a steel net, the flexibility and durability of modern bureaucracy vary over time. The lower down the bureaucratic hierarchy one travels, the less scope there is for personal innovation, for any private appropriation of formal procedures and resources; the higher one ascends, on the other hand, the weaker the constricting power of the net, as organizational roles demand and allow greater flexibility. Thus, in industrialized societies, corruption occurs more often and is more salient at a higher level of the hierarchy.[63] Bureaucracy in China has shown itself to be a "bamboo stick," the flexibility and durability of which also varies, but in an exactly opposite way: the farther from the top, the more flexible it becomes and the more discretion local officials have; the closer to the top, the more rigid it is, and the tighter the supervision and control.

THE TRADITIONAL ADMINISTRATIVE ELITE

Since one of the defining aspects of organizational involution is the reinforcement of pre-existing modes, it is worthwhile discussing the traditional Chinese elite. In the traditional Chinese administrative system, there were two types of administrative staff belonging to a broadly defined "officialdom": appointed officials, or *guan*, who had passed formal examinations and were selected by the imperial court, and hired clerks and runners, or *li*, underlings who worked in the local administration, the *yamen*. The former, selected and appointed by the emperor, were well trained in Confucian ethics and administration. They were assigned to places other than their home towns by the law of avoidance, and thus they often had to depend on the *li*—who were from the local area and whose families had for generations kept up close relations with the *yamen*—to manage routine affairs and deal with powerful local gentry. It was the *li*, large in number and often more powerful than appointed officials in local affairs, who became the "pivot between the state and people."[64] They were often beyond the control of the ruler and were frequently accused of being corrupt and "unclean" (*wuli*).

Local administrations suffered constantly from financial and political squeezes by the imperial court and powerful local private interests. The central government demanded tax revenues from the localities, and local gentry often deprived the local administrators of adequate income by refusing to pay or scheming to get off taxes. Tensions had long existed. As John Watt shows, by the end of the Ming dynasty the magistrate found himself at the center of the tangled conflict between the public and the private.[65] As an official he had been accepted into the exclusive public sphere and also had been appointed its chief representative in the private domain.

One generic feature of patrimonial bureaucracy, according to Weber, was the lack of a clear delineation between public and private: officials took public office as their private domain. This was certainly the case in imperial China, one reason being the relatively low salaries of local officials. Local officials had to pay out of their own pocket to hire runners and clerks, who were an indispensable part of the administration. In other words, running a magistrate's *yamen* was like running a family business. According to a study of salaries and expenditures of local magistrates in the Qing dynasty, hiring an administrative assistant required several hundred taels per year from a magistrate whose regular salary from the central government before the Yongzheng reform was 45 taels.[66] In addition, miscellaneous runners and clerks working for the county *yamen* received insubstantial subsidies, hardly enough for food. They had their own ways of making money—extorting and imposing levies on peasants and squeezing magistrates for various services. They charged, when a newly appointed magistrate arrived, first a "vicious custom" (*lougui*), a kind of payment for getting accepted by the local elite.[67] In turn, higher officials also often expected county magistrates to send them part of the illicit surcharges.[68] "Gifts" of this kind helped to shield local officials from investigation or punishment. Thus in imperial China, corruption was always linked to "venal officials and unclean clerks" (*tanguan wuli*). It is worth noting that although the latter group—the *li*—was regarded as having the lowest moral standing and social status, at the same time their jobs were sought after for their income.[69]

Tax and levy collection was a major function of traditional state agents. It was a much more limited role than that of state agents in a Communist order. Official corruption, the aspect of moral degeneration notwithstanding, was rather narrowly defined. It usually referred to embezzlement of funds and bribery, whereas much of what today would be regarded as corruption was legitimate. For example, sale of office was often invoked as an acceptable way to raise revenue when armed conflicts occurred or the revenue reserves of the central treasury were low.[70] Not only were practices such as forced donations (*juanshu*) or voluntary tributes (*baoxiao*) legitimate, they were widespread. Interestingly enough, these practices are very similar to the forced donations and levies imposed by local government agencies on units and individuals today—only the current impositions are treated as illicit and are prohibited by central as well as by local government decrees.

A host of preventive measures were adopted by the rulers to guard against corrupt behavior by officials. Of the many such institutions and methods dating from the late imperial period, three appear as most significant: the *huibi* system (law of avoidance), the local taxation reform under Emperor Yongzheng, and the censor system. The law of avoidance was designed to prevent nepotism and the use of non-official relationships to influence decisions.[71] In the Qing dynasty, specific administrative rules were put in place to prohibit some old customs among local officials. These included such offenses as offering presents to bribe or to "please" other officials and paying friendly calls on metropolitan officials at the time of receiving provincial appointments. Newly appointed officials were also not permitted to receive friendly visits from examination graduates (i.e., local gentry). After the arrival of the official, local gentry were forbidden to present themselves as his "students" or propose "clan affiliations." New officials accepting such contacts would be dismissed.[72] Transferring officials to places other than their home towns in order to prevent their building up a local following was a common practice in other patrimonial administrations, too.[73] As an instrumental institution to curb corruption in a kinship-oriented society, the law of avoidance and its actual practice were seriously limited in effectiveness.

Bringing the Staff Back In

One of the analytical focuses of this study is the conflict between the state and officialdom, between the ruling party organization and its cadres. It points to the need for recasting the conceptual dichotomy of state and society in which the interests of the state and officialdom are viewed as one and the same.[74] Recognition that the power of the state and the power of officials are not identical, in fact, flows directly from the classical tradition in political sociology, especially from Weber's distinction between the patrimonial (and charismatic) ruler and administrative staff. Under charismatic rule, according to Weber, the tension between the charismatic ruler and the staff, which embodies routinizing impulses, "takes the form of the appropriation of powers of control and of economic advantages by the followers or disciples."[75] In a patrimonial polity, however, officials and retainers who obtain office through a grant from the ruler try to protect their right to that benefice for themselves and, if possible, their descendants.[76] Weber's model of political interaction yields telling insights into power relations in reforming Communist systems.

An essential feature of a patrimonial polity is that due to the absolute power of the ruler over their lives, careers, and fortunes, the subordinate elite constantly seek to modify and dilute patrimonial rulership, a process Weber calls "appropriation."[77] Processes of appropriation are accelerated by the weak or nonexistent separation of public and private in patrimonialism. In Weber's view, the decentralized appropriation of central power gives rise to localized power structures that are rigid, inadequate to new tasks, and unamenable to reform, rationalization, or regulation. The present volume is much informed by this Weberian conceptual orientation. The predatory, corrupt behavior of state agents today resembles that of pre-revolutionary Chinese local elites, who not only were predatory vis-à-vis peasants and businesses but also encroached upon the interests of the rulers.

Since the reforms began two decades ago, there have existed two parallel and, at times contradictory, trends: a weakening in the power of the state in rural and urban localities, on the one hand, and on the other the increasing abuse of power of office by local officials. A popular analytical emphasis adopted by scholars is the role of local government vis-à-vis the center. Some contend that the reforms have led local officials to tap into their entrenched power base to thwart or distort the policies of the central government in both rural and urban sectors.[78] Others adopt a contrasting view, arguing that there is an increasingly effective penetration of local society by (central) state power that extracts resources as a result of expansion of market forces and an increasing separation of political, economic, and social authority compared to the pre-reform "honeycomb polity."[79] Still others regard the conflicts between the central and local states as a long-term problem in the PRC that still haunts the regime, particularly at the policy implementation stage.[80] In the words of one scholar, "to transfigure the revenue that should have belonged to the central treasury or enterprises into local revenue and to transfigure the expenditure of the local government into that of the central treasury or enterprise is the game local governments are good at."[81]

My findings suggest that we need to go beyond the dichotomies of both state versus society and central state versus local state and to focus on the often-overlooked distinction between party/state cadres on the one hand, and on the other the party/state, which they are supposed to represent and serve. We need to bring the *staff* back in. In addition to fiscal conflicts between the central and local states, stemming from a "cellularization" of the economy,[82] there have been growing tensions between the state and its agencies and agents, as reflected in official deviance by units and individual cadres, resulting from an involution of organization. The cellular economy, which existed long before reform, has been shown to pose obstacles to marketization, but involuted officialdom, over which the state's control has diminished, is rife with deviance, including corruption.[83] What we are witnessing is conflicts of economic interests not only between the central and local states, but also, and perhaps more important, between the state and its agencies and agents utilizing state authority to achieve ends that ultimately serve their private interests. In the post-Mao period, the capacity of the state is hampered by the non-separation or collusion of local government and local enterprises—a pivotal source of revenue for local authorities through both formal and informal ties. That is, there are two parallel trends of decentralization of state power: one *vertical*, as reflected in the center-locality relationship, which has been keenly discussed among scholars; the other *horizontal*, as manifested in the growing independence and uncontrollability of agencies and agents of the state. This latter aspect of decentralization has been overlooked, but it is closely related to irregularities and the deviance of officialdom.

To be sure, such a horizontal decentralization of power—a *deconcentration of power*—is an age-old problem in Chinese politics. It had existed long before the Communists took power. Official deviance in post-revolution China as examined in this book shows the persistence of this long-standing battle. In an effort to interpret contemporary Chinese politics via a Weberian model, Joseph Levinson captured the essence of traditional Chinese political life—a patrimonial polity characterized by a creative tension between the ruler and agents, underscoring the vital opposition of interests that has long invigorated Chinese politics.[84] The pre-revolutionary patrimonial Chinese state, personified by autocratic emperors, never ceased to struggle with officialdom. Both institutional arrangements (e.g., the law of avoidance, censor systems, taxation reforms, legalization of local tax surcharges) and ethical tenets (e.g., the indoctrination of Confucian ethics and clean-government standards) were designed to prevent deviance by officials. Officials, however, did not relish their dependence on the state and sometimes attempted to serve their own private ends.[85]

The State, Agents, and Market Reforms

The erosion of the Chinese party/state's ability to maintain a disciplined and effective administrative corps has major implications for the state in its changing role in the economy. As the Chinese state undergoes a transformation from a predominantly *redistributive* state to a *regulatory* state, the transition has thus far incurred some unintended consequences for the government. The state—"midwife of the emergent market structure"[86]—has yet to deliver a healthy baby while herself being preoccupied with other matters. The prediction that "the organizational dynamics of regulatory intervention will likely result in increased rationalization of the state bureaucracy"[87] has yet to prove itself the case. As I have shown, the ability of the party/state to control its agents has been on the decline, but the power of state agencies and agents has been rapidly enhanced. Equipped with regulatory power, but without effective institutional constraints, state agencies have tapped into the new opportunities to seek profits from the rapidly growing number of businesses and other profit or non-profit organizations. This process takes place at two levels: the department level and the individual level. When an individual is implicated in a corruption case, it may not be difficult to determine the venality of his or her action. But when government agencies or other types of public units are involved, an action is often marginal between "illegal," which entails severe sanctions, and "irregular," which is often condoned. This issue bears theoretical as well as practical implications.

On the one hand, as Karl Polanyi argued from the experience of Western industrialization, the state has "had to be constantly on the watch to ensure the free working of the system"; he adds: "the road to the free market was opened and kept by an enormous increase in continuous, centrally organized and controlled interventionism."[88] In the context of a transforming state socialist economy, the role of the state in creating and regulating markets becomes even more vital. On the other hand, neoclassical economists such as James Buchanan and Anne Krueger view the role of the state as exactly the opposite: state regulatory intervention will inevitably increase transaction costs, and, more germane to our present concern, it will increase opportunities for rent-seeking behavior.[89] In an essay on the new regulatory role of the reforming socialist state, Victor Nee observes that the qualities of a Weberian ideal-typical bureaucracy were greatly weakened in the Maoist mobilization state, which stressed the moral and ethical orientation of cadres and their leadership quality, and states that Maoist *kadijustice* proved inadequate to the new regulatory demands imposed on the state in its quest to establish regulated markets.[90] Based on what I have addressed in this volume, however, one may argue that the augmentation of state regulatory power in the marketplace may also generate incentives for officials to use their power for personal gains, entrenching vested "minor public" interests in the interface between the state and the economy, and thus intensifying neotraditional rather than legal-rational authority.[91] The process of transforming the mobilization state under state socialism into a regulatory state under market socialism—a proclaimed goal of the Chinese regime—is far from a smooth one.

Official deviance and corruption in contemporary China point to the dilemma faced by any reforming socialist state: the state needs to play an active role to create and regulate markets in order to ensure an orderly transition and maintain market order;[92] at the same time, the intervention of the state places extra burdens on already overloaded administrative budgets, pressing the state to further expand rather than reduce the size of its administrative machine, regardless of the rhetoric of "small government, big society." The PRC's haphazard, economy-only approach to political reform hitherto has not helped the matter, either. As a result, a neotraditionalized officialdom was afforded opportunities to cash in on the regulatory power and seek rents. The key to ending this quandary is perhaps not so much in the quantitative improvement of regulations—China is on a fast track to promulgate new laws and new regulatory agencies—but the building of an effective regulatory bureaucracy by facilitating a legal-rational mode of authority.

A growing body of scholarship centers on the changing capacity of the state as a consequence of the reforms. Different contentions abound concerning the role of local government in overall economic development. Whereas some stress the harmful impact of the growing fiscal discretion of local governments[93] or the policy distortions by local authorities in the foreign investment sector,[94] others are proponents of local government–led industrialization, especially in rural areas.[95] My findings suggest that in the post-Mao reform era the capacity of the state is hampered both by the growing power of local authorities and by the party/state's ineffective control over its own organizations and officialdom. These two parallel trends in the disintegration of the power of the central state have far-reaching implications in terms of the relationships between the state, society, and the market. In this study, I have highlighted the behavior of state agencies in this changing relationship.

State agencies, whether central, provincial, or local, have become more and more corporate-like, seeking to maximize their profits and turn over as little as possible to the state treasury.[96] Both corruption by state agencies and corruption by individual public officials essentially reflect the inability of the state to control its own agencies and agents. Rather than dismantling the honeycomb polity, the cellularization and feudalization that existed even before the reform have been exacerbated.

The government has attempted to reverse these trends. It took measures to reduce its intervention in routine operations of enterprises and to prohibit state agencies from extracting non-tax funds from the enterprises. However, so far results are limited. Even if the state sheds its direct control over enterprises and turns them into bona fide modern firms, as the reforms are attempting to do, the regulatory requisites of the marketplace will inevitably grant government agencies of various levels different kinds of interventionist power. The state's capacity can still be distorted when such power is abused, as the many cases of institutional corruption by state agencies indicate. Again, the unsolved question of the state (i.e., the regime organization) versus officialdom (i.e., state agents) still remains as the crux of the problem.

Technocratization, Bureaucratization, or Neotraditionalization?

What, then, is an accurate characterization of Chinese officialdom today? The reforms have brought some significant changes to the Chinese socioeconomic system and have had some enduring effects on the party/state and its agents. The Communist party has been at the forefront of these changes despite its leadership's refusal to endorse any wholesale reform of the political system. The party has made efforts to revitalize its organization after years of disruption, in order for it to meet the needs of economic development. Faced with a gigantic yet inefficient bureaucratic system, the CCP has launched some reforms in China's administrative systems such as new personnel policies, elimination of life tenure for officials, transformation of the cadre corps into a civil service (though not in the sense of being politically neutral and independent), and the downsizing of an overstaffed state apparatus and its conversion into self-financed economic entities.

It remains debatable what impact the reforms have had on regime organization and how the reforms should be interpreted. One argument suggests that the post–Cultural Revolution shift of priority to modernization and economic development has inevitably led to a technocratization (or the beginning of it) of the cadre corps, replacing revolutionaries with technocrats.[97] Echoing this view, another argument, namely the "bureaucratization" thesis, holds that "some limited but dramatic steps have been taken that reduce the level of structural bureaucratization of Chinese society." If successful, it is argued, "these reforms will make China both less bureaucratic structurally and more bureaucratic in organizational functioning."[98] The technocratization thesis takes the educational and age background of officials as primary indicators of their ability to make behavioral and attitudinal changes. The bureaucratization argument, on the other hand, places a premium on the dominant operational modes of the bureaucracy. It notes that there are two kinds of conceptualization of bureaucratization: the first is based on the scope of power, characterized by "the extension of the bureaucracy's sphere of activities and power either in its own interests or those of some of its elite";[99] the second is based on the nature of power, characterized by an organization that is operated under impersonal, rational-legal domination.[100] In fact, Weber himself noted the conceptual difference when he distinguished formal and substantive rationalities of bureaucracy. However, he assumed that, in practice, in modern societies these two aspects of bureaucratization would tend to develop together, with ever more large-scale organizations and the increasing dominance of the legal-rational form of functioning within those organizations. The Chinese experience has proven this is not always the case.[101]

My findings challenge both the technocratization and bureaucratization arguments regarding Chinese officialdom. There is little doubt that an overall increase in the educational level of public officials has occurred, yet the implications of such a trend are not readily discernible. Both arguments fail to differentiate the members of two significant strata of elite—those in leading positions in central and provincial party/state agencies versus those in leading positions in grassroots units, whose behavioral patterns may be quite different. The argument here is not so much about whether these new cohorts of cadres are better educated, technically oriented, and pragmatic. Indeed, the demographic dimension of the cadre corps has changed dramatically. However, in spite of the technocratization of personnel and rationalization of formal procedures, what characterized the change of the post-Mao cadre corps is the continuation of the dominance of neotraditional modes. The lack of a transformation of cadres remains one of the direst weaknesses of the Chinese transition, and it is exposed even more starkly by the growing obstacles the deepening market reforms now face.

In this sense, we have not seen a bureaucratization approximating the Weberian ideal type, whereas an Eisenstadtian (structural) bureaucratization continues. Nor was there a serious *de-bureaucratization*, which Eisenstadt defines as "subversion of the goals and activities of the bureaucracy in the interests of different groups with which it is in close interaction," where society has gained considerable control over bureaucracy.[102] The scope of bureaucratic power has been *changing*, but it may not necessarily be *shrinking*. As the government juggled with reducing and re-expanding state administrative agencies and staff as part of its half-hearted "political reform" in the last two decades, the capacity of the party/state to control the behavior of these agencies and individual officials has been greatly attenuated. The real effect of the recent round of downsizing that was set in motion in March 1998 under the new premier, Zhu Rongji—the seventh major administrative restructuring since 1949—remains to be seen.

The question is, what does the future hold for these cadres as markets expand and the economic systems continue to change? Can they really become Weberian bureaucrats, or are they going to be a *bureaucratic bourgeoisie*, who, according to Randall and Theobald, use political power to acquire wealth—a phenomenon that is well entrenched in the development literature?[103] Are politics and administration going to be the only routes to power and in turn to wealth, as in the Philippines in the 1960s?[104] As Hong Yung Lee has pointed out, "the historical transformation in the makeup of the ruling political elite had been accompanied by limited changes in the party-state structure, its relation to society, and its mode of operation."[105] The fact that informal modes of operation still play a significant, if not dominant, role in routine organizational politics has led us to believe that the Chinese officialdom will more likely remain neotraditional in the near future, nurtured by a "booty capitalism"—a fragmented but administratively managed market economy.[106]

CHAPTER ONE

1. Bo Yibo, *Ruogan zhongda juece* (1991), 156–57.

2. According to surveys done by Transparency International, in 1997 China was ranked the seventh most corrupt country to do business in, after Nigeria, Bolivia, Colombia, Russia, Pakistan, and Mexico. See *Economist*, March 7, 1998; *New York Times*, March 6, 1998.

3. Some scholars are more explicit in portraying corruption as a galvanizing factor in the popular demonstrations in China in 1989 and Poland in 1980. See, particularly, Perry, "Intellectuals and Tiananmen"; Shue, "China: Transition Postponed?"; Ostergaard and Petersen, "Official Profiteering and the Tian'anmen"; Yan Sun, "The Chinese Protest of 1989"; Peter Lee, "Bureaucratic Corruption"; and Tarkowski, "A Centralized System and Corruption." Others raise more questions than answers. See, e.g., Dittmer, "Tiananmen Reconsidered," 534.

4. *RMRB*, April 21, 1990.

5. Siu, *Agents and Victims in South China*, 291.

6. Kang Youwei, *Lunyu zhu*, 184–85.

7. Barker, *The Politics of Aristotle*, 373.

8. L. White, *Policies of Chaos*.

9. Etzioni-Halevy, "Exchange Material Benefits."

10. Jowitt, *New World Disorder*, 40.

11. Noonan, *Bribes*.

12. Perry Link, a specialist in Chinese literary works, commented, "*reportage* is a modern Chinese genre that falls between literary art and news report. Good reportage differs from ordinary news reporting in several ways: it is longer and more carefully written, and while it may begin from an event in the news, its author seeks to uncover aspects of social background that are more basic and enduring than the news event itself." See Liu Binyan, *People or Monster*? See also Moran, *Unofficial Histories*.

13. Friedrich, "Political Pathology," 74.

14. Scott, *Comparative Political Corruption*, 3.

15. Heidenheimer, Johnston, and LeVine, *Political Corruption*, 9.

16. Philp, "From *'Asabiya'* to Moral Aptitudes," 18.

17. Nye, "Corruption and Political Development," 416.

18. Brooks, *Corruption in American Politics and Life.*

19. R. Price, *Society and Bureaucracy*, 146–47.

20. There was also a controversial "crime of speculation" (*touji daoba*) both by individuals and public units. It was related to the once-pervasive *guandao* (official profiteering or speculation). At the height of the anti-corruption drive in 1989, the government made it a crime for public units to engage in "speculative activities to seek illegal profits for units." (See Zheng and Qi, *Lianzheng jianshe ziliao xuanbian*, 214.) However, in practice it was difficult to determine, as many legal experts pointed out, what "illegal profits" are, especially given the changing policies on marketization. A few cases of this kind were, however, actually prosecuted.

21. The title of a study by Stephen Ma—"Reform Corruption: A Discussion on China's Current Development"(1989)—indicates the tendency among authors interested in corruption to focus on a narrow frame of definitions. See also Findlay and Chiu, "Sugar Coated Bullets"; Sands, "Decentralizing an Economy"; Ostergaard and Petersen, "Official Profiteering and Tian'anmen."

22. Grossman, "The 'Second Economy.'"

23. There are, however, subtly different implications of the terms in the Chinese political context. The term *fubai* has a connotation of a serious, and likely fatal, condition of decaying. People are still nervous about using such negative terms to describe the party because of the risk of political repercussions. *Fuhua* has a narrow meaning when used to refer to a person, though it is literally a synonym of *fubai*. It usually refers to a lifestyle of conspicuous consumption and amoral behavior that is opposed to the simple and ordinary lifestyle called for by the party. *Buzheng zhifeng* and *dangfeng wenti*, on the other hand, are two euphemistic phrases used by the regime to refer to a wide range of disciplinary problems.

24. Some scholars have noted the problem of applying a narrow definition of corruption in the Chinese context. Alan Liu, for example, suggested the term "venality," instead of "corruption," to refer to malfeasance and misfeasance committed by party cadres. See Liu, "Kleptocracy on Mainland China."

25. Buchanan et al., *Toward a Theory of the Rent-Seeking Society.*

26. Root, *The Fountain of Privilege.*

27. The term "prebendal" has limited use in contemporary social science analysis. Its first general application was made by Max Weber, who discussed prebendal organization of office in patrimonial societies. In his original formulation, prebendalism was not a deviant practice, in that incumbency or control of an office entitled the holder to rents or payments for undertaking real or fictitious duties. See Weber, *From Max Weber: Essays in Sociology*, 207. Students of

contemporary African politics have also applied the term. See, for example, R. Joseph, *Democracy and Prebendal Politics*, and P. Lewis, "From Prebendalism to Predation."

28. Weber, *From Max Weber: Essays in Sociology*, 207.

29. Sampson, "Bureaucracy and Corruption," 69.

30. R. Joseph, *Democracy and Prebendal Politics*.

31. Again, the key criterion here is personal benefit from *public office*. Jean Oi made an insightful distinction between corruption and clientelism: "clientelism implies an exchange process involving a reciprocal flow of private benefits between cadres and peasants," whereas "corruption implies only a one-way flow of goods or resources." See Oi, "Market Reforms and Corruption," 225. Insofar as public office being exploited for private purposes, the two belong to the same category of official deviance.

32. Some scholars call this type of corruption "internal corruption," for it occurs within an organization, involving only public officials. Embezzlement is a typical case. See Klitgaard, *Controlling Corruption*, 20.

33. Trotsky, *The Revolution Betrayed*.

34. Ma Yanwen, "Guanliao jieji."

35. According to one prominent leader of the Red Guard movement, during the Cultural Revolution in cities throughout China a number of independent political groups appeared that wanted a new Leninist revolution in order to overthrow the bureaucratic class formed after the 1949 Communist takeover. See the interview of Yang Xiaokai, in *Zhengming*, September (1986): 62–65. For a detailed analysis of the Marxist argument of socialist bureaucratization, see the chapter by Meisner, Kraus, and Friedman, in Nee and Mozingo, *State and Society in Contemporary China*.

36. See Meyer, "Communism and Leadership"; Hirszowicz, *The Bureaucratic Leviathan*; Rogovin, "The Problems of Corruption in Soviet Society."

37. Hope, "Politics, Bureaucratic Corruption, and Maladministration," 1.

38. Chan and Unger, "Grey and Black."

39. Ji Yan, "Dangnei buzhengzhifeng suoyuan"; Xue Yin'e, "Zaitan dangnei fubai."

40. Harris, "Socialist Graft."

41. S. Ma, "Reform Corruption"; Sands, "Decentralizing an Economy."

42. Rose-Ackerman, *Corruption*; MacRae, "Underdevelopment and the Economics of Corruption"; Kiser and Tong, "Determinants of the Amount and Type of Corruption." For a general application of a principal-agent model in corruption study, see Klitggard, *Controlling Corruption*.

43. Andvig, "Why Do Corruption Rates Differ?" 53.

44. Krueger, "The Political Economy"; Bates, *Markets and States*.

45. Tilman, "Emergence of Black-Market Bureaucracy," 440.

46. Grossman, "The 'Second Economy.' "

47. Wu Jinglian, "Xunzulilun"; Hu Heli, "Lianzheng sanze"; Zhi and Yi, "Shuangguizhi ba zhongguo"; Hu Angang, *Tiaozhan zhongguo*.

48. Levi, *Of Rules and Revenue*, 24.

49. Ibid.

50. Philp, "From '*Asabiya*' to Moral Aptitudes," 18.

51. McMullan, "A Theory of Corruption"; Huntington, *Political Order*; Price, *Society and Bureaucracy*.

52. Scott, "Corruption, Machine Politics."

53. Mars and Altman, "The Cultural Bases"; Sampson, "Bureaucracy and Corruption"; Klugman, *The New Soviet Elite*; Meyer, "China: Modernization and 'Unhealthy Tendencies' "; M. Yang, "Between State and Society"; and M. Yang, "The Gift Economy."

54. Riggs, *Administration in Developing Countries*.

55. Scott, "Corruption, Machine Politics."

56. I have in mind Robert Price's study of Ghanaian bureaucratic corruption and his concept of "malintegration." See Price, *Society and Bureaucracy*.

57. A. Liu, "The Politics of Corruption," 603.

58. J. Meyer, "China: Modernization."

59. Jiang Siyi, "Suqing fengjianyidu"; Su Shaozhi, "Zhengzhi tizhi."

60. The Chinese employ a somewhat different definition and usage of "feudal" (*fengjian*) or "feudalism" (*fengjian zhuyi*) from those of the West. In the West, feudal refers to a particular type of power relationship as well as to a pre-capitalist historical period. In China, feudal has come to mean things, especially unwanted ones, which are traditional or pre-revolutionary.

61. Lin and Chen, "Suqing fengjianzhuyi"; Song, "Jianchi jitilingdao."

62. P. Lee, "Guanyu zhongguo."

63. Jowitt, "Soviet Neotraditionalism."

64. Ibid.

65. Herein lies the most significant difference between the two models of Communist neotraditionalism. Andrew Walder's neotraditional model of industrial authority offers a convincing depiction of the patterns of relationship in the Chinese workplace under the Communist regime. However, the neotraditionalism in his study differs from that of Jowitt's. The proposition that Communist neotraditionalism is a *modern* type of industrial authority (Walder, *Communist Neo-Traditionalism*, 10, emphasis in original) represents a departure from Jowitt's thesis. While both emphasize the novelty of the Communist regime, Walder's neotraditional image of relations in the Communist state/society claims only to be analytical, not historical (ibid., 9). It deals with the *nature of*, not any *change in*, Communist regimes. Jowitt's thesis is regime-centered, exploring the generic features of Leninist organization rather than its interaction with society. Studies in Chinese politics and society that were influ-

enced by Walder's thesis focus on how non-official sectors of society are affected by the state or how the state is affected by society.

66. In social sciences, "involution" has been used to refer to a changing process in which an organism facing external impingement for change turns inward and increasingly elaborates existing modes of operation and internal relationships rather than turning outward and adopting new modes. Hence in agriculture, economies in Indonesia were found to be post-traditional rather than modern as a result of involution (see Geertz, *Agricultural Involution*). Recent efforts by students of Chinese history and rural society to apply the idea of involutionary change have made valuable contributions to our understanding of Chinese rural economic development (see P. Huang, *The Peasant Family*) and the Chinese state-building process (see Duara, "State Involution"; Siu, *Agents and Victims*; Wang Shaoguang, "From Revolution to Involution"). They have adopted and refined the concept of involution to depict both "technological involution," the main concern of Geertz, and what the Potters call "sociological involution" in Chinese social history (see Potter and Potter, *China's Peasants*). The former type, as in the works of Philip Huang, is described as the "involutionary growth—without labor productivity development"—of Chinese rural economy from pre-revolutionary times up to the reform era (Huang, *The Peasant Family*). The latter, rather than depicting a discrepancy between the growth of production output and development of productivity, is applied in an analysis of the relationship between state and society in both pre- and post-1949 China. Historian Prasenjit Duara uses the concept of "state involution" to describe the state-building process in China in which state organizations expand not through the increasingly efficient use of existing or new inputs, but through the replication, expansion, and elaboration of an inherited pattern of state-society relations (Duara, "State Involution"; Siu, *Agents and Victims*). Derived from this perspective, some speak of the deepening of state penetration in local society as not being accompanied by the strengthening of central political integration (Wang Shaoguang, "From Revolution to Involution").

67. Andrew Janos calls the bureaucratization argument that views the charismatic Leninist regimes as changing from "extraordinary" to "ordinary" qualities the neo-Weberian "devolution" model. See Janos, *Politics and Paradigms*, 110–11. I have taken my cue from his term in calling such a developmental path *devolutionary*.

68. See Hong Yung Lee, *From Revolutionary Cadres*.

69. Harding used "semi-bureaucracy" to refer to a similar phenomenon. Jowitt drew an image of "undeployable party principals" when Leninist regimes became neotraditionalized. Duara used "quasi-broker" to describe the result of involutionary state-building in pre-revolutionary China. See Harding, *Organizing China*; Jowitt, "Soviet Neotraditionalism"; and Duara, "State Involution."

70. Human relation theory of organizations emerged as a critical response to Weber's ideal-typical bureaucratic rational domination in modern administrative organizations, and particularly, to rationalist theory of scientific management. This group of scholars, including Robert Merton, Elton Mayo, Alvin Gouldner, Philip Selznick, and Michel Crozier, raised the challenge that bureaucratic impersonalism may have its dysfunctional effects on organization and management. The main argument of this school is that mechanically seeking rationalization and standardization will not increase efficiency or predictability, both of which are the primary goals of modern rationality domination. On the contrary, formal organizations "never succeed in conquering the non-rational dimensions of organizational behavior," and the pressure coming from pursuit of secondary norms of impersonality and conformity will drive the primary norms of human relations within the organization to resist, with informal means, formal rules and standards, causing uncertainty and hence dysfunction. To them, "organizations become institutions as they are infused with value, that is, prized not as tools alone but as sources of direct personal gratification and vehicles of group integrity." See Selznick, *Leadership in Administration*, 5.

71. Siu, "Socialist Peddlers."

72. Bendix, *Nation-Building*.

73. It should be noted that the dialectic between the formal (*zhengshi* or *xingshi*) and the informal (*feizhengshi* or *shizhi*) is not to be simply juxtaposed onto the dichotomy between the procedural (*chengxu*) and the substantive (*neirong*). Though related and sometimes overlapping, the two sets are meaningful but are not quite in the same category: the former reflects a relationship between formal organizational structures and real social ties operating in it, while in the latter both are variants of organizational means of "rationality domination" (see Schluchter, *The Rise of Western Rationalism*). Weber has paid attention to the contradiction between procedural rationalization, which he identified with legality and modern bureaucracy, and substantive rationalization, which appears as a component of a counter- principle that disables the machine of a predictable administrative apparatus (Weber, *Economy and Society*, 811). In Weber's view, substantive rationalization produces lack of calculability and ultimately "regression." It is precisely on this ground that the post-Weberian school departed from Weber. The organizational involution thesis intends to bring back attention to the problems associated with the predominant means of substantive rationalization of Leninist organizations.

74. Schurmann, *Ideology and Organization*.

75. Jowitt has elaborated eloquently on the concept of "combat task," which, according to him, is one of the defining factors of the existence and development of Leninist movements (see Jowitt, "Soviet Neotraditionalism"; Jowitt, *New World Disorder*). Alan Liu also touched upon this issue by applying the anthropological concept of "threat-dependent institution" to analyze the

Chinese Communist party (see Liu, "Kleptocracy on Mainland China"). Continuing dependence on threat or combat even during a peaceful time of consolidation, I think, reflects the fatal weakness of revolutionary movements that refuse to adapt and transform themselves into a modern bureaucratic mode of operation. Indeed, when armed struggle no longer exists, "warfare" of some kind has to be created in order to keep cadres proficient and on constant alert. In China this warfare appeared to be numerous political campaigns with language full of fighting spirit. I will elaborate on this point in more detail elsewhere in this book.

76. Although the main empirical inquiry herein concerns the Chinese case, this study will make an effort to bring in the experience of other Leninist regimes, particularly the Soviet, via secondary literature, in order to attempt more generalized theorizing.

77. Weber, *Economy and Society.*

78. McMullan, "A Theory of Corruption."

79. Here I borrow Jowitt's useful concept, in which he separates *regime culture*—the norms and values promoted by a regime—from *community culture*—the norms and values prevailing in society. See Jowitt, "An Organizational Approach."

80. Whitaker used the term to describe a changing process of traditional society where a good deal of the structure and behavior of preexisting social systems has sustained itself in the face of penetration by Western institutional forms. See Whitaker, "A Dysrhythmic Process," and R. Price, *Society and Bureaucracy,* 207–8. Whereas Whitacker's is an image of disparity between state and society, mine is between organization and members and between form and substance.

81. Dittmer, *China's Continuous Revolution,* 266.

82. Merton, *Social Theory and Social Structure.*

83. Caiden and Caiden, "Administrative Corruption," 306.

CHAPTER TWO

1. Shortly before the final victory, the Communists had some 800,000 cadres, far short of the number needed to manage the whole nation. See Zhu, Xie, and Fan, *Zhongguo gongchandang,* 262.

2. In March 1949, the CCP Central Committee decided to adopt a policy of "retaining all useful personnel from KMT executive, judiciary, military, and police agencies." This administrative expansion created further fiscal strain on the already financially pressed new government. See ibid.

3. For example, in Tianjin, among the 93,531 cadres, 75,826 (82 percent) were retained personnel, most of them in such functional agencies as banks, trade, and enterprises. See ibid. Lieberthal, however, identified only 12,391. See

Lieberthal, *Revolution and Tradition*, 35. The larger number may reflect the broader definition of "cadres," which included all staff on the state payroll.

4. Gao Shudong, "Lun jianguo chuqi dangde ganbu tizhi," 99.

5. *RMZG* 1, no. 8 (1950).

6. Mao, *Mao Zedong xuanji*, 4: 1438.

7. Xie Juizhai, "Minzhu zhengzhi," 26.

8. Li Zhaobing, "Xiaomie zibenzhuyi," 26.

9. We should note that the usage of the term "corruption" was rather broad here, as was always the case throughout CCP history. In this case, during the 1942 party rectification, it included illicit actions such as gambling, visits to prostitutes, and improper sexual relationships, underlining the need for a better understanding of what "corruption" meant in the Chinese context and how to differentiate among various types of deviance. See Chen Yung-fa, *Making Revolution*, 313.

10. Zhang Zhenglong, *Xuebai xuehong*.

11. Ibid.

12. Jowitt has noted the distinction between the social and the cultural mobilization of uprooted peasants (see Jowitt, *New World Disorder*, 15–17). The Chinese case bears out his point that not all mobilizations of uprooted peasants provided proof of the stripping of their cultural orientation. Desertion, petty graft, and other deviance in the Chinese revolutionary ranks show both the convergence and conflict between the orientations of the party and the peasants. In the meantime, one should not dismiss the rational base of peasant behavior. Indeed, the inability of the party to inhibit those who deviated and deserted and to maintain members as disciplined, dedicated, and deployable cadres indicates that it is questionable whether a Leninist party was always able to "offer itself as an intelligible medium for recruits and transformation of 'imperfect' materials" (ibid., 15). Many members of the revolutionary movement remained "unperfected," longing only for material betterment.

13. Feng Ding, "Lun fanxing," 59–60.

14. Zhang Zhenglong, *Xuebai xuehong*, 338.

15. Ibid., 127.

16. At the time, there was no salary-rank (*jibie*) differentiation in the communist troops, so perquisites were granted on the basis of the actual position (*zhiwei*) one held. In the three decades that followed the abolition of the free supply system, the discrepancies between salary-rank and position became increasingly greater. One might hold a section-chief (*chuzhang*) position yet receive a salary comparable to a superior bureau chief, because salary-ranks were primarily based on seniority whereas positions were not necessarily tied to salary. This structure has been reformed in recent years. Salaries are now tied more closely to positions than to seniority, although the latter is not totally irrelevant. See Chapter 5 for further discussion.

17. Soon after the guerrillas entered the cities, it became popular for veterans to divorce their wives, who were usually older and less educated. Many remarried better-educated, urban females.

18. Zhang Zhenglong, *Xuebai xuehong*, 317.

19. *JYZWX*, 1992.

20. Jiang Yi, *Zhongguo gongchandang*, 431.

21. *RMRB*, December 29, 1951.

22. Li Weiyi, *Zhongguo gongzi*, 143

23. One should not, however, exaggerate the effects of material incentives in inducing misconduct by cadres. In fact, the agency where personal corruption cases most frequently occurred was the police. Not totally by coincidence, the police departments had the largest group of personnel retained from the old regime.

24. The famous Wang Shiwei affair is a case in point. Wang, an intellectual from an urban bourgeois background, came to Yan'an to join the Communist movement. He was later disappointed to find out that among his supposedly egalitarian comrades, some enjoyed better material treatment than others. He bluntly voiced his criticism, which led to deadly sanctions: he became a victim in the Yan'an Rectification Campaign of 1942 and was secretly executed in 1947. For a discussion of this case, see Goldman, *Literary Dissent*, chap. 2.

25. We should keep in mind that before the implementation of a scaled salary system in 1955, there was indeed no formal differentiation in terms of salary-ranking (*jibie*) as Ezra Vogel has noted (see Vogel, "From Revolutionary to Semi-bureaucrat," 38). However, the absence of a formal ranking system tied to salary did not entail an absence of differentiation of status (*diwei*) and the treatment normally derived from it. Thus position (*zhiwu*) substituted for rank as the basis of treatment and status.

26. Mao, *Jingji wenti*.

27. *ZJQG*, 77. See also Selden, *The Yenan Way*, 250–51.

28. See *ZJQG*, 78. The directive did warn, however, that the army units should take a cautious approach to operating commercial businesses.

29. This popular Chinese phrase refers to individuals or units, usually non-business types, getting into business.

30. Li Weiyi, *Zhongguo gongzi*, 135.

31. Caizheng kexue yanjiusuo, *Geming genjudi*.

32. Zhang Zhenglong, *Xuebai xuehong*, 128.

33. Shan and Liu, *Zhongguo lianzhengshi*, 293.

34. According to the "Rules on the Supply Work of the Eighth Route Army" (1940), army units above the regiment level were allowed to run shops or co-ops, thus engaging in commercial activities. See *HQGZ*, 51–52.

35. *HQGZ*, 84–85.

36. *KZSGN*, vol. 8.

37. Xing and Zhang, *Kangri zhanzheng*.

38. *SFDD* (1952), 29.

39. Zhao Chaogou, *Mao Zedong xiansheng*.

40. *HQGZ*, 366–68.

41. For a discussion of the results of the production campaign, see Peter Schran, *Guerrilla Economy*, chap. 6; and Selden, *The Yenan Way*. Selden also emphasized the intentional aspect of cadre participation in manual labor as a way of organizational integration.

42. These two principles were initially advanced, by Mao and Li Fuchun, who was the CCP's chief official in charge of financial and economic affairs at the time. See *KSCSX*, 1344. See also Li Fuchun, *Li Fuchun xuanji*, 33–42.

43. See the directive on the production campaign from the CCP committee of the Taihang region and the political affairs department of the Taihang garrison, in *KSCSX*, April 13, 1944.

44. This was the "Plan for Production and Austerity by the Mess Units," named after Teng Daiyuan, then chief of staff of the Front Command of the Eighth Route Army, and Yang Lizhi, deputy chief of staff.

45. *KSCSX*, 1344.

46. Ibid., 1345.

47. *TGGS* 1987:212.

48. Mao, *Jingji wenti*, 128.

49. *TGGS*, 213–14.

50. See *KSCSX*, 1474. This document was originally issued as "Financial Decree Number 216" on June 15, 1944. The anti-corruption and austerity drive refers to the campaign launched alongside the rectification campaign in some base areas in the 1942–43 period.

51. Ibid.

52. According to Mao, factories run by various units "should install 10-hour work days and a wage system based on the output each staff produces because egalitarian supply systems obliterate the discrepancy between skilled and unskilled labor." See Mao, *Jingji wenti*, 115.

53. In fact, the term *danwei* began to take on a practical economic meaning during this period. Under the supply system, all army and administrative units were divided into "mess units" (*huoshi danwei*); thus, each of these units was an independently budgeted body and ran its own dining services. While the main expense was for meals (hence "mess"), each unit needed more than it received from its budget allocation. The term "mess unit" gave a meaning close to what we now call *danwei*. See Lü, "Minor Public vs. Greater Public."

54. *KSCSX*.

55. Ibid. Note here that even during the guerrilla period there already were instances of impoundment of fines by government agencies. See my discussion of a similar phenomenon in the reform era in Chapter 5.

56. Ibid., 1475.

57. Ibid.

58. I should point out that fraudulent reporting and dissimulation by units, also present in periods after 1949, were driven by economic interests rather than by the mobilization mode of operation and ethos as rendered in the *fukuafeng* during the Great Leap Forward and the *dabiao* in the 1990s.

59. *BJZ*, November 1939, emphasis added.

60. Mao, *Jingji wenti*, 160.

61. Retail business by government agencies and army units was banned soon after the Communist victory. See discussion below.

62. Zhu, *Dongbei jiefangqu*, 1987.

63. Ibid., 287.

64. *JYZWX*, vol. 1, 67–69.

65. Mao, *Mao Zedong sixiang* (1969), 1, emphasis added.

66. *JYZWX*, vol. 1, 201.

67. This is the earliest CCP document found hitherto on the subject. To my knowledge, no one else has cited these documents.

68. Wang Zhufa, "Jiefang zhanzheng shiqi."

69. *JYZWX*.

70. *RMRB*, January 10, 1952.

71. *RMRB*, March 13, 1952.

72. *RMSC* (1952), 58.

73. Not included are regular logistic operations (e.g., weapon repair factories, uniform factories, and the like) or the defense industry under the central ministries. Unlike the procurement system in the West, the Chinese armed forces run their own production units and produce most of their own basic supplies. It is necessary to distinguish this system from the other types of business activities, which were (are) mainly profit seeking.

74. The production and business activity in the military saw a new surge in 1967 after Mao issued his famous "May Seventh Instruction," in which he re-embraced the image of an army being both a "combat corps" and a "production corps." See Xu Guangyi, *Dangdai zhongguo jundui*, 46–77; Qu Yizhi, "Lun zhonggong junban qiye wenti."

75. Lu, Shi, and Wu, *Zhongguo fanfubai*.

76. *RMSC* (1952), 57, emphasis added.

77. Ibid.

78. Zhang Xiangling, *Heilongjiang sishinian*, 207.

79. Xiao Su, "Jianguo chuqi Harbin."

80. Financial and economic centralization was first set in motion in March 1950. As Bo Yibo, a main figure in the decision-making process, pointed out in his memoirs, many cadres "who were used to fragmented operations in the base areas, were reluctant to make such a transition." Aware of the opposition

among local leaders, the State Council, in its "Decision to Unify Financial and Economic Work" (March 3, 1950), warned that "if party members are found to have fraudulently reported statistics, embezzled, or thwarted the rules in financial and economic work, they must be punished resolutely, both by state laws and party discipline." See Bo Yibo, *Ruogan zhongda juece* (1991), 81–85.

81. *CJRB*, February 9, 1952. Frederick Teiwes notes the existence of "independent kingdoms" in his discussion of party rectification in 1950–1953. See Teiwes, *Politics and Purges in China*, 169–70. Two additional aspects warrant further discussion, however. First, the tendency of units and localities to manipulate information had its roots in the pre-1949 Communist wartime experience; second, individual cadre corruption was also related to departmentalism of this sort.

82. The latter aspect of the malpractice of state agencies, that is, predatory actions against private interests, was not as prominent in the early period of the PRC as in the post-Mao reform period. It was nonetheless an inseparable part of deviance by state institutions. For a more detailed empirical discussion of this aspect, see Chapter 6.

83. As a part of the supply system privileges, the state provided many officials with cars, bodyguards, and housekeepers.

84. Although the Three Anti Campaign and the subsequent central planning and growing state sector did much damage to *benwei zhuyi* (departmentalism), especially in terms of financing and material supply, the problem persisted in the years that followed. The reforms of the 1980s have in fact brought *benwei zhuyi* to the fore again.

85. *RMRB*, December 16, 1951.

86. *JYZWX*, vol. 2, 386.

87. *NFRB*, January 23, 1952.

88. *DBRB*, September 15, 1951, emphasis added.

89. *DBRB*, October 30, 1951.

90. Sun Ruiyi, *Sanfan wufan yundong*, 31.

91. *RMRB*, January 8, 1952.

92. For studies that contain discussions of this anti-corruption campaign, see Teiwes, *Politics and Purges in China* (especially chapter 4); Barnett, *Communist China*; Lieberthal, *Revolution and Tradition*.

93. *RMRB*, December 25, 1951.

94. Campaign-style mobilization is a defining characteristic of Leninist organization. As Gordon Smith aptly describes campaigns in Leninist orders, they serve four separate functions: (1) to uncover, punish, and, by example, prevent violations; (2) to communicate new policies or laws to officials and the public; (3) to inform party and state officials of the state of legality in a region; and (4) to provide an outlet for ritualistic participation in government. See Smith, *Public Policy and Administration in the Soviet Union*.

95. *JYZWX*, vol. 2, 473.

96. *JGFZX*, 318. The appointment of non-party activists appears to be an attempt both to woo more people from outside the CCP organization and to make the anti-corruption campaign more legitimate through the participation of non-party members, particularly when corruption was being targeted outside the government.

97. These telegrams were published by the Documents Research Center of the CCP Central Committee. Mao personally drafted a number of the directives concerning the pace, strategy, and rules of the anti-corruption campaign. See *JYZWX*, vols. 2 and 3.

98. *RMRB*, December 21, 1951.

99. Jiang Yi, *Zhongguo gongchandang*.

100. Interview with author, October 1991.

101. *JYZWX*, vol. 3, 51–52, 68–70.

102. An Ziwen, "Wei xiaochu."

103. Lynn White calls the campaign a method of administration designed more to achieve results than to plan them. His lucid comment on campaigns is worth quoting at length here: Campaigns "are aimed at effectiveness more than predictability. It seems to be most useful when the 'organizational weapon' that is launching assaults has too few resources to achieve goals without keeping subordinates or non-members off balance. Not only do campaigns lower the need for administrative resources because they raise compliance through inspiring fears of repression. Just as important, they gather new administrative resources by raising hopes of career advancement among activists" (White, *Policies of Chaos*, 18). White went so far as to treat the constant official campaigns as a cause of the Cultural Revolution. In our present analysis, the Three Anti Campaign itself, as an "administrative policy" (ibid., 9), did not directly cause corruption and was cost-effective in inhibiting corruption in the short run. However, I too have reasons to suspect that the long-term impact of campaigns, which may induce dissimulated habits from citizens and officials alike, was much more significant with respect to officials' behavior, as my later analysis of the Great Leap Forward and the Cultural Revolution will show.

104. *ZYSXB*.

105. Lin Daizhao, *Zhongguo xiandai renshi*, 388.

106. Ibid., 389.

107. *WQXZ*, 579.

108. Yi Jin, "Shanghaishi de sanfan."

109. See a report by An Ziwen to the Central Committee on the conclusion of the Three Anti Campaign, recently published in *JYZWX*, vol. 3, 384–88.

110. This is evidenced in a number of primary and secondary documents on the Three Anti Campaign. See, for instance, Bo Yibo's recollections of the campaign (Bo, *Ruogan zhongda juece* [1991], 144–45); An Ziwen's report to the

Central Committee. See *JYZWX*, vol. 3, 384–88; and Yi Jin, "Shanghaishi de sanfan."

111. The statistics come from three sources, none of which has ever been cited in studies of the Three Anti Campaign. The first, *Sanfan wufan yundong zhong tongji ziliao* (Statistics of the Three and Five Anti Campaigns), no. 10, October 31, 1952, was compiled by the Central Austerity Inspection Commission (see *ZJDZ*, 523). The other two are An Ziwen's report (*JYZWX*, vol. 3, 384–88) and Bo Yibo's memoirs (Bo, *Ruogan zhongda juece* [1991], 145). There are some discrepancies in the figures. But the most reliable ones seem to be those in *ZJDZ*. Note that the numbers here are all exclusive of the corruption cases committed by non-officials, usually those in the private sector.

112. County-level government staff, however, were also mobilized, according to some county gazetteers. The Three Anti Campaign can be regarded as mainly targeted at state administrative personnel.

113. *LTXZ*.

114. Wang and Chen, *Zhongguo gongchandang*, 136–39. For a detailed discussion of the party rectification in rural areas during this period, see Bernstein, "Keeping the Revolution Going"; Teiwes, *Politics and Purges in China*.

115. Lu, Shi, and Wu, *Zhongguo fanfubai*.

116. *RMRB*, December 30, 1951.

117. Lu, Shi, and Wu, *Zhongguo fanfubai*, 22.

118. *ZGFZB*, January 27, 1986.

119. *HBRB*, February 15, 1952.

120. *RMRB*, January 10, 1952.

121. In the contemporary Chinese political and legal vocabulary, *feifa,* or "illegality," is one of the most abused and arbitrary adjectives: it is used even when there are no legal or other norms to speak of.

122. It is worth noting that although since the 1950s *nuoyong gongkuan* (diversion or misappropriation of public funds) has always been a punishable action, it was not until January 1988 that a legal statute made it a crime. *Nuoyong gongkuan* is defined as a diversion for use other than a prescribed purpose, private or non-private (e.g., work unit), with the intention of paying back the funds in the future. There has been some debate as to whether the diversion (or peculation) of funds for non-private use is a criminal or a disciplinary act. See Zhongguo jiancha xuehui, *Chengzhi tanwu huilu.*

123. In the city of Changzhou, for example, 85 agents of the municipal tax bureau were caught taking bribes from some 300 businessmen who received help to evade taxation (see *JFRB*, December 30, 1951). For an excellent study of traditional Chinese tax agents and corruption, see Zelin, *The Magistrate's Tael.*

124. Bo Yibo, *Ruogan zhongda juece* (1991), 161.

125. For a case study of the Five Anti Campaign in the city of Tianjin during 1949–52, see Lieberthal, *Revolution and Tradition*, especially chap. 7.

126. Bo Yibo, *Ruogan zhongda juece* (1991), 164.

127. Jiang Yi, *Zhongguo gongchandang*, 413.

128. Ibid., 415.

129. Bo Yibo, *Ruogan zhongda juece* (1992), 170.

130. Lieberthal, *Revolution and Tradition*, 141–42.

131. Jiang Yi, *Zhongguo gongchandang*.

132. Bo Yibo, *Ruogan zhongda juece* (1991), 168.

133. Ibid.

134. In his memoirs, Bo Yibo offers a reliable account of how Mao regarded the campaign as a "large-scale class struggle," a "ruthless battle." According to Bo, Mao insisted on weakening but not destroying the capitalist class.

135. *DBRB*, December 15,1951.

136. Schurmann, *Ideology and Organization in Communist China*.

137. See Chen Dejin, "Jianguo chuqi dangfeng"; and Zhang Xiangling, *Heilongjiang sishinian*, 208.

138. Unlike their Soviet counterparts, the Chinese Communists never granted total vertical leadership to functional ministries, including the judiciary and procurate. Although there have been changes, most of the time the mode of leadership was "dual leadership," both horizontal (i.e., local party/ state) and vertical (i.e., functional ministries).

139. Qiu Dunhong, "Tan woguo fazhi jianshe."

140. See Bo Yibo, *Ruogan zhongda juece* (1991), 144; Zhou Jizhong, *Zhongguo xingzheng jiancha*, 588. According to a report by the Central Supervision Commission, 28,000 cases were investigated and disciplined by the supervisory system in 1951–52, among which 37 percent were graft and squandering, 12 percent were bureaucratism, and 25 percent were violations of party or administrative discipline. Altogether, 17,800 officials received disciplinary action. See Zhou, *Zhongguo xingzheng jiancha*.

141. Ibid.

142. Ibid., 599.

143. Zhao Shenghui, *Zhongguo gongchandang*, 264.

144. Zhu, Xie and Fan, *Zhongguo gongchandang jianshe shi*, 296–97.

145. Zhao Shenghui, *Zhongguo gongchandang*.

146. For a discussion of *biaoxian*, see Chapter 3.

147. An Ziwen, *An Ziwen zuzhi gongzuo wenxuan*, 10–12.

148. Zhao Shenghui, *Zhongguo gongchandang*, 269.

149. Ibid., 290; An Ziwen, *An Ziwen zuzhi gongzuo wenxuan*, 118.

150. Li Weiyi, *Zhongguo gongzi zhidu*.

151. Harding, *Organizing China*.

152. Liu Shaoqi, "Yao fangzhi lingdao renyuan teshuhua."

153. This information is found in a report by the CCP Municipal Committee

of Beijing to the Central Committee on December 4, 1951. See *JYZWX*, vol. 2, 496–97.

154. Jiang Yi, *Zhongguo gongchandang*, 410.

155. Harry Harding was correct in regarding the period following the Three Anti Campaign as one of organizational rationalization. See his *Organizing China*, chap. 3.

156. Vogel, "From Revolutionary to Semi-bureaucrat."

157. Existing studies of the politics of the early period of the PRC tend to focus on the regime's attacks on the traditional social order, particularly the capitalist class. Thus the Five Anti Campaign has received relatively more attention than the Three Anti Campaign. See, for example, Lieberthal, *Revolution and Tradition*; Lynn White, "Changing Concepts of Corruption in Communist China" and his *Careers in Shanghai*. A notable exception is Teiwes' work (*Politics and Purges in China*) on elite discipline during the 1950–53 period.

158. Cf. Lieberthal, *Revolution and Tradition*; L. White, *Careers in Shanghai*; "Changing Concepts of Corruption in Communist China."

159. *JYZWX* 1992: 482.

160. An Ziwen revealed that as early as October 1952, many people who had received disciplinary or penal punishment had begun to petition to have their cases re-evaluated or their penalties rescinded (*JYZWX* 1992 [v3]). Several county gazetteers contain information supporting An's claim.

CHAPTER THREE

1. Harding, *Organizing China*, 152.

2. Zhao Shenghui, *Zhongguo gongchandang*.

3. Participation of cadres in manual labor had a long history. During the production movement in Yan'an and other communist base areas in the early 1940s, cadres of administrative agencies and army units participated in farming, craft, and other production activities. See Selden, *The Yenan Way*.

4. Mao, *Mao Zedong xuanji*, vol. 5, 419.

5. Mao first raised the issue of "continuous revolution" in his "Sixty Work Methods" in January 1958. He wrote: "There should be one revolution after another.... Last year we had socialist revolution in thought and on the political fronts, now we should engage in a technological revolution so that we can catch up with Britain in 15 or more years." See Cong Jin, *1949–1989 de Zhongguo*, 109–10.

6. According to Bo Yibo, Mao made the point several times after 1956 that China's economic development had to rely on "our tradition of mass work and the mass line," not on Soviet methods. See Bo, *Ruogan zhongda juece* (1993), 721.

7. Since devastating events took place in this period, it remains one of the most sensitive topics in CCP history. Little has been written about the Great

Leap Forward inside China for lack of publicized materials. In the West, the Great Leap Forward is given some attention in studies of Chinese politics in general, but few detailed studies exist. See David Bachman's volume on the bureaucratic origin of the Great Leap Forward (*Bureaucracy, Economy, and Leadership*). See also Domenach, *The Origins of the Great Leap Forward*; D. Yang, *Calamity and Reform*; M. Whyte, "Who Hates Bureaucracy?" Harding, *Organizing China*; Bernstein, "Stalinism"; W. Joseph, "A Tragedy of Good Intentions"; MacFarquhar, *The Origins of the Cultural Revolution*, vol. 2.

8. The issue of speed of socialist construction was very much in the minds of the CCP leaders. At the Second Plenum of the Eighth Party Congress in May 1958, the Central Committee pronounced the primary goals of rapid development. Even during the meeting, the goals were adjusted several times, from catching up with the United Kingdom in fifteen years and the United States in twenty-some years to five and fifteen years. Note that these goals were set not only by Mao himself but by many ministries of the State Council. See Xie Chuntao, *Dayuejin kuanglan*, 50–51; also Liu Shaoqi, the Political Report on the Second Plenum of the Eighth Party Congress.

9. Shanghai shiwei, *Zhongguo gongchandang*, 356.

10. Mao, *Mao Zedong sixiang wansui* (1969), 204, 216

11. Shanghai shiwei, *Zhongguo gongchandang*, 357.

12. Huang and Liu, *Zhongguo gongchandang lianzheng fanfu shiji*.

13. Zhao Shenghui, *Zhongguo gongchandang*, 314.

14. On the practice of *xiafang*, see Rensselaer Lee, "The *Hsia Fang* System"; Teiwes, *Politics and Purges in China*, 35–36; J. Lewis, *Leadership in Communist China*, 220–32.

15. *RMRB*, January 25, 1958.

16. Zhao Shenghui, *Zhongguo gongchandang*.

17. Qi Liaozhou, "Chuanbo gongchanzhuyi."

18. Mao spoke several times at the Second Plenum of the Eighth Party Congress in May 1958 about the issue of challenging authority (*pochu mixin*) and liberalizing thinking (*jiefang sixiang*). See Mao, *Mao Zedong sixiang wansui* (1969), 186–219.

19. *RMRB*, January 31, 1958.

20. See Renmin chubanshe, *Di'erjie quanguo renmin daibiao dahui*, 99. Throughout its first eight years (1950–58), there were constant debates over how independent supervisory agencies should be of the party leadership, and how centralized they ought to be. In 1986, the supervision agencies were reinstalled after almost three decades of absence. But they never regained their autonomy vis-à-vis party/state structures of various levels, which they once had in the early 1950s. See Chapter 2. See also Zhou Jizhong, *Zhongguo xingzheng jiancha*; Cai Dingzhao, *Guojia jiandu zhidu*.

21. Lenin, *The Works of Lenin*, vol. 43, 195–96.

22. The Chinese procuracy has followed a similar path to that of the Soviet. Both originally were intended to be powerful institutions. On the Chinese procuracy, Harding gives a detailed discussion in "The Study of Chinese Politics." See also the three articles by George Ginsburg and Arthur Stahnke (1964; 1965; 1968) about the Chinese procuracy in *China Quarterly*, no. 20, (1964), 1–37; no. 24 (1965), 53–91; no. 34 (1968), 82–132.

23. This term is widely used to describe meetings or sessions spent reflecting on non-professional-related theoretical or political issues. Its origins can be traced back to Mao's speech at a CCP Central Committee meeting in Nanning in January 1958. Mao called on the people who were in *shiye* (substantial professions) to engage in more political activities, and the people who were in *xuye* (non-substantial work) to gain more professional knowledge. Since then, *wuxu* has become a familiar ritual as part of many professional meetings. See Mao, *Mao Zedong sixiang wansui* (1969), 146.

24. Li Shiying, *Dangdai Zhongguo de jiancha zhidu*.

25. Ibid., 145–46.

26. Ibid., 130.

27. Mao said at this meeting: "When we were in the base areas, we operated under the supply system. People had rectitude. There was no bickering over treatment. After liberation we installed the salary and rank systems which caused many problems. This has facilitated the capitalistic mode of behavior, such as longing for rank and privilege." See Mao, *Mao Zedong sixiang wansui* (1969), 362.

28. Ibid., 250.

29. For example, in Heilongjiang province almost every rural commune installed the free supply system. Under this system "meals were free," and other daily necessities were supplied by the communes. See Heilongjiang, *Heilongjiang nongye hezuoshi*, 339.

30. Li Weiyi, *Zhongguo gongzi zhidu*, 49.

31. Cellularity and multifunctionality are hallmarks of a self-sufficient, exclusive traditional community. Some of the "modern" Chinese institutions during the Republican period continued a number of these traditional features, not unlike those in the Great Leap Forward. See, for example, the study of the Bank of China by Wen-hsin Yeh in Lü and Perry, *Danwei*. For a detailed discussion of the enforcement of the *hukou* system, see Tiejun Cheng, *The Household Registration*. Lynn White (*Policies of Chaos,* 148–62) also cogently suggested that both Leninist organizational tenets of exclusiveness and traditional cellularity were at work in intensifying the *danwei*-ization during this period. Indeed, this development can be seen as a watershed in the direction pursued by the Chinese regime in the following decade.

32. Li Rui, *Lu Shan huiyi shilu*; Chen Shihui, "1959 nian de fanyouqing douzheng."

33. *WAXZ*, 583.

34. Author's interview, October 1991.

35. Lenin used a similar method in "socialist competition" in such campaigns as the *Subbotnik* (Work on Saturday) and Communist Youth Shock brigades as early as the early 1920s.

36. Zhao Shenghui, *Zhongguo gongchandang*, 310.

37. The origin of the flag metaphor is perhaps Mao's speech at the Second Plenum of the Eighth CCP Central Committee on May 20, 1958, when he made the following point: "Erect red flags and detect the direction of the wind. The red flag is our [national] flag with five stars. Where there are inhabitants, there are flags, be they red or white. Don't be afraid of raising red flags everywhere. There should be red flags on all mountain tops, in all villages, party committees, state agencies, army units, factories, and co-ops. Not all places have red flags. Some had just erected red flags before they soon became backward and the flag color faded. Red flags need to be constantly renewed." See Mao, *Mao Zedong sixiang wansui* (1969), 212.

38. Luan, "Jingxing dayuejin yishi," 30.

39. Zhao Shenghui, *Zhongguo gongchandang*.

40. *ZBSH* 5 (1958).

41. Chen and Han, *An Ziwen zhuanlüe*.

42. Zhao Shenghui, *Zhongguo gongchandang*, 315–16.

43. The population figures for 1959, 1960, and 1961 were 672,070,000, 662,070,000, and 658,590,000, respectively (see Ma and Huang, *Zhongguo de zuotian yu jintian*, 568).

44. Zhao Shenghui, *Zhongguo gongchandang*.

45. Walder, *Communist Neo-Traditionalism*, 160.

46. Ibid., 136.

47. Lynn White also took note of the organizational operational modes of the Chinese regime and went so far as to suggest that a similar practice, labeling, was one of the organizational causes of the Cultural Revolution. He did not pay attention, though, to the labeling of work units such as brigades, party branches, or production teams, which I think was equally significant in inducing certain behavioral patterns such as dissimulation, "Janus-facedness," and dependency on superiors.

48. I cannot help but note that such tripartition finds its roots in the philosophical component of Chinese party ideology, which sees the world as consisting of three dimensions—left, center, and right.

49. Zhang Yigong, "Fanren Li Tongzhong de gushi," 172.

50. *RMRB*, September 10, 1958; Xie Chuntao, *Dayuejin kuanglan*.

51. Luan, "Jingxing dayuejin yishi," 28.

52. Before the Communists came to power, the term had been used frequently during the Yan'an Rectification to denote a prevalent style or tendency

among the party cadres such as *xuefeng* (style of ideological study), *wenfeng* (writing style), and *gongzuo zuofeng* (work style). In Chinese, *zhengfeng* (rectification) as a method of organization building has connotations of rectifying one's "style" or "orientation."

53. Jowitt, *New World Disorder*, 79–80.

54. *RMRB*, September 22, 1958.

55. *RMRB*, September 18, 1958. The reports of rice and other grain production output appeared in newspapers in the summer of 1958. Other absurd reports include a report of a pumpkin harvest at 202,735 *jin* per *mu* (see *RMRB*, August 9, 1958), and a report of grape production at 26,115 *jin* per *mu* (see *Shanxi ribao*, September 23, 1958).

56. *RMRB*, August 11, 1958.

57. Ma and Huang, *Zhongguo de zuotian yu jintian*, 568.

58. *HBXZ*.

59. Sun Zhijie, "Ji Xushui gongchanzhuyi," 26.

60. Interview with author, September 1991.

61. The "Three Red Flags" consist of the general line of the party, the people's commune, and the Great Leap Forward.

62. *SLXZ*, 385.

63. Liu Binyan, "Bijing yousheng sheng wusheng," 239–40.

64. Li Rui, *Lu Shan huiyi shilu*, 87.

65. Yang Xianzhen, "Yijiu wujiu nian jishi."

66. Mao, *Mao Zedong sixiang wansui* (1969), 294.

67. Li Shiying, *Dangdai Zhongguo de jiancha zhidu*, 151.

68. *RMRB*, December 13, 1985.

69. Li Shiying, *Dangdai Zhongguo de jiancha zhidu*, 152.

70. The information about this case came from an unpublished official investigation I was able to obtain.

71. Sun Zhijie, "Ji Xushui gongchanzhuyi."

72. *SYXZ*, 782. As Bo Yibo pointed out, through the power of the local officials over the public canteen in the commune system, the villagers became more dependent on the collective and more susceptible to abuse by these officials. See Bo, *Ruogan zhongda juece* (1993), 762.

73. The information is contained in an internal report on the situation of rural party organizations in Hebei province. See *Siqing gongzuo jianbao*, no. 2, Office of the Four Cleanup Campaign, CCP Hebei provincial committee, September 1964.

74. Sun Zhijie, "Ji Xushui gongchanzhuyi," 19–20.

75. *WAXZ*, 581–82.

76. Bo Yibo, *Ruogan zhongda juece* (1993), 765.

77. This information is revealed in a self-criticism report from the Gansu

Provincial CCP Committee to the CCP Central Committee. See *ZDJCZ*, vol. 23, 409.

78. Later, as part of an effort to rectify the illicit leveling, the government twice issued directives (November 1960 and June 1961) ordering that all the land and assets obtained from rural communes by government units be returned to the villages. See *ZDJCZ*, vol. 23, 373–74, 475–78.

79. See Bo Yibo, *Ruogan zhongda juece* (1993). What is worth noting here is the reappearance of the production activities of government agencies, military units, and other units after they were banned in the wake of the Three Anti Campaign. One can assume that along with other policy measures such as the *hukou* system and consumer goods rationing in the same period, it helped to shape the post-revolutionary *danwei* regime in China.

80. Deng Zihui, who was in charge of agricultural work in the Central Committee, revealed this in a major policy statement on the communes on May 24, 1962. See *JNSH*, 707.

81. As a matter of fact, Mao defended the use of "irregularity," "peasant style," and "guerrilla mentality" by the people who voiced doubts about the rationality of the mass campaign style of steel production (see Mao, *Mao Zedong sixiang wansui* [1967], 248). In an editorial, the party's major journal, *Hongqi* (Red Flag), criticized the "faction of doubters": "This 'great chaos' is actually a great order. Without chaos, there is going to be no order. Revolutionary masses welcome this 'chaos.' Only those who doubt the revolution are afraid of it." This is probably the first time the CCP leadership openly advocated *luan* (chaos) as a positive factor. The term was often used during the Cultural Revolution. See *HQ*, no. 12, 1958.

82. These levels were province, prefecture, county, commune, brigade, and production team.

83. Cong, *1949–1989 de Zhongguo*, 248. Interestingly, estimating a problematic "one-third" of a given institution, based on the well-known tripartition method, is a constant exercise of the CCP leadership. Later, in the Four Clean Campaign, the estimate of the "rotten elements" and the party branches that were in the hands of class enemies was again one-third.

84. Ibid., 534.

85. Luan, "Jingxing dayuejin yishi."

86. Wu and Zhang, "Luelun zhonggong bada luxian."

87. It is worth noting that such information was revealed by delegates from the usually disciplined PLA during a session of PLA delegates at the 1962 CCP enlarged central committee conference, attended by some 7,000 officials from various levels. See Cong, *1949–1989 de Zhongguo*, 431.

88. See ibid., 432. It can be detected from these slogans that the general interests of the whole people (nine fingers) were purported to be placed above those of individual localities and units (one finger). Local leaders who said such

things showed their commitment to national planning and their willingness to sacrifice local interests.

89. Mao, *Mao Zedong sixiang wansui* (1967), 110–11.

90. Jia and Rong, "Zhide chensi de niandai."

91. Ibid.

92. Zhao Shenghui, *Zhongguo gongchandang.*

93. Xie, *Dayuejin kuanglan*, 183.

94. Heilongjiang, *Heilongjiang nongye hezuoshi*, 373.

95. Ibid., 374–77.

96. Chen and Han, *An Ziwen zhuanlüe.*

97. Zhao Shenghui, *Zhongguo gongchandang*, 337.

98. Cai, *Guojia jiandu zhidu*, 269.

99. It should be noted, though, that these figures reflect only cases of economic corruption, as narrowly defined, and other illegal actions. The more prevalent, yet subtle, forms of deviant behavior were not within the jurisdiction of the public procurate.

100. Zhou Enlai made such an observation in his "On Some Issues of the Twenty-second Congress of the CPSU" speech of November 19, 1992. See Cong Jin, *1949–1989 de Zhongguo*, 504.

101. Deng made this speech at a meeting in the Central Committee's High Party School on July 11, 1962. See ibid., 504.

102. See, for example, Wang Shaoguang, "From Revolution to Involution."

103. *RMRB*, January 27, 1958.

104. For example, the state supervisory system was one of such institutions that came under fire for the reasons stated here.

105. Alan Liu has suggested that Mao intentionally resorted to what he called "strategic corruption" in order to implement his own program, and that rectitude was the least of Mao's considerations—so much so that "he was willing to use hoodlums." See his "Kleptocracy on Mainland China," 161. I do not agree with such assumptions. On the contrary, I think Mao was very much concerned about the rectitude of cadres albeit perceiving a wrong source for the problem and employing the wrong methods to solve it.

106. Selznick, *Leadership in Administration*, 143.

107. Ibid., 148.

108. Xie Chuntao, *Dayuejin kuanglan*, 287.

109. Harding, *Organizing China*, 17.

110. Mao made his most comprehensive and open criticism of the Stalinist road of socialist development in a detailed comment on Stalin's book, *Problems of the Socialist Economy*. Mao commented, "The significance of human agency, of laborers, was neglected [by Stalin]. . . . Without a communist campaign, the transition to communism is very difficult to achieve." See Mao, *Mao Zedong sixiang wansui* (1969), 248–49.

111. Bachman, *Bureaucracy, Economy, and Leadership*, 228.

112. On several occasions Mao openly expressed his displeasure with the economic planners in the ministries, such as the state planning commission, for their "blocking of information" and "presenting things nobody really understands including themselves." For Mao's view, see Li Rui's recollections (see Li, *Lu Shan huiyi shilu*) on the Lushan Meeting. See also Mao, *Mao Zedong sixiang wansui* (1969).

113. Dittmer, *China's Continuous Revolution*, 44, emphasis added.

114. See, e.g., Friedman, Pickowicz, and Selden, *Chinese Village, Socialist State*; Shu-Min Huang, *The Spiral Road*.

115. Friedman, Pickowicz, and Selden, *Chinese Village, Socialist State*, 272–73.

116. It is perhaps in this sense that MacFarquhar suggested viewing the Great Leap Forward as a state of mind, a belief on the part of the CCP leadership in bringing about rapid changes in all socioeconomic and political aspects. For this view, see Bachman, *Bureaucracy, Economy, and Leadership*, 3n.

117. Harding, *Organizing China*, 115.

118. Whyte, "Who Hates Bureaucracy?" 243.

119. Some historical events were misinterpreted by Whyte. For instance, he cited the "vigorous efforts" of the central leadership to eliminate local autonomy and traditional customs (see Whyte, "Who Hates Bureaucracy?" 243). In fact, decentralization was taking place during the Great Leap Forward. The main flaw of his argument, I think, lies in his perception that the attacks on traditional institutions and norms came from a "bureaucratic" direction, neglecting the possibility of their coming from a revolutionary, charismatic direction.

120. Merton, *Social Theory and Social Structure*.

121. Etzioni, *A Sociological Reader*, 385.

122. The term "bureaucracy" has two kinds of meanings: one relating to the administrative sector of the state (as opposed to its political sector), and the other concerned with the mode of operation of a regime, as in Weber's famous typology. In the former sense, I do not think it is possible to make a clear definition of exactly what constituted "bureaucracy" in China. As for the latter, I see a sharp distinction between the bureaucratic and cadre modes of organizational behavior as Schurmann has aptly suggested. Thus it is analytically meaningful to use different terms when the meaning is different. It is out of this contention that, as noted earlier, I have chosen to avoid using the term "bureaucracy" to denote the administrative body of the Chinese state.

123. Schurmann, *Ideology and Organization*, 235, emphasis added.

CHAPTER FOUR

1. Even though an increasing volume of information has come to light in recent years, the studies of party organization and cadres before and during the

Cultural Revolution remain sketchy and limited. Methodological problems make the analysis of official deviance, including corruption during the 1960s, more tentative than in studies of other periods. To remedy the problem, I was able to obtain information from unpublished archival documents dated from 1964 to 1965 such as internal reports, investigations, and bulletins issued by the Office of the Four Cleanup Campaign of the CCP Hebei provincial committee. These documents are complementary to the Lianjiang Documents, dating from 1962 to 1963, upon which Western researchers once relied. In addition, information was also drawn from published primary sources such as local gazetteers and personal memoirs.

2. For example, there were the "Big Four Cleanup" and "Small Four Cleanup" campaigns during the Socialist Education Campaign; and the "One Attack, Three Anti" (*yida sanfan*) and "Cleanup Class Ranks" (*qingli jieji duiwu*) campaigns during the Cultural Revolution.

3. In May 1963, the CCP held an important meeting in Hangzhou on issues concerning rural areas. It passed a resolution that later became known as the "Initial Ten Points," an important policy guide for the Four Clean Campaign. In it, the CCP for the first time raised the point that the "grafters, speculators, and corrupt elements *within* the administration and collectives" were new bourgeois elements (*xinde zichanjieji fenzi*), setting the tone for the class warfare that would soon follow. This development seems to indicate that the party, or at least Mao, began to recognize that serious danger of cadre corruption existed. See *NJZWH*, 1982.

4. Zhou Enlai, *Zhou Enlai xuanji.*

5. Cong Jin, *1949–1989 de Zhongguo,* 407.

6. Ibid., 410.

7. Ibid., 414.

8. Zhou Enlai made this observation in a speech, "On Several Issues Concerning the 22nd CPSU Congress," on November 19, 1961. The speech was not included in his published selected works. See ibid., 504.

9. Liu Shaoqi, *Liu Shaoqi wenxuan,* vol. 2, 305.

10. See Wang Guangmei's 1964 report on the Four Cleanup Campaign in Hebei province in *JNSH*, 779.

11. For a cogent analysis of the Maoist discourse of "continuous revolution," see Dittmer, *China's Continuous Revolution.*

12. Mao, *Mao Zedong sixiang wansui* (1969), 642.

13. For information on these speeches, see Cong Jin, *1949–1989 de Zhongguo,* 156n1. It was apparent that the salary-ranking scheme was intended to be a target of the Cultural Revolution, though this aspect was never implemented.

14. Mao, *Mao Zedong sixiang wansui* (1969), 499.

15. Mao's comments were made on December 12, 1964, but only became

known on June 18, 1976, in a CCP Central Committee directive. See Wang Nianyi, *1949–1989 de Zhongguo*, 589.

16. During the Sino-Soviet ideological debate of the early 1960s, the CCP published nine commentaries in the *People's Daily*. In the third installment, it assailed the Yugoslavian Communists for allowing the degeneration of socialism and for forming a "new capitalist bureaucratic class" (*RMRB*, September 26, 1963). In the final commentary a year later, the Soviet Union was accused of having formed a "privileged strata" consisting of apparatchiks, managers of *kolkotz* and state enterprises, and an elite intelligentsia (*RMRB*, July 14, 1964). The comments by the Chinese leaders resembled some of Trotsky's and Djilas' arguments about post-revolutionary Communist cadres.

17. Mao made his comments at a Central Committee meeting in February 1962 (Cong Jin, *1949–1989 de Zhongguo*, 527). It was at this meeting that the CCP decided to launch the Socialist Education Campaign. The problems of grassroots cadres were not entirely exaggerated by the CCP leadership in its appraisal of the post-Leap situation. There were two mutually reinforcing dimensions at work at the time. On the one hand, local officials were the ones who carried out all the feverish acts under pressure from above, and who later were reprimanded for their acts. They were victims of their own activities and more. On the other hand, the leadership became aware of the cadres' dissimulation, and thus blamed the cadres for much of the crisis that its own policies had caused. In addition, the prospect of a Chinese repetition of Khrushchev revisionism also alarmed the leadership.

18. Jin Chunming, *Jianguo hou sanshisan nian*, 164.

19. As an indication of the politicization of officialdom, the Four Cleanups were later changed to "cleaning up political affairs, the economy, thoughts, and organization," or the so-called Big Four Cleanups.

20. Mao, *Mao Zedong sixiang wansui* (1969), 445, 590, 609.

21. Ibid., 445.

22. For studies on this campaign, see Baum, *Ssu-Ching*; Baum, *Prelude to Revolution*; Teiwes, *Politics and Purges in China*; MacFarquhar, *The Origins of the Cultural Revolution*, vol. 2.

23. While the rural segment of the broader Socialist Education Campaign, the Four Cleanups, has received considerable attention among Chinese and Western scholars, little has been written about its urban equivalent, due in part to the lack of information. In his detailed study of disciplinary problems among Chinese cadres, Teiwes, *Politics and Purges in China*, did not identify correctly the Five Antis. See Teiwes, *Politics and Purges in China*, 507n.g. The campaign was far from inconsequential with regard to the overall organizational development of the Chinese party/state, despite the fact that some of its original goals were later swept aside and overshadowed by the new, even broader mobilization of the Cultural Revolution.

24. The earliest use of the term *houmen* (back door) in official documents can be found in a directive on improving work in the commercial sector that was issued by the CCP Central Committee and the State Council on June 19, 1961. The directive prohibited staff in state stores and co-ops from "opening the back door" (*kai houmen*). The document is reprinted in *ZDJCZ*, vol. 23, 484–89.

25. Unless otherwise noted, the information about the Five Anti Campaign of 1963–64 is from an internal report by the CCP Central Supervisory Commission to the Central Committee dated November 8, 1963, as well as from several interviews the author conducted with three retired officials and one former salesperson in a state-run department store. For the report, see *JGFZX*, 18–27.

26. *NJXZ*, 15.

27. Zhang Xiangling, *Heilongjiang sishinian*, 334.

28. *ZDJCZ*, 193–94.

29. Zhang Xiangling, *Heilongjiang sishinian*.

30. Sun, *Dazhai hongqi de shengqi yu zhuiluo*, 362.

31. See Mao, *Mao Zedong sixiang wansui* (1969), 587. It is not clear, though, whether Mao meant that the top leaders themselves also "took too much" because they had to rely on officially provided privileges, or whether he meant that the top leaders had no need to take too much because they already were sufficiently provided.

32. Dorothy Solinger has suggested that in Maoist China, Marxism meshed with a long-term Chinese bias against commerce to perpetuate distrust of the commerce staff and downgrading of its material foundation (see her "Marxism and the Market in Socialist China," 199). There was indeed animosity toward the commercial sector in Maoist China. The perception of unfair and illicit practices such as *zouhoumen* by cadres and staff in the commercial sector may also have contributed to such hostility.

33. He Kailong, *Dangdai zhongguo de gongshang xingzheng guanli*, 101.

34. Ibid., 105. I should point out that the criteria for "illegal economic activities" were based on the political judgments of the time. All activities outside of state planning were deemed illegitimate to a certain degree.

35. Cong, *1949–1989 de Zhongguo*, 579.

36. He Kailong, *Dangdai zhongguo de gongshang xingzheng guanli*.

37. Andrew Walder also noted that *caigouyuan* became crucial operators for factories who obtained needed materials by creating networks of connections. See Walder, "Some Ironies of the Maoist Legacy in Industry," and also Dittmer, *China's Continuous Revolution*, 168–69.

38. During the Cultural Revolution, these offices were accused of being institutions for spying on the Central Committee. Most survived the political storms, however. With the market reforms, their functions changed. Some provided economic information and lobbied for contracts for local interests, while others simply became a place for retired officials to settle in a big city.

39. In capitalist economies, similar but generically different types of economic activities (i.e., the "informal economy," the "unregulated economy") also exist. On the Soviet "second economy," see Grossman, "The 'Second Economy' of the USSR"; Katsenelboigen, "Colored Markets in the Soviet Union"; O'Hearn, "The Consumer Second Economy: Size and Effects"; and Feldbrugge, "Government and Shadow Economy in the Soviet Union." Soviet scholars also had extensive discussions of this problem in a leading journal of economics, *Problems of Economics*. On the Chinese second economy, see Chan and Unger, "Grey and Black"; Mayfair Yang, "The Gift Economy and State Power in China." For an excellent study by Chinese scholars on the similar phenomenon, see Huang Weiding, *Zhongguo de yinxing jingji*.

40. He Kailong, *Dangdai zhongguo de gongshang xingzheng guanli*, 105. This finding also supports the argument that China really never had a completely centrally planned economy, and that its economy was even less centrally planned than that of the Soviet Union, which also experienced a boom in the second economy during the Khrushchev period. For such arguments see Riskin, *China's Political Economy*; Solinger, "Marxism and the Market in Socialist China"; and Pei, "Microfoundation of State Socialism and Patterns of Economic Transformation."

41. The CCP Central Committee issued a directive on May 15, 1960, to launch this new campaign in the countryside. See Lu Cheng et al., *Dangde jianshe qishinian jishi*, 388.

42. Ibid., 399.

43. Sun Huairen, *Shanghai shehui zhuyi jingji*, 363.

44. This survey is contained in an internal bulletin, *Siqing gongzuo jianbao* (*SQGJ*, no. 28 [February 20, 1965]), by the Office of Four Cleanup Campaign of the CCP Hebei provincial committee.

45. Ibid.

46. Ibid.

47. One notable aspect of these data is the use of the "family" or "household" as a unit of analysis by the investigators. It reflects the unusual stature of Chinese rural cadres: they are agents of the state on one hand, and they are family men of the peasantry on the other. For many of them, serving as a local official or staff person is an opportunity to get ahead economically. Note also the relatively large proportion of peasants who became "cadres" (in rural areas, it meant anyone holding a public office, from village head to bookkeeper).

48. At a high-level meeting in Beijing in May 1964, the CCP Central Committee made this estimate and called for further mobilization of the masses to "trace the roots up to higher authorities." See Zhao Shenghui, *Zhongguo gongchandang*, 354.

49. The CCP leadership was still somewhat ambiguous on this subject during the Four Cleanup Campaign. At times, corrupt officials were called "new

exploitative elements" (*fenzi*), but not a "stratum" (*jieceng*) or "class" (*jieji*). See Mao, *Mao Zedong sixiang wansui* (1969), 582–83. However, cadre problems were regarded as deriving from a "faction in power" (*dangquanpai*).

50. *RMRB*, March 26, 1963; *NFRB*, May 23, 1963.

51. *SQGJ*, no. 4 (October 30, 1964).

52. *SQGJ*, no. 28 (February 28, 1965).

53. The replacement of officials during the campaign was only part of a large-scale effort to rejuvenate the cadre ranks. The decision to reexamine party/state personnel originated in a 1963 investigation in Fujian by a deputy director of the CCP central organization department, who had reported to the Central Committee that there were two growing problems among county-level officials: they were old, and few were from local areas. Mao, departing from this finding, raised the issue of "successors of the proletariat revolution" in May 1964. See Zhao Shenghui, *Zhongguo gongchandang*, 356.

54. Ibid., 360.

55. *SQGJ*, no. 1 (May 3, 1964).

56. *HQ*, 1970, no. 1.

57. Ibid.

58. *BSXZ*, 456.

59. *CCXZ*, 149.

60. Dangdai, *Zhonghua renmin gongheguo shangye*, 101.

61. Ibid.

62. Huang and Liu, *Zhongguo gongchandang lianzheng*.

63. Dangdai, *Zhonghua renmin gongheguo shangye*, 248.

64. Interestingly, this meeting was never publicly reported by the official media. On November 20, 1961, the CCP Central Committee issued a circular containing a report of the State Council's Office of Finance and Commerce that called for a "mass campaign against *zouhoumen*." It is worth noting that soon after this document was issued, the important "Meeting of Seven Thousand Officials of Various Levels" was held in January 1962.

65. Li Xian-nian, *Li Xian-nian lun caizheng*, 488.

66. Ibid., 489.

67. Dangdai, *Zhonghua renmin gongheguo shangye*.

68. Ibid., 301.

69. *ZDJCZ*, vol. 23.

70. Namely, the CCP Central Committee directive to launch the new Five Anti Campaign, issued on March 1, 1963.

71. Zhou, *Zhou Enlai xuanji*, vol. 2, 418–22.

72. Huang and Liu, *Zhongguo gongchandang lianzheng*.

73. Li Xian-nian, *Li Xian-nian lun caizheng*, 491.

74. Ibid., emphasis added.

75. As a result of the instructions of a directive from the CCP Central

Committee on "Continuously Carrying Out Socialist Transformation of Residual Private Industries, Small Merchants and Vendors" (April 2, 1958), both rural free markets and urban businesses were on the verge of total extinction. See Cong Jin, *1949–1989 de Zhongguo*, 385–86.

76. MacFarquhar, *The Origins of the Cultural Revolution*; Chan, "Dispel Misconceptions about the Red Guard Movement"; Joseph, Wong, and Zweig, *New Perspectives on the Cultural Revolution*; Wang Shaoguang, *Failure of Charisma*.

77. Thomas Gold raised the provocative question as to whether revolutionary comradeship ever replaced friendship in communist China. See Gold, "After Comradeship." Evidence suggests that it never did.

78. Interview by author, December 1993.

79. Shu-min Huang, *The Spiral Road*.

80. Lü and Perry, *Danwei*.

81. In Chinese, *si* (private) carries a strong sense of "selfishness." Under the Communist regime, especially during the Maoist era, the negative aspect associated with the *si* was increased, even demonized.

82. *Wenhuibao*, January 16, 1967.

83. Mosher, *Broken Earth*, 88.

84. One type of informal relations that grew out of the Cultural Revolution, factionalism, is also noted by Keith Foster in his study of Zhejiang province. Weak and discredited structures and institutions, he noted, had little success in exercising authority over strong and risk-taking informal groups. See Foster's chapter in Joseph, Wong, and Zweig, *New Perspectives*. *Guanxi* is closely related to factional groupings, but the two are not the same. *Guanxi* is often formed on the basis of factional relationships, yet factional relationships are not the only manifestation of *guanxi*.

85. *RMRB*, February 7, 1982.

86. *RMRB*, February 1, 1982.

87. Lin Yimin noted this aspect of the utility of the *guanxi* mode. He argues that effective *guanxi* networking with state agents was necessary to the success of economic organizations in the 1980s. However, with the changes brought about by the new rounds of market reforms, *guanxi* has become less important, ironically because of the money factor. State agencies can be bought if the price is right. An enterprise need not cultivate *guanxi* but has to pay an unspecified amount of money. This is not to deny the utility of *guanxi*, for it is still a cheap and effective way of getting through when other conditions (e.g., the amount of money paid) are equal. See Li Yimin, "Personal Connections."

88. Interview by author, September 1991.

89. Ibid.

90. *GMRB*, November 20, 1980.

91. Ibid.

92. *RMRB*, August 7, 1981.

93. *TJRB*, December 9, 1981.

94. *ZGTX*, no. 305, December 15, 1983.

95. Although most scholars accept the notion that the Cultural Revolution lasted from 1966 through 1976, when Mao died, some have voiced strong disagreement. They argue that the Cultural Revolution actually ended in 1969, when the Red Guard movement was crushed and young rebels were either co-opted into a new organizational system or sent away to the countryside. The significance of such different periodizations, they suggest, is more than analytical convenience. They reflect different paradigms in analyzing the Cultural Revolution. Anita Chan, among others, most forcefully insists that the re-periodization of the Cultural Revolution from three years to ten was a conscious attempt of the Dengists to try to obfuscate what actually happened in the years between 1966 and 1969. See Chan, "Dispel Misconceptions About the Red Guard." For our current analysis, the periodization is significant not because of paradigm differences in treating the event itself, but because of the consequences of the Cultural Revolution, particularly the Red Guard phase, on overall regime organization and the cadre ranks.

96. According to a study by Li Xun based on internal archival materials, a survey was conducted in 1972 of worker-rebels-turned-officials in Shanghai. It found that among former worker rebels who became leaders, 28.7 percent were relegated or purged due to "serious political, economic, or life-style problems" including corruption. I thank Li Xun for letting me cite this information from her unpublished manuscript, "Gongren zaofanpai: Zhongguo wenhua dageming zuizhongyao de biaoben" (Worker rebels: The most important species in the Chinese Cultural Revolution).

97. Power was understood here as any discretion over human or material resources. In a society where the state had discretion over so many aspects of life, the scope of power was much broader, and the power of public office was much greater. Thus a shop manager in a factory had power because of his control over personnel and other production-related matters. A meat store attendant also had power thanks to her discretion over goods in short supply and sought after. But it was the officials at various levels who held powerful positions that were unmatched by those who were merely staff.

98. Wang Shouxin, a middle-aged female official in Bin county, Heilongjiang province, began her career as a cashier in a state-owned company. She allegedly worked her way up during the Cultural Revolution and became an official in her unit. She was found to have committed massive corruption. For a detailed discussion of this case, see Liu Binyan, *People or Monster?*

99. *JCRB*, January 22, 1997.

100. Ibid.

101. Interview by author, December 1993.

102. *GMRB*, November 9, 1980.

103. Jiang Wei, "Yianran huishou," emphasis added.

104. The author had the experience of borrowing *neibu* books such as Chinese translations of Ernesto "Che" Guevara's *Diary* and the *Memoirs of Charles de Gaulle* from a friend whose father was an official and who was able to buy the books. It was quite ironic that some of these *neibu* books were written by world-famous Communist leaders.

105. See Chen Erjin, "Lun wuchan jieji minzhu geming." The *neibu* phenomenon was one of the major targets of the democratic movement of the late 1970s. See, for example, Xiao Ming, "Neibu dianying heshiliao?" and also "Tantan neibu zhege mingzi." See also *DDKH*, vols. 4 and 15.

106. *DDKH*, vol. 8, 104.

107. Wang Hui, *Zhongguo de kuanchangbing*, 6–7.

108. Huo, *Guangrong yu mengxiang*.

109. Lin, Liu, and Shi, *Renmin gongheguo chunqiu shilu*.

110. Ibid., 966.

111. Ibid.

112. Wang Zhixiang, "Dui ganbu zinü de diaocha yu sikao."

113. This once widely noted phenomenon was soon forgotten and has only received attention in recent years from authors who personally experienced the episode. See Xiao Qinfu et al., *Wuci langchao*; Zhou Li, *Manhadun de nüren*. The information here is based on my interviews with several people who tried to get into the PLA in the 1970s. Some succeeded, some failed. One informant, who did not get in even with help of some connections of her father, was beaten out by someone whose father's "old comrades" had stronger ties or were in better positions in the government. She was later sent to the countryside, like many others of her generation.

114. Xiao Qinfu et al., *Wuci langchao*, 14–15.

115. Ibid.

116. Ibid.

117. Wang Yongxin, "Jiaoyu de chuntian."

118. Huang and Liu, *Zhongguo gongchandang lianzheng*.

119. *RMRB*, January 18, 1974.

120. Huang and Liu, *Zhongguo gongchandang lianzheng*, 218.

121. See, for example, Huang Yao et al., *Huihuang de zhiqingmeng*.

122. An Zhi, *Zhiqing chenfu lu*, 260.

123. Huo Mu, *Guangrong yu mengxiang*.

124. In the post-Mao official press, official deviance including corruption that had become pervasive since the Cultural Revolution has been often attributed to the radical "Gang of Four." The saying, "Power will expire if you don't wield it," was alleged to have been coined by them. This attribution is unfair, to say the least. On the contrary, the radicals including Jiang Qing and her confidants Chi Qun and Xie Jingyi were more vocal than others in their opposition to

official privilege and other status-oriented preferential treatments enjoyed by officials, their political motives and hypocrisy (given their own indulgence in such privileges) notwithstanding.

125. *QSND*, December (1979), 9.

126. Zhong Yan, "1977 nian huifu gaokao neiqing."

127. The phrase "sent-down youths" (*xiaxiang zhiqing*), also termed "educated youths" (*zhishi qingnian*, or simply *zhiqing*), refers to the cohort of young urban middle-school or high-school graduates who were, voluntarily or not, sent down to the countryside to receive "re-education" by peasants. (For a detailed study of this historical event, see Bernstein, *Up to the Mountains*). It has been estimated that since 1955, when the movement of "going to the countryside" began, until 1980, when it finally ended, some 1.8 million *zhiqing* were sent down. See *ZLRN*, 1872.

128. Zhang Lipu, "1978," 64.

129. The desperate and tragic efforts made by *zhiqing* were captured in this recollection of a former sent-down youth. Some even risked their lives by taking medicines with strong side effects in order to induce falsely positive lab tests in order to be sent home for medical reasons. See Huang Yao et al., *Huihuang de zhiqingmeng*, 229–36.

130. Huo Mu, *Guangrong yu mengxiang*.

131. Ibid.

132. Walder, "Some Ironies of the Maoist Legacy in Industry," 234–35.

133. For the Romanian case, see Sampson, "The Informal Sector in Eastern Europe," and his "Bureaucracy and Corruption."

134. This view of corruption is evidenced in several speeches on cadre problems made by CCP leaders during the early 1960s, including one by Liu Shaoqi at a meeting on party organizational work in November 1962. The term "corruption" used in this period also reflected such an understanding—*fuhua* rather than *fubai*, as is used today. See Huang and Liu, *Zhongguo gongchandang lianzheng*, 184–85.

135. Harding, *Organizing China*, 15.

136. In one place it was written, "The Party is composed of the most advanced elements of the proletariat; it is a vigorous vanguard organization leading the proletariat and the revolutionary masses in the fight against class enemies." See *The Ninth National Congress of the Communist Party of China* (Documents), 111.

137. Whyte, "Who Hates Bureaucracy?" 242.

138. Involution could also be seen in other aspects of socio-political life. In an interesting study of the language used in the Cultural Revolution, Wang Yi argued that the method of "mass criticism" resembled the use of curses in traditional society, for both used cruel language to obtain their aim of banishing demons. Indeed, rudeness and lack of courtesy became common in Chinese

society as a consequence of the relentless mass criticism during the Cultural Revolution. See Wang Yi, "Mass Criticism in the Cultural Revolution."

CHAPTER FIVE

1. Deng Xiaoping, *Deng Xiaoping wenxuan*, 190.

2. Chen Zhili, *Zhongguo gongchandang jiansheshi*, 1014.

3. In February 1920, the Bolshevik government under Lenin established a new and expanded body of popular control, the People's Commissariat of Workers' and Peasants' Inspection, empowered to monitor "all the organs of state administration, the economy, and social organizations." Later, at the Eleventh Party Congress in 1922, this independent body was incorporated into the Central Control Commission, the control commission of the party. The two supervisory bodies would remain unified until 1934, when Stalin separated the state control organizations from those of the party. For a detailed discussion of the history of the Soviet control institutions, see Clark, *Crime and Punishment in Soviet Officialdom*. The similarity in historical development of the Soviet and Chinese supervisory-disciplinary organs is striking. The PRC also had separate supervisory bodies of both the party and state, which also merged at one point.

4. Renmin chubanshe, *Di'erjie quanguo renmin daibiao dahui wenjianji*.

5. Ibid.

6. Ibid., 165.

7. Fu and Gao, "Zai guoji gongyun shi shang dangnei jiandu jizhi tuihua qishilu."

8. The state supervisory apparatus (as opposed to those of the Communist party) was originally established in 1931 in the Jiangxi Soviet region under CCP rule. Under the name of "Worker-Peasant Procurate Commission," it was the main organ dealing with corruption and administrative misconduct in the Chinese Soviet government. An innovation of this new organ was to set up "shock teams," composed of ordinary citizens, to inspect government agencies or public enterprises without notice. See Zhou Jizhong, *Zhongguo xingzheng jiancha*, 554–64; Wu and Liu, *Zhongguo gongchandang lianzheng*, 64–70. During the anti-Japanese war, no separate supervisory organ existed in the communist-controlled base areas. Nominal power of supervision was given to the Council of Deputies (*can yi hui*), a united-front body elected by popular votes. This period saw the beginning of the party's direct control over administrative supervision through its own apparatus—the Party Supervisory Commission (the predecessor of the Party Disciplinary Inspection Commission) following the principle of the party's absolute leadership. Evidence shows that the power mandated to the council of deputies was more symbolic than substantive. After the People's Republic was established, the new government established the People's Supervisory Commission, which later became the State Supervisory Ministry. It existed until 1959. See Chapters 2 and 3.

9. The disciplinary inspection commission of the CCP was originated in 1927 under the name of "Party Supervisory Committee." It existed throughout the history of the CCP, except during the Cultural Revolution, when it ceased functioning, along with many other party organs.

10. *Liaowang*, no. 31, 1997.

11. I attended one of these conferences in Kunming in 1983. It would take many years before some of the recommendations made at this conference on administrative reforms were implemented.

12. Hong Yung Lee's volume offers a detailed, insightful analysis of the cadre system since 1949. On the changes since reform began in 1978, see Hong Yung Lee, "From Revolutionary Cadres to Party Technocrats." See also Burns, *The Chinese Communist Party's Nomenclature System*; Saich, "Cadres"; Manion, "The Cadre Management System."

13. *Zhongguo gongchandang di shisanci quanguo daibiao dahui wenjian huibian*, 4.

14. The earliest public iteration of the *si hua* (four criteria) of cadre selection was in a speech by Deng Xiaoping in which he states: "to guarantee the construction of the four modernization and the continuity of our policies, our cadres should meet four criteria based on the premise of upholding socialism— revolutionary loyalty, youth, education and professionalizations." See *RMRB*, September 19, 1981. The idea of these criteria was, apparently, originally raised by Deng himself in his now-famous 1980 speech at a Politburo meeting ("On the Reform of the System of Party and State Leadership" [Deng, *Deng Xiaoping wenxuan*, 280–302]). He explicitly added to the (*de cai jianbei*) "revolutionary virtue plus ability" criteria the three others. They were formally written into the Party Charter at the Twelfth Party Congress in 1982.

15. *FZRB*, August 14, 1997.

16. *RMRB*, May 2, 1998.

17. Ibid., June 7, 1997.

18. *FZRB*, August 14,1997.

19. *RMRB*, April 15, 1998.

20. *SJRB*, May 4, 1998.

21. *Liaowang*, no. 39, 1997. There were six major administrative restructuring drives during the Maoist period (in 1952–53, 1958–59, 1960–65) and three during the past two decades (in 1982, 1988, and 1993).

22. Blecher and Shue, *Tethered Deer*.

23. I am grateful to a scholar at the Henan Academy of Social Sciences for providing me with the results of this survey, conducted in October 1997.

24. *Renshi*, no. 7, 1986.

25. *RMRB*, May 30, 1991.

26. *Liaowang*, no. 39, 1997.

27. There was a slight decrease in the number of employees in administra-

tive agencies, from 10.3 million in 1993 to 10.27 million in 1994, as a result of administrative downsizing. See *Chinese Statistical Yearbook*, 1995; *SJRB*, May 4, 1998; *Liaowang*, no. 4, 1998.

28. Su Ming, "Zhongguo caizheng zhichu guanli toushi."

29. Blecher and Shue, *Tethered Deer*.

30. Xu Gongmei, "Zoufang songshuyu."

31. Li Kang, *Zhongguo nongcun jiceng shequ zuzhi*.

32. *Zhengzhi yu Falü*, no. 4, 1991.

33. *SJRB*, March 12, 1997.

34. Cheng Ying, "Qianbaiwan ganbu mianlin dajingjian."

35. For these documents, see Huang and Liu, *Zhongguo gongchandang lianzheng*.

36. *RMRB*, May 15, 1979.

37. *RMRB*, May 17, 1979.

38. *RMRB*, August 15, 1979.

39. *RMRB*, January 15, 1980.

40. *RMRB*, August 15, 1980.

41. A personal experience during my research trip in 1991 shows how such coping works. An acquaintance of mine, a policeman, got frustrated with heavy traffic in the streets of Beijing and decided to put a police siren on the top of his car as he drove me from the airport. I was surprised to see a car not on official duty rushing through the streets with its siren on. Later, I was told that this practice is not uncommon. There were people who as a favor lent police and paramilitary police license plates to non-police vehicles. I noticed that in the streets of many Chinese cities and towns, a large number of official vehicles (the ones with noticeable plates and sirens belonging to the police, the paramilitary police, the courts, the procurate, and road management, and the like) were actually being used to carry non-work-related items and personnel who obviously had no official duties.

42. Deng, *Deng Xiaoping wenxuan*, 207.

43. H. Y. Lee, *From Revolutionary Cadres to Party Technocrats*.

44. *RMRB*, June 11, 1982.

45. *SXRB*, May 12, 1982.

46. *ZGTX*, no. 190, 1981.

47. Zhang Yun, "Quanmian tigao dangyuan suzhi."

48. Wang Zongru, "Bixu gaodu hongshi dangde jicengzuzhi jianshe."

49. *RMRB*, March 31, 1989.

50. *HBZTX*, no. 403, 1989.

51. Jowitt, *New World Disorder*.

52. Before reform, state cadres were assigned according to state needs and personal qualifications (and sometimes class background) to posts in different areas with little regard for the personal preference of individual cadres. This

practice resulted in many separated couples. Other factors included the closed *danwei* system, which gave people no freedom to move in or out, and the household registration (*hukou*) system, under which urban and rural populations were strictly separated.

53. Due to restrictions on urban residency, peasants with rural residency could not freely become urban residents. The fact that many cadres were recruited from rural areas and their spouses still legally resided in the countryside made it vital to acquire urban residency for them. The practice is called *nongzhuanfei* (switching from agricultural to non-agricultural residency). Rankings of the work unit and of the person himself also made a crucial difference.

54. *ZGTX*, no. 584, 1988.

55. Tong, *Guojia gongwuyuan gailun*; Xiao Qinfu et al., *Wuci langchao*.

56. Liu, *Liu Shaoqi Wenxuan*, vol. 2, 305.

57. Hu and Cao, "Rong guan yousilu."

58. Ibid.

59. In the most tangible terms, difference of *rank* in the pre-reform period was reflected in salary. A regular promotion of salary rank thus was necessary. Yet all regular salary rank promotions were unified nationwide actions—that is, only during such promotion drives were individual cadres considered for promotion. There had been only a few occasions where such promotions were implemented between 1956 (when the salary-ranking system was first set up) and the mid-1980s (when cadre salary ranks and post ranks were made comparable).

60. Interview by author, November 1991.

61. *RMRB*, November 8, 1995.

62. *ZGTX*, no. 457, 1986.

63. Ibid.

64. *RMRB*, March 12, 1998.

65. Dissimulation, scholars of comparative communism have pointed out, is typical of regimes with "mobilization ethos and structure." See Berliner, *Factory and Manager in the USSR*; Jowitt, "Soviet Neotraditionalism." The Soviet practice of *ochkovitiratelstvo* (cheating) is mirrored in the Chinese practice of *fukua* (exaggeration and showing off).

66. XH, March 10, 1997.

67. CNA, July 16, 1997.

68. *BYT*, no. 6, 1994.

69. *RMRB*, March 11, 1997.

70. Burawoy, "View from Production."

71. *RMRB*, March 12, 1998.

72. Shen, *Difang zhengfu de jingji zhineng*, 173.

73. *JCRB*, February 15, 1999.

74. See reports in *RMRB*, July 23, 26, 27, 1999; *New York Times*, July 27, 1999.

75. *RMRB*, June 1, 1993.

76. Yang and Tang, *Zhongguo 1992*.

77. In one case, a city government review found that there were over 15,000 different circulars or directives from several hundred national and local agencies, departments, and bureaus on economic affairs alone. Among them, some 7,000 contradicted one another or several other circulars. See Yang and Tang, *Zhongguo 1992*, 291.

78. *FZRB*, September 5,1997.

79. Jowitt, *New World Disorder*.

80. For similar findings, see T. White, "Postrevolutionary Mobilization in China."

81. Lü, "Politics of Peasant Burdens in Reform China."

82. *BYT*, no. 11, 1993.

83. *BYT*, no. 1, 1993.

84. Ibid.

85. *FZRB*, June 7, 1996.

86. *RMRB*, March 6, 1996.

87. Li Kang, "Jiceng zhengquan yu jiceng shequ."

88. Ibid.

89. Anthropological and sociological studies of Chinese society have paid much attention to *guanxi*, both in contemporary and traditional forms. On *guanxi* and informal relations in contemporary China, see Walder, "Organized Dependency and Cultures of Authority"; Mayfair Yang, "Between State and Society"; "The Modernity of Power in the Chinese Socialist Order"; J. Lewis, *Political Networks and the Chinese Policy Process*. On Chinese kinship organization, see Freedman, *Chinese Lineage and Society*. On informal business practices, see DeGlopper, "Doing Business in Lukang." See Nathan, *Peking Politics*, on elite factions and informal relations in pre-revolutionary China.

Mayfair Yang suggests that the art of *guanxi* is rooted in a Chinese cultural tradition that has survived the revolutionary transformation. This mode of exchange, or what she calls "the gift economy," is engendered by the material shortages under state socialism characterized by a "redistributive economy." Thomas Gold also sees *guanxi* as a way to cope with structural constraints, influenced by residual traditional social behavior (see Gold, "After Comradeship"). Walder, on the other hand, emphasizes the novel dimension of such relations, which resulted from Communist neo-traditionalist structure and patterns. See also Wang Feng, "State Socialism and *Guanxi* in China." While these scholars try to make a case for explaining the origins of the pervasiveness of *guanxi*, others attempt to determine the resources and processes *guanxi* networks can tap into. See, for example, Lin Yimin, "Personal Connections."

90. Zhang Yun, "Quanmian tigao dangyuan suzhi."

91. Huang and Liu, *Zhongguo gongchandang lianzheng fanfu shiji*.

92. See, for example, the commentary in *Guangming Ribao* entitled "Guan-

296 Notes to Chapter 5

xihu poxi" (An analysis of connected persons and units), November 20, 1980; and the commentary in *People's Daily* entitled "Jianjue dujue guanxihu" (Resolutely abolish connected units and persons), August 7, 1981.

93. See, for example, Yu Yingjie, "Gaohao dangfeng bixu changpo guanxi-wang" (On connection webs); Gao, Niu, and Liu, "Dapo guanxiwang" (Break connection webs); Qian Weiping, "Guanxiwang xianxiang fenxi" (An analysis of connection webs). There are subtle differences between these seemingly synonymous terms. The parties engaged in a *guanxihu* relationship are usually units rather than individuals. According to one definition, *"guanxihu* are those targets to whom one's self-interests are closely tied and it is imperative to treat them specially . . . between *guanxihu*, principles are pushed aside yet transactions are done in the name of the *'gongjia'* (public family)" (*RMRB*, August 7, 1981).

94. *ZGTX*, no. 384, 1985.

95. Interview by author, December 1991.

96. *GRRB*, December 10, 1997.

97. Pearson, *Joint Venture in the People's Republic of China*; *Liaowang*, no. 3, 1998.

98. *NCXB*, 1990. The issue number is unclear.

99. Jin Longze, "Xinshiqi dangyuan weijifanfa de tedian."

100. Zheng Yanming, "Zhongguo nongmin falü yishi de xianshi bianqian."

101. *Liaowang*, no. 3, 1998.

102. *GRRB*, December 10, 1997.

103. *Liaowang*, no. 3, 1998.

104. Interview by author, January 1994.

105. Ibid.

106. Ibid.

107. Interview by author, December 1993.

108. *RMRB*, May 4, 1993.

109. See, for example, Oi, *State and Peasant in Contemporary China*; Walder, *Communist Neo-Traditionalism.*

110. *RMRB*, February 2, 1986.

111. Xia, "Huibi, weile qinglian."

112. *Liaowang*, no. 28, 1996.

113. Cheng Ying, "Qianbaiwan ganbu mianlin dajingjian."

114. Yu and Dai, "Guanyu danwei neibu ganbu qinshujuji."

115. Ibid.

116. This investigation was conducted by the personnel bureau of Yiyang prefecture, Hunan province, in 1989. In China, the "section" level is the lowest tier of administrative ranking in an agency or enterprise. Administrators below this level are usually referred to as "general staff" (*yiban ganbu*).

117. Yang Guan, "Qiye 'jiazu' xianxiang."

118. Liu and He, *Huibi zhidu jiangxi.*

119. Jin Bang, "Zhide yinqi renmen yanzhong zhuyi de wenti."

120. Liu and He, *Huibi zhidu jianxi.*

121. Li Jianzhong, "Renshi renmian zhongde fubai xianxiang."

122. The term "protectionism" was used by a Russian scholar to refer to cronyism or patronage in the Soviet Union. See Rogovin, "The Problems of Corruption in Soviet Society."

123. Ibid.

124. Ibid.

125. This letter originally appeared in *Szabad Fold,* September 20, 1970, and is cited in Peter Bell's study on Hungarian rural development under the Communists. In Bell's opinion, the charges made here are generally credible, though not verified. See Bell, *Peasants in Socialist Transition.*

126. See Tamas Reni, "A Politically-Motivated Suicide in Hungary." The Misko scandal erupted in 1988 when a town council president was caught demanding that a local school teacher give the son of his political crony better grades than he deserved. The scandal was widely reported by the Hungarian media and Misko was investigated. It was found that favoritism was a common practice in this town under the leadership of Misko, who had ruled for over twenty years. During the course of the investigation Misko committed suicide. For this case, see ibid. Misko apparently overestimated the disgrace and punishment he would have had to face, for had he survived, it is likely he would have turned into an entrepreneur as did many other Communist officials, who benefited from the transition.

127. Gao, Niu, and Liu, "Dapo guanxi wang."

128. For example, the authorities in Tongling city, Anhui province (where 89 percent of the *ke*-rank and 10 percent of the county-rank officials had relatives in the same units), announced their decision to implement a system of avoidance in 1988. See Liu and He, *Huibi zhidu jianxi,* 206–7.

129. *China Daily,* June 11, 1996.

130. XH, November 21, 1996.

131. *FZRB,* August 14, 1997.

132. In the Chinese context, "localism" refers to factionalism centered around local ties as well as to the unwarranted pursuit of local political and economic interests. The former is a problem of organization, the latter is a problem of policy. Here I use it in the first sense. It is worth noting that while Beijing pursued a policy of decentralization in economic management during the Great Leap Forward in the late 1950s, it assailed (organizational) localism in some southern provinces such as Guangdong. See Wang Kuang, "Fandui difang zhuyi."

133. Harding, *Organizing China*; Wang Kuang, "Fandui difang zhuyi."

134. Liu and He, *Huibi zhidu jianxi,* 209, emphasis added.

135. To be sure, nepotism is not a unique socialist phenomenon. In Hong Kong, for example, where "entrepreneurial familialism" is a prevalent form of capitalist development, nepotism can be found in about half of Hong Kong Chinese firms. See Siu-lun Wong, "The Applicability of Asian Family Values," 138. According to some authors, nepotism facilitates economic development and is widely accepted. In such cases, it may not even be regarded as a form of corruption. The PRC case, however, is quite distinct from the case of Chinese in Hong Kong or Taiwan for two reasons. First, in the PRC, nepotism is embedded mainly in public ownership and in government units rather than in the private ownership of family firms, a predominant form of business organization in Hong Kong and Taiwan. Second, an employer in the PRC (e.g., a public unit) hires relatives not solely for rational managerial reasons, as is more often the case with Hong Kong Chinese firms.

136. The earliest practice of replacement of retired workers with their children or *dingti* appeared in 1956 as an ad hoc measure adopted by some sectors to help overcome difficulties faced by retiring workers. It became a regular practice after 1962, but only within certain sectors such as mining and lumber, and among geological workers in the field. A notable aspect is the restrictions and qualifications the government put on the *dingti* practice. It was limited to sectors such as mining, field survey, and logging, which attracted few people. That it was always reactive rather than active is clear in that most of the documents were *replies* from central authorities to local or ministerial inquiries on the matter. This factor has led some scholars to suggest that the regulations are a consolidation of practices already established and codification of decisions reached at lower levels when decision-making power was transferred to *danwei*. See Korzec, "Occupational Inheritance in the People's Republic of China."

The official endorsement of *dingti* as well *neizhao* (internal recruitment) for all sectors was announced in December 1978. It stipulated that urban *danwei*, both productive and non-productive, be given the right to hire people from within, and that one child of retired employees be allowed to "replace" the parent. With thousands of returned youths from the countryside and thousands more graduating from high schools, the government gave a green light to its implementation in order to reduce the pressure of urban unemployment. Both practices lasted until October 1986, when another State Council document formally invalidated them. The same decree, however, also left some room for certain categories of workers to be replaced by their children after 1986. This exemption remains valid. See Chen Li, "Qianyi guoyou qiye yonggong zhidu de liangge wenti." See also *ZLRN*; Henderson and Cohen, *The Chinese Hospital*; Gold, "Back to the City."

What concerns us here, however, is not the practice itself but its consequences. As Korzec noted, the actual process of replacing retired workers or cadres was often plagued by irregularities and the use of *guanxi*.

137. Due to restrictions on migration and personnel mobility between work units before the reforms, many married couples worked in different localities for years. Although the problem had existed since the founding of the PRC, the Cultural Revolution disrupted the regular process of reuniting separated couples. By 1979, there were some one million cadres separated from their spouses. Some had to give up their cadre status in order to reunite with their spouses. See *ZLRN*, 892–93.

138. To absorb this large labor force and to avoid unemployment, the government was pressed to allow practices such as *dingti* and *neizhao*. Each work unit, to a certain degree, was required to find work for the children of its own employees. One method was the opening of "labor service companies." See Gold, "Back to the City."

139. *ZLRN*, 1651.

140. Liu and He, *Huibi zhidu jianxi*, 50–51.

141. For a brief discussion of this issue, see Kraus, "The Chinese State and Its Bureaucrats," 141.

142. Liu and He, *Huibi zhidu jianxi*; Yu and Dai, "Guanyu danwei neibu ganbu qinshujuji."

143. Studies of Chinese lineage organizations and kinship groups have been conducted mainly by anthropologists. While some emphasize the marked continuity with the past of lineage organizations, others see more transformation in rural society, including lineage and kinship ties, by the state since 1949. For the former view, see Cohen, "Lineage Organization in North China." For the latter, see Potter and Potter, *China's Peasants,* and Siu, *Agents and Victims in South China.* I take the view that the revival of traditional relations in rural areas reflects both persisting values and the effects of changing economic and political alignments.

144. Cheng Ying, "Zhonggong dangzuzhi zai nongcun shiwei."

145. Mao Shaojun, "Nongcun zongzu shili manyan."

146. *Qingming* is a traditional Chinese holiday to memorialize the dead, particularly one's ancestors and other kin. It is a key part of the clan organizations' ritual activities.

147. Mao Shaojun, "Nongcun zongzu shili manyan."

148. Cheng Ying, "Zhonggong dangzuzhi zai nongcun shiwei."

149. Mao Shaojun, "Nongcun zongzu shili manyan."

150. Wang Xijia, "Nongcun ganqun guanxi heyi ruci jinzhang," 18.

151. Mao Shaojun, "Nongcun zongzu shili manyan."

152. Wang Xijia, "Nongcun ganqun guanxi heyi ruci jinzhang."

153. Cheng Ying, "Zhonggong dangzuzhi zai nongcun shiwei."

154. Qian and Xie, "Qinzu qunju xianxiang yu woguo."

155. Chen and Li, "Zongzu shili."

156. Ibid.

157. Zhang Yun, "Quanmian tigao dangyuan suzhi."

158. Minzhengbu, "Guanyu jiejue cunji zuzhi tanhuan wenti de baogao."
159. Mao Shaojun, "Nongcun zongzu shili manyan."
160. *RMRB*, October 14, 1986.
161. Qian and Xie, "Qinzu qunju xianxiang," 162–63.
162. Li Kangyi, "Guanyu cunmin weiyuanhui xuanju."
163. The Falungong, a semi-religious group founded in 1992 by a self-proclaimed reincarnation of Buddha that preaches practicing health-promoting meditation, has successfully recruited many CCP members, including high-level officials. Its rapid organizational development, tight discipline, and mobilization capacity stunned the CCP leadership. A well-organized practice-in participated by nearly 10,000 people outside the central government compound in April 1999 forced a negotiation between representatives of the Falungong, who were CCP members and held high positions in the government, and officials from the State Council. It was the stark contrast between a well-disciplined organization with more than 20 million believers and a ruling party whose organizational capacity to keep its members committed was weak at best that finally prompted the CCP to disband and suppress the Falungong. The fierce crackdown—which in some of its language and methods recalls the Cultural Revolution—is another indication of the deep-rooted fear of the CCP leadership to lose its already weak ability to maintain an effective ruling organization.

CHAPTER SIX

1. It is pertinent to examine the evolution of terms for "corrupt activities" used by members of the Chinese regime. In the early days of the post-Mao era, they were known as *"buzheng zhifeng"* (unhealthy tendencies), then in the early 1980s, *"jingji fanzui huodong"* (economic criminal activities) (see *People's Daily* editorial of February 2, 1982); in the late 1980s, *"fubai xianxiang"* (corrupt phenomena); the first time this term appeared in official literature was in a CCP and State Council directive in December 1985. This evolution reflects both the objective increase of corruption and the subjective recognition of that increase by the government.
2. Zheng and Qi, *Lianzheng jianshe ziliao xuanbian*.
3. Hebeisheng jiwei, "Guanyu fupingxian xiaoji fubai xianxiang yanzhong."
4. Ibid.
5. Xiao Yang, the current chief justice of the Supreme People's Court and a former minister of justice, made a similar observation on changing patterns of corruption. See Yang and Gao, *Woguo dangqian jingji fanzui yanjiu*, 151.
6. In fact, during the Cultural Revolution, people who owned real estate felt more pressure from radicals' attacks than people who did not. My family owned a private residence at that time, and turned it over to the state voluntarily without any charge, for a number of reasons. For one, without an unusually

high income, the family was unable to maintain the house, which was rather old. Under state ownership it could be taken care of, and our family could still rent the space from the state. But more significant, my family, particularly my father, who was then a mid-level official, believed there was little future for private real estate and that it was a political liability at the time.

7. *JJCK*, August 19, 1989.

8. Zhang, Zhou, and Shi, "Zui'e de tudi hongjiang."

9. Hebeisheng jiwei, "Guanyu fupingxian xiaoji fubai xianxiang yanzhong."

10. *Liaowang*, no. 17, 1989.

11. Zhang, Zhou, and Shi, "Zui'e de tudi hongjiang."

12. As recently as 1995, housing in China was primarily "public," owned by the state or public units. See World Bank, *From Plan to Market*. The state, through work units, allocated housing to urban employees. Criteria for housing allocation included rank, seniority, number of family members, generation, and so on. Higher-ranking officials often had an advantage over others when it came to housing space. To regulate housing assignments and to curb corruption, the CCP made it a violation of regulation for officials to have more space than others with similar needs. In 1990, the situation began to change with the emergence of the real estate market and as the state began to release the burden of providing public housing. The state expects that, with the most drastic reform measure implemented since the housing reform began, the public housing system will be fundamentally transformed as the 1998 reform unfolds.

13. *RMRB*, March 21, 1990.

14. *RMRB*, September 24, 1997.

15. Huang Weiding, *Zhongguo de yinxing jingji*, 175.

16. Zhongjiwei, *Zhengyi yu xie'er*.

17. Hebeisheng renmin jianchayuan, "Hebeisheng jiancha jiguan shinianlai zhengzhi tanwu huilu."

18. Zhongjiwei, *Zhengyi yu xie'er*.

19. Ye Tan, "Dalu sida fubai xianxiang."

20. Both of these features—direct, face-to-face tax collection and the semi-legal retention of a certain part of tax revenues—are reminiscent of the traditional Chinese taxation bureaucracy. See Zelin, *The Magistrate's Tael*.

21. In China's complex social relationships, *shuren* (familiar person) is a basic, personal connection that one may count on for instrumental purposes.

22. Interview by author, August 1997.

23. Ibid.

24. Hua Sheng, "Wuguan butan daozhi wushang bujian."

25. Yang and Gao, *Woguo dangqian jingji fanzui yanjiu*, 229.

26. *Liaowang*, no. 2, 1998.

27. Ibid., no. 10, 1997.

28. Yang Xingguo, "Rangtanwuzhe wuzangshenzhidi."

29. *JCRB*, February 15, 1999.

30. *Zhongguo Jiancha*, no. 8, 1998.

31. Ye Tan, "Dalu sida fubai xianxiang."

32. Ibid.

33. *Zhongguo Jiancha*, no. 8, 1998.

34. Interview by author, December 1997.

35. Hebeisheng renmin jianchayuan, "Hebeisheng jiancha jiguan shinianlai chengzhi tanwu huilu."

36. Chang and Xu, *Zhongguo facaifeng*, 34.

37. *Liaowang*, no. 27, 1997.

38. *Wenzhai Zhoubao*, July 4, 1993.

39. *Liaowang*, no. 29, 1996.

40. Xiao Li, "Yiqi maiguan maiguan an shimo."

41. *Liaowang*, no. 29, 1996.

42. *Liaowang*, no. 4, 1997.

43. *Liaowang*, no. 10, 1997; *JCRB*, January 25, 1997; Li Jianzhong, "Renshi renmian zhongde fubai xianxiang."

44. *RMRB*, January 21, 1998.

45. For the origins and nature of the concept of "minor public," see Lü, "Minor Public vs. Greater Public."

46. By contrast, collective graft may involve people from *different* departments or agencies. Inter-departmental collective corruption can be found in many countries. For example, James Scott found that in Indonesia under President Sukarno, there was widespread "clique-based" corruption, in which bureaucrats and army officers formed inter-departmental cliques and engaged in graft. See Scott, *Comparative Political Corruption*.

47. *JCRB*, January 30, 1997.

48. These kinds of businesses affiliated with government agencies are qualitatively different from enterprises under the administrative control of certain government agencies under central planning. Strictly speaking, the purpose of administrative control during the pre-reform period was not profit-making. Not for the agencies alone, at least. In an effort to clarify the distinction between these businesses, Marc Blecher calls this new form the "entrepreneurial state." See Blecher, "Developmental State, Entrepreneurial State."

49. *BYT*, no. 19, 1988. One may note the resemblance of this phenomenon to the practice of *guandu shangban* (official supervision and merchant management) of the late nineteenth century and the "bureaucratic capitalism" of the KMT government in the late 1940s, which was vehemently attacked by the Communists. In each of the earlier cases, the official-business collusion had a negative impact on the economy and featured rampant corruption by bureaucrats. For the practice of *guandu shangban*, see Feuerwerker, *China's Early Industrialization*.

50. *Statistical Yearbook of China* (1990), 447; *RMRB*, March 7, 1989.

51. *GRRB*, August 24, 1988. A more subtle and recent pattern in official firms is the "company that flipped its name plate" (*fanpai gongsi*)—former state administrative agencies that altered into "corporate groups" (*qiye jituan gongsi*)—which is an outgrowth of administrative downsizing and the transformation of state control over enterprises. Claiming to be economic legal persons, these companies, which have changed overnight from state administrative bureaus, still exercise control over the management of an enterprise that was previously under the control of the same people who now control the new entity. The only difference is that, whereas in the old days the agencies were provided for by the state budget, now they are financed by revenues from enterprises under their umbrella (*FZRB*, December 5, 1992). This new phenomenon distorts the purpose of the deepening administrative and economic reforms and worries the government (*RMRB*, March 2, 1993).

52. Chang and Xu, *Zhongguo facaifeng*, 30.

53. Huang and Liu, *Zhongguo gongchandang lianzheng fanfu shiji*.

54. *RMRB*, August 1, 1985.

55. Chang and Xue, *Zhongguo facaifeng*.

56. The information on this case is from the interview conducted by the author in May 1993.

57. Several Chinese visitors to the United States whom I interviewed told similar stories based on their personal experience. A visitor from Shanghai interviewed in 1995 mentioned a dramatic increase in the cost of getting a passport: for seven-day processing, 350 *yuan* (roughly equal to an average monthly salary); for three-day pick-up, 500 *yuan*; and for same-day pick-up, 600 *yuan*.

58. Yang and Tang, *Zhongguo 1992*, 153. Note here the difference between this practice and the actions of individual bank credit agents taking bribes discussed earlier. Corrupt practice in state bank branches as a whole is conducted under a much more sophisticated guise.

59. Huang and Liu, *Zhongguo gongchandang lianzheng fanfu shiji*, 367.

60. *RMRB*, September 24, 1997.

61. *RMRB*, January 14, 1999, and February 15, 1999.

62. Chen Zuolin, "Jianjue jiuzheng hangye buzheng zhifeng."

63. There is little discussion in English language scholarship of this type of corrupt practice. Hsi-Sheng Chi has noted in passing what he calls "hegemons"—public agencies that can hold people hostage and demand a ransom. See Chi, *Politics of Disillusionment*, 175–76.

64. Jia and Su, *Heimao baimao*, 143. Uniforms, a symbol of both authority and discipline, are usually worn by regulatory and law enforcement agents. In China, uniforms have an additional utility. They are clothes provided free by the state, and in poor rural areas clothing was, and still is, expensive for many people.

65. *Jiansu Jijian*, no. 8, 1993.

66. Xu Gongmei, "Zoufang songshuyu."

67. Note here that the method of *pingbi* is still being used but in a notably different way from the days of the Great Leap Forward. See Chapter 3.

68. Clause 6 of the "Supplementary Rules on Punishing Graft and Bribery Crimes" passed by the National People's Congress stipulates: "seeking or accepting materials and properties of others and pursuing the interests of others by state-owned enterprises, non-profit units, agencies, organizations, if serious, are subject to fines and the main responsible persons shall be sentenced to five years or less imprisonment or arraignment" (*JGFZX*, 116).

69. Wu Liucun, *Huiluzui ge'an yanjiu*.

70. Wang Shaoguang, "From Revolution to Involution."

71. Huang and Liu, *Zhongguo gongchandang lianzheng fanfu shiji*.

72. *Liaowang*, no. 14, 1997.

73. *SJRB*, June 19, 1993; *Baokan Wenzhai*, February 5, 1996; *NCXB*, no. 2, no. 4, no. 16, 1996; *FZRB*, April 10, 1996; *FZRB*, June 7, 1996. On how much the peasants resent the heavy financial burdens, see also Lü, "Politics of Peasant Burdens in Reform China."

74. Jia and Su, *Heimao baimao*.

75. *Liaowang*, no. 24, 1997.

76. In December 1991, the State Council issued a "Regulation on Payments and Labor From Peasants," which was intended to regulate the payments peasants make to both the state and the local community.

77. Chen Youfu, "Nongmin fudan wenti de shenceng toushi."

78. Li Qin, "Dui woguo nongmin fudan zhuangguang de fenxi."

79. Lü, "Politics of Peasant Burdens in Reform China."

80. *Henan Tongji*, no. 7, 1992.

81. Hua, "Wuguan butan daozhi wushang bujian."

82. *FZRB*, July 18, 1997.

83. *FZRB*, September 9, 1997.

84. *SJRB*, March 21, 1994.

85. *RMRB*, March 16, 1996.

86. The central government convened a meeting on the progress of the assessment-collection separation in July 1999. There, Wei Jianxing, a Politburo member in charge of anti-corruption, gave a mixed report on its progress. See *RMRB*, July 21, 1999.

87. When asked about the grand new office building of a county tax bureau, a tax agent told me that the income of the tax agents in the bureau is "not too bad." He admitted that the most important power the bureau has is tax exemption. It is an open secret that the bureau (like all other tax agencies in China) uses it to extract money, and nobody knows how much the heads of the bureau have kept for themselves. This money is what is known today in China as "fuzzy income" (interview by author, December 1993).

88. Liu, Li, and He, "Shuishi shouyizhe."

89. Jiang Jixing, "Qingshui yamen zhong de shouru chayi."

90. *RMRB*, December 5, 1995.

91. *FZRB*, January 20, 1996.

92. See *Jingbao Yuekan* (Mirror), April 1994. I personally saw it in action and reported it twice to Shenzhen city authorities, but the practice continued for at least several months in 1994.

93. Scholars have focused attention on the cooperative relations between local enterprises and government. See, e.g., Oi, "Fiscal Reform"; Huang Yasheng, "Web of Interests and Patterns of Behavior." In a study of the relationships between local economic bureaucracies and enterprises during the reforms, Huang Yasheng made the point that the two parties form a coalition characterized by collusive patterns of behaviors, which helps to stabilize the system. Here, I am suggesting something broader and less functional. The collusive patterns, once entered into to achieve the goals of the two parties involved, can be venal in nature and damaging in consequence.

94. See, for example, Thomas Gold, "The Resurgence of Civil Society in China"; Merle Goldman, "The Men Who Took the Rap in Beijing"; Andrew Nathan, *China's Crisis*.

95. One such new association is the Hebei Public Relations Association. The founder of the association, a retired official, insisted that it did not have any "forced marriage" with enterprises (Author's interview, January 1994). However, I found out later that it does run a company and publishes a journal whose board consists of twenty-five "joint sponsor units" (*lianban danwei*). All of them are business firms.

96. Yang and Tang, *Zhongguo 1992*, 97–98.

97. Ibid., 157. This kind of behavior of local state agencies and officials has been categorized as mainly non-corrupt by some scholars. According to Jean Oi, "the new budget constraints imposed by fiscal reforms compel local officials to keep their own greed in check and use the profits and revenues from local enterprises to fund local expenditures and for reinvestment." See Oi, "Fiscal Reform." I would take issue with such assumptions. Oi treats economic growth in rural China as a phenomenon unexplainable by corruption. Budget constraints indeed have led local officials to seek more funds to reinvest in local projects, but they have also compelled officials to seek their own private (or in the form of collectives) profits at the same time. The two are not necessarily mutually exclusive.

98. Zhou Jizhong, *Zhongguo xingzheng jiancha zhidu*, 615.

99. Xu Hongbing, "Danwei sishe 'xiaojinku' xingwei dingxing chutan," 33.

100. The data on these three cases are from an internally circulated study of the Hebei provincial government I was able to obtain.

101. Yang and Tang, *Zhongguo 1992*, 95.

102. *Liaowang*, no. 22, 1997.

103. Xu Hongbing, "Danwei sishe 'xiaojinku' xingwei dingxing chutan."

104. *Zhongbao*, January 26, 1987.

105. *GJJ*, no. 10, 1998, 80–81.

106. *RMRB*, August 19, 1993; Jia and Su, *Heimao baimao*, 200.

107. *FZRB*, September 11, 1997.

108. Jia and Su, *Heimao baimao*.

109. Interview by author, December 1993.

110. Interview by author, October 1991.

111. Zheng Xuwei, "Dangqian woguo caizheng kunjing."

112. According to one report, as many as 90 percent of the cases of fiscal discipline violation and corruption are related to off-budget funds. See Qu Liansheng, "Xiangzhen zichou zijin guanli gaige chuyi."

113. The relevant statutes are the PRC Penal Code, the "Supplementary Rules on Crimes of Graft and Bribery" (1988), and the NPC's "Decision on Punishing Criminal Offense in Violation of Company Law" (1995).

114. The "Administrative Penalty Law," which took effect on October 1, 1996, was meant to change the situation. One of this law's main objectives is to regulate fines assessed and collected by government agencies, and thus reduce the possibility of corruption. See *RMRB*, March 16, 1996, and May 17, 1996. So far, no public units have been prosecuted under this law.

115. For information on and discussion of this legal provision, see *FZRB*, September 10, 1997.

116. The analogy to the Great Leap Forward was not lost on farmers: "Things were done in a big way in the past, which caused us disasters. Today, with this type of fund-raising, we are made to suffer again."

117. *HBRB*, March 10, 1997.

118. *SJRB*, August 6, 1996.

119. *China Daily*, August 13, 1996.

120. *RMRB*, September 24, 1997.

121. *RMRB*, December 23, 1999.

122. *SJRB*, June 11, 1996.

123. *Zhongguo Jiancha*, no. 2, 1998.

124. Ibid.

125. *New York Times*, April 9, 1996.

126. *Far Eastern Economic Review*, December 14, 1997.

127. Political and Economic Risk Consultancy, Internet publication, 1997, http://www.asiarisk.com/.

128. These include "Disciplinary Action Rules of the CCP," "Implementation Measures on Intra-Party Supervision," "Ethical Code of CCP Cadres," "Rules Against Luxury Spending," and "Administrative Supervision Law." See *Liaowang*, no. 18, 1997.

129. An official document of the Supreme People's Procurate reveals, for example, that during the 1986 campaign the focus of the crackdown was economic crime cases (mostly graft and bribery) of the second half of 1984 and the first half of 1985. The result was to put a temporary halt to potential violations. But later the Supreme People's Procurate found that more and larger cases had taken place since the second half of 1985. See Zhongguo jiancha xuehui, *Chengzhi tanwu huilu fanzui lunwenji*, 62–63.

130. During these campaigns, certain not-so-standard measures were applied—such as assessing heavier criminal penalties than usual, including capital punishment.

131. In early 1995, the government announced that public officials were required to declare their incomes and register gifts; and that state-owned enterprises are required to report the use of entertainment funds to the workers' councils. According to official statistics, 80 percent of the large- and medium-sized units have adopted the new rules, while 85 percent of cadres made income declarations. However, government officials have also admitted that a large number of units still have not adopted the new rules, and the real effects of the rules remain unclear. See *RMRB*, August 17, 1996.

132. XH, January 14, 1997.

133. *Gonggong Guanxibao*, January 18, 1997.

134. XH, August 13, 1996.

135. In 1993, the party disciplinary inspection commission (PDIC) system and the administrative supervisory system began operating jointly for the purpose of the improvement of the inspection of Party discipline and administrative supervision under the unitary leadership of the Party. See *RMRB*, January 14, 1993.

136. Namely, *jiuzheng hangye buzhengzhifeng bangongshi*. It was first set up in 1990 under the auspices of the State Council. Since then, it has become a semi-permanent office. See Huang and Liu, *Zhongguo gongchandang lianzheng fanfu shiji*.

137. Namely, *caijin jilü dajiancha ban'gongshi*.

138. The "invited special monitor" (*teyao jianchayuan*) system was established in 1989. Under this system, disciplinary and supervisory agencies invite certain citizens from various professions and units to be unpaid monitors of party and administrative discipline. By 1996, there were some 20,000 such monitors in over half of the counties. See *RMRB*, November 28, 1996.

139. *China Daily*, August 13, 1996.

140. Huang and Liu, *Zhongguo gongchandang lianzheng fanfu shiji*, 448.

141. Several informants expressed the former view when they voiced their doubts about how high the party's top leadership was willing to go to punish violators. Such doubt is only natural because of the overall distrust and lack of confidence in all government policies. For the latter view, see Shirk, *The Political*

Logic of Economic Reform in China, 143–44, 188–89. From a rational-choice perspective, Shirk suggests that corruption and the lax attitudes toward it are used by leaders as a strategy to win political support.

142. Huang and Liu, *Zhongguo gongchandang lianzheng fanfu shiji*, 292.

143. Yang Minzhi, "Fandui fubai baohuzhuyi."

144. For example, in the case of Chen Xitong, former CCP Politburo member and mayor of Beijing, the Central Committee formed a special case group in order to conduct the investigation that eventually led to the prosecution of, or disciplinary actions against, many former city officials in 1996.

CHAPTER SEVEN

1. Lowenthal, "The Post-Revolutionary Phase in China and Russia."

2. Harding, *Organizing China.*

3. Here I borrow the taxonomy of four images of bureaucracy—Marxian, Machiavellian, Weberian, and anthropological—illuminated by Alfred Meyer. See Meyer, "Communism and Leadership." See also Esherick and Perry, "Leadership Succession."

4. See Meisner, *Mao's China*, 386.

5. See Cirtautas, "Neo-Traditionalism and the Feudalization of Post-Leninist Polities."

6. Shaoguang Wang, "From Revolution to Involution."

7. Potter and Potter, *China's Peasants.*

8. H. Y. Lee, *From Revolutionary Cadres to Party Technocrats.*

9. Harding used "semi-bureaucracy" to refer to a similar phenomenon. See his *Organizing China*. Duara used "quasi-broker" to describe the result of involutionary state building in pre-revolution China. See Duara, "State Involution."

10. For this school of thought, see Barrington Moore's path-breaking work, *Terror and Progress, USSR*. See also Huntington, *Political Order in Changing Societies*, 3–47; Johnson, *Change in Communist Systems*, 1–33.

11. See Djilas, *The New Class*; Johnson, *Change in Communist Systems*; Lowenthal, "Development vs. Utopia in Communist Policy."

12. Jowitt, "Soviet Neotraditionalism."

13. See, for example, Pye, *The Mandarin and the Cadre.*

14. Walder, "Organized Dependency and Cultures of Authority," 72; see also McCormick, "Leninist Implementation."

15. The term is used here to distinguish it from "nation building" as a historical process in which a national community is to be integrated, and "state building" as a process of the state's defining its capacity and legitimacy vis-à-vis society. "Regime building" refers to the process whereby the regime organization defines and/or redefines goals and modes of operation. Due to the changing environment and the instability of the post-revolutionary regimes, regimes

of such an order have realized, and I think quite correctly, that regime building is far from a foregone conclusion.

16. Pye, *The Mandarin and the Cadre*; Shue, *The Reach of the State*; Madsen, *Morality and Power in a Chinese Village*.

17. P. Huang, *The Peasant Family and Rural Development*, 192; See also Walder, *Communist Neo-Traditionalism*; Siu, *Agents and Victims in South China*.

18. Although the authors did not explicitly advance the thesis of neo-traditionalism or involution, the study of a northern Chinese village laid out "four continuities" that can all be regarded as strong denominators of the involutionary development of Chinese society. These are a peasant political culture, a new nationalism (blaming outsiders), personal loyalty (particularism), and a lack of well-educated human resources. One should note, though, that "continuities" were meant to describe the constant currency that transcended shifting policies rather than simply denoting the continuities of pre-revolution factors. See Friedman, Pickowicz, and Selden, *Chinese Village, Socialist State*.

19. Ibid., 269.

20. See Kwong, *The Political Economy of Corruption in China*; Gong Ting, *The Politics of Corruption in Contemporary China*; Ostergaard, "Explaining China's Recent Corruption"; Sands, "Decentralizing an Economy."

21. McCormick, "Leninist Implementation"; see also Walder, "Organized Dependency and Cultures of Authority."

22. See Lü, "Booty Socialism, Bureau-preneurs, and the State in Transition."

23. For a discussion of the phenomenon in African countries, see Mbaku, *Corruption and the Crisis of Institutional Reforms*; Williams, *Political Corruption in Africa*. An interesting comparison is with the "syndicated corruption" found in the police department in Hong Kong prior to the mid-1970s. In Hong Kong, a group of police officers from the same unit (e.g., a precinct) were involved in the extortion and distribution of payments from private citizens. There were existing "rules of the game": no officer was allowed to retain the money personally and distribution was according to the rank of the officers—the higher the rank, the more spoils one got. Similar cases were found in other departments of the Hong Kong government (Blair-Kerr, *Second Report of the Commission of Enquiry*). The pattern is close to corruption by public units in China yet not quite the same.

24. Researchers in China have noted that it is also more difficult to prosecute cases that belong to the structural corruption category. Most corruption cases that have been prosecuted are of the non-structural type. See Cheng Guoyou, "Jiegouxing fubai qianyi."

25. Indeed, some Chinese scholars have explicitly called the pervasive use of *guanxi*, nepotism, and collusive behaviors "political corruption," which behaviors, they suggest, are together more threatening than economic corruption. See Hu, Bao, and Tian, "Fubai xianxiang tanyou."

26. Scott, *Comparative Political Corruption*, 88–90.

27. Rogovin, "The Problems of Corruption in Soviet Society."

28. Although in Maoist China, administrative illness categories also included these phenomena, cadre corruption was nonetheless treated as a serious political threat, particularly after the Great Leap Forward.

29. Steven Sampson has produced excellent studies of informal relations and corruption in Romania under the Ceausescu regime. I draw from his cases and insightful analyses. See Sampson, "Bureaucracy and Corruption as Anthropological Problems."

30. Ibid., 90.

31. See Bell, *Peasants in Socialist Transition*, 253–54.

32. See Shefield, *"Pripiskii"*; W. Clark, *Crime and Punishment in Soviet Officialdom*.

33. Klugman, "The Psychology of Soviet Corruption."

34. Tucker, *The Soviet Political Mind*.

35. Jowitt, "Soviet Neotraditionalism"; Klugman, "The Psychology of Soviet Corruption."

36. Sampson, "Bureaucracy and Corruption as Anthropological Problems," emphasis in the original.

37. See Clark, *Crime and Punishment in Soviet Officialdom*. Perhaps not by coincidence, almost every control and anti-corruption body in China can find its counterpart in the Soviet Union. For example, the Party Disciplinary Inspection Commission (PDIC) in China and the Party Control Committee recreated under Brezhnev; the merged working relationship of PDIC and the Ministry of Supervision in China since 1993 and the Party-State Control Committee (KPGK) created under Khrushchev two decades earlier; the Ministry of Supervision (and its predecessor, the Commission of State Control) and the USSR's Ministry of State Control (and its predecessor, the People's Commissariat of State Control); as well as the economic crime division of the People's Procurate in both countries.

38. Bell, *Peasants in Socialist Transition*.

39. Ibid., 250.

40. Sampson, "Bureaucracy and Corruption as Anthropological Problems."

41. Schwartz, "Corruption and Political Development in the USSR"; Grossman, "The 'Second Economy' of the USSR."

42. Sampson, "The Informal Sector in Eastern Europe," 46.

43. Tarkowski, "Endowment of Nomenclature."

44. This development is somewhat different from the early experience of the Chinese regime, which also underwent several rounds of administrative streamlining, in that only a few former officials turned into private entrepreneurs then. For one thing, the private sector was more thoroughly eliminated in China before the reforms. For another, the Chinese leadership tried to retain

these officials' cadre quality even when they were not in a state agency or position. Thus in China, *jingjian* (streamlining) often meant *xiafang* (sending down) rather than "sending out." When a cadre was sent down, he was likely to remain in the nomenklatura list though at a lower level. In most cases, they would come back to the old agencies or be reassigned to other ones. As I pointed out when discussing these features earlier, this was an area where heavy informal maneuvering among cadres took place in the wake of the Cultural Revolution.

45. Tarkowski, "A Centralized System and Corruption"; "Endowment of Nomenclature."

46. Tarkowski, "Endowment of Nomenclature."

47. Treisman, "Korruptsia."

48. Templer, *Shadows and Wind*, 112.

49. Ibid., 198.

50. Ibid., 119.

51. Treisman, "Korruptsia."

52. Cirtautas, "Neo-Traditionalism and the Feudalization."

53. Theobald, *Corruption, Development and Underdevelopment*, 64; Medard, "The Underdeveloped State in Tropical Africa," 185.

54. Theobald, *Corruption, Development and Underdevelopment*, 88.

55. Joseph, *Democracy and Prebendal Politics in Nigeria*, 30; see also Leftwich, "States of Underdevelopment."

56. Namely, units of the party or state sector tried to use the power they had to take advantage of the liberal economic policy in order to build a solid economic base for the unit as a whole. Tarkowski used the term "collective endowment of nomenclatura" to describe the phenomenon in Poland in the early 1990s. See also Harsch, "Accumulators and Democrats."

57. Scott, *Comparative Political Corruption*.

58. Myrdal, *Asian Drama*, 229.

59. See, e.g., Roth, "Personal Rulership, Patrimonialism, and Empire-building"; Theobald, *Corruption, Development and Underdevelopment*; Williams, *Political Corruption in Africa*.

60. Jowitt, *New World Disorder*.

61. R. Price, *Society and Bureaucracy in Contemporary Ghana*.

62. In a study of Soviet corruption, William Clark applies the idea of the "soft state" and notes the "softness" of the post-Leninist state in Russia. He contends that many problems connected with corruption (e.g., black markets and organized crime) can be traced to the weaknesses of the Soviet state. His findings and analysis may lend support to a generalization of the involution argument beyond China. See Clark, *Crime and Punishment in Soviet Officialdom*.

63. Theobald, *Corruption, Development and Underdevelopment*, 161–62.

64. Watt, *The District Magistrate in Late Imperial China*.

65. Ibid.

66. Wang Shi, "Bofeng yu lougui," 57.

67. Ibid.

68. Li Longjian, *Mingqing jingjishi.*

69. For a discussion of the *li*, see Zhao Shiyu, "Liangzhong butong de zhengzhi xintai yu mingqing xuli de shehui diwei." See also Wang Shi, "Bofeng yu lougui."

70. In the West, growth in the sale of offices is associated with the expansion of the trade and commerce that marked the transitional stage between the patrimonial "jungle of particularistic dependencies of the high Middle ages" and rational-legal bureaucracy. See Anderson, *Lineages of the Absolute State*, 33–35. See also Theobald, *Corruption, Development and Underdevelopment*, 28. In China, the growth of the sale of offices had more to do with the fiscal needs of the ruler/state for military purposes. One can find a clear pattern in Ming-Qing history: whenever a war or military expedition took place, there would be a dramatic increase in the sale of offices and titles.

71. In English, the word "nepotism" derives from the practice of popes awarding positions to their *nipoti* or "nephews" (usually illegitimate sons). In Chinese, interestingly, the equivalent word is *qundai*, or "skirt string," which derives from the practice of acquiring office and power through a marital relationship with the royal court by a female relative (usually a daughter or sister).

72. Watt, *The District Magistrate in Late Imperial China*; see also Wei Xiumei, *Qingdai zhi huibi zhidu.*

73. Theobald, *Corruption, Development and Underdevelopment*, 22.

74. Such assumptions can be detected almost everywhere in scholarly writings on contemporary China, particularly when changing relations between state, market, and society are discussed.

75. Weber, *The Theory of Social and Economic Organization*, 347.

76. Bendix, *Max Weber.*

77. Weber, *Economy and Society*, 1028–33.

78. See, for example, Siu, *Agents and Victims in South China*; Oi, *State and Peasant in Contemporary China*; Pearson, *Joint Venture in the People's Republic of China.*

79. Shue, *The Reach of the State.*

80. Lampton, *Policy Implementation in Post-Mao China.*

81. Wang Shaoguang, "From Revolution to Involution"; see also Shirk, "Playing to the Provinces."

82. For this argument, see Lampton, *Policy Implementation in Post-Mao China*, particularly the chapters by David Bachman and Barry Naughton. See also Donnithorne, "China's Cellular Economy."

83. In a review essay, Steven Goldstein points out the need to look into the balance of power between leaders and bureaucracy in pre-reform China in

order to test the proposition that "bureaucracy has become dominant" in the post-Mao era. His insistence on a historical perspective is well taken here. See Goldstein, "Reforming Socialist Systems." My analysis is in line with Goldstein's general assumption that the leader-versus-staff conflict preceded the reform. My particular angle, however, is different from those who focus on *policy making and outcome* as indicators of such conflict. Mine is on *behavioral outcome* of cadres and on control and deviance.

84. Levinson, *Confucian China and Its Modern Fate*; see also Kraus, "The Chinese State and Its Bureaucrats," 141–42.

85. Kraus, "The Chinese State and Its Bureaucrats."

86. Nee, "Peasant Entrepreneurship and the Politics of Regulation in China," 173.

87. Ibid., 177.

88. Polanyi, *Great Transformation*, 140.

89. See Buchanan, *Toward a Theory of the Rent-Seeking Society*; Krueger, "The Political Economy of the Rent-Seeking Societies."

90. Nee, "Peasant Entrepreneurship and the Politics of Regulation in China," 178.

91. A similar point was made by Lin Yimin in his study of how enterprises use *guanxi* networks to deal with state agents under a "particularistic state" framework. See Lin, "Personal Connections, the State, and Inter-Organizational Stratification."

92. In the early stages of market formation, the need to maintain order in the marketplace is particularly crucial. This has been borne out by current market reforms in China, where fraud, copyright infringement, fake products, below-standard products, and price gouging are hindering the healthy growth of the consumer market.

93. Naughton, "Implications of the State Monopoly"; Wang Shaoguang, "From Revolution to Involution"; C. Wong, "Fiscal Reform and Local Industrialization"; Huang Yasheng, "Web of Interests and Patterns of Behavior of Chinese Local Bureaucracies."

94. Pearson, *Joint Venture in the People's Republic of China*.

95. See Oi, *Rural China Takes Off*, and her "Fiscal Reform and the Economic Foundation of Local State Corporatism."

96. This trend has been noted by Chinese and Western scholars alike. Jean Oi has coined the phrase "local corporatism" to denote a similar phenomenon. Her focus, in line with her overall argument, is nonetheless narrower than my concerns here. The dichotomy between central and local states misses an important dimension of the "corporatization" of the state agencies *at all levels*. Normatively, the suggestion that local corporatism facilitates economic development is problematic, also. When state agencies and agents, central, provincial or local, act like firms or businessmen, the legitimate functions of the state are inevitably

jeopardized. Such activity can create a distorted marketplace, where power is converted to money and regulators become unregulated, thus unable to regulate fairly and effectively.

97. Lee, *From Revolutionary Cadres to Party Technocrats*. Li and White, "Mainland China and Taiwan: Empirical Data and the Theory of Technocracy."

98. Whyte, "Who Hates Bureaucracy?" 249.

99. Eisenstadt, "Bureaucracy, Bureaucratization, and Debureaucratization," 307. China scholar Martin King Whyte makes a similar observation. He calls this type of bureaucratization a "structural" one. See Whyte, "Who Hates Bureaucracy?"

100. Weber, *Economy and Society*.

101. For example, Stanley Udy Jr. presents empirical evidence to show that these two kinds of bureaucratization tend to be negatively correlated. See Udy, " 'Bureaucracy' and 'Rationality' in Weber's Organizational Theory."

102. Eisenstadt, "Bureaucracy, Bureaucratization, and Debureaucratization," 307.

103. Randall and Theobald, *Political Change and Underdevelopment*.

104. Huntington, *Political Order in Changing Societies*, 67.

105. H. Y. Lee, *From Revolutionary Cadres to Party Technocrats*, 9.

106. For the concept of "booty capitalism," see Hutchcroft, "Booty Capitalism." For similar views on the post-Communist regimes, see Jowitt, "Dizzy with Democracy"; Root, "Corruption in China."

Abueva, Jose. "The Contribution of Nepotism, Spoils and Graft to Political Development." *East-West Center Review* 3, no. 1 (1966): 45–54.

———. "What Are We in Power For? The Sociology of Graft and Corruption." *Philippino Sociological Review* 8 (1970): 203–10.

Afanas'ev, M. "On the Analysis of Bureaucracy Under Real Socialism." *Problems of Economics* 32, no. 5 (1989): 69–88.

Alam, M. S. "Some Economic Costs of Corruption in LDCs." *Journal of Development Studies* 27, no. 1 (1990): 89–97.

Alatas, Syed Hussein. *The Problem of Corruption.* Singapore: Times Books International, 1986.

An Zhi. *Zhiqing chenfu lu* (The rise and fall of educated youths). Chengdu: Sichuan renmin chubanshe, 1988.

An Ziwen. "Wei xiaochu tangzuzhi nei de xiaojide he bu jiankangde xianxiang er douzheng" (Fight for the elimination of the negative and unhealthy tendencies in the party organization). *Xuexi* (Study), no. 3 (1953): 20–25.

———. *An Ziwen zuzhi gongzuo wenxuan* (Collected articles and speeches of An Ziwen on organizational work). Edited by Han Jincao. Beijing: Zhonggong zhongyang dangxiao chubanshe, 1988.

Anderson, Perry. *Lineages of the Absolute State.* London: New Left Books, 1979.

Andvig, Jens. "The Economics of Corruption: A Survey of Issues and Methods of Analysis." *Norsk Utenrikspolitiks Institutt Rapport* (Norway), no. 104 (1986).

———. "Why Do Corruption Rates Differ?" Unpublished manuscript, 1987.

Anhui sheng renminzhengfu bangongting, ed. *Anhui shengqing, 1949–1983* (The reality of Anhui province, 1949–1983). Hefei: Anhui renmin chubanshe, 1985.

Aquino, Belinda. *The Politics of Plunder: The Philippines Under Marcos.* Manila: Great Books Trading and College of Public Administration (University of Philippines), 1987.

Bachman, David. *Bureaucracy, Economy, and Leadership in China: The Institutional*

Origins of the Great Leap Forward. Cambridge: Cambridge University Press, 1991.

Barker, Ernest, trans. and ed. *The Politics of Aristotle*. Oxford: Clarendon Press, 1946.

Barnard, Chester. *The Functions of the Executive*. Cambridge, Mass.: Harvard University Press, 1938.

Barnett, A. Doak. *Communist China: The Early Years, 1949–55*. New York: Praeger, 1964.

———. *Cadres, Bureaucracy, and Political Power in Communist China*. New York and London: Columbia University Press, 1967.

Bates, Robert. *Markets and States in Tropical Africa: The Political Basis of Agricultural Policies*. Berkeley: University of California Press, 1981.

Baum, Richard. *Ssu-Ching: The Socialist Education Movement of 1962–1966*. Berkeley: China Research Monographs (University of California), 1968.

———. *Prelude to Revolution: Mao, the Party, and the Peasant Question, 1962–66*. New York: Columbia University Press, 1975.

Bayley, David. 1966. "The Effects of Corruption in a Developing Nation." *Western Political Quarterly* 19, no. 4 (1966): 719–32.

Bell, Peter D. *Peasants in Socialist Transition: Life in a Collectivized Hungarian Village*. Berkeley: University of California Press, 1984.

Ben Dor, Gabriel. 1974. "Corruption, Institutionalization, and Political Development: The Revisionist Theses Revisited." *Comparative Political Studies* 7, no. 1 (1974): 63–83.

Bendix, Renhard. *Nation-Building and Citizenship*. Berkeley: University of California Press, 1964.

———. *Max Weber: An Intellectual Portrait*. Berkeley: University of California Press, 1977.

Benson, George, Steven Maaranen, and Alan Heslop. *Political Corruption in America*. Lexington, Mass.: D. C. Heath, 1978.

Berliner, Joseph. *Factory and Manager in the USSR*. Cambridge, Mass.: Harvard University Press, 1957.

Bernstein, Thomas. "Keeping the Revolution Going: Problems of Village Leadership after Land Reform." In John Wilson Lewis, ed., *Party Leadership and Revolutionary Power in China*. New York: Cambridge University Press, 1970.

———. *Up to the Mountains and Down to the Villages*. New Haven: Yale University Press, 1977.

———. "Stalinism, Famine, and Chinese Peasants: Grain Procurement during the Great Leap Forward." *Theory and Society* 13, no. 3 (1984): 339–77.

Blair-Kerr, Alastair. *Second Report of the Commission of Enquiry under Sir Alastair Blair-Kerr*. Hong Kong: n.p, 1973.

Blecher, Marc. "Developmental State, Entrepreneurial State: The Political

Economy of Socialist Reform in Xinji Municipality and Guanghan County." In Gordon White, ed., *The Chinese State in the Era of Economic Reform.* Armonk, N.Y.: M. E. Sharpe, 1991.

———. Review of Walder's *Communist Neo-traditionalism. Pacific Affairs* 60, no. 4 (1987): 657–59.

Blecher, Marc, and Vivienne Shue. *Tethered Deer: Government and Economy in a Chinese County.* Stanford: Stanford University Press, 1996.

Blecher, Marc, and Gordon White. *Micropolitics in Contemporary China: A Technical Unit during and after the Cultural Revolution.* Armonk, N.Y.: M. E. Sharpe, 1979.

Bo Yibo. *Ruogan zhongda juece yu shijian de huigu* (Recollections of some major decision making and events), vols. 1 and 2. Beijing: Zhonggong zhongyang dangxiao chubanshe, 1991, 1993.

Boyne, Roy. 1984. "Weber on Socialism and Charisma: A Comment." *Soviet Studies* 36, no. 4 (1984): 602–5.

Brooks, Robert. *Corruption in American Politics and Life.* New York: Dodd, Mead, 1910.

Buchanan, James, et al. *Toward a Theory of the Rent-Seeking Society.* College Station: Texas A and M University Press, 1980.

Burawoy, Michael. "View from Production." In Chris Smith and Paul Thompson, eds., *Labour in Transition: The Labour Process in Eastern Europe and China.* London: Routledge, 1992.

Burns, John. *Political Participation in Rural China.* Berkeley: University of California Press, 1988.

———. *The Chinese Communist Party's Nomenclature System.* New York: M. E. Sharpe, 1989.

Butterfield, Fox. *China: Alive in a Bitter Sea.* New York: Times Books, 1982.

Cai Dingzhao. *Guojia jiandu zhidu* (The system of administrative supervision). Beijing: Zhongguo falü chubanshe, 1991.

Caiden, Gerald E. 1988. "Toward a General Theory of Official Corruption." *Asian Journal of Public Administration* 10, no. 1 (1988): 3–26.

Caiden, Gerald E., and Naomi Caiden. "Administrative Corruption." *Public Administration Review* 37 (1977): 301–9.

Caizheng kexue yanjiusuo. *Geming genjudi caizheng jingji* (Finance and economy in the revolutionary bases). Beijing: Zhongguo caizheng jingji chubanshe, 1985.

Caizhengbu and Jianchabu. *Caizheng jiancha gongzuo wenjian ziliao xuanbian* (A selection of documents and materials on financial supervision work), vol. 3. Beijing: Zhongguo caizheng jingji chubanshe, 1990.

Carino, Ledivina. "The Politicization of the Philippine Bureaucracy: Corruption or Commitment?" *International Review of Administrative Science* 1 (1985): 13–18.

Carino, Ledivina, ed. *Bureaucratic Corruption in Asia: Causes, Consequences and Controls*. Quezon City: JMC Press, 1986.

Chan, Anita. 1993. "Dispel Misconceptions About the Red Guard Movement." *Papers of the Center for Modern China* 4, no. 6 (1993): 1–29.

Chan, Anita, and Jonathan Unger. 1982. "Grey and Black: The Hidden Economy of Rural China." *Pacific Affairs* 55, no. 3 (1982): 452–71.

Chang Xin and Xu Hui. *Zhongguo facaifeng* (The fever to make money in China). Shenyang: Shengyang chubanshe, 1988.

Chen Dejin. "Jiangguo chuqi dangfeng yu lianzheng jianshe" (Party building and good governance in the early period of the PRC). *Sixiang Zhanxian* (Ideology Front), no. 3 (1991): 13–18.

Chen Erjin. "Lun wuchan jieji minzhu geming" (The proletarian democratic revolution). Originally published in *Siwu Luntan* (April 5th Forum), no. 10 (1979). *DDKH*, vol. 1: 73–218.

Chen Feng. "Zhuanxingqi ganbu jieceng de diwei biandong he fubai de liyi genyuan ji zhili" (Changes in cadres' social status and the sources of corruption and its control). *Shehuixue Yanjiu* (Sociological Studies), no. 5 (1997): 93–101.

Chen Jianxin. "Jingti jiti fubai" (Vigilance against collective corruption). *Minzhu Yufazhi* (Democracy and Legality), no. 9 (1997).

Chen Kuide. "Zhonggong jiazu zhengzhi de xingqi" (The rise of communist familial politics in China). *Minzhu Zhongguo* (Democratic China) (June 1992): 71–74.

Chen Li. "Qianyi guoyou qiye yonggong zhidu de liangge wenti" (Two problems in SOE hiring practice). *Sichuan Daxue Xuebao* (Journal of Sichuan University), no. 4 (1996).

Chen Shihui. "1959 nian de fanyouqing douzheng" (The anti-rightist orientation campaign of 1959). *Dangshi Yanjiu* (Studies of CCP History), no. 3 (1986): 9–15.

Chen Yeping and Han Jincao. *An Ziwen zhuanlüe* (A short biography of An Ziwen). Taiyuan: Shanxi renmin chubanshe, 1985.

Chen Yongping and Li Weisha. "Zongzu shili: Dangqian nongcun shequ shenghuo zhong yigu qianzai de pohuai liliang" (Clans: A potential destructive force in current rural communities). *Shehuixue Yanjiu* (Sociological Study), no. 5 (1991): 31–36.

Chen Youfu. "Nongmin fudan wenti de shenceng toushi" (A deeper understanding of the peasant burden problem). *Gaige Yu Lilun* (Reform and theory), no. 1 (1994): 52–55.

Chen, Yung-fa. *Making Revolution: The Communist Movement in Eastern and Central China, 1937–1945*. Berkeley: University of California Press, 1986.

Chen Zhili. *Zhongguo gongchandang jiansheshi* (The history of party building of the CCP). Shanghai: Shanghai renmin chubanshe, 1991.

Chen Zuolin. "Jianjue jiuzheng hangye bucheng zhifeng, gaohao dangfeng he lianzheng jianshe" (Resolutely stop the vocational unhealthy tendencies and build a clean government and party). *Qiushi* (In Search of Truth), no. 20 (1990): 9–13.

Cheng Dinghe. "Lüelun ganbu zhidu gaige" (On the reform of the cadre system). *Jianghuai Lun Tan* (Jianghuai Forum), no. 6 (1986): 35–37.

Cheng Guoyou. "Jiegouxing fubai qianyi" (A discussion of structural corruption). *Shehui* (Society) (January 1994): 13–15.

Cheng Tiejun. *The Household Registration (Hukou) System in China*. Ph.D. dissertation, State University of New York at Binghamton, 1991.

Cheng Ying. "Zhonggong dangzuzhi zai nongcun shiwei" (The weakening power of the CCP in the countryside). *Jiushi Niandai* (The Nineties) (June 1990): 70–71.

———. "Qianbaiwan ganbu mianlin dajingjian" (Hundreds of thousands of officials are facing streamlining). *Jiushi Niandai* (The Nineties) (November 1992): 31–33.

Chi, Hsi-sheng. *Politics of Disillusionment: The Chinese Communist Party Under Deng Xiaoping, 1978–1989*. Armonk, N.Y.: M. E. Sharpe, 1990.

Cirtautas, Arista. "Neo-Traditionalism and the Feudalization of Post-Leninist Polities." Conference paper, American Political Science Association, 1994.

Clark, William. *Crime and Punishment in Soviet Officialdom*. Armonk, N.Y.: M. E. Sharpe, 1993.

Clarke, Michael, ed. *Corruption: Causes, Consequences and Control*. London: Frances Pinter, 1983.

Cohen, Myron. "Lineage Organization in North China." *Journal of Asian Studies* 49, no. 3 (1990): 509–34.

Cong Jin. *1949–1989 de Zhongguo: Quzhe fazhan de suiyue* (China, 1949–1989: the era of difficult development), vol. 2. Zhengzhou: Henan renmin chubanshe, 1989.

Connor, Walter. *Socialism's Dilemmas: State and Society in the Soviet Bloc*. New York: Columbia University Press, 1988.

Critchlow, James. "Corruption, Nationalism, and the Native Elite in Soviet Central Asia." *Journal of Communist Studies* 4, no. 2 (1988): 143–61.

Crozier, Michel. *The Bureaucratic Phenomenon*. Chicago: University of Chicago Press, 1964.

Dangdai zhongguo shangye bianjibu. *Zhonghua renmin gongheguo shangye dashiji, 1958–1978* (A chronology of major events in the commercial sector of the PRC, 1958–78). Beijing: Zhongguo shangye chubanshe, 1990.

Davis, Deborah. "Patrons and Clients in Chinese Industry." *Modern China* 14, no. 4 (1988): 487–97.

DeGlopper, Donald. "Doing Business in Lukang." In W. Willmott, ed., *Economic Organization in Chinese Society*. Stanford: Stanford University Press, 1972.

Deng Xiaoping. *Deng Xiaoping wenxuan, 1975–1982* (Selected works of Deng Xiaoping, 1975–1982). Beijing: Renmin chubanshe, 1983.

Ding Shu. *Renhuo* (Disaster by human: The Great Leap Forward and Great Famine). Hong Kong: The Nineties Monthly Press, 1991.

Ding Shuimu. "Guanyu dangnei buzhengzhifeng de shehuixue sikao" (A sociological reflection on the intra-party unhealthy tendencies). *Shehui Kexue* (Social Science), no. 8 (1988): 61–63.

Dittmer, Lowell. "The Structure of the Chinese State." In Yu-ming Shaw, ed., *Power and Policy in the PRC*. Boulder: Westview Press, 1985.

———. *China's Continuous Revolution: The Post-Liberation Epoch: 1949–1981*. Berkeley: University of California Press, 1987.

———. "Patterns of Elite Strife and Succession in Chinese Politics." *China Quarterly*, no. 123 (1990): 405–30.

———. "Zhonggong dangzuzhi zai nongcun shiwei" (The weakening power of the CCP in the countryside). *Jiushi Niandai* (The Nineties) (June 1990): 70–71.

———. "Tiananmen Reconsidered." *Pacific Affairs* 64 (Winter 1991–92): 529–35.

Djilas, Milovan. *The New Class: An Analysis of the Communist System*. New York: Praeger, 1957.

Domenach, Jean-Luc. *The Origins of the Great Leap Forward: The Case of One Chinese Province*. Boulder: Westview Press, 1995.

Dong Xuetao. "Dangnei buzhengzhifeng chansheng de guilü, tezheng he genyuan" (The patterns, characteristics and roots of intra-party unhealthy tendencies). *Lilun Xuekan* (Study of Theory), no. 5 (1988): 34–36.

Donnithorne, Audry. "China's Cellular Economy: Some Economic Trends Since the Cultural Revolution." *China Quarterly*, no. 52 (1972): 605–19.

Douglas, Jack, and John M. Johnson. *Official Deviance: Readings in Malfeasance, Misfeasance, and Other Forms of Corruption*. Philadelphia: J. B. Lippincott Company, 1977.

Dow, Thomas E., Jr. "The Theory of Charisma." *Sociological Review* 10 (1969): 306–18.

Dowse, Robert. "Conceptualizing Corruption." *Government and Opposition* 12, no. 2 (1977): 244–54.

Duara, Prasenjit. "State Involution: A Study of Local Finances in North China." *Comparative Studies in Society and History* 29, no. 1 (1987): 132–61.

———. *Culture, Power, and the State: Rural North China, 1900–1942*. Stanford: Stanford University Press, 1988.

Dwivedi, O. P. "Bureaucratic Corruption in Developing Countries." *Asian Survey* 7, no. 1 (1967): 18–36.

Eisenstadt, E. S. "Bureaucracy, Bureaucratization, and Debureaucratization." In A. Etzioni, ed., *A Sociological Reader on Complex Organizations*. New York: Holt, Rinehart & Winston, Inc., 1969.

Ekpo, Monday. *Bureaucratic Corruption in Sub-Saharan Africa*. Washington, D.C.: University Press of America, 1979.

Elster, Jon. *Sour Grapes*. Cambridge: Cambridge University Press, 1983.

Endicott, Stephen. *Red Earth: Revolution in a Sichuan Village*. London: I. B. Tauris & Co. Ltd. Publishers, 1988.

Esherick, Joseph, and Elizabeth Perry. 1983. "Leadership Succession in the People's Republic of China: 'Crisis' or Opportunity?" *Studies in Comparative Communism* 16, no. 3 (1983): 171–77.

Etzioni, Amitai. *The Active Society: A Theory of Societal and Political Process*. New York: Free Press, 1968.

Etzioni, Amitai, ed. *A Sociological Reader on Complex Organizations*. New York: Holt, Rinehart & Winston, Inc., 1969.

Etzioni-Halevy, Eva. "Exchange Material Benefits for Political Support: A Comparative Analysis." In Heidenheimer, Johnston, and LeVine, eds. *Political Corruption*. New Brunswick, N.J.: Transaction Publishers, 1989.

Feldbrugge, F. J. "Government and Shadow Economy in the Soviet Union." *Soviet Studies* 36, no. 4 (1984): 528–43.

Feng Ding. "Lun fanxing" (On self-reflection). *Fu Xiao* (Dawn), no. 4 (1943).

Feng Jianfu et al. *Zhongguo guoqing congshu (bai xianshi jingji shehui diaocha): Hailin* (Series on China's state of the nation [a 100 county-city socioeconomic study]: Hailin). Beijing: Zhongguo dabaike quanshu chubanshe, 1991.

Feuerwerker, Albert. *China's Early Industrialization: Sheng Hsuan-Hui, 1844–1926, and Mandarin Enterprises*. Cambridge, Mass.: Harvard University Press, 1958.

Findlay, Mark, and Thomas Chor-Wing Chiu. "Sugar Coated Bullets: Corruption and the New Economic Order in China." *Contemporary Crisis* 13, no. 2 (1989): 145–61.

Foster, George M. "Peasant Society and the Image of Limited Good." *American Anthropologist* 67 (1965): 293–315.

Freedman, Maurice. *Chinese Lineage and Society: Fukien and Kwangtung*. New York: Humanities Press, 1966.

Friedman, Edward, Paul Pickowicz, and Mark Selden. *Chinese Village, Socialist State*. New Haven: Yale University Press, 1991.

Friedrich, Carl. "Political Pathology." *Political Quarterly* 37 (1966).

Fu Yong and Gao Hongguo. "Zai guoji gongyun shi shang dangnei jiandu jizhi tuihua qishilu" (The revelation of the devoluted inner-party control mechanism in the history of the international communist movement). *Mao Zedong Sixiang Yanjiu* (Studies of Mao Zedong Thoughts), no. 3 (1989): 43–46.

Gao Shudong. "Lun jianguo chuqi dangde ganbu guanli tizhi de miange" (The changes in the cadre management system in the early years of the PRC). *Dangshi Yanjiu* (Research in CCP History), no. 6 (1987): 98–101.

Gao Xin. "Zhu Rongji neng tengshang zaixiang baozuo?" (Can Zhu Rongji become the prime minister?) *Tansuo* (Probe) (February 1992): 67–68.

Gao Zongmin, Niu Shuchen, and Liu Zhanzhong. "Dapo 'guanxi wang.'" In Xing Chongzhi, ed., *Duanzheng dangfeng wenji* (A collection of works on keeping an upright party style). Shijiazhuang: Hebei renmin chubanshe, 1987.

Ge Yaoliang. "Guanyu woguo shimin zhengzhi gaige yishi he xintai de fenxi" (An analysis of the psychological state and opinions of Chinese citizens on political reform). *Juece Yu Xinxi* (Decision-making and Information), no. 1 (1989): 36–40.

Geertz, Clifford. *Agricultural Involution: The Process of Ecological Change in Indonesia*. Berkeley: University of California Press, 1963.

Gillespie, Kate, and Gwenn Okruhlik. "The Political Dimensions of Corruption Cleanups: A Framework for Analysis." *Comparative Politics* 24, no. 1 (1991): 77–95.

Gold, Thomas. "Back to the City: the Return of Shanghai's Educated Youth." *China Quarterly*, no. 84 (1981).

———. "After Comradeship: Personal Relations in China Since the Cultural Revolution." *China Quarterly*, no. 104 (1985): 657–75.

———. "The Resurgence of Civil Society in China." *Journal of Democracy* 1 (1990): 18–31.

Goldman, Merle. *Literary Dissent in Communist China*. New York: Athenaeum, 1971.

———. "The Men Who Took the Rap in Beijing." *World Monitor* (August 1991): 16–19.

Goldstein, Steven. "Reforming Socialist Systems: Some Lessons of the Chinese Experience." *Studies in Comparative Communism* 21, no. 2 (1988): 221–37.

Gong, Ting. "Corruption and Reform in China: An Analysis of Unintended Consequences." *Crime, Law, and Social Change* 19, no. 6 (1993): 311–27.

———. *The Politics of Corruption in Contemporary China: An Analysis of Policy Outcomes*. Westport, Conn.: Praeger, 1994.

Gong Xiaoxia. "Ganbu xingwei fangshi de bianhua" (Changes in behavioral modes of cadres). *Zhongguo Zhichun* (China Spring) (March 1992): 52–54.

Gonggong Guanxibao (Public Relations Daily). Beijing.

Grossman, Gregory. "The 'Second Economy' of the USSR." *Problems of Communism* 26, no. 5 (1977): 25–40.

Guojia Tongjiqu. *Zhongguo shehui tongji ziliao* (Social statistics of China, 1990). Beijing: Zhongguo tongji chubanshe, 1990.

Hann, C. M. *A Village Without Solidarity: Polish Peasants in Years of Crisis*. New Haven: Yale University Press, 1985.

Harding, Harry. *Organizing China: The Problem of Bureaucracy 1949–1976*. Stanford: Stanford University Press, 1981.

————. "The Study of Chinese Politics: Toward a Third Generation of Scholarship." *World Politics* 36 (1984): 283–307.

Harris, Peter. "Socialist Graft: The Soviet Union and the People's Republic of China—A Preliminary Survey." *Corruption and Reform* 1 (1986): 13–32.

————. "Corruption and Responsibility in the PRC." Unpublished manuscript, 1988.

Harsch, Ernest. "Accumulators and Democrats: Challenging State Corruption in Africa." *Journal of Modern African Studies* 31, no. 1 (1993): 31–48.

He Kailong, ed. *Dangdai zhongguo de gongshang xingzheng guanli* (Business and commercial administration in contemporary China). Beijing: Dangdai zhongguo chubanshe, 1991.

He Ping. "Lun zuzhi guannian" (On organizational consciousness). *Lilun Daokan* (Journal of Theory), no. 1 (1989): 31–34.

He Yuwen. *Zhonggong caizheng jiepao* (An anatomy of finance of the Chinese Communists). Hong Kong: Asia Press, 1953.

Hebeisheng jiwei (Hebei PDIC). "Guanyu fupingxian xiaoji fubai xianxiang yanzhong zizhang manyan qingkuang de diaocha" (An investigation of the growing corruption and passivity in Fuping county). Internal report, 1991.

Hebeisheng renmin jianchayuan (Hebei procurate). "Hebeisheng jiancha jiguan shinianlai chengzhi tanwu huilu fanzui qingkuang jianjie" (A brief introduction to the anti-corruption cases of the Hebei procurate in the last decade). Unpublished document, 1991.

Hebeisheng zonggonghui. "Hebeisheng zhigong duiwu diaocha ziliao" (An investigation of the workers of Hebei province). Unpublished document, 1986.

Heidenheimer, Arnold, Michael Johnston, and Victor LeVine, eds. *Political Corruption: A Handbook*. New Brunswick, N.J.: Transaction Publishers, 1989.

Heilongjiang nongye hezuoshi bianweihui. *Heilongjiang nongye hezuoshi.* (History of the agricultural collectivization in Heilongjiang province). Beijing: Zhonggong dangshi ziliao chubanshe, 1990.

Henan Tongji (Henan Statistics) (Zhengzhou).

Henderson, Gail, and Myron Cohen. *The Chinese Hospital: A Socialist Work Unit*. New Haven: Yale University Press, 1984.

Hirszowicz, Maria. *The Bureaucratic Leviathan: A Study in the Sociology of Communism*. Oxford: Martin Robertson, 1980.

Hope, Kempe. "Politics, Bureaucratic Corruption, and Maladministration in the Third World." *International Review of Administrative Science* 1 (1985): 1–6.

Hu Angang. *Tiaozhan zhongguo* (China's challenges). Taipei: Xinxin wen wenhua shiye gufeng gongsi, 1995.

Hu Heli. "Lianzheng sanze" (Three solutions to corruption). *Jingji Yu Shehui Tizhi Bijiao* (Comparative Studies of Society and Economy), no. 2 (1989).

Hu Jiayong. "Woguo zhengfu guimo weishenmo chixu bengzhang?" (Why has the government kept growing?) *Gaige* (Reform), no. 3 (1998): 87–92.

Hu Shizu and Cao Guanghui. "Rong guan yousilu" (A worrisome report about the explosion of official ranks). *Neican Xuanbian* (Selected Internal References), no. 22 (1992).

Hu Xiaohan, Bao Yonghui, and Tian Wenxi. "Fubai xianxiang tanyou" (An inquiry into corruption phenomena). *Guoqing Yanjiu* (Study of State of the Nation), no. 3 (1989).

Hu Zhihe. "Tantan dangnei buzhengzhifeng yu fubai xianxiang de lianxi yu qubie" (The connection and differences between intra-party unhealthy tendencies and corruption). *Dangzheng Ganbu Xuekan* (Journal of Party and Government Cadre Study), no. 9 (1990): 27–29.

Hua Sheng. "Wuguan butan daozhi wushang bujian" (Corruption of officials causes corruption of merchants). *Tansuo* (Quest) (April 1993).

Huang, Philip. *The Peasant Economy and Social Change in North China*. Stanford: Stanford University Press, 1985.

———. *The Peasant Family and Rural Development in the Yangzi Delta, 1350–1988*. Stanford: Stanford University Press, 1990.

Huang Rongkun. "San ling wu shen yu lü jin bu zhi de fansi" (A reflection on the inefficacy of orders and decrees). *Dangxiao Luntan* (Party School Forum), no. 2 (1989): 59–62.

Huang Shu-min. *The Spiral Road: Change in a Chinese Village in the Eyes of a Communist Party Leader*. Boulder: Westview Press, 1989.

Huang Weiding. *Zhongguo de yinxing jingji* (Hidden economy in China). Beijing: Zhongguo shangye chubanshe, 1996.

Huang Xiurong and Liu Songbin. *Zhongguo gongchandang lianzheng fanfu shiji* (A history of anti-corruption in the CCP). Beijing: Zhongguo fangzheng chubanshe, 1997.

Huang Yao et al. *Huihuang de zhiqingmeng* (Glorious dream of educated youths). Changsha: Hunan wenyi chubanshe, 1990.

Huang, Yasheng. "Web of Interests and Patterns of Behavior of Chinese Local Bureaucracies and Enterprises during Reforms." *China Quarterly*, no. 123 (1990): 431–58.

Humphrey, Caroline. *Karl Marx Collective: Economy, Society and Religion in a Siberian Collective Farm*. Cambridge: Cambridge University Press, 1983.

Hunan yiyang diqu renshiju. "Ganbu 'jinqin fanzhi' de biduan jiqi duice" (The maladies and solution of cadre "inbreeding"). In Liu and He, eds., *Huibizhidu jiangxi*. Beijing: Zhongguo renshi chubanshe, 1990.

Huntington, Samuel. *Political Order in Changing Societies*. New Haven and London: Yale University Press, 1968.

Huntington, Samuel, and C. Moore, eds. *Authoritarian Politics in Modern Societies*. New York, 1977.

Huo Mu. *Guangrong yu mengxiang: Zhongguo zhiqing ershi wunian shi* (Glory and dream: Twenty-five years of history of Chinese educated youths). Chengdu: Chengdu chubanshe, 1992.

Hutchcroft, Paul. "Booty Capitalism: Business-Government Relations in the Philippines." In Andrew MacIntyre, ed., *Business and Government in Industrializing Asia*. Ithaca: Cornell University Press, 1994.

Hutchings, Robert L. " 'Leadership Drift' in the Communist Systems of Soviet Union and Eastern Europe." *Studies in Comparative Communism* 22, no. 1 (1989): 5–9.

Janos, Andrew. *Politics and Paradigms*. Stanford: Stanford University Press, 1986.

Ji Guolian. "Dangqian junren tanwu huilu fanzui de qushi yuanyin ji duice" (Tendency, reasons and solution of current graft and bribery crimes in the military). In Zhongguo jiancha xuehui, ed., *Chengzhi tanwu huilu fanzui lunwenji*. Beijing: Zhongguo jiancha chubanshe, 1990.

Ji Yan. "Dangnei buzhengzhifeng suoyuan" (Tracing the sources of intra-party unhealthy tendencies). *Shanxi Shida Xuebao* (Journal of Shanxi Normal University), no. 1 (1989): 26–27.

Jia Guangqi and Rong Shouli. "Zhide chensi de niandai" (The years worth reflecting on). *Dangshi Bocai* (Highlights of Party History), no. 1 (1990): 8–11.

Jia, Hao, and Lin Zhimin. *Changing Central-Local Relations in China*. Boulder: Westview Press, 1994.

Jia Lusheng and Su Ya. *Heimao baimao: Zhongguo gaige xianzhuang toushi* (Black cat, white cat: Perspectives on current reforms in China). Changsha: Hunan wenyi chubanshe, 1992.

Jianchabu zhengce faguisi. *Jiancha yewu fagui zhengce xuanbian* (Selected laws, regulations, and policies governing supervision work, 1989–90). Beijing: Zhongguo zhengfa daxue chubanshe, 1990.

Jiang Jixing. "Qingshui yamen zhong de shouru chayi" (Income disparity among the non-profit agencies). *Shehui* (Society), no. 9 (1991): 13–15.

Jiang Siyi. "Suqing fengjianyidu shi yixiang zhongyao renwu" (An important task: Cleaning up the poisonous residue of feudalism). *RMRB*, August 1, 1986.

Jiang Sui. "Liu Huaqing gui xing tanmi" (The truth about Liu Huaqing's Guangxi trip). *Cheng Ming* (Contention) (February 1993): 18–19.

Jiang Wei. "Yianran huishou" (Looking back). *Baogao Wenxue* (Reportage), no. 12 (1989).

Jiang Yi et al. 1992. *Zhongguo gongchandang zai Shanghai: 1921–1991* (The Chinese Communist Party in Shanghai: 1921–91). Shanghai: Shanghai renmin chubanshe, 1992.

Jiangsu Jijian (Disciplinary Inspection in Jiangsu). Nanjing: PDIC of Jiangsu Province.

Jin Bang. "Zhide yinqi renmen yanzhong zhuyi de wenti: Hebeisheng bufen shixian jiguan qinshuhua wenti diaocha" (A serious problem worth our attention: An investigation of familialization in some cities and counties of Hebei province). *Hebei Shelian Tongxun* (Bulletin of Hebei Social Science Association) (December 1986): 44–46.

Jin Chunming. *Jianguo hou sanshisan nian* (The thirty-three years after the founding of the state). Shanghai: Shanghai renmin chubanshe, 1987.

Jin Longze. "Xinshiqi dangyuan weijifanfa de tedian, yuanyin ji fangfancuoshi" (Patterns, causes and preventive measures of behavior violating laws and disciplines). *Tianchi Xuekan* (Journal of Tianchi) (March 1988): 30–35.

Jin Xiaoming. "Fakuan beihou de heidong" (The black hole behind fines). *Neican Xuanbian* (Selected Internal References), no. 7 (1990): 17–20.

Jingji Shehui Tizhi Bijiao. *Fubai: Huobi yu quanli de jiaohuan* (Corruption: An exchange of money and power). Beijing: Zhongguo zhanwang chubanshe, 1989.

Johnson, Chalmers. "Tanaka Kakuei, Structural Corruption, and the Advent of Machine Politics in Japan." *Journal of Japanese Studies* 12, no. 1 (1986): 1–28.

Johnson, Chalmers, ed. *Change in Communist Systems*. Stanford: Stanford University Press, 1970.

Johnston, Michael. "The Political Consequences of Corruption: A Reassessment." *Comparative Politics* 18, no. 3 (1986): 367–91.

Johnston, Michael, and Yufan Hao. "China's Surge of Corruption." *Journal of Democracy* 6, no. 4 (1995): 80–94.

Jones, Edwin. "Politics, Bureaucratic Corruption, and Maladministration in the Third World: Some Commonwealth Caribbean Considerations." *International Review of Administration Science* 1 (1985): 19–23.

Joseph, Richard. *Democracy and Prebendal Politics in Nigeria*. Cambridge: Cambridge University Press, 1987.

Joseph, William. "A Tragedy of Good Intentions: Post-Mao Views of the Great Leap Forward." *Modern China* 12, no. 4 (1986): 419–57.

Joseph, William, Christine Wong, and David Zweig, eds. *New Perspectives on the Cultural Revolution*. Cambridge, Mass.: Harvard University Press, 1991.

Jowitt, Kenneth. "An Organizational Approach to the Study of Political Culture in Marxist-Leninist Systems." *American Political Science Review* 68 (1974): 1171–91.

———. "Inclusion and Mobilization in European Leninist Regimes." *World Politics* 8, no. 1 (1975): 69–96.

———. "Soviet Neotraditionalism: The Political Corruption of a Leninist Regime." *Soviet Studies* 25, no. 3 (1983): 275–97.

———. *New World Disorder: The Leninist Distinction*. Berkeley: University of California Press, 1992.

————. "Dizzy with Democracy." *Problems of Post-Communism* (January–February 1996): 3–6.

Kaminski, Antoni. "The Privatization of the State: Trends in the Evolution of (Real) Socialist Political Systems." *Asian Journal of Public Administration* 10, no. 1 (1988): 27–47.

————. "Coercion, Corruption, and Reform: State and Society in the Soviet-type Socialist Regimes." *Journal of Theoretical Politics* 1, no. 1 (1989): 77–101.

Kang Youwei. *Lunyu zhu* (An annotation of Analects). Beijing: Zhonghu shuju, 1984.

Katsenelboigen, Atarah. "Colored Markets in the Soviet Union." *Soviet Studies* 29, no. 1 (1977): 62–85.

Kim, Ilpyong. *The Politics of Chinese Communism: Kiangsi under the Soviets.* Berkeley: University of California Press, 1973.

Kiser, Edgar, and Xiaoxi Tong. "Determinants of the Amount and Type of Corruption in State Fiscal Bureaucracies: An Analysis of Late Imperial China." *Comparative Political Studies* 25, no. 3 (1992): 300–331.

Klitgaard, Robert. *Controlling Corruption.* Berkeley: University of California Press, 1988.

Klugman, Jeffrey. "The Psychology of Soviet Corruption, Indiscipline, and Resistance to Reform." *Political Psychology* 7, no. 1 (1986): 67–82.

————. *The New Soviet Elite: How They Think and What They Want.* New York: Praeger, 1989.

Korzec, Michel. "Occupational Inheritance in the People's Republic of China." Amsterdam Asia Studies Paper, no. 57. University of Amsterdam, 1985.

Kramer, John. "Political Corruption in the USSR." *Western Political Quarterly* 30, no. 2 (1977): 213–24.

Kraus, Richard. "The Chinese State and Its Bureaucrats." In Nee and Mozingo, eds., *State and Society in Contemporary China.* Ithaca: Cornell University Press, 1983.

Krueger, Anne. "The Political Economy of the Rent-Seeking Societies." *American Economic Review* 64, no. 3 (1974): 291–303.

Kwong, Julia. *The Political Economy of Corruption in China.* Armonk, N.Y.: M. E. Sharpe, 1997.

Lai Chaojian et al. *Yibaige jianzheng* (One hundred witnesses). Taipei: Liming wenhua shiye gongsi, 1975.

Lampert, Nicholas. *Whistle Blowing in the Soviet Union.* New York: Schocken, 1985.

Lampton, David, ed. *Policy Implementation in Post-Mao China.* Berkeley: University of California Press, 1987.

Lane, David, ed. *Elite and Political Power in the USSR.* Hants, UK: Edward Elgar, 1988.

Lardy, Nicholas. 1989. "Zhongguo jiage gaige chizhi yu difangbaohuzhuyi zaocheng de 'xunzu shehui' " (The rent-seeking society formed by the stagnation of the price reform and local protectionism). *Jingji Shehui Tizhi Bijiao* (Comparative Social and Economic Systems), no. 2 (1989).

Lee, Hong Yung. "From Revolutionary Cadres to Bureaucratic Technocrats." In Brantly Womack, ed., *Contemporary Chinese Politics in Historical Perspective*. London: Cambridge University Press, 1991.

———. *From Revolutionary Cadres to Party Technocrats in Socialist China*. Berkeley: University of California Press, 1991.

Lee, Peter N. S. "Guanyu Zhongguo fubai wenti de yanjiu" (A study of corruption in China). *Jingji Shehui Tizhi Bijiao*, no. 1 (1989).

———. "Bureaucratic Corruption during the Deng Xiaoping Era." *Corruption and Reform* 5, no. 1 (1990): 29–47.

Lee, Rance P. L., ed. *Corruption and Its Control in Hong Kong*. Hong Kong: Chinese University Press, 1981.

Lee, Rensselaer. "The *Hsia Fang* System: Marxism and Modernization." *China Quarterly*, no. 28 (1966): 43–49.

Leff, Nathaniel. "Economic Development through Bureaucratic Corruption." *American Behavioral Scientists* 8, no. 3 (1964): 8–14.

Leftwich, Adrian. "States of Underdevelopment: The Third World State in Theoretical Perspective." *Journal of Theoretical Politics* 6, no. 1 (1993): 55–74.

Lenin, Vladimir. *The Works of Lenin* (Chinese translation). Beijing: Renmin chubanshe, 1978.

Lepak, Keith J. "Prelude to Crisis: Leadership Drift in Poland in the 1970s." *Studies in Comparative Communism* 22, no. 1 (1989): 11–22.

Levenson, Joseph. *Confucian China and Its Modern Fate*. Berkeley: University of California Press, 1972.

Levi, Margaret. *Of Rules and Revenue*. Berkeley: University of California Press, 1988.

LeVine, Victor. "Supportive Values of the Culture of Corruption in Ghana." In Heidenheimer, Johnston, and LeVine, eds., *Political Corruption*. New Brunswick, N.J.: Transaction Publishers, 1989.

Lewis, John Wilson. *Leadership in Communist China*. Ithaca: Cornell University Press, 1963.

———. *Political Networks and the Chinese Policy Process*. Occasional Paper of the Northeast Asia–US Forum on International Policy. Stanford University, 1986.

Lewis, Peter. "From Prebendalism to Predation: The Political Economy of Decline in Nigeria." *Journal of Modern African Studies* 34, no. 1 (1996): 79–103.

Li, Cheng, and Lynn White. "Mainland China and Taiwan: Empirical Data and the Theory of Technocracy." *China Quarterly*, no. 121 (1990): 1–35.

Li Ching et al. *Zhongguo ziben zhuyi gongshangye de shehui zhuyi gaizao* (The socialist transformation of capitalist industry and commerce in China: [Beijing], [Shenyang]). Beijing: Zhonggong dangshi chubanshe, 1991, 1992.

Li Fuchun. *Li Fuchun xuanji* (Selected works of Li Fuchun). Beijing: Zhongguo jihua chubanshe, 1992.

Li Jianzhong. "Renshi renmian zhongde fubai xianxiang" (Corrupt practices in personnel appointment). *Dangxiao Luntan* (Party School Forum) 5 (1994): 37–38.

Li Jun and Zhou Tiegen. "Remmen xinmu zhong de lianzheng jianshe" (Public opinion on the clean-government building). *Shehui Kexuejia* (Social Scientists), no. 1 (1991): 78–83.

Li Kang, ed. "Jiceng zhengquan yu jiceng shequ" (Grassroots government and grassroots community: An investigation). *Shehui Gongzuo Yanjiu* (Studies in Social Work), no. 3 (1990).

———. *Zhongguo nongcun jiceng shequ zuzhi jianshe xintansuo* (A new study of grassroots community organizations in rural China). Beijing: Zhongguo gexue jishu chubanshe, 1992.

Li Kangyi. "Guanyu cunmin weiyuanhui xuanju de diaocha yu sikao" (Some reflections on village council elections). *Nongcun Gongzuo Yanjiu* (Study in Rural Work), no. 4 (1997).

Li Longqian. *Mingqing jingjishi* (Economic history of the Ming and Qing dynasties). Guangzhou: Guangdong jiaoyu chubanshe, 1988.

Li Qin. "Dui woguo nongmin fudan zhuangguang de fenxi" (An analysis of the current situation of peasant burden in China). *Zhongguo Nongcun Jingji* (Chinese Rural Economy), no. 8 (1992).

Li Rui. *Lushan huiyi shilu* (Recollections of the Lushan meeting). Beijing: Chunqiu chubanshe, 1989.

Li Shiying, ed. *Dangdai Zhongguo de jiancha zhidu* (The procuratorial system in contemporary China). Beijing: Zhongguo shehui kexue chubanshe, 1988.

Li Weiyi. *Zhongguo gongzi zhidu* (Salary system in China). Beijing: Zhongguo laodong chubanshe, 1991.

Li Xian-nian. *Li Xian-nian lun caizheng jinrong maoyi, 1950–1991* (Selection of Li Xian-nian's works on finance and trade). Vol. 1. Beijing: Zhongguo caizheng jingji chubanshe, 1992.

Li Zhaobing. "Xiaomie zibenzhuyi yishi zai liushou budui zhong de fanying" (Eliminate the influence of capitalist mentality in the army). In Zhongyang gaizao wenyuanhui, ed., *Feidang de zuzhi yu celui luxian* (The organization and strategy of the bandit party). Taipei: Zhongyan wenwu gongyingshe, 1952.

Liao Gailong et al., eds. *Gongchandangyuan xiuyang quanshu* (A complete volume on the cultivation of Communists). Dalian: Dalian chubanshe, 1991.

Liao Jianming. "Yi quan mou si de nanzhi yu genzhi" (The difficulty and elimination of abuse of power). *Guangxi Dangxiao Xuebao* (Journal of Guangxi Party School), no. 5 (1988): 33–36.

Liaowang (Outlook). Beijing.

Lieberthal, Kenneth. *Revolution and Tradition in Tientsin 1949–1952*. Stanford: Stanford University Press, 1980.

Lin Daizhao. *Zhongguo xiandai renshi zhidu* (Modern Chinese personnel system). Beijing: Laodong renshi chubanshe, 1989.

Lin Jingyao and Chen Yuan. "Suqing fengjianzhuyi canyu yingxiang yao zhuozhong zai zhidushang jinxing gaige" (To clean up the residual influence of feudalism requires reforms of the system). *Hongqi* (Red Flag), no. 1232 (1980): 34–39.

Lin, Yimin. "Personal Connections, the State, and Inter-Organizational Stratification in Post-Mao China." Manuscript, 1992.

Lin Yu. "Rudang buying shi yizhong rongyu" (Joining the party should be regarded as an honor). *Gongren Ribao* (Workers' Daily), April 29, 1988.

Lin Yunhui, Liu Yong, and Shi Bonian. *Renmin gongheguo chunqiu shilu* (An authentic history of the People's Republic). Beijing: Zhongguo renmin daxue chubanshe, 1992.

Liu, Alan. "The Politics of Corruption in the People's Republic of China." *American Political Science Review* 77 (1983): 602–23.

———. "The Dragon's Teeth of Mao Tse-tung: Cadres in Mainland China." *Issues and Studies* 21, no. 8 (1985): 12–33.

———. "Kleptocracy on Mainland China: A Social-Psychological Interpretation." In Yu-ming Shaw, ed., *Mainland China: Politics, Economics and Reform*. Boulder: Westview Press, 1985.

Liu Binyan. *People or Monster?* Bloomington: Indiana University Press, 1983.

———. "Bijing yousheng sheng wusheng" (Sound is better than soundless after all). In Perry Link, ed., *Liu Binyan Zuopin jingxuan*. Hong Kong: Wenxue yanjiushe, 1988.

Liu Jialin and He Xian. *Huibi zhidu jianxi* (An analysis of the law of avoidance). Beijing: Zhongguo renshi chubanshe, 1990.

Liu Mingjiu. *Weiji chuli gongzuo wenda ji* (Questions and answers on dealing with violations of discipline). Beijing: Zhongguo qingnian chubanshe, 1990.

Liu Rongqin et al. *Zhongguo guoqing congshu (bai xianshi jingji shehui diaocha): Zhucheng* (Series on China's state of the nation [a 100 county-city socioeconomic study]: Zhucheng). Beijing: Zhongguo dabaike quanshu chubanshe, 1991.

Liu Shaoqi. *Political Report on the Second Plenum of the Eighth Party Congress*. Beijing: Renmin chubanshe, 1958.

———. *Liu Shaoqi wenxuan* (Selected works of Liu Shaoqi). Beijing: Renmin chubanshe, 1979.

———. *Three Essays on Party-Building*. Beijing: Foreign Languages Press, 1980.

———. "Yao fangzhi lingdao renyuan teshuhua" (Privilege of leading officials should be prevented). (1956.) *Dangde Wenxian* (Party Documents), no. 5 (1988).

Liu Xianquan. "Tan jiti sifen xingwei de dingxing" (On the nature of collectively dividing up spoils). *Jiancha Yu Lianzheng* (Supervision and Clean-Government), no. 1 (1993): 40–41.

Liu Xiaozhu. "Zhongguo dalu jishu guanliao de xingqi jiqi zhengzhi yiyi" (The rise of technocrats in mainland China and its political implications). *Tansuo* (Quest) (February 1993): 75–76.

Liu Xinxin, Li Xiaolin, and He Daxin. "Shuishi shouyizhe: Liaoning sheng yinxing shouru diaocha zhiyi" (Who benefits: An investigation of hidden income in Liaoning province). *Neican Xuanbian* (Selected Internal References), no. 44 (1990): 5–7.

Liu Zhenqi. "Guanyu cunmin weiyuanhui zuzhi zhuangkuang de diaocha yu sikao" (An investigation and reflection on the situation of the village council). Unpublished manuscript, 1989.

Liu Zhenru. "Dangnei fubai xianxiang genyuan chutan" (A preliminary study of the sources of intra-party corruption). *Lilun Jiaoxue* (Theory Teaching), no. 4 (1989): 37–38.

Lowenthal, Richard. "Development vs. Utopia in Communist Policy." In Johnson, ed., *Change in Communist Systems*. Stanford: Stanford University Press, 1970.

———. "The Post-Revolutionary Phase in China and Russia." *Studies in Comparative Communism* 16, no. 3 (1983): 191–201.

Lu Bing, Shi Yuxin, and Wu Yongzhao. *Zhongguo fanfubai diyi da an* (The most serious case of corruption of the new China). Beijing: Falü chubanshe, 1990.

Lu Cheng et al. *Dangde jianshe qishinian jishi* (Seventy years of party building). Beijing: Zhonggong danshi chubanshe, 1991.

Lu Jianhong. "Shilun qingmo jiceng keceng zhidu de gaige" (On the reforms of the local bureaucratic rule of the late Qing). *Zhengzhixue Yanjiu* (Political Science Research), no. 3 (1989): 55–59.

Lü, Xiaobo. "Minor Public vs. Greater Public." In Xiaobo Lü and Elizabeth Perry, eds., *Danwei: The Changing Chinese Workplace in Historical and Comparative Perspective*. Armonk, N.Y.: M. E. Sharpe, 1997.

———. "Politics of Peasant Burdens in Reform China." *Journal of Peasant Studies* 25, no. 1 (1997): 113–38.

———. "Booty Socialism, Bureau-preneurs, and the State in Transition: Organizational Corruption in China." *Comparative Politics* 32, no. 3 (2000): 273–94.

Lü, Xiaobo, and Elizabeth Perry, eds. *Danwei: The Changing Chinese Workplace in Comparative and Historical Perspective*. Armonk, N.Y.: M. E. Sharpe, 1997.

Luan Kexin. "Jingxing dayuejin yishi" (Some recollections of the Great Leap

Forward in Jingxing). *Hebei Wenshi Ziliao* (Historical Materials of Hebei), no. 2 (1992): 27–50.

Ludz, Peter. *The Changing Party Elite in East Germany*. Cambridge, Mass.: MIT Press, 1968.

Lui, Adam Y. C. *Corruption in China during the Early Ch'ing Period 1644–1660*. Hong Kong: University of Hong Kong Press, 1979.

Lupher, Mark. "Power Restructuring in China and the Soviet Union." *Theory and Society* 21 (1992): 665–701.

Ma, Stephen K. "Reform Corruption: A Discussion on China's Current Development." *Pacific Affairs* 62, no. 1 (1989): 40–52.

Ma Yanwen. "Guanliao jieji yu wuchanjieji zhuanzheng" (Bureaucratic class and the dictatorship of the proletariat). *Beijing Daxue Xuebao* (Journal of Peking University), no. 4 (1976): 3–12.

Ma Yuping and Huang Yuchong, eds. *Zhongguo de zuotian yu jintian: 1840–1987 guojing shouce* (China's yesterday and today: A handbook of the national conditions, 1840–1987). Beijing: Jiefangjun chubanshe, 1989.

MacFarquhar, Roderick. *The Origins of the Cultural Revolution*. Vol. 2, *The Great Leap Forward*. New York: Columbia University Press, 1983.

———. "Prospects: Half Gloomy or Half Bright?" *Problems of Communism* 41, no. 1–2 (1992): 168–69.

MacRae, John. "Underdevelopment and the Economics of Corruption: A Game Theory Approach." *World Development* 10, no. 8 (1982): 677–87.

Madsen, Richard. *Morality and Power in a Chinese Village*. Berkeley: University of California Press, 1984.

Manion, Melanie. "The Cadre Management System, Post-Mao: The Appointment, Promotion, Transfer and Removal of Party and State Leaders." *China Quarterly*, no. 102 (1985): 203–33.

———. "Corruption by Design: Bribery in Chinese Enterprise Licensing." *Journal of Law, Economics, and Organization* 12, no. 1 (1996): 167–95.

Manz, Gunther. "The Shadow Economy in the GDR." *Eastern European Economics* (Spring 1991): 69–79.

Mao Shaojun. "Nongcun zongzu shili manyan de xianzhuang yu yuanyen fenxi" (The current situation and analysis of the rampancy of clan power in the countryside). *Zhejiang Shehuikexue* (Social Science in Zhejiang), no. 2 (1991): 51–55.

Mao Zedong. *Jingji wenti yu caizheng wenti* (On economic and financial problems) (1942). Hong Kong: Xinminzhu chubanshe, 1949.

———. *Mao Zedong sixiang wansui* (Long live Mao Zedong thoughts). n.p. 1967.

———. *Mao Zedong sixiang wansui* (Long live Mao Zedong thoughts). Hong Kong: n.p. 1969.

———. *Mao Zedong xuanji* (A collection of Mao Zedong's writings). Beijing: Renmin chubanshe, 1978.

Mars, Gerald, and Yochanan Altman. "The Cultural Bases of Soviet Georgia's Second Economy." *Soviet Studies* 35, no. 4 (1983): 546–60.

Matthews, Mervyn. *Privilege in the Soviet Union: A Study of Elite Lifestyles under Communism.* London: George Allen & Unwin, 1972.

Mayer, Robert. "Marx, Lenin and the Corruption of the Working Class." *Political Studies* 41 (1993): 636–49.

Mbaku, John, ed. *Corruption and the Crisis of Institutional Reforms in Africa.* Lewiston, N.Y.: E. Mellen Press, 1998.

McCormick, Barrett. "Leninist Implementation: The Election Campaign." In David Lampton, ed., *Policy Implementation in Post-Mao China.* Berkeley: University of California Press.

McMullan, M. "A Theory of Corruption." *Sociological Review* 9 (1961): 181–200.

Medard, J. F. "The Underdeveloped State in Tropical Africa: Political Clientelism or Neo-Patrimonialism." In C. Clapham, ed., *Private Patronage and Public Power.* London: Pinter, 1982.

Meisner, Maurice. *Mao's China: A History of the People's Republic.* New York: Free Press, 1977.

Merton, Robert. *Social Theory and Social Structure.* New York: Free Press, 1968.

Meyer, Alfred. "Communism and Leadership." *Studies in Comparative Communism* 16, no. 3 (1983): 161–69.

Meyer, James T. "Another Look at Corruption: Lessons of the Career of the '"God of Fortune."'" *Issues and Studies* 23, no. 11 (1987): 28–49.

———. "China: Modernization and 'Unhealthy Tendencies.'" *Comparative Politics* 21, no. 2 (1989): 193–214.

Migdal, Joe. *Strong States and Weak Societies: State and Society Relations and State Capacity in the Third World.* Princeton: Princeton University Press, 1988.

Minzhengbu. "Guanyu jiejue cunji zuzhi tanhuan wenti de baogao" (Report on the problem of paralyzed village organization). Unpublished manuscript, 1989.

Montias, J. M., and Susan Rose-Ackerman. *Corruption in a Soviet-Type Economy: Theoretical Considerations.* Kennan Institute for Advanced Russian Studies Occasional Paper, no. 110. 1980.

Moore, Barrington. *Soviet Politics: The Dilemma of Power.* Cambridge, Mass.: Harvard University Press, 1950.

———. *Terror and Progress, USSR: Some Sources of Change and Stability in the Soviet Dictatorship,* Cambridge, Mass.: Harvard University Press, 1954.

Moran, Thomas. *Unofficial Histories.* Boulder: Westview Press, 1994.

Morris, Stephen. *Corruption and Politics in Contemporary Mexico.* Tuscaloosa: University of Alabama Press, 1991.

Mosher, Steven. *Broken Earth: The Rural Chinese.* New York: Free Press, 1983.

Mueggler, Erik. "Money, the Mountain, and State Power in a Naxi Village." *Modern China* 17, no. 2 (1991): 188–226.

Myrdal, Gunnar. *Asian Drama: An Inquiry into the Poverty of Nations*, vol. 2. New York: Twentieth Century Books, 1968.

Nahirny, Vladimir, C. "Some Observations on Ideological Groups." *American Journal of Sociology* 67, no. 4 (1962): 397–405.

Nathan, Andrew. *Peking Politics*. Berkeley: University of California Press, 1976.

———. *China's Crisis: Dilemmas of Reform and Prospects for Democracy*. New York: Columbia University Press, 1990.

Naughton, Barry. "Implications of the State Monopoly over Industry and Its Relaxation." *Modern China* 18, no. 1 (1992): 14–41.

Nee, Victor. "Peasant Entrepreneurship and the Politics of Regulation in China." In Nee and Stark, eds., *Remaking the Economic Institutions of Socialism: China and Eastern Europe*. Stanford: Stanford University Press, 1989.

Nee, Victor, and David Mozingo, eds. *State and Society in Contemporary China*. Ithaca: Cornell University Press, 1983.

Nelson, Daniel, ed. *Local Politics in Communist Countries*. Lexington: University of Kentucky Press, 1980.

The Ninth National Congress of the Communist Party of China (Documents). Peking: Foreign Language Press, 1969.

Noonan, John. *Bribes*. New York: Macmillan, 1984.

North, Douglas. *Structure and Change in Economic History*. New York: Norton, 1981.

Nye, Joseph. "Corruption and Political Development: A Cost-Benefit Analysis." *American Political Science Review* 61, no. 2 (1967): 417–27.

O'Hearn, D. "The Consumer Second Economy: Size and Effects." *Soviet Studies* 33, no. 2 (1981): 218–34.

Oi, Jean. "Market Reforms and Corruption in Rural China." *Studies in Comparative Communism* 22, nos. 2–3 (1989): 221–33.

———. *State and Peasant in Contemporary China*. Berkeley: University of California Press, 1989.

———. "Fiscal Reform and the Economic Foundation of Local State Corporatism in China." *World Politics* 45, no. 1 (1992): 99–126.

———. *Rural China Takes Off: Institutional Foundations of Economic Reform*. Berkeley: University of California Press, 1999.

Ostergaard, Clement. "Explaining China's Recent Corruption." *Corruption and Reform* 1, no. 3 (1986): 209–33.

Ostergaard, Clement, and Christina Petersen. "Official Profiteering and the Tian'anmen Square Demonstrations in China." *Corruption and Reform* 6, no. 2 (1991): 87–107.

Palmier, Leslie. *The Control of Bureaucratic Corruption: Case Studies in Asia*. New Delhi: Allied Publishers, 1985.

Pearson, Margaret. *Joint Venture in the People's Republic of China*. Princeton: Princeton University Press, 1991.

Pei, Minxin. "Microfoundation of State Socialism and Patterns of Economic Transformation." *Communist and Post-Communist Studies* 29, no. 2 (1996): 131–45.

Perry, Elizabeth. "State and Society in Contemporary China." *World Politics* 41, no. 4 (1989): 579–91.

―――. "Intellectuals and Tiananmen: Historical Perspective on an Aborted Revolution." In Daniel Chirot, ed., *Crisis of Leninism and the Decline of the Left*. Seattle: University of Washington Press, 1991.

―――. "Introduction: Chinese Political Culture Revisited." In Elizabeth Perry and Jeffrey Wasserstrom, eds., *Political Protest and Political Culture in Modern China: Learning from 1989*. Boulder: Westview Press, 1992.

Philp, Mark. "From '*Asabiya*' to Moral Aptitude: A Case Study in the Definition of Political Corruption." Unpublished manuscript, 1989.

Polanyi, Karl. *Great Transformation*. Boston: Beacon Press, 1957.

Political and Economic Risk Consultancy (PERC). "Corruption in Asia in 1997." http://asiarisk.com./lib10.html (1997).

Potter, Sulamith, and Jack M. Potter. *China's Peasants: The Anthropology of a Revolution*. Cambridge: Cambridge University Press, 1990.

Price, Jane. *Cadres, Commanders, and Commissars: The Training of the Chinese Communist Leadership 1920–45*. Boulder: Westview Press, 1976.

Price, Robert. *Society and Bureaucracy in Contemporary Ghana*. Berkeley: University of California Press, 1975.

Przeworski, Adam. *Democracy and the Market: Political and Economic Reforms in Eastern Europe and Latin America*. Cambridge: Cambridge University Press, 1991.

Pye, Lucian. *The Mandarin and the Cadre: China's Political Culture*. Ann Arbor: University of Michigan Press, 1988.

Qi Liaozhou. "Chuanbo gongchanzhuyi de yishixingtai" (Disseminate the ideology of communism). *Xuexi* (Study), no. 19 (1958).

Qian Hang and Xie Weiyang. "Qinzu qunju xianxiang yu woguo dangqian nongcun de zongzu huodong" (Conglomeration of kinsmen and the clan activities in rural areas). *Xueshu Jikan* (Academic Quarterly), no. 3 (1991): 157–63.

Qian Weiping. "Guanxiwang xianxiang fenxi" (An analysis of personal networks). *Xuexi Yu Shijian* (Study and Practice), no. 5 (1989).

Qiu Dunhong. "Tan woguo fazhi jianshe de chengji he buzu" (The achievements and weakness of the legalization in our country). *Hebei Faxue* (Hebei Legal Science), no. 3 (1992).

Qu Liansheng. "Xiangzhen zichou zijin guanli gaige chuyi" (A preliminary discussion on the reform of township self-raised funds). *Zhongguo Nongcun Jingji* (Chinese Rural Economy), no. 3 (1997).

Qu Yizhi. "Lun zhonggong junban qiye wenti" (The problem of the enterprises by the military). *Zhonggong Yanjiu* (CCP Study) 26, no. 12 (1992): 49–57.

Rajkumar, Renuka. "Political Corruption: A Review of the Literature." *West African Journal of Sociology and Political Science* 1, no. 2 (1976): 177–85.

Randall, Vicky, and Robin Theobald. *Political Change and Underdevelopment: A Critical Introduction to Third World Politics*. Durham, N.C.: Duke University Press, 1985.

Reni, Tamas. "A Politically Motivated Suicide in Hungary." Unpublished manuscript, IPSA Political Finance/Political Corruption Study Group, 1989.

Renmin chubanshe. *Di'erjie quanguo renmin daibiao dahui wenjianji* (A collection of the documents of the 2nd National People's Congress). Beijing: Renmin chubanshe, 1959.

——. *Zhongguo gongchandang dangzhang huibian* (A compilation of the CCP charters). Beijing: Renmin chubanshe, 1983.

Renshi (Personnel). Beijing.

Riggs, Fred, ed. *Administration in Developing Countries*. Boston: Houghton Mifflin, 1964.

——. *Frontiers of Development Administration*. Durham, N.C.: Duke University Press, 1970.

Riskin, Carl. *China's Political Economy: The Quest for Development Since 1949*. London: Oxford University Press, 1987.

Rocca, Jean-Louis. "Corruption and Its Shadow: An Anthropological View of Corruption in China." *China Quarterly*, no. 130 (1992): 402–16.

Rogovin, V. S. "The Problems of Corruption in Soviet Society: The Experience of Historical and Sociological Analysis." Unpublished manuscript, 1989.

Rogow, A. A., and Harold Lasswell. *Power, Corruption and Rectitude*. Englewood Cliffs, N.J.: Prentice-Hall, 1963.

Roldan, Antonio. "A Brief Psychology of Corruption." *Psychology* 26, no. 4 (1989): 53–55.

Root, Hilton. *The Fountain of Privilege*. Berkeley: University of California Press, 1994.

——. "Corruption in China: Has It Become Systemic?" *Asian Survey* 36, no. 8 (1996): 741–57.

Rose-Ackerman, Susan. *Corruption: A Study in Political Economy*. New York: Academic Press, 1978.

Roth, Guenther. "Personal Rulership, Patrimonialism, and Empire-building in the New States." *World Politics* 20, no. 2 (1968): 194–206.

Rowe, William. "The Public Sphere in Modern China." *Modern China* 16, no. 3 (1990): 309–29.

Ruan Ming. "Cong Lu Dingyi dao Deng Liqun: Zhonggong liren xuanchuan buzhang" (From Lu Dingyi to Deng Liqun: The ministers of propaganda works of the CPC). *Minzhu Zhongguo* (Democratic China), no. 9 (1992): 63–70.

Saich, Tony. "Cadres: From Bureaucrats to Managerial Modernizers?" In Birthe Arendrup, Carlten Thogersen, and Anne Wedell-Wedellsborg, eds., *China in the 1980s and Beyond*. London: Curzon Press, 1986.

Sampson, Steven. "Bureaucracy and Corruption as Anthropological Problems: A Case Study from Romania." *Folk* 25 (1983): 64–96.

———. "Rumors in Socialist Romania." *Survey* 28 (Winter 1984): 142–64.

———. "The Informal Sector in Eastern Europe." *Telos* 66 (Winter 1985): 44–66.

Sands, Barbara. "Decentralizing an Economy: The Role of Bureaucratic Corruption in China's Economic Reforms." *Public Choice* 65, no. 1 (1990): 85–91.

Scalapino, Robert. "Modernization and Revolution in Asia." *Problems of Communism* 41, no. 1–2 (1992): 180–81.

Schluchter, Wolfgang. *The Rise of Western Rationalism*. Berkeley: University of California Press, 1981.

Schmidt, Steffen, et al., eds. *Friends, Followers, and Factions*. Berkeley: University of California Press, 1977.

Schram, Stuart. *Mao Unrehearsed*. New York: Pelican, 1974.

Schran, Peter. *Guerrilla Economy*. Albany: State University of New York Press, 1976.

Schroeder, G., and R. Greenslade. "On the Measurement of the Second Economy in the USSR." *Association for Comparative Economic Studies Bulletin* 21, no. 1 (1979): 3–22.

Schurmann, Franz. *Ideology and Organization in Communist China*. Berkeley: University of California Press, 1968.

Schwartz, Charles. "Corruption and Political Development in the USSR." *Comparative Politics* 11, no. 4 (1979): 425–43.

Scott, James. "Corruption, Machine Politics, and Social Change." *American Political Science Review* 63, no. 4 (1969): 1142–59.

———. "The Analysis of Corruption in Developing Nations." *Comparative Studies on Society and History* 11, no. 3 (1969).

———. *Comparative Political Corruption*. Englewood Cliffs, N.J.: Prentice-Hall Inc., 1972.

Sedov, L. "From Bureaucracy to Logocracy." *Problems of Economics* 32, no. 5 (1989): 89–94.

Selden, Mark. *The Yenan Way in Revolutionary China*. Cambridge, Mass.: Harvard University Press, 1971.

Selznick, Philip. *The Organizational Weapon: A Study of Bolshevik Strategy and Tactics*. New York and London: McGraw-Hill, 1952.

———. *Leadership in Administration*. Berkeley: University of California Press, 1957.

Shan Yuanmu and Liu Yian. *Zhongguo lianzhengshi* (A history of anti-corruption in China). Zhengzhou: Zhongzhou guji chubanshe, 1991.

Shanghai shiwei zuzhibu. *Zhongguo gongchandang Shanghaishi zuzhishiliao* (Historical materials of the CCP organization in Shanghai). Shanghai: Shanghai renmin chubanshe, 1991.

Shaw, Carl. "Hegel's Theory of Modern Bureaucracy." *American Political Science Review* 86, no. 2 (1992): 381–89.

Shefield, Stephen. *"Pripiskii:* False Statistical Reporting in Soviet-type Economies." In M. Clarke, ed., *Corruption: Causes, Consequences and Control.* London: Frances Pinter, 1983.

Shen Liren. *Difang zhengfu de jingji zhineng he jingji xingwei* (The economic functions and behavior of local governments). Shanghai: Shanghai yuandong chubanshe, 1998.

Shi Huasheng. "Lun women guandian zhi yitong" (On the similarities and differences between us). In *Zhongguo dalu zhengzhi xiandaihua lunji* (A collection of articles on the political modernization in mainland China). Taipei: Youshi wenhua shiye gongsi, 1983.

Shils, Edward. "Primordial, Personal, Sacred and Civil Ties." *British Journal of Sociology* 8, no. 2 (1957): 130–45.

———. "Charisma, Order, and Status." *American Sociological Review* 30, no. 2 (1965): 199–213.

Shirk, Susan. *Competitive Comrades: Career Incentives and Student Strategies in China.* Berkeley: University of California Press, 1982.

———. "Playing to the Provinces: Deng Xiaoping's Political Strategy of Economic Reform." In *Studies of Comparative Communism* 23, nos. 3–4 (1990).

———. *The Political Logic of Economic Reform in China.* Berkeley: University of California Press, 1993.

Short, Philip. *The Dragon and the Bear: Inside China and Russia Today.* London: Hodder & Stoughton, 1982.

Shue, Vivienne. *The Reach of the State: Sketches of the Chinese Body Politic.* Stanford: Stanford University Press, 1988.

———. "China: Transition Postponed?" *Problems of Communism* 41, nos. 1–2 (1992): 157–68.

Sichuan wenxue chubanshe, ed. *Heise wangguo de yunluo* (The fall of the black kingdom). Chengdu: Sichuan wenxue chubanshe, 1988.

Simis, Konstantin. *USSR: The Corrupt Society.* New York: Simon & Schuster, 1982.

Simon, Herbert. *Administrative Behavior.* New York: Macmillan, 1948.

Siu, Helen. *Agents and Victims in South China: Accomplices in Rural Revolution.* New Haven: Yale University Press, 1989.

———. "Socialist Peddlers and Princes in a Chinese Market Town." *American Ethnologist* 16, no. 2 (1989): 195–212.

Smart, Alan. "The Political Economy of Rent-Seeking in a Chinese Factory Town." *Anthropology of Work Review* 14 (1993): 15–19.

Smelser, Neil. *Theory of Collective Behavior.* New York: Free Press of Glencoe, 1963.

Smith, Gordon. *Public Policy and Administration in the Soviet Union.* New York: Praeger, 1980.

Smith, Hendrick. *The Russians.* London: Time Books, 1976.

Solinger, Dorothy. "Marxism and the Market in Socialist China." In Nee and Mozingo, eds., *State and Society in Contemporary China.* Ithaca: Cornell University Press, 1983.

Solomon, Richard. *Mao's Revolution and the Chinese Political Culture.* Berkeley: University of California Press, 1971.

Song Bai. "Jianchi jitilingdao fandui jiazhangzhi zuofeng" (Uphold collective leadership, oppose patriarchalism). *Hongqi* (Red Flag), no. 944 (1980): 6–10.

Statistical Yearbook of China. Beijing: Zhongguo tongji chubanshe.

Strand, David. "Civil Society and Public Sphere in Modern China: A Perspective on Popular Movements in Beijing, 1919–1989." *Working Papers in Asian/ Pacific Studies.* Durham: Duke University Asian/Pacific Studies Institute, 1990.

Su Hua, ed. *Dangdai Anhui dashiji: 1949–1985* (A chronology of major events in contemporary Anhui: 1949–1985). Hefei: Anhui renmin chubanshe, 1987.

Su Meifeng and Zhuo Songsheng. *Zhongguo gongwuyuan zhidu* (The civil service in China). Wuhan: Huazhong ligong daxue chubanshe, 1988.

Su Ming. "Zhongguo caizheng zhichu guanli toushi" (The management of fiscal spending in China). *Liaowang*, no. 4 (1998): 10–16.

Su Shaozhi. "Zhengzhi tizhi gaige yu fandui fengjianzhuyi yingxing" (Political reforms and opposition to the influence of feudalism). *RMRB*, August 15, 1986.

———. "Zhongguo zhengzhi tizhi gaige de hongguan yanjiu" (A macroanalysis of the political system reform in China). *Cheng Ming* (Contention) (June 1990): 56–63.

Sun Huairen. *Shanghai shehui zhuyi jingji jianshe fazhan jianshi* (A short history of socialist reconstruction in Shanghai, 1949–85). Shanghai: Shanghai renmin chubanshe, 1990.

Sun Lun-kee. *Zhongguo wenhua de shenceng jiegou* (The deep structure of Chinese culture). Hong Kong: Yishan chubanshe, 1983.

Sun Qitai and Xiong Zhiyong. *Dazhai hongqi de shengqi yu zhuiluo* (The rise and fall of the Dazhai red flag). Zhengzhou: Henan renmin chubanshe, 1990.

Sun Ruiyi. *Sanfan wufan yundong* (The Three Anti and Five Anti campaigns). Beijing: Xinhua chubanshe, 1991.

Sun, Yan. "The Chinese Protest of 1989: The Issue of Corruption." *Asian Survey* 31, no. 8 (1991): 762–82.

Sun Zhijie. "Ji Xushui gongchanzhuyi" (Xushui communism). *Hebei Wenshi Ziliao* (Historical Materials of Hebei), no. 2 (1992): 1–26.

Swart, Koenraad. *Sale of Public Office in the Seventeenth Century*. The Hague: Martinus Nijhoff, 1949.

Taihang geming genjudi shigao bianweihui. *Taihang geming genjudi shigao, 1937–49* (Historical materials of the Taihang base area, 1937–49). Taiyuan: Shanxi renmin chubanshe, 1987.

Tang Jinsu and Wang Jieshi. "Nongcun qianfu de weiji buke diku" (The potential crisis in the countryside is not be taken lightly). Unpublished manuscript, 1989.

Tang Zhongxin. *Nongcun liangchule huangpai* (Rural areas have shown the yellow [foul] card). Beijing: Zhongguo funü chubanshe, 1989.

"Tantan neibu zhege mingzi" (A few words about "internal"). *Siwu Luntan* (April Fifth Forum), no. 4 (1979). Reprinted in *DDKH*, vol. 1: 35–44.

Tarkowski, Jacek. "A Centralized System and Corruption: The Case of Poland." *Asian Journal of Public Administration* 10, no. 1 (1988): 48–70.

———. "Old and New Patterns of Corruption in Poland and the USSR." *Telos* 80 (Summer 1989): 51–62.

———. "Endowment of Nomenclature, or Apparatchiks Turned into Entrepreneurchiks, or from Communist Rank to Capitalist Riches." *Innovation* 4, no. 1 (1990): 89–105.

———. "The Decay and Fall of the Polish Workers' Party." Unpublished manuscript, 1991.

Tarrow, S. G. *Peasant Communism in Southern Italy*. New Haven: Yale University Press, 1967.

Teiwes, Frederick. *Politics and Purges in China: Rectification and Decline of Party Norms, 1950–1965*. Armonk, N.Y.: M. E. Sharpe, 1979.

Templer, Robert. *Shadows and Wind: A View of Modern Vietnam*. New York: Penguin Books, 1999.

Theobald, Robin. *Corruption, Development and Underdevelopment*. Durham, N.C.: Duke University Press, 1990.

Tidrick, Gene, and X. Chen, eds. *China's Industrial Reform*. New York: Oxford University Press, 1987.

Tilman, Robert. "Emergence of Black-Market Bureaucracy: Administration, Development, and Corruption in the New State." *Public Administration Review* 28, no. 5 (1968): 437–44.

Tong Zhimin, ed. *Shehuizhuyi guojia ganbu guanlitizhi gaige* (The reforms of the management system of state cadres in socialist countries). Beijing: Guangming ribao chubanshe, 1988.

———. *Guojia gongwuyuan gailun* (Theories of state public servants). Beijing: Zhongguo renmin daxue chubanshe, 1989.

Transparency International. "Corruption Perception 1996." http://www.gwdg.de/~uwvw/rank-96.jpg (1996).

Triesman, Daniel. "Korruptsia." *New Republic* (May 11, 1992): 14–17.

Trotsky, Leon. *The Revolution Betrayed.* New York: Pathfinder Press, 1972.

Tsou, Tang. "Western Concepts and China's Historical Experiences." *World Politics* 21 (1969): 655–91.

———. "Back from the Brink of Revolutionary 'Feudal' Totalitarianism." In Victor Nee and David Mozingo, eds., *State and Society in Contemporary China.* Ithaca: Cornell University Press, 1983.

Tucker, Robert. *The Soviet Political Mind: Stalinism and Post-Stalin Change.* New York: Norton, 1971.

Udy, Stanley, Jr. " 'Bureaucracy' and 'Rationality' in Weber's Organizational Theory: An Empirical Study." *American Sociological Review* 24 (1959): 761–65.

Van Roy, Edward. "On the Theory of Corruption." *Economic Development and Cultural Change* 19, no. 1 (1970): 86–110.

Vogel, Ezra F. "From Friendship to Comradeship: The Change in Personal Relations in Communist China." *China Quarterly,* no. 21 (1965): 46–60.

———."From Revolutionary to Semi-bureaucrat: The 'Regularization' of Cadres." *China Quarterly,* no. 29 (1967): 36–60.

Voslensky, Michael. *Nomenclature: The Soviet Ruling Class.* Garden City, N.Y.: Doubleday, 1984.

Wakeman, Frederic. "The Civil Society and Public Sphere Debate." Unpublished manuscript, 1992.

Walder, Andrew. "Some Ironies of the Maoist Legacy in Industry." In Mark Selden and Victor Lippit, eds., *The Transition to Socialism in China.* Armonk, N.Y.: M. E. Sharpe, 1982.

———. "Organized Dependency and Cultures of Authority in Chinese Industry." *Journal of Asian Studies* 43, no. 1 (1983): 51–76.

———. *Communist Neo-Traditionalism: Work and Authority in Chinese Industry.* Berkeley: University of California Press, 1986.

———. "A Reply to Womack." *China Quarterly,* no. 126 (1991): 333–39.

Wang Feng. "State Socialism and *Guanxi* in China." Occasional Papers of the Center for Modern China, no. 9. 1991.

Wang Hui. *Zhongguo de kuanchangbing* (The bureaucratic disease in China). Beijing: Zhongguo funü chubanshe, 1989.

Wang Huning. *Fanfubai: Zhongguo de shiyan* (Anti-corruption: China's experiment). Haikou: Sanhuan chubanshe, 1990.

Wang Jianjun. "Nongcun ganqun guanxi: Kunjing ji chulu" (Rural cadres-masses relations: Predicaments and solutions). *Shehuizhuyi Yanjiu* (Studies of Socialism), no. 5 (1990): 56–60.

Wang Kuang. "Fandui difang zhuyi" (Against localism). *Xuexi* (Study), no. 3 (1958): 9–12.

Wang Nianyi. *1949–1989 de Zhongguo: Dadongluan de niandai* (China, 1949–1989: vol. 3, The years of great chaos). Zhengzhou: Henan renmin chubanshe, 1989.

Wang, Shaoguang. "From Revolution to Involution: State Capacity, Local Power, and (Un)governability in China." Unpublished manuscript, 1991.

———. *Failure of Charisma: The Cultural Revolution in Wuhan.* Hong Kong: Oxford University Press, 1995.

Wang Shi. "Bofeng yu lougui" (Low salary and venal customs). *Wenshi Zazhi* (Journal of Humanities) 3, nos. 1–2 (1944): 53–72.

Wang Sibin. "Cunganbu de bianji diwei yu xingwei fenxi" (An analysis of the marginal status and behavior of village cadres). *Shehuixue Yanjiu* (Sociological Studies), no. 4 (1991): 46–51.

Wang Xijia. "Nongcun ganqun guanxi heyi ruci jinzhang" (Why are cadre-peasant relations so tense?). *Shehui* (Society), no. 11 (1991): 18–19.

Wang Yanzhong. "Gongchang ban shehui de xingcheng yuanyin yu shehui houguo" (Society run by factory: Its origins and social consequences). *Beijing Daxue Yanjiusheng Xuekan* (February 1991): 99–105.

Wang Yi. "Mass Criticism in the Cultural Revolution and Ancient China's Curse Sorcery." *Hong Kong Journal of Social Sciences*, no. 7 (Spring 1996): 122–39.

Wang Yifan and Chen Mingxian. *Zhongguo gongchandang lici zhentang zhenfeng* (Rectification in CCP history). Harbin: Heilongjiang renmin chubanshe, 1985.

Wang Yongxin. "Jiaoyu de chuntian" (The spring of education). *Dangde Wenxian* (CCP Archives), no. 4 (1997): 84–87.

Wang Zhaojun. "Lun Zhongguo shehui de 'pizi' xianxiang" (On the phenomenon of 'riffraff' in Chinese society). *Dang Dai News Weekly* (Hong Kong) (September 1990): 24–25.

Wang Zhenyao and Wang Shihao. "Guanjian zaiyu jishi tiaozheng dang he guojia yu renmin de zhengzhi guanxi" (The key lies in readjusting the political relations between the state and peasants). *Shehui Gongzuo Yanjiu* (Research in Social Work), no. 3 (1990).

Wang Zhixiang. "Dui ganbu zinü de diaocha yu sikao" (Investigation and reflections on children of officials). *Qingnian Yanjiu* (Youth Study), no. 7 (1987): 9–14.

Wang Zhufa. "Jiefang zhanzheng shiqi dongbei genjudi de lianzheng jianshe" (The clean-government building in the northeastern base areas during the liberation war period). *Dangde Wenxian* (Party Documents), no. 4 (1991): 87–90.

Wang Zongru. "Bixu gaodu zhongshi dangde jicengzuzhi jianshe" (Grassroots organizational building must be given attention). *Dangjian Yanjiu* (Studies in Party Building), no. 3 (1990): 37–39.

———. "Nongcun gangqun guanxi shuli de diaocha yu fansi" (Some reflections and investigation on the estranged relationship between cadres and the masses). *Kexui Shehuizhuyi Yanjiu* (Studies in Scientific Socialism), no. 1 (1990): 41–46.

Waterbury, John. "Corruption, Political Stability and Development: Comparative Evidence from Egypt and Morocco." *Government and Opposition* 11, no. 4 (1976): 426–45.

Watt, John. *The District Magistrate in Late Imperial China.* New York: Columbia University Press, 1972.

Weber, Max. *The Theory of Social and Economic Organization.* Translated by A. M. Henderson and T. Parsons. New York: Free Press, 1964.

———. *From Max Weber: Essays in Sociology.* Translated by Hans Gerth and Wright Mills. New York: Oxford University Press, 1965.

———. *Economy and Society.* New York: Bedminster Press, 1968.

Wei Xiumei. *Qingdai zhi huibi zhidu* (The avoidance system in the Qing dynasty). Taipei: Institute of Modern History, Academia Sinica, 1992.

Werner, Simcha B. "The Development of Political Corruption: A Case Study of Israel." *Political Studies* 31, no. 4 (1983): 620–39.

Whitaker, C. S., Jr. "A Dysrhythmic Process of Political Change." *World Politics* 19, no. 2 (1967): 190–217.

White, Gordon. "Corruption and Market Reform in China." *IDS Bulletin* 27, no. 2 (1996): 40–47.

White, Lynn. "Deviance, Modernization, Rations, and Household Registration in Urban China." In A. Wilson, S. Greenbalt and R. Wilson, eds., *Deviance and Social Control in Chinese Society.* New York: Praeger, 1977.

———. *Careers in Shanghai.* Berkeley: University of California Press, 1978.

———. "Changing Concepts of Corruption in Communist China: Early 1950s Versus Early 1980s." In Yu-ming Shaw, ed., *Changes and Continuities in Chinese Communism,* vol. 2. Boulder: Westview Press, 1988.

———. *Policies of Chaos.* Princeton: Princeton University Press, 1989.

White, Tyrene. "Postrevolutionary Mobilization in China." *World Politics* 43 (1990): 53–76.

Whyte, Martin King. "Who Hates Bureaucracy? A Chinese Puzzle." In Victor Nee and David Stark, eds., *Remaking the Economic Institutions of Socialism: China and Eastern Europe.* Stanford: Stanford University Press, 1989.

Whyte, Martin King, and William Parish. *Urban Life in Contemporary China.* Chicago: University of Chicago Press, 1983.

Williams, Robert. *Political Corruption in Africa.* Aldershot, UK: Gower, 1987.

Wnuk-Lipinski, E. "Dimorphism of Values and Social Schizophrenia—A Tentative Description." *Sisyphus* (Warsaw) 3 (1982).

Wolf, Eric. "Kinship, Friendship, and Patron-Client Relations in Complex Societies." In Steffen Schmidt et al., eds., *Friends, Followers, and Factions.* Berkeley: University of California Press, 1977.

Womack, Brantly. "Transfigured Community: Neo-traditionalism and Work Unit Socialism." *China Quarterly,* no. 126 (1991): 313–32.

Wong, Christine. "Fiscal Reform and Local Industrialization: The Problematic Sequencing of Reform in Post-Mao China." *Modern China* 18 (April 1991).

Wong, Siu-lun. "The Applicability of Asian Family Values to Other Sociocultural Settings." In Peter Berger and Hsin-Huang Hsiao, eds., *In Search of an East Asian Development Model.* New Brunswick, N.J.: Transaction Publishers, 1988.

World Bank. *From Plan to Market: World Development Report.* Oxford: Oxford University Press, 1996.

Wu Chuanhuang and Liu Lukai, eds. *Zhongguo gongchandang lianzheng jianshe shi* (History of clean-government building by the CCP). Lanzhou: Gansu renmin chubanshe, 1992.

Wu Jinglian. "Xunzulilun yu woguo jingji zhongde mouxie xiaoji xianxiang" (Rent-seeking theory and some negative phenomena in our nation's economy). *Jingji Shehui Tizhi Bijiao* (Comparative Studies of Society and Economy), no. 5 (1989).

Wu Li and Zhang Faling. "Lüelun zhonggong bada luxian weineng guanche daodi de jingji yuanyin" (The economic reasons why the line of the 8th Congress was not carried out to the end). *Zhonggong Dangshi Yanjiu* (CCP History Research), no. 4 (1993).

Wu Liucun, ed. *Huiluzui ge'an yanjiu* (Case studies of the crime of bribery). Chengdu: Sichuan daxue chubanshe, 1991.

Xia Xin. "Huibi, weile qinglian" (Avoidance, for the sake of being clean and upright). In Liu Jialin and He Xian, eds., *Huibi zhidu jiangxi* (An analysis of the law of avoidance). Beijing: Zhongguo renshi chubanshe, 1990.

Xiao Li. "Yiqi maiguan maiguan an shimo" (A case of selling and buying public office). *Zhongguo Jiancha* (Supervision in China), no. 6 (1998): 25–28.

Xiao Ming. "Neibu dianying heshiliao?" (When are "internal movies" going to end?). *Renmin Zhisheng* (People's Voice), no. 9 (1979).

Xiao Qinfu et al. *Wuci langchao* (Five big waves). Beijing: Zhongguo renmin daxue chubanshe, 1989.

Xiao Su. "Jianguo chuqi Harbin zai lianzheng jinashe shang caiqu de cuoshi ji jingyan" (Measures and lessons of the early days of the PRC in Harbin). *Longjiang Dangshi* (Party History of Heilongjiang), no. 6 (1990): 15–17.

Xie Baogui. "The Function of the Chinese Procuratorial Organ in the Combat against Corruption." *Asian Journal of Public Administration* 10, no. 1 (1988): 71–79.

Xie Chuntao. *Dayuejin kuanglan* (The turbulence of the Great Leap Forward). Zhengzhou: Henan renmin chubanshe, 1990.

Xie Juizhai. "Minzhu zhengzhi de shiji" (The reality of democratic politics). In Zhongyang gaizao wenyuanhui, ed. (1952), *Feidang de zuzhi yu celui luxian* (The organization and strategy of the bandit party). Taipei: Zhongyan wenwu gongyingshe, 1939.

Xing Guang and Zhang Yang. *Kangri zhanzheng shiqi Shaan-Gan-Ning bianqu caizheng jingji shigao* (A brief history of finance and economy in the Shaan-Gan-Ning border region during the anti-Japanese war). Xi'an: Xibeidaxue chubanshe, 1988.

Xingzhengguanli kexue yanjiusuo. *Guojia gongwuyuan zhidu jianghua* (On the civil service). Beijing: Laodong renshi chubanshe, 1988.

Xu Bin, Xu Hui, and Long Duo. *Zhongguo de qundaifeng* (Chinese nepotism). Dalian: Dalian chubanshe, 1989.

Xu Gongmei. "Zoufang songshuyu" (A visit to Songshuyu village). *Tansuo* (Quest), no. 4 (1993).

Xu Guangyi, ed. *Dangdai zhongguo jundui de houqin gongzuo* (The logistical work of the contemporary Chinese armed forces). Beijing: Zhongguo shehui kexue chubanshe, 1990.

Xu Hongbing. "Danwei sishe 'xiaojinku' xingwei dingxing chutan" (A preliminary study of illicit work-unit small treasuries). *Zhengzhi Yu Falü* (Politics and Law), no. 1 (1992): 32–33.

Xue Jiaji et al. *Zhongguo guoqing congshu (bai xianshi jingji shehui diaocha): Changshu* (Series on China's state of the nation [a 100 county-city socio-economic study]: Changshu). Beijing: Zhongguo dabaike quanshu chubanshe, 1991.

Xue Yin'e. "Zaitan dangnei fubai xianxiang riyi yanzhong de genben yuanyin shi zhidu bujianquan" (The root of increasing intra-party corruption is the lack of institutionalization). *Lilun Daokan* (Journal of Theory), no. 4 (1989): 14–19.

Yang Chunxi and Gao Ge. *Woguo dangqian jingji fanzui yanjiu* (A study of economic crimes in our country today). Beijing: Beijing daxue chubanshe, 1996.

Yang, Dali. *Calamity and Reform in China: State, Rural Society, and Institutional Change Since the Great Leap Forward*. Stanford: Stanford University Press, 1996.

Yang Guan. "Qiye 'jiazu' xianxiang" (The phenomenon of 'familialization' in enterprises). *Shehui* (Society), no. 4 (1991): 42–45.

Yang Huiming and Tang Buyun. *Zhongguo 1992: Beishui zhizhan* (China 1992: A battle without a way to retreat). Chengdu: Sichuan renmin chubanshe, 1992.

Yang Jie. *Xinshiqi lianzhengjianshe* (Clean government building in the new era). Guangzhou: Guandong gaodeng jiaoyu chubanshe, 1989.

Yang, Mayfair. "The Modernity of Power in the Chinese Socialist Order." *Cultural Anthropology* 3, no. 4 (1988): 408–27.

———."Between State and Society: The Construction of Corporateness in a Chinese Socialist Factory." *Australian Journal of Chinese Affairs*, no. 22 (1989).

———. "The Gift Economy and State Power in China." *Comparative Studies in Society and History* 31, no. 1 (1989): 25–54.

Yang Minzhi. "Fandui fubai baohuzhuyi" (Against corruption protectionism). *Liaowang* (Outlook), no. 31 (1997): 7–9.

Yang Xianzhen. "Yijiu wujiu nian jishi" (Some recollections of 1959). *Qiusuo* (Probe) 5 (1984): 27–32.

Yang Xingguo. "Rangtanwuzhe wuzangshenzhidi" (Let there be no resting place for corrupters). *Liaowang* (Outlook), no. 4 (1998): 20–21.

Ye Tan. "Dalu sida fubai xianxiang" (Four major corruption patterns in China). *Jingbao Yuekan* (Mirror) (Hong Kong), no. 3 (1998): 34–36.

Yeh, Milton. "Modernization and Corruption in Mainland China." *Issues and Studies* 23, no. 11 (1987): 11–27.

Yi Jin. "Shanghaishi de sanfan, wufan yundong" (The Three Anti and Five Anti Campaigns in Shanghai). *Shanghai Dangshi* (CCP history in Shanghai), no. 6 (1990): 17–25.

Yi Ren, ed. *Dangdai zhongguo sutan* (Anti-corruption in contemporary China). Beijing: Zhongguo jiancha chubanshe, 1993.

Yu Jianliang. "Dui nongcun wenti de yului ji duice" (Worries about and solutions to rural problems). Unpublished manuscript, 1989.

Yu Shaojun and Dai Guanxong. "Guanyu danwei neibu ganbu qinshujuji zhuangkuang de diaocha" (An investigation on the internal conglomeration of relatives in work units). *Lilun Xuekan* (Journal of Theoretical Studies), no. 5 (1986): 22–26.

Yu Tingge. "Xinxingshi xia jiaqiang cunji ganbu duiwu jianshe de sigao" (Some reflections on the cultivation of village cadres under the new situation). Unpublished manuscript, 1989.

Yu Xianyang. "Danwei yishi de shehuixue fenxi" (A sociological analysis of the work-unit mentality). *Shehuixue Yanjiu* (Sociology Research), no. 5 (1991): 76–81.

Yu Yingjie. "Gaohao dangfeng bixu chongpo 'Guanxiwang' " (Connection networks must be broken in order to maintain a healthy party). *Shehui Kexue* (Social Science), no. 10 (1986): 25–27.

Zafanolli, Wojteck. "A Brief Outline of China's Second Economy." *Asian Survey* 25, no. 7 (1985): 715–36.

Zelin, Madeleine. *The Magistrate's Tael*. Berkeley: University of California Press, 1984.

Zhang Bingsen, Zhou Xiaonong, and Shi Xinrong. "Zui'e de tudi hongqiang" (Criminal land grabs). *Neibu Cankao* (Internal References) (1990).

Zhang Lipu. "1978: Xishuangbanna bawan zhiqing fancheng fengchao" (1978: The incident of 80,000 youths in Xishuangbanna trying to return home). In Huang Yao et al., *Huihuang de zhiqingmeng* (Glorious dream of educated youths). Changsha: Hunan wenyi chubanshe, 1990.

Zhang Xiangling. *Heilongjiang sishinian* (Heilongjiang's forty years). Harbin: Heilongjiang renmin chubanshe, 1986.

Zhang Xinxin and Sang Hua. *Beijing ren: Yibai ge putongren de zishu* (People of Beijing: The stories of 100 ordinary people). Shanghai: Shanghai wenyi chubanshe, 1986.

Zhang Yigong. "Fanren Li Tongzhong de gushi" (The story of prisoner Li Tongzhong). In Youshi Wenhua Shiyegongsi, ed., *Renyao zhijian* (Between human and monster [reportage]). Taipei: Youshi wenhua shiye gongsi, 1982.

Zhang Yun. "Quanmian tigao dangyuan suzhi shi dangfeng genben haozhuan de jianshi jichu" (Improving the quality of party members is the foundation for improvement of the party's orientation). *HQ*, no. 10 (1986).

Zhang Zhenglong. *Xuebai xuehong* (Snow white, blood red: An investigatory reportage of the northeast theater of China's last civil war). Beijing: Jiefangjun chubanshe, 1989.

Zhao Chaogou. *Mao Zedong xiansheng fangwen ji* (Meeting with Mao Zedong). (1945). Wuhan: Changjiang wenyi chubanshe, 1990.

Zhao Chi et al. *Zhongguo guoqing congshu (bai xianshi jingji shehui diaocha): Dingzhou* (Series on China's state of the nation [a 100 county-city socio-economic study]: Dingzhou). Beijing: Zhongguo dabaike quanshu chubanshe, 1991.

Zhao Shenghui. *Zhongguo gongchandang zuzhi shigang* (An organizational history of the Chinese Communist party). Hefei: Anhui renmin chubanshe, 1987.

Zhao Shiyu. "Liangzhong butong de zhengzhi xintai yu mingqing xuli de shehui diwei" (Two different kinds of political attitudes and the social status of clerks and runners in Ming-Qing periods). *Zhengzhixue Yanjiu* (Political Science Research), no. 1 (1989): 50–56.

Zheng Ming and Qi Lian. *Lianzheng jianshe ziliao xuanbian* (A collection of clean government building documents). Beijing: Zhongguo caijing chubanshe, 1989.

Zheng Xuwei. "Dangqian woguo caizheng kunjing de chengyin ji duice" (Current financial difficulties and solutions). *Jingji Tizhi Gaige* (Economic System Reform), no. 4 (1997): 88–91.

Zheng Yanming. "Zhongguo gongchandang fanfubai douzheng de lishi gaocha" (A historical investigation of the anti-corruption struggle in the CCP). *Qiushi* (Seeking Truth), no. 5 (1990): 47–49.

Zheng Yongliu et al. "Zhongguo nongmin falü yishi de xianshi bianqian"

(Changes in legal consciousness of the Chinese peasants). *Zhongguo Faxue* (Chinese Legal Science), no. 1 (1992): 92–97.

Zhi Yanji and Yi Shi. "Shuangguizhi ba zhongguo yinxiang hechu" (Where is the dual-track system leading China to?). *Jingjixue Zhoubao* (Economics Weekly), March 26, 1989.

Zhong Yan. "1977 nian huifu gaokao neiqing" (Behind the decision to resume entrance exams in 1977). *Gejie* (All Walks of Life), no. 1 (1997).

Zhongbao (Central Daily). New York.

Zhonggong Tianmenshi jiwei (Tianmen city PDIC). *Ganbu zhongde fubai xianxiang yu quanli zhiyue* (The corruption phenomenon among officials and restraints on power). *Dangde Jijian Jiaoyu Cangao Ziliao* (Reference Materials on Party Discipline Inspection Education), no. 8 (1988): 7–10.

Zhongguo gongchandang di shisanci quanguo daibiao dahui wenjian huibian (The compilation of documents of the 13th Party Congress of the CCP). Beijing: Renmin chubanshe, 1987.

Zhongguo jiancha xuehui, ed. *Chengzhi tanwu huilu fanzui lunwenji* (A collection of papers on crimes of graft and bribery). Beijing: Zhongguo jiancha chubanshe, 1990.

Zhongguo zuojia xiehui, ed. *Quanguo youxiu baogao wenxue pingxuan huojiang zuopinji* (A selection of prize-winning reportage: 1985–86), vols. 1–2. Beijing: Zuojia chubanshe, 1988.

Zhongjiwei (Central PDIC). *Zhengyi yu xie'er* (Justice and vice). Beijing: Zhongguo fangzheng chubanshe, 1995.

Zhou Enlai. *Zhou Enlai xuanji* (Selected works of Zhou Enlai). 2 volumes. Beijing: Renmin chubanshe, 1978.

Zhou Jizhong. *Zhongguo xingzheng jiancha zhidu* (The administrative supervision system in China). Nanchang: Jiangxi renmin chubanshe, 1989.

Zhou Li. *Manhadun de nüren* (A woman in Manhattan). Beijing: Beijing chubanshe, 1992.

Zhu Hanguo, Xie Chuntao, and Fan Tianshun. *Zhongguo gongchandang jianshe shi* (The history of party building). Chengdu: Sichuan renmin chubanshe, 1991.

Zhu Jianhua. *Dongbei jiefangqu caizheng jingji shigao* (A history of finance and economy of the northeast liberated region). Harbin: Heilongjiang renmin chubanshe, 1987.

Zinoviev, Alexander. *The Reality of Communism*. London: Victor Gollancz Ltd., 1984.

Zuckerman, A. "Social Structure and Political Competition: The Italian Case." *World Politics* 24 (1972).

Zuigao renmin fayuan. *Jijian jiancha gongzuo shouce* (Handbook on disciplinary inspection and supervisory work). Beijing: Renmin fayuan chubanshe, 1991.

ban sanchan　辦三產　to operate businesses in the tertiary (i.e., service) sector

benwei zhuyi　本位主義　departmentalism

buzheng zhifeng　不正之風　unhealthy tendencies

chuangshou　創收　to create income

chuanxiaoxie　穿小鞋　to give someone tight shoes to wear, i.e., make things hard for someone

chuji ganbu　處級干部　cadres of the division-chief rank

da baitiao　打白條　(1) to write blank receipts (an irregular accounting method prone to embezzlement); (2) to write IOUs

dabiao　達標　to reach a certain standard

dachi dahe　大吃大喝　to wine and dine

daiyu　待遇　treatment

damaifu　打埋伏　to conceal (the real financial situation)

dangfeng　黨風　work style or ethos of the party

dangfeng buzheng　黨風不正　unhealthy, undesirable tendencies in the party

danwei　單位　work unit

daomai daomai　倒買倒賣　to profiteer

dingti　頂替　to replace one's parent with one's child (for employment)

duochi duozhan　多吃多占　eating and taking more than one is entitled to

fan tanwu huilu ju　反貪污賄賂局　anti-graft and bribery bureau

fanpai gongsi　翻牌公司　companies that just flipped their name plate (i.e., transfigured themselves from state administrative organs to business firms)

fanyouqing　反右傾　anti-rightist-orientation (campaign)

fang weixing　放衛星　to launch satellites; refers to the boasting of higher achievements during the Great Leap Forward

fensan zhuyi　分散主義　decentralism, departmentalism
fubai　腐敗　decay, corruption
fuhua　腐化　decadent; often refers to lifestyle
fukua　浮夸　to exaggerate (results)

gongkuan qingke　公款請客　wine and dine with public funds
gongsi bufen　公私不分　non-segregation of public and private
guakao　挂靠　to attach to (a work unit, usually a government agency)
guanban gongsi　官辦公司　official firms
guanbenwei　官本位　primacy of public office (i.e., being an official)
guandao　官倒　official speculation, profiteering
guanxi　關系　connections
guanxihu　關系户　connected units or persons
guanxiwang　關系綱　networks of connections

hangye buzhengzhifeng　行業不正之風　unhealthy vocational tendencies
huibi　回避　to avoid (according to law of avoidance)
huicheng　回城　return to the city (said of the "educated youths" who were
　　sent to the countryside)
huilu　賄賂　bribery
hukou　户口　residency

jiadi　家底　household accumulation, wealth
jiagong jisi　假公濟私　seek private gains in the name of public
jiancha　監察　to supervise, control
jiancha yuan　檢察院　procurate
jiawu　家務　family business, family wealth; here refers to business and
　　assets of Communist army and government units
jibie　級別　ranking, level
jieliu　截留　to impound
jijian　紀檢　discipline inspection
juanshu　捐疏　to donate (to local officials)
jubao　舉報　to expose, report (corruption cases)

keji ganbu　科級干部　cadre of the section-chief rank

la guanxi　拉關系　to establish connections
langfei　浪費　to squander, waste
lianzheng　廉政　clean government
linghui jingshen　領會精神　to grasp the spirit of (a document or speech
　　from higher authorities)

lougui 陋規 vicious customs

luan tanpai 亂攤派 unruly levies

neizhao 內招 to recruit internally

nuoyong 挪用 peculation, diversion of (public) funds

paidui 排隊 to place (a person or a unit) in proper order or category; this method, aimed at defining various classifications according to the ideological progressiveness of a person or a unit, was widely used during the Maoist period

paoguan 跑官 to pursue an official position by lobbying higher authorities

pingbi 評比 to compare and compete

qiankui 潛虧 hidden loss

qiaoli mingmu 巧立名目 to cunningly create items (so that public units can allocate money or materials as bonuses to their staff and workers by circumambulating fiscal rules)

qundai guanxi 裙帶關系 nepotism

renren weiqin 認人為親 to treat people on the basis of personal relations

sanluan 三亂 the three unrulies (unruly levies, forced donations, and fines)

shangyou zhengce, xiayou duice 上有政策, 下有對策 where there is a policy from higher authorities, there is a counter-policy from local authorities

shiti 實體 economic entity; usually refers to businesses run by administrative or non-profit units

shoufei 收費 to charge fees

shouhui 受賄 to accept bribes

sungong feisi 損公肥私 to feed private interests at the cost of public interests

suohui 索賄 to solicit bribes

tanpai 攤派 apportionment of levies

tanwu 貪污 graft, embezzlement

taogou 套購 to fraudulently purchase (commodities under state monopoly); under state socialism, any attempt to buy (for selling later) commodities controlled by the state was regarded as taogou, which was an economic crime

tegong　特供　special consumer supplies (for high-ranking officials)
tequan　特權　privilege
teyao jianchayuan　特邀監察員　special (anti-corruption) monitors
tiba　提拔　to select and promote (cadres)
tigan　提干　to be selected or promoted to be state officials or military officers
touji daoba　投機倒把　speculation, profiteering
tuogou　脱鉤　to divest or de-link (from business by government agencies)

waifeng　歪風　unhealthy ethos, evil tendency
weifa luanji　違法亂紀　violation of laws and discipline
weiji jin'e　違紀金額　retained revenue that violates fiscal discipline (usually by public units)
weiji zijin　違紀資金　money made by violating (fiscal) discipline

xiahai　下海　to take a plunge into the ocean (of business)
xialou　下樓　to step downstairs; a technique of mass campaign where cadres had to pass the test of confession and self-criticism
xiantuanji　縣團級　(cadres or units) of the county or regiment-chief rank
xiaogong　小公　minor public; refers to (the interests of) work-units
xiaojinku　小金庫　small coffers, slush funds
xinghui　行賄　to give bribes
xishou xizao　洗手洗澡　to wash hands and take a bath; refers to confession and self-criticism; a phrase originated in the Yan'an rectification; techniques of mass campaign
xuansong　選送　select and send (to college, factory, or military service)

yinxing jingji　隱型經濟　hidden economy
yinxing shouru　隱性收入　hidden income
youling buxing, youjin buzhi　有令不行, 有禁不止　where there is an order, there is no implementation; where there is a ban, there is still the prohibited practice
yusuanwai　預算外　extra-budgetary, off-budget
yusuanwai zijin　預算外資金　extra-budgetary funds, off-budget funds

zhan xiaopianyi　占小便宜　to gain petty advantages
zheng ren　整人　to fix someone (politically)
zhongxin gongzuo　中心工作　core task
zichou zijin　自籌資金　self-raised funds
zouguochang　走過場　to stage a show (in order to demonstrate compliance or achievement)
zouhoumen　走後門　going through the back door

Wuxu, 79, 276n23

Xiafang, 107, 109, 152, 311n44; manual labor and, 76–77; origin of, 77
Xiaogan County: disciplinary violations / misconduct in, 128 (table); fine revenue in, 214 (table)
Xiaogong, 43
Xingshizhuyi, 27
Xushui County: free supply system in, 95; inspection of, 91

Yamen, 248; *li* and, 247
Yan'an period, 41, 55; corruption during, 69
Yan'an Rectification Campaign, 267n24, 277n52
Yang, Mayfair: on *guanxi*, 295n89
Yanshou, 208, 226
Ye Jizhuang, on departmentalism, 44
Yongzheng Emperor: reform under, 248, 249

Zhang Guozhong, 90; on detention, 94
Zhang Xidong, case of, 99
Zhang Zishan, case of, 58
Zhao shuren, 151
Zhao xiaopianyi, 121
Zhengdun, 152
Zhiqing, 290nn127, 129
Zhou Enlai, 280n100; anti-*zouhoumen* campaign and, 132; on cadre disciplinary problem, 115; proposal by, 78–79
Zhuanji wenxue, information from, 7
Zhu Rongji: on *dabiao*, 174; downsizing and, 257
Ziazhihui feng, described, 95–96
Zouguochang, 189
Zouhoumen, 130–34, 141, 150, 175, 179; beginning of, 130, 131, 137, 144; curbing, 131, 132, 145, 286n64; incidents of, 132–33; rationale/opportunities for, 149; using, 136, 177, 178
Zou Jiahua, 217
Zunyi Meeting (1935), Mao at, 156